Baby Matters

Baby Matters

What Your Doctor May Not Tell You About Caring for Your Baby

Dr. Linda Folden Palmer

Lucky Press

LANCASTER, OHIO

Published by Lucky Press, LLC
126 S. Maple Street
Lancaster, Ohio 43130
www.luckypress.com/babymatters

While the author has taken great pains to bring the reader the most
accurate information and interpret it wisely, no part of this text is a
substitute for medical diagnosis or treatment prescription.

PRINTED IN THE UNITED STATES OF AMERICA
Back cover photo by Shugrue Photography

Palmer, Linda Folden
    Baby matters : what your doctor may not tell you
about caring for your baby / Linda Folden Palmer. -- 1st
ed.
    p. cm.
    Includes bibliographical references and index.
    ISBN: 0-9676050-7-5
    LCCN: 00-110124

    1. Infants--Care. 2. Child care. 3. Pediatrics--
Popular works. I. Title.

RJ61.P35 2001   618.92
                                 QBI00-909

To Joseph Kennedy, George, Tracy,

and all those at IGO involved in the conception of my son,

and oh yes, my husband, to Douglas, for giving me a beautiful son.

Acknowledgments

I WOULD LIKE TO ACKNOWLEDGE AND SINCERELY THANK EDITOR ELLYN Roberts for giving me some solid beginning directions; editor Peter Bumpus for long, hard, and unrelenting work on turning my awkward words into beautiful prose, and strong guidance in embellishing and trimming the text; Janice Phelps and Lucky Press for providing me with the opportunity to bring my book to the public; Michael Vidor and Anne Sheldon for placing their faith in me and motivating me to finish my text; Rosalind Haselbeck for plowing through the text and providing valuable scientific comment and review; and Mary Galbraith, Jeannie Israel, and Lauri for their helpful contributions.

A special thank you to my son, Corlin, for hugs and kisses, and not minding to nurse and nap lying in my desk drawer as I typed at the computer across his body; and to my husband, Douglas, for opening my eyes about cow's milk, and encouraging me to write this book.

I would also like to thank the thousands of scientists for their valuable research, whose work provided me the basis upon which to derive my text. I applaud La Leche League International for recollecting the maternal wisdom, and just for being there to support new mothers. A warm recognition and gratitude to all those of the Attachment Parenting Support Group who kept me going as a mother, as a writer, as a woman, and especially those who have encouraged me most with their enthusiastic responses to my book. Mostly, I would like to acknowledge mothers, around the world, throughout the ages.

Preface

BECAUSE SO MUCH OF THE INFORMATION IN THIS BOOK IS NEW TO bookshelves, controversial, or just very poorly understood, and because, as a whole, this kind of material has not previously been supported by a firm scientific foundation, and because this highly valuable information belongs to those who performed the research, I felt it was important to strongly document this text. At the same time most have found that *Baby Matters* is easily understood and hard to put down because the material is priceless for parents and health care providers alike. I ask the reader to not be frightened of the many citations or some scientific terminology, but to know that this work was not gone into lightly. If there is too much information, which I have heard, just consider that you have obtained several books for the price of one; a lot of the information is just too valuable to leave out. I hope you'll pull out that ol' highlighter pen and go to it. You'll be very glad you did. Then share your favorite parts with your friends, colleagues, and health care providers.

Prologue

DURING THE LATE NINETEENTH CENTURY, IT WAS SUSPECTED THAT "miasmas" or "vapors" in the air caused disease, which led to a heightened concern about sharing breath while sleeping. Especially in England and the U.S., married mates who could afford to do so began sleeping in separate beds. This soon became a fashionable trend. Poor families tried to emulate the wealthy by having separate bedrooms for each member of the family.

At the same time, the industrial revolution was changing family life. Speedy transportation was moving nuclear families away from extended families and friends. Mothers had less help with household and child care chores and began to value early independence in their children. As a result of these trends, even babies were pushed out into beds or cribs of their own. Unfortunately, a new problem developed for families — that of crying, sleepless infants vying for attention.

Enter Dr. Luther Emmett Holt, considered the father of pediatrics. Around the turn of the century, he started to teach that babies should never be played with. He came up with the idea that infants would be "spoiled" if parents gave in to their requests for "indulgences." A baby's desires to be frequently fed, carried, rocked, comforted, and to have something to suck on were "bad habits" that should not be obliged. Infant crying increased from this advice, but mothers were relieved by the (very erroneous) advice that infants needed to be allowed to cry for extended periods in order to develop their lungs.

> Suddenly, male doctors, educated only by formula companies, became experts on how mothers should feed their babies.

Also during the early 1900s, as sanitation awareness increased, orphans and other infants were starting to survive on artificial feeding formula far more often than they had in the past. Nestlé and other formula manufacturers mounted enormous campaigns to promote their infant feeding substitutes. They even sent saleswomen dressed as nurses to hospitals or to new mothers' homes as "milk nurses." Companies also gave gifts and grants to doctors and hospitals to encourage them to distribute free formula samples. They used aggressive TV, billboard, radio, and neon sign campaigns to convince mothers that they may not have enough breastmilk, and that formula was elite, convenient, sterile, and "scientific." These companies provided huge grants to promote the development of the American Academy of Pediatrics. Suddenly, male doctors, educated only by formula companies, became "experts" on how mothers should feed their babies. The companies' milk stations, which promoted their formulas, were soon converted to "well-child" clinics. Eventually these became the first pediatricians' offices, providing "nutritional advice" and regular weighing for infants. "Scientific" weight charts developed by the formula companies were used to convince the majority of mothers they were not supplying enough nourishment for their infants. In truth, these charts only reflected the obesity of malnourished formula-fed infants. Nevertheless, an "epidemic" of imagined breastmilk insufficiency occurred, which led to a real insufficiency as mothers breastfed less and started producing less, and soon, artificially feeding infants with cow's milk formulas became the norm.

Robbed of the proper nutrition and immune protection of mother's milk, these infants suffered untold cases of diarrhea, illness, and death. Additionally, some doctors began to recognize that not all symptoms related to formula and cow's milk were caused by infection or malnutrition. Cow's milk allergies became widely recognized. Later, however, this observation went out of vogue in favor of describing the problem as colic, colitis, and nervous mothers.

As women began to work outside the home, and scheduled bottle feedings became the norm, pediatric and hospital visits for illnesses became more and more frequent, behavior problems increased, and nighttime crying issues and night terrors became common problems. A new kind of child expert, the sleeping specialist, became popular.

In the middle of the twentieth century, after noticing that certain kinds of behavior problems were increasing in children, Dr. John Bowlby and others began to study parent–child bonding. They noticed that children who had been evacuated from war zones (and separated from their parents) were far more disturbed by their wartime experiences than those who had stayed with their mothers during the bombing of London. It became clear to these researchers that the availability of parents was a key factor in the behavior patterns developed by children. In recent decades, the diagnosis of "hyperactivity" has become very common. Researchers have linked such symptoms not only to a need for greater parental attention, but often to cow's milk sensitivities and other food reactions, all products of "modern" parenting. Still, these observations are seldom taken into account when recognizing such hyperactive behaviors. The usual treatment for this behavior is addictive stimulant drugs. Now we see up to 35% of children in some classrooms being diagnosed and medicated for attention-deficit disorder even as we teach the mantra "just say NO to drugs."

While new sanitation practices and miracle medicines have been curing diseases and saving the lives of young and old alike, many children's health problems have actually increased by orders of magnitude.

Thanks to medicine and sanitation, the infant death rate has dropped drastically over the last hundred years (after rising greatly with the onset of industrialization). But there is an enigma in our country — while often leading the way in medicine, we actually have one of the lowest infant survival rates among industrialized nations. Childhood diseases and behavior problems are considerably higher than in most other nations as well.

Now that many of these twentieth-century babies are beyond their third or fourth decades of life, we are faced with geometric increases in bowel diseases, obesity, and several kinds of cancers and autoimmune diseases.

We have also been watching puberty occur at increasingly earlier ages. Now that many of these twentieth-century babies are beyond their third or fourth decades of life, we are faced with geometric increases in bowel diseases, obesity, and several kinds of cancers and autoimmune diseases. We have also noticed that the "unspoiled," "early independence" children are having more problems than ever with adult independence, intimacy issues, and lasting marital relationships.

Science is just now finding some keys to what is going on in our children's bodies. First, we are learning, at a chemical level, about the consequences of our lost art of touch. Additionally, we are discovering some of the adverse effects of children's exposures to pesticides, antibiotics, vaccinations, and consumption of milk from cows.

This volume represents my wish to give parents the tools to evaluate their young children's environment and understand how it can affect their development. The intent is to arm parents with information, so they can make better parenting and health care choices.

1

Finding Out What Matters

TODAY, MANY OF THE PROBLEMS PARENTS HAVE WITH THEIR BABIES are linked to new parenting and feeding techniques that have been implemented during the recent century. Colic, for instance, is far more common in the U.S. than in many other places around the world. I will show how two chief causes for its rise are the stress suffered by babies being regularly separated from their mothers and the common difficulties babies have tolerating the large cow's milk proteins in infant formulas and breastfeeding mothers' diets. Cow's milk is a foreign substance that has pervaded every corner of our diets — starting with artificial infant feeds, but finding its way into mother's breastmilk through the foods she eats as well. As it turns out, health problems such as diabetes, obesity, bowel disease, and cancer, on the rise in both children and adults, are strongly linked to infant feeding choices. This book discusses the most important problems that have flourished over the last century, and those that parents have the most power to change.

We begin with a story about a mother, who we'll call Jenny, whose newborn behaved wildly at the breast — wanting to nurse, but not wanting to nurse, flailing his head back and forth. After his first several days of life, he would do little more than scream and cry. Even though Jenny was a new mother, she was sure this was a cry of pain and frustration. Her baby's bowels did not move, except for a weekly watery explosion that no diaper on the planet could hold. He would awaken during naps and during the night with screams. He lost more than the usual amount of weight for a newborn, and then did not show much gain.

The doctors diagnosed Jenny's infant with colic and sent her back home, assuring her that he would "grow out of it" someday. They provided an "increased" feeding schedule, which was actually much less frequent than his attempts already. But making him wait to eat only found him in such a crying frenzy that he couldn't even try to nurse. Well-meaning visitors tried to force him to nurse, which made him protest more, force bottles of formula on him, which made him vomit, or force pacifiers and water bottles, which made him lose interest in feeding at all. The doctor also eventually recommended formula supplements, but these still were not tolerated. Jenny looked frantically through all her baby books to find out just what colic was, and what could be done. She found an answer: crying 2 hours per day is "normal"; crying 3 hours or more per day is "colic" — a condition of crying a lot.

This, she thought, was no diagnosis; it was simply an excuse. But why? Apparently hers was not the first child to ever behave this way. The first clue came from another mother. She suggested that the baby might be allergic to something in Jenny's milk. Jenny had never heard of this, but she thought back over her diet before the miserable night that had just passed. It contained three of the foods her friend mentioned as most common offenders. She went home and found a couple vague references to these food reactions in her baby books, so she tried eliminating a few foods from her diet and saw immediate improvement, although her son was far from recovery.

Jenny thought she was well educated in diagnosis, health, and nutrition. Her training included basic pediatric concerns as well. Not only that, but she owned quite a stack of the standard baby care books, and her pediatrician was so popular that he was frequently seen on local TV. She felt rather embarrassed and concerned that her education did not include such basic dietary information. She wondered why it was not readily available.

Okay, so this mom's name wasn't Jenny. It's Linda, Linda Palmer — me, the author.

By this time, it was very clear that my son was in pain. He would arch his back and clench his fists. I began searching through medical textbooks and found little help. Finally I began to find information in some well-recognized research journals. Strangely, however, I noticed that most of the helpful research and information came from Europe, Australia, Israel, and many parts of the world, but almost nothing from the U.S.

The more answers I found, the more questions I had. It would take a book to tell you about even a small portion of the vast amount of, shall I say, "secret" research and information out there about colic and many other challenges that parents might face. Then I found some incredible reasons for why this sound, scientific, and important information is not available in most medical offices in this country: Basically, a few stray misconceptions and a century of exploitation for industry profit are behind the story. It would take a book to tell you even a little of what I learned…and you are reading that book.

Herein, I only discuss situations where choices can be made and where there are important potential differences in the mental and physical outcomes for children based on those choices. Of course, it is precisely these matters, those where there are choices, that are influenced by industry and advertising (propaganda). Some child-rearing ideas are woven so deeply into the fabric of our culture that even most of our well-meaning infant care scholars are victims of the scheme.

To understand the problems of modern child rearing, we must recognize the impact of industrialization, which brought rapid and frequent transport of families from their friends and extended families. Busy people in rapid transit, who were also busy watching their new radios and televisions at home, lost a great deal of community interaction, and therefore support. Industrialization has also shaped a society where both parents often work, reducing contact not only with the neighborhood, but even within the nuclear family. The "village" is now a thing of the past. The village not only more easily provided the significant attention and stimulation a child needs, but it also gathered and passed on a collection of parenting knowledge and discoveries.

Why did it take me so long to realize that my baby, although still suffering food sensitivity problems, did actually feed quite well first thing in the morning and during the night — after the hospital stay that is? Rather than relying on a stream of lactation nurses and relatives hovering around, trying to force my baby to feed, I finally found some mothers who explained that my sensitive and already uncomfortable young baby was hyperstimulated by all the noise and strangers. Having recently arrived from a peaceful womb, where he mainly heard only two voices, my son finally found one peace in his new existence, one break from his crying and frustration. Babies are not all alike, but finally, alone with me in a quiet, dimly lit room, my tiny son could nurse soundly and happily, in between his bouts of painful crying and snatches of sleep. In fact, he seemed to find relief from pain in the act of nursing itself. This, I found later, could be soundly explained by some of the secret science.

I should have known all about child rearing since playing house as a child; I should have learned this from being a part of a village. The truth is, however, that I had never even seen a baby nurse before. I am most frightened to realize that I may never have "gotten" it, that my son may never have begun to gain weight, that…who knows?

Since our villages are all but gone in this country, La Leche League, International, has taken it upon themselves to again gather up the wisdom from experienced mothers and share these experiences, the trials and the successes. This breastfeeding organization, founded in 1956, now acts as a valuable information source for new mothers. Hopefully, with efforts such as theirs and others, our new generation of babies will not have to be the guinea pigs of modern society. Hopefully, mothers can collect evidence and experience and pass this information on, for more consistently healthy, happy, and brighter results.

I came into parenting with little agenda beyond every parent's hope for a healthy child. Challenges came quickly however, and answers were limited and generally were not well supported with sound research. I embarked on a large amount of research and established contact with hundreds of families whose lives I purposefully probed, all aimed initially at solving my own parenting dilemmas. Over time, it became apparent that infant care choices could make huge differences, and that the research evidence pointed to certain choices rather definitely. It is stunning that this information is widely unknown in parenting circles, parenting books, and in pediatric offices. The information in this volume will empower parents by revealing a large amount of the latest scientific, medical, sociological, and psychological research about how babies are affected by parenting choices.

Somewhat insidiously over time, child care has drifted into a regimen that aims to make strong, independent "adults" out of our innocent children, starting from day one. Parents have been encouraged to ignore baby's cries and their own very strong instinctual urges to respond, to disconnect themselves from their infant very quickly, to create a detached, "independent" infant. I've certainly obtained this programming from social cues all my life: If you pick up the baby, coddle him, "give-in" to baby's requests, you will "spoil" him — "Don't spoil the baby!" Yet, I have found that there is no sound research to support any long-term benefit from this advice. In fact, mountains of psychology studies suggest the opposite, and a look at cultures with differing practices bears this truth out.

This reminds me of an incredible embarrassment. I am haunted by a sick feeling every time I recall the number of times I regurgitated my own cultural programming to my patients — that babies need to cry frequently and at length to develop their lungs.

Quite contrary to the popular idea that babies are out to control their parents, I intend to demonstrate that babies are helpless immature beings with feelings and instinctual drives for survival and social imprinting. They thrive when they are tenderly cared for, nursed, and closely nurtured. Psychology and sociology researchers have found that, in reality, the significant result of today's coveted early independence is poorly bonded children who often become poorly functioning adults. The outcome of our ubiquitous detached parenting is most clearly seen during adolescence when poorly attached children often exhibit highly destructive behavior toward themselves or others — often gently referred to as "antisocial" behavior. This behavior is the independent behavior that was sought — now, unfortunately, independent of the wishes of parents or society. It is the consequence of successfully preventing close bonding from birth.

> This behavior is the independent behavior that was sought — now, unfortunately, independent of the wishes of parents or society. It is the consequence of successfully preventing close bonding from birth.

Self-destructive and violent behavior has been a growing problem throughout the twentieth century. Nearly all who study it find it is strongly linked to the earliest treatment of children. In fact, it has been found that the level and quality of maternal care, especially during the earliest months, provides an incredibly consistent indicator of a child's future behavior and socialization. Well-bonded, securely attached children are more responsive to parental requests, a kind of "dependence" that is preferable. Of course, the results of this behavior carry on into adult life. Furthermore, many adult diseases, both mental and physical, including the now common inability to form long-bonded marital or partner relationships, stem from this lack of strong early attachment.

Leaving babies crying alone in cribs and otherwise maintaining physical distance through plastic bottles, playpens, and plastic baby carriers contributes to poor attachment. Although the results are obvious, those who study the functioning of our nerves and hormones have now demonstrated that a hormonally conducted bonding occurs when two people consistently touch, protect, and care for each other, and that brain patterns are permanently altered by bonding patterns between parent and child.

Most would agree that children probably do not consciously remember the way they were treated during early infancy. Many recount this observation as support or comfort for their ideas about ignoring babies' cries for attention and providing minimal stimulation. Yet, it can be shown that while the specifics may be lost, unconscious memories are developed on the neurological and biochemical level from birth — a baby's brain develops according to its environment, from day one. Childhood, adolescence, and adulthood are all affected by this early programming. And as far as the coveted independence goes, it has been shown that

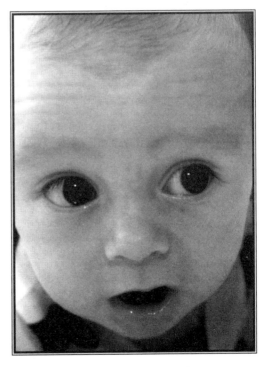

those who receive the most affection early on display the highest levels of independence as adults.

At the same time that emotion and behavior are being influenced by detached parenting, health and survival are also taking a beating. Formula feeding is a facet of detached parenting. Not only does withholding breastmilk lead to more illness and death when this important part of an infant's immune protection is lost, but an untold number of babies, children, and adults suffer from physical and behavioral ailments linked to food intolerance reactions. These reactions are an immune system response, stemming especially from the early introduction of cow's milk and milk formulas.

We know that the intestinal irritation and bleeding commonly associated with infants consuming cow's milk proteins eventually allows heavy proteins to pass through the intestinal walls before they have been digested, causing further destructive immune reactions. Our increasing exposure to chemical contaminants in our environment and the enormous amount of drugs and chemicals fed to milk-producing cows may be partially responsible for the ever-increasing numbers of food allergies, asthma, and autoimmune illnesses. At the same time, medical recognition of these immune mechanisms has actually waned considerably, especially in the U.S. Therefore, treatable cases of colic and many other problems remain unrecognized, and children continue to suffer and parents continue to be frustrated. At the same time that milk formulas became popular infant feeds, huge numbers of children suddenly started suffering from a wide array of symptoms that were recognized as food sensitivities. Unfortunately, it appears that the response to this "coincidence" was to change the definition of food allergy. Today, most reactions to milk products are still considered to be somehow different from other validly recognized allergies, causing them to become entities unto themselves, such as "colic," or they are attributed to psychological behavior problems of the child or the parents.

Other connections between cow's milk and disease are also not widely advertised. Today, there is little doubt that early and frequent feeding of dairy products leads to a greatly increased incidence of childhood diabetes. It has been confirmed that high cow's milk consumption is a major cause of osteoporosis. Alas, this information has been stifled, apparently because the National Dairy Council governs the National Osteoporosis Foundation. With huge contributions to pediatric education, the dairy industry and formula manufacturers have managed to keep their products in the high regard of baby doctors. Their other advertising efforts have caused these products to become widely accepted in the eyes of the public as well. Pediatricians and the public have been successfully convinced that formula is a quite reasonable substitute for mother's milk. In fact, however, formula-fed infants suffer twice as many illnesses as breastfed ones, and approximately twice as many bottle-fed infants die compared to breastfed babies (from all causes, as an average). Supplementing breastfed babies with formula not only slows early weight gain, but interferes greatly with the valuable immunity provided by breastmilk. In our nation, this information never quite makes it into *Parenting* magazine, whose chief advertisers are…you guessed it. Even after infancy, a significantly higher risk of childhood cancer exists for those who never received breastmilk compared to those who nursed exclusively and for extended periods.

Other parenting practices changed as a result of formula feeding. Today's babies are kept in a separate room so that breastfeeding is not encouraged. Since these babies don't nurse throughout the night while mom and dad sleep, they frequently wake up crying, wanting to eat. Babies often also suffer from chronic intestinal inflammation or indigestion due to irritating and difficult-to-digest foreign bovine proteins, which also makes them wake up crying many times during the night. Parents of these formula babies have to find ways to get a good night's sleep. Measures designed to alleviate this sleep dilemma, such as imposing deep sleep by having babies sleep unnaturally on their stomachs, or exhausting children by allowing long periods of crying, have greatly backfired. We are now discovering that this once-coveted deep sleep has led to countless sudden infant deaths. Formula-fed crib babies also miss the comforting nursing and warm breastmilk throughout the night, as well as the sleep-inducing hormones acquired from nursing closely between two warm parents. Nature designed everything for the most peaceful, restful night for the entire family.

Other potentially harmful practices may be motivated by other industries. Fever-reducing medications are strongly advertised and prescribed, yet for most infections, illness and death increase when fevers are reduced. These are the statistics, the research findings, yet, what message do we receive? Antibiotics continue to be prescribed for ear infections even though there is little doubt that there is a higher rate of recurring ear infections in those who receive antibiotic therapy than in those who do not. In fact, the return of chronic middle ear fluid is 2 to 6 times higher in those treated with antibiotics. Serious sinus infections (mastoiditis) are currently on the rise as a direct result of strongly resistant bacteria developed through the common use of antibiotic therapy for ear infections. Ear infection is a topic well covered in this text because it is so pervasive, but its frequent occurrence doesn't make sense and is not universal. It is largely preventable.

Although some of these modern problems have been mostly ignored, the number of people who react to cow's milk is so significant that the problem can't be entirely swept under the rug. Instead, the discussion has become misguided. People and doctors have been led to believe that the chief cause of intestinal pain from dairy consumption is lactose intolerance, a condition that can be easily overcome even without excluding dairy products from the diet. Lactose intolerance *is* a real problem that increases with age (evidently, adults are not intended to drink milk, a baby food). It occurs sooner and more often in genetic populations who have consumed dairy for a much shorter history: actually most of the world except for those of Northern European descent. But lactose is a chief component of mother's milk, and, until quite recently, a baby who could not digest lactose would never have lived to pass on his genes. Intestinal intolerance to *cow's milk protein, not lactose*, is the major cause of undiagnosed colic in infants, and of other GI symptoms in the young and old alike.

I have come across many other startling matters. For example, did you know that vitamin K injections at birth are associated with childhood leukemia? Did you know that how you feed and treat your infant can strongly affect your child's IQ? There are also some important concerns surrounding common practices such as vaccination and circumcision that I feel parents have the right to know about.

I have found overwhelming evidence for these assertions and others. I will explain how the health, behavior, intelligence, and success of our children, and the adults they become, can be positively influenced by parental behavior. For various reasons this information does not permeate our common medical or social knowledge; therefore, I wish to arm parents with the best information available. I hope that parents and parents-to-be will find this data provocative, so they will be aware that they have choices and will understand what some of the consequences of their choices may be. I wish parents to know that what you feed your baby matters. How you treat your baby matters. Our future will be significantly affected by the choices that parents make today.

I have high hopes for the children of the twenty-first century.

2

The Attachment Advantage

"The spoiled baby is not one who is pampered, it is one who is being disciplined...its trust in mother and father is being eroded — in the true sense, it is being spoiled."

— Desmond Morris, *Human Beings*, a television documentary

GRADUALLY, MORE AND MORE PARENTS ARE FINDING THAT BY FOLLOWING their deep inborn instincts for baby care, they feel attuned to their child rather than confused about child rearing. They are rewarded for their efforts as their children reach school age, adolescence, and adulthood. However, without appropriate support from doctors and the community, isolated from their extended families who are often in conflict and lacking information about child rearing themselves, and with much of the maternal wisdom of the ages lost, new families often have to blaze their own trails.

The Big Experiment

For a brief period in man's multimillion-year history (the twentieth century), in a small part of the world (Western civilization), one of nature's miraculous innate powers was terribly abused. Down through ages of natural selection, mothers and their infants learned how to recognize each other, how to communicate, and how to imprint and bond. Mothers also knew how to provide all the necessary nurturing, nutritional, and developmental care for their infants, and how to warmly, lovingly, and gently develop a sense of security that allowed their offspring to grow and eventually achieve a healthy independence. While extraordinary medical advances have increasingly provided for the physical survival of the mother and infant, emotional well-being has taken a beating. Failure to thrive, behavior disorders, morbidity, and occasionally even mortality are some of the unfortunate consequences.

At the end of the nineteenth century Dr. Luther Emmett Holt Sr., considered the father of pediatrics, published *Care and Feeding of Children*, which became a child care bible. This book and others instructed parents to never give in to babies' cries for "indulgences." Indulgences included being picked up, held, rocked, comforted, or provided something to suck on, whether it was for attention, warmth, or simply because baby was hungry, or for any other "bad habit." Dr. Holt demanded that infants should never be played with and should never be allowed in their parents' bed. Next came the psychologists such as John Watson. Watson preached in his widely revered 1928 book, *Psychological Care of Infant and Child*, that children should never be hugged or kissed or allowed on your lap — except for maybe a good-night kiss on the forehead, a morning handshake, or an occasional pat on the head for a job well done.[1]

Throughout the twentieth century infant care "professionals" pushed tremendously for artificial feeding, they insisted that children should "cry it out," and they advised that responding to infants would seriously "spoil" them. This advice forced bewildered mothers to repress the very essence of their maternal instincts, creating an unnaturally cold, harsh environment for infants. Over time, as weak bonds occurred, this method became easier for mother to uphold. And as more and more people who had failed to form deep attachments during infancy and childhood became parents, these insidious rules became easier and easier for each successive generation to follow. Many problems developed, but there were "expert" answers around every corner. Some mothers weakened and secretly gave in to their infants' needs behind closed doors, but would then provide mixed messages to their babies when others were near. In the end, many lived with incredible guilt over the whole ordeal. Certainly, no power on earth can prevent mothers from deeply loving their babies or from finding ways to reveal their love. For attempting to provide the best possible environment for us, our foremothers' finest intentions must be highly honored, but at the same time, we must be aware that there were consequences to the negligence that was culturally imposed upon both mother and child.

Over the last decades, we have been encouraged to avoid comforting our infants for fear they may ask for more. On one hand we have been told that babies are totally blank slates to be molded as we please. On the other hand we are supposed to believe that they are devious scheming creatures who spend their days conniving to control the household and come between the parents. If we allow them to have their way, they will become spoiled and will continue to cry for more and more indulgence.

This hands-off approach has not been the only experiment in infant care, but it

> *The explosion of aggressive children, socially irresponsible adolescents, insecure and behaviorally disordered adults, and growing divorce rates stemmed from frequent rejection by caretakers who ignored the infants' earliest and most primal needs: security, a deep bonding with a primary caregiver, and tender, responsive maternal care.*

has been notably unsuccessful, as were many others, and it is the one we need to correct now. The consequences of this great experiment in human health and nature have been far from healthy, and often very destructive. Mid-century researchers such as John Bowlby and Mary Ainsworth studied in depth the psychology behind the explosion of aggressive children, socially irresponsible adolescents, insecure and behaviorally disordered adults, and growing divorce rates. They found the strongest links to the individuals' early environments. Their studies provided powerful insight into what they labeled "insecurely attached" children. These psychologists found that many developmental and adult shortcomings stemmed from frequent rejection by caretakers who ignored the infants' earliest and most primal needs: security, a deep bonding with a primary caregiver, and tender, responsive maternal care.

As time passed, these psychologists' words were partially heeded, and a gradual softening of position started to appear in the writings of child care experts. Consider the career of one of the most popular advisors, Dr. Benjamin Spock. Much evolution can be seen from his first 1945 baby care book to his last 1998 edition. But as far as matching advice to psychological and scientific findings, there is a long way to go. At the same time that we've seen some softening, we've developed a new hardening of sorts. We have become masters of the baby container. Children are carried in plastic carriers from crib to car seat, transported in strollers, strapped into bouncy seats, and otherwise confined in high chairs, walkers, jumpers, and playpens — often for 95% of their day.

Mixed Feelings

Generations of parents following the advice of the experts who cautioned them not to allow their babies to develop strong attachments to them, or to expect comfort from them, have come to wonder why their teenagers won't trust and confide in them. By withholding parental responsiveness and affection, we have grown generations of adults who are unable to trust, and who act out to acquire attention. Many lack the foundation, security, and trust required to maintain a lasting relationship with a mate. By not respecting the feelings of our infants, we raise children who do not respect the feelings of their peers, adolescents who do not respect the feelings of their parents, and adults who often can't respect even their own feelings.

One major facet of the advice given to parents was the counsel that "autonomy" or "independence" must be developed in their infants. Infants, however, are not meant to be independent, and humans are not solitary animals. Out of a totally pro-tective, secure, nutritive, life-sustaining, and nurturing womb, we are born, helpless and premature, to adults who are tuned by evolution to provide nutrition, protection, and social development during our contin-ued growth. As a reward, this relationship forms the foundation for continued nurtur-ing and guidance, and eventually creates a loving, self-sustaining adult. Not respond-ing to infants' needs has been shown to often reduce their efforts to have their needs met, sometimes resulting in a less-demanding "good baby." In others, prolonged periods of crying ensue, unheeded, when baby is hungry or alone in a crib. Either way, the mother and baby have successfully avoided becoming "too attached" to each other, as the standard advice recommends, so that separations will be easy. Withdrawn or crying alone, whichever path the infant takes, she may appear to be more independent, but ulti-mately the sad fact is — she is merely very much on her own.

> Withdrawn or crying alone, whichever path the infant takes, she may appear to be more independent, but ultimately the sad fact is — she is merely very much on her own.

Countless investigations have revealed the behavioral conse-quences of these methods: a high risk for behavioral disorders in growing children as well as in the adults they will become. School-age children may be more outwardly aggressive and less in control of themselves, or sometimes they are quite withdrawn. Parents often have little control over their detached and now very independent teenagers, and these teens often demonstrate a wide variety of anti-social behaviors. Anxiety disorders, depression, intimacy issues, and an inability to form stable, lasting bonds are also prominent in adults from insecurely attached beginnings.

To put this issue more simply, when infants' feelings are consistently ignored, they cannot be expected to confide in their caretakers when they become teenagers. When their needs and desires (which are one and the same at this age) are consistently unmet early on, the resulting teenagers cannot be expected to trust that their parents are the ones to turn to. Furthermore, fear may appear to work well as a behavior control for young children, but this tactic runs out of steam for young adults. Only strong bonding and deeply embedded respect and trust will positively influence behavior at this stage of life and beyond.

Popular Psychological Models of Attachment

Children from very understaffed orphanages, such as those in Rumania, who were supplied almost no affection or stimulation, provide a sad view of the opposite extreme to strong infant bonding with a responsive, affectionate caregiver. Even in institutions where food and medical treatment are adequate, few of the infants live. Those who do may cry for long hours, but more often a trance-like state manifests. They have minimal intellectual development and poor motor development. Those who are rescued into homes become very difficult to control. They show little response to caregiver overtures, but may be overly friendly to strangers. They often grow into adolescents and adults whose pathological behavior seems unresponsive to nearly any kind of therapy. Many of these males end up institutionalized for crimes, while females frequently become victims. The more "successful" ones use their interpersonal detachment in pathological ways to advance their careers and to frequently enter into and out of relationships. The fate of these emotionally abandoned youngsters is explained by their lack of early bonding to a consistent caregiving figure. As they grow up, they lack a secure emotional foundation, they are unable to develop trust in others, and they seldom initiate fulfilling affectionate relationships. In short, the skills necessary for productive interpersonal interactions have never been learned. These children are not neurologically well developed and are unable to form bonds with other human beings. They suffer from severe attachment disorder.

Boosted by her work with Bowlby, and after years of painstaking observation and research during the 1950s and 1960s, Mary Ainsworth divided children, chiefly from less severe situations than just described, into three categories. According to her nomenclature, which continues to be used in psychology today, children can be "avoidantly attached," "ambivalently attached," (two forms of insecure attachment), or "securely attached." As defined in this work, secure attachment is observed in just over half of all infants. A "disorganized attachment" category was later added by psychologist Mary Main and is sometimes, but not always, used in studies. Seeking to find a standard for measurement of infant attachment, Ainsworth recorded detailed observations of infant behavior toward their mothers and strangers in a consistently performed laboratory sequence of events dubbed the "strange situation." Her work became very popular in the 1970s because she was able to recognize distinct behaviors in infants that consistently reflected distinct maternal practices. Many others went on to confirm and expand her work, and some investigators even followed infants into adolescence and adulthood.

According to the widely accepted Ainsworth model, infants develop secure attachment when their mothers provide tender, responsive care from the very beginning. Their mothers quickly respond to their cries, validate their feelings, and are affectionate, well attuned to them, and consistently concerned. Securely attached infants are confident, display upset when mother leaves, greet her warmly when she returns, respond to her soothing, and enjoy her comfort. They explore away from their mother, glancing back or returning frequently to their mother, using her as a secure base, and seeking her comfort when alarmed or upset. The secure child develops good peer relationships and expresses empathy. While occasionally testing limits, they are elementally trustworthy.

Avoidantly attached infants come from mothers whose availability, both emotionally and physically, has been limited. This child's mother pushes for his independence and doesn't like his "neediness." She often rejects him and is emotionally unresponsive. While Ainsworth never directly implied any connection, this perfectly describes the expert pediatric advice of the times — force independence and do not respond to cries. Avoidantly attached infants do not look for physical contact with their mothers, and they don't respond to an embrace, although they may express upset at being put down. They actively ignore mother's return after separation and avoid mother when in distress. This is the "good" or "independent" baby many have been told to strive for. The avoidant child often appears complacent and less distressed over separation, although he eventually can become very demanding. The avoidant child may be alternatively clingy, demanding, withdrawn, aggressive, and angry. He may randomly attack or express anger at his mother, and isolate himself when in pain. As he grows, he is unenthusiastic and has poor peer relations.

The ambivalently attached baby is anxious, cries a lot, does not explore, and resists being soothed. Her body does not mold to that of her caregiver when being held, rather she may arch away or become limp. She may act overly cute and ply for favor. She actively seeks her parents' affections yet responds with hostility. As she grows, she shows immaturity and often becomes the victim of the avoidant child's aggressiveness. This infant's behavior is the result of receiving inconsistent attention from her parents. (These parents tried to follow the no-spoiling rules, but often gave in.) She becomes angry and unsure of her parents' ability to be there when needed.

More seriously abused or neglected infants generally fall into the disorganized attachment classification. To the less familiar observer, they may appear very attached, but they may greet a parent with actions such as falling to the floor or leaning their heads against a wall. As children, they attempt to control their parents as well as take care of them. They seldom make eye contact, seldom smile, and often exhibit speech problems. They act overly attractive and cute toward strangers. They are least able to regulate their emotions and may exhibit self-destructive behaviors.

Securely Attached

I emphasize the mid-century models of attachment because a great number of studies are available, based on these models, that give us insight into the results of various parenting attitudes. The idea of secure attachment has now grown. Many parents seek a greater depth of attachment through even more natural means, such as breastfeeding on cue, than these early researchers were ready for.

Having been provided with consistently responsive and affectionate care, children classified as securely attached, and the adults they become, usually develop more successful marriages, maintain better relationships with their parents, suffer fewer behavioral disorders, and show higher levels of integrity, including the ability to trust. In contrast to the results of trying to instill "independence" through early detached parenting, which creates emotionally insecure adults, securely attached infants become secure adults of high self-esteem who are strongly independent, but who can also be interdependent in relationships.

> In contrast to the results of trying to instill "independence" through early detached parenting, which creates emotionally insecure adults, securely attached infants become secure adults of high self-esteem who are strongly independent, but who can also be interdependent in relationships.

Researchers investigating various attachment levels in mother–infant pairs report that mothers of securely attached infants seem to enjoy their babies more, are better able to recognize and understand their cues, and are better able to use those cues to guide their infants' behavior.[2] It is logical to view the maternal ability to act on cues as a cause of attachment as much as a result of it.

Greater joy for all participating family members is the typical outcome.

Securely attached children are able to delay gratification much longer than their poorly attached peers (a measure of independence).[3] Higher IQ, regardless of mother's working status, and greater success in school, regardless of intelligence, are shown to be other benefits reaped by securely attached children.[4,5] It has even been shown that securely attached infants use acute care services about half as often,[6] perhaps because the attuned mother has better skill at determining the actual level of illness in her child, or feels more secure about her observations and her ability to care for him. Also, it is more likely that these children have been breastfed, and a reduction in illness results from breastfeeding alone. Although it is sometimes difficult to ascertain how much influence each of the factors in child rearing has, a healthier child is the common denominator of a more secure attachment.

Many studies have shown successful outcomes from training mothers of high-risk mother–infant pairs to be sensitively responsive to their babies' cues. One study specifically reported more pleasingly socialized babies who cried less and performed more intellectually challenging types of exploration.[7] A preschool-age follow-up showed that the effects of sensitive mothering were lasting, finding that the babies had become secure children who displayed positive peer interactions.[8]

One valuable achievement in young children that helps promote positive social behavior for years to come is developing a good conscience. Research on children between the ages of 2 and 5 discerned that while gentle maternal discipline (one attachment guideline) successfully promoted conscience in fearful toddlers, only a high level of responsiveness from mother and secure attachment resulted in a well-developed conscience in toddlers classified as fearless.[9]

Although pacifier use does not disqualify a child from being described as attached, securely attached children are seldom found to have strong attachments to pacifiers.[10] Looking beyond the securely attached classification to the "attachment-parented" child (soon to be described), one will see that these children seldom develop long-term attachments to thumbs, pacifiers, or inanimate objects of any kind.[11] The key is that these children are more attached to their caretakers. Later on, this ability to derive more long-term security and satisfaction from a mate than from "things" is reported to be an advantage for developing a more secure marriage.

Seeds of Behavior Disorders

So what happens to the many children who do not gain the benefit of strong bonding experiences with a consistent caretaker? Inborn temperaments cause all children to respond to a given caregiving environment in their own way. However, certain strong patterns do reveal themselves in sociological studies, which provide insight and help us predict the general results of certain parenting patterns for children of all temperaments. A large number of studies have confirmed that weakly or insecurely attached children manifest unproductive behaviors throughout their lives as a result of their relationship with their mothers and the level and quality of caregiving they were provided, but not generally as a result of genetic or other factors.[12,13]

Insecurely attached youngsters, those from "early independence" and "let them cry" households, often evolve into adults who dread emotional intimacy or are hostile, insecure, or manipulative with romantic partners.[14,15] Not only does poor attachment lead to poor adult romantic relationships, but often to the development of psychological disorders.

Psychologists know well that a child's level of attachment strongly predicts behavior problems at school age.[16] In addition, *researchers have found that anxiety disorders,[17] deviant behavior,[18] and other personality disorders[19] during adolescence are strongly linked to poorly developed early bonding,* with only a minimal influence from other factors such as parental death, maternal anxiety, or initial temperament. Aggressive and self-destructive behavior, eating disorders, and substance abuse are some of the results[20] — all common problems in recent decades. Adolescents hospitalized for psychiatric disorders overwhelmingly display insecure attachment patterns,[21] as do those involved in criminal behavior and hard drug use.[22]

As attachment theory studies gradually worked their way up to studying the effects on adulthood, romantic failings were the first focus. Gradually the connections between infant attachment and adult mental behavior and stress reactions became recognized. In fact, a recent large survey confirms that most adults with mental disorders suffer from childhood-based attachment disorders.[23] Much current research has shown interest in the strong connection between impaired attachment and the development of depression.[24,25] New hormone studies reveal that adults with poor coping abilities for dealing with stress were infants whose stress hormone regulation did not organize well due to poor maternal responsiveness (*as explained in the next chapter*). And, today's ever-so-prominent workaholics are considered to be adults raised insecurely attached, now hiding from the intimacies of real life.

> *It has been proposed that the increasing incorporation of standard U.S. child-rearing practices over generations is responsible for the declining rate of mental health seen in successive generations of immigrants.*

Clues from Immigration

The psychological results of different bonding practices are clearly revealed by following the health patterns of people from cultures who transition from one kind of child-rearing society to another. The people of Mexico, who generally practice a more attached style of parenting than people in the U.S., suffer mental disorders only half as much as non-Hispanic U.S. whites. This difference persists in recent Mexican immigrants to the U.S.; however, the mental health of their U.S. born children is reduced. By the third generation, U.S. born Mexican Americans have rates of mental illness just as miserable as those in non-Hispanic U.S. whites. This same effect has been shown for other Central and South American regions studied. It has been proposed that the increasing incorporation of standard U.S. child-rearing practices over generations is responsible for the declining rate of mental health seen in successive generations of immigrants.[26-29]

Seeds of Violence

Psychologists, psychiatrists, sociologists, and others agree that reduced motherly responsiveness leads to the poor early attachment patterns that predispose children to aggressive behavior.[30,31] In addition to being associated with mild and moderate behavior disorders such as depression and anxiety, the quality of infant attachment has been found to be strongly linked to aggression, violence, and criminality in adolescence and adulthood.[32] These patterns are found to be remarkably unyielding to change throughout a child's development and during adulthood.[33] Once seen, childhood aggression and associated poor peer relations are strong predictors of aggressive adolescent behaviors,[34] which in turn can often result in adult violence. Dr. Ken Magid, author of *High Risk: Children without a Conscience*, has studied the issue of adolescent and adult violence in depth and concludes that poor early attachment is the key.

Bonding Effects on Puberty

One striking consequence of the childhood stress of insecure attachment is early puberty. While this has been noticed in both males and females, the early onset of menstruation in girls, the most objective measurement, is the most frequently measured indicator in puberty studies.[35-37] There are several unfortunate results from early puberty. One is that children develop adult feelings before they are old enough to understand and handle them. Another, encouraged by the behavioral results of parental detachment, is an increase in teen pregnancy. Possibly the most devastating result is the increased risk of breast cancer and other cancers associated with early menstruation.[38,39] The incredible rise in consumption of cow's milk during the 1900s, also a factor in decreased attachment (via decreased breastfeeding), provides an additive effect to the early onset of puberty as well as to increased cancer rates (*as discussed in the chapter on cow's milk*).

Psychologist Jay Belsky provides a possible explanation for this accelerated maturity. He has proposed that a pattern of detached parenting has naturally occurred throughout our history, and in animals as well, in response to hard times when food is scarce or survival is otherwise in danger.[40] Ample food and safety generate the time and stability for providing warm, responsive care, thereby resulting in quality evolution of the species; hard times switch the focus to mere survival. Theoretically, reduced attachment would serve to reduce the pain of lost family members. Harsh parenting would lead to the development of early puberty and would encourage behaviors that promote multiple sexual partners, thus increasing chances for survival of the species during bleak times. Detached parenting would also foster aggressive behavior, increasing the ability to compete for food and mating opportunities.

Other Factors

Certainly, an increasing level of psychological aftermath, aggression, or violent behavior correlates with a more insecure level of attachment. Most researchers agree that withholding maternal responsiveness, often characterized as "not spoiling the child," which was encouraged by experts over the last one hundred years, is the major source of undesirable behavior, but other factors compound these problems. These are the more obvious elements of marital conflict, divorce, parental substance abuse, parental crime or psychiatric disorder, and overprotective and controlling parents. Note however that these conditions are those that occur chiefly in parents with insecurely attached beginnings. Fortunately, it is comforting to know that, at least statistically, the effects on children experiencing hardships such as divorce can be mostly overridden when at least one long-term caregiver maintains a strong sensitive bond with them.

Another major cause of infant and child behavior problems is food sensitivity reactions and other allergies. These are much more far-reaching than most are led to believe. The reduction in breastfeeding and the resultant mass use of cow's milk largely causes this growing predicament. (*This topic is covered in depth in the last chapters of this book.*) It's clear that less-responsive parenting and formula use often go hand-in-hand, making it sometimes difficult to entirely discern which of these factors is leading to which behavioral effects. Yet, with the thousands of studies on the adverse effects of dairy consumption, it is quite clear that this ingredient on its own is highly responsible for many behaviorial problems now becoming prevalent. Over and over again, we will see similar behavior and health problems from detached parenting practices and from early and heavy cow's milk feeding.

Separation Sensitivity

Extended mother–infant separation is another key issue affecting infant bonding. In the early years, repeated long separations, such as parental vacations, can be harmful to the attachment relationship.[41] Children may learn that they can't depend on mother to always be there, and trust diminishes. Along with long-term separation comes the delicate issue of daylong separations and day care. There were bursts of studies on this issue in the mid 1980s as well as the late 1990s, but the results are very conflicting. None of the results appear to be overwhelming. Overall, it appears that less-attached mother–infant pairs may decide to use day care somewhat more frequently, which may perpetuate the reduced attachment, but many of these infants end up finding attachments through day care that instill the ability to trust. Infants who repetitively lose predominant caregivers seem to suffer most. Using data on the *quality* of day care produces more certain statistics, but ideas on quality also vary. When visiting a day care center, one tends to notice beauty and cleanliness, at least at first, but the nature and level of the attention given to each child is far more important. There seems to be agreement that part-time day care has less effect on the mother–infant bond than does full-time, and other factors being the same, many behavioral differences between in-home and day care children seem to fade over time after kindergarten. Unfortunately, most families, having generally lost the valuable access to a close-knit neighborhood or tribe or highly available extended families, are sometimes caught today between what parenting levels are desired and what is emotionally (and financially) possible.

Twins:
The "Beginnings Don't Matter" Studies

Lawrence Wright, a staff writer for the *New Yorker*, wrote *Twins and What They Tell Us about Who We Are*.[42] He summarizes and speculates from studies performed on twins who were raised in separate households. Studies of separated twins aim to discover how totally different environments affect the outcome of genetically identical humans, in an attempt to throw light on the age-old nature versus nurture debate. Because Wright found similar behaviors in adults who came from supposedly different beginnings, Wright suggests that early environment has little effect on behavior. Judith Harris, in *The Nurture Assumption*, uses the same arguments to suggest that only peers influence how children will behave and what kind of people they will become — that the actions of the parents matter little. Again, she bases her arguments on the assumption that the separated twins in the studies had entirely different beginnings, having been adopted by different families. Although parenting practices were not strongly altered by the large number of attachment studies of the 1970s and 1980s, which added much weight to the parental nurture side of the equation, there has been a sigh-of-relief reaction from factions of society for these new nature and peers-based arguments, demonstrating that the issue has remained a prominent concern in the minds of many.

I believe however that the subjects in these studies had much more similar beginnings than Wright and Harris realize, and this, I feel, is a very critical point that washes out their arguments from the start. First of all, each pair shared the same womb and intrauterine exposure to maternal emotions, stress levels, nutrition, drugs, and so forth. Since the subjects were nearly all adopted, few, if any, were breastfed. Since most or all of the adoptive families were unaware they were raising separated twins, it can be assumed that none of the adoptive parents were present at the births or were available for early bonding experiences. In fact, the average age of these subjects at adoption was *5 months!* (Only after the severe effects of institutionalizing babies were recognized in the 1960s did newborn adoptions occur to any degree.) Since most twins are low-birth-weight babies, in all likelihood most of these babies spent their first weeks in hospitals. Then these children, depending on the year of their birth, spent the next months of their lives either in inattentive orphanages, or in foster homes where caretakers typically protect themselves by not becoming too attached to the infants. Furthermore, all these subjects not only shared a critical separation with their first bonded caretakers (after non-bonded hospital beginnings), but they also suffered separation from their closely bonded twin, whom they knew for several months in the womb plus for whatever time they spent together after birth. Initially, their adoptive parents would not have been influenced by the hormonally induced reorganization of brain receptors that goes on during pregnancy, promoting early parental behaviors. Additionally, the infants would not have an initial imprinting on these adoptive parents, generally formed in the womb and the first weeks of life. Their bottle-feeding and less intimate relationships would predict more of a crib-crying, textbook-of-the-times (stressful) upbringing. Finally, and particularly at the time of these births, there were set parameters for families who were allowed to adopt, creating more similarity.

None of this is meant to suggest that adoption is anything less than an absolutely priceless opportunity. Adopted infants can develop just as strong an attachment as any other baby — and can even be breastfed in most cases if the desire is there. I make this comparison only to point out that Wright's and Harris's subjects have far less random beginnings than they suggest.

For instance, Wright describes two girls who similarly displayed prolonged thumb-sucking and "blanket clenching." Neither girl could be easily controlled, both had poor peer relations, and both hid their emotions. Each girl told the researchers that she received a very low level of affection from her mother — the one who reported a somewhat higher level being the one with better behavior and peer relations. To me, the girls' behavior sounds like genetically similar responses to similar low-attachment environments and the shared early loss of primary caregivers and a sibling. Other symptoms they displayed, such as prolonged bedwetting and learning disorders, are often signs of intolerance to cow's milk products (beginning with formula feeding) and possibly other foods. This sensitivity and the resulting behavior require a certain genetic disposition, but depend on environmental circumstances to manifest.

Because researchers found close similarities in behavior in many sets of separated twins, they conclude that early environment has little to do with shaping personality. However, when one examines the truly important factors, the early environments of these twins were very similar indeed. The early conditions these twins shared are the ones that attachment researchers emphasize as the most important for shaping behavior.

> Social behavior, discipline, criminality, and depression were all influenced more by family environment than by genetics, as was "happiness."

Consider another example. Other researchers showed that when one twin was divorced, there was a much higher than average chance the other would be.[43] This *could* demonstrate a genetic predisposition for divorce, as they suggest; more likely (to me) however, divorce was a genetically similar response to the shared experience of poor attachment and separations during infancy.

Most importantly, when these studies reported "similar behaviors," they usually described shared personality quirks. In contrast, more reliable statistics, gathered by comparing identical twins (identical genetics) to fraternal twins (some dissimilar genetics) who were all raised together, indicate that *social* behavior, discipline, criminality, and depression were all influenced more by family environment than by genetics, as was "happiness." Attachment studies suggest the very same thing; furthermore, these behaviors are the most important aspects of personality, not the mere quirks of personality upon which much of the nature and peers arguments were built.

As with our appearance, much of our personality, preferences, and mannerisms are genetically determined. So are the ways we will personally respond to certain kinds of social exposure. But there is a definite pattern to the responses that correlate most strongly with the earliest environment, which then governs how we will react later on in life. I find no contradiction between the studies on twins and the attachment study findings. No one discounts genetics, but it seems clear that parental responsiveness and bonding also play a major role in psychological and social outcomes.

Reattachment

Psychologists do have ways of mediating when poor attachment has occurred in a child. Before the age of 7 months, extra holding, nurturing, and availability generally do the trick. Children adopted or placed into foster homes before this age show little difficulty in forming healthy attachments when strong measures are taken. Professional intervention needs to be more focused the older the child is. Fairly good results are still expected when efforts begin before the age of 7 years.[44] These windows of opportunity also exist for the father who was not involved from the beginning. Beyond this age, positive lasting change is very difficult to produce and treatments become more radical. For this reason, psychologists and sociologists emphasize the overwhelming importance of nurturing parenting from the very beginning.

Breaking the Cycle

The findings of attachment research suggest that insecurely attached children not only end up in poorly attached marriages and relationships, but in their turn they also raise insecurely attached children. Fortunately, however, it has been shown that some adults who explore their own insecurely attached shortcomings can heal and become more attached as adults and parents. Belsky found that adults who simply have a coherent understanding of the negative consequences of their own insecure attachment, and who can remain effective parents during highly stressful situations, are able to raise securely attached children.[45] He calls these adults "earned secures." Others have similarly found that the cycle can be broken through intellectual means.[46] Ultimately, many heal themselves by successfully developing a strongly attached relationship with a mate or child.[47]

Going Beyond Secure Attachment

The distinct categories of secure or insecure attachment serve to provide a valuable basis for research into the outcomes of various parental patterns, but the picture is certainly not as simple as some literature describes it, namely, as attached either securely or insecurely. There are very severe examples of improper attachment resulting from abandonment and abuse, but there are many shades of attachment between this and the securely attached infant, whose parents respond quickly and sensitively to cries, and provide consistent affectionate attention.

Many also believe there are many levels of secure attachment, or possibly a level beyond it of highly attuned, strongly bonded, gentle and intimate relationships. Today, parents around the U.S. are rediscovering their natural parenting options and are following a style that has become known as "attachment parenting." The results of the multitude of in-depth studies on attachment have lent permission to many to provide the responsive, affectionate care parents are naturally driven to offer. Some deeper issues are not addressed in the popular psychological models of the twentieth century, such as the immense value of nursing for emotional, physical, and intellectual development, as well as for physical health. Even beyond this, there is a huge gap between common breastfeeding advice and the most beneficial nursing measures. The provision of skin-to-skin contact and frequent holding and carrying may not be part of these models either, but the great value of around-the-clock close contact has been described by many and can be clearly seen around the world.

> Cultures around the world that practice more natural forms of parenting have healthier infants who cry much less, toddlers who do not exhibit "terrible twos," generally respectful teenagers, and independent adults who participate in family matters.

Thus, the attachment-parenting model may look at traditional twentieth-century parenting as the cause of mild to moderate forms of attachment disorders. Moreover, some of the relationships approved as securely attached may be viewed as still lacking some ideal qualities. While only 41% of U.S. infants have been classified as insecurely attached, the percentage of adults who generally suffer from security, trust, control, or intimacy issues, who are not able to sustain long healthy relationships, who are depressed or anxious, or who deal poorly with stress, is larger than this.

Cultures around the world that practice more natural forms of parenting have healthier infants who cry much less, toddlers who do not exhibit "terrible twos," generally respectful teenagers, and independent adults who participate in family matters.

Attachment parenting practices are based on the wisdom of our natural parenting instincts and baby's natural abilities to provide instructions for care. In addition to instinctual guidance, more complex species are known to pass wisdom down from generation to generation. But we have lost a few generations. It's no wonder new mothers in the Western world have so many problems and questions. Most have never witnessed a birth before their own child's nor seen a baby nurse — the most basic essentials are not there. Actually, a large portion of attachment-parented infants are the third or fourth child in a family that has given up "modern" methods in favor of practices they found over time to be easier and to provide superior results.

Those who wish to gain all the benefits of securely attached parent–child relationships find it easy to follow their natural drives to feed baby when hunger is expressed, to nurse, console, and comfort him in response to his needs, to hold and be with their infants as much as possible, using snuggies, slings, and backpacks to give the infant moment-to-moment body contact, to provide consistent caretaker availability and response, and enriching exposure to the daily world. Nightly cries of abandonment and hunger, which tear at a parent's heart, are enjoyably avoided by naturally sharing sleep and nursing throughout the night.

Follow Your Instincts

Human babies are born much more prematurely than most babies are. While most animal babies can walk or swim at birth, humans are unable to even make their way to mother's milk or other food for a year. Two years must pass before they can recognize danger signs. At birth, they only have needs: to be fed when their tummies are hungry, to be kept warm by warm bodies, to be protected and cared for, and to develop social attachments for emotional security.

Nature and evolution have provided sufficient means for babies to have all their needs met. Their tiny size, softness, precious smiles, and heart-rending cries elicit powerful drives in adult females to respond to them and hold them, and in males to protect them. When there is no interference, human instincts, hormones, neurotransmitters, and neurons provide for a strong bonding process between infants and their caretakers so that the providers of the infants' milk and safety will never be far away. At the same time, infants' brains are stimulated and educated by regular social interaction, expressions, touching, and words from caretakers, and they are therefore nurtured into intelligent, independent, secure, trusting beings. A gesture or a whimper and mother knows they need to be fed, dried, spoken to, or warmed. When you pick up a crying baby, you provide security and comfort and build the baby's trust in her caretakers. An infant who is fed when he is hungry feels satiated, loved, and respected, and trusts that he is safe. A baby whose parents respond to her feelings knows she can confide in them.

> *An infant who is fed when he is hungry feels satiated, loved, and respected, and trusts that he is safe. A baby whose parents respond to her feelings knows she can confide in them.*

By following Mother Nature, rather than fighting her, parenting can be far more fulfilling, as can the results. Many parents are comforted to discover permission to be with their children in the way their hearts tell them. The idea of being natural parents includes considering what feels natural for each person in the relationship. Thus, *every family will practice parenting in its own unique way* — and even differently with each child. Most find that parenting is easier when the feeling is right.

3

Bonding: The Inside Story

FALLING IN LOVE CAN BE INTOXICATING. WE MAY FEEL EUPHORIC, giddy, or forgetful as our minds become saturated with endorphins (natural opioids, pleasure hormones) and norepinephrine (adrenaline). These are our rewards for closeness. Furthermore, our bodies maintain relationships by secreting hormones such as oxytocin, prolactin, and vasopressin that make us feel good when we interact with others. Under proper conditions, this experience can emerge during parent–infant bonding. If it does, we as parents will follow the advice of our hormones and will continue to nurture our babies and maintain physical closeness with them. We "fall in love" with our babies over and over as our brains undergo physical changes that reinforce parenting behaviors. The infant experiences similar hormonal responses and is permanently affected by them, becoming strongly attached to his closest caretakers.

Humans could not have become complex, intelligent creatures without a long evolutionary social development that taught them to live with each other, learn from each other, care for each other, and depend upon each other for survival and fulfillment. This social development begins in the womb, where we become accustomed to the scent and sounds of our mother, and to the rhythm of her day. Once we are born, our hormonal control systems and brain synapses begin to permanently organize according to the human interactions we experience. We are designed to seek fulfillment for all our basic health and social needs so we can blossom into healthy, intelligent, and socially well-adapted individuals; however, we may find ourselves in an environment where our solicitations do not always receive a healthy response. When this is the case, we are programmed to become more self-centered and aggressive and less-bonded, in proportion to the severity of conditions. Toward the harsher extreme, where touching is seldom experienced and comfort rarely received, we stop secreting growth hormone and reduce brain development in order to conserve energy for a more independent survival.

In the brains of infants and children, permanent patterns are created. Unneeded brain receptors and neural pathways are disposed of, while those appropriate to the given environment are enhanced. Early social responses, stress responses, and intellectual attention build a foundation that will guide our interaction with our environment for the rest of our lives

> While an adult may be able to be romantically neglected, deceived, or totally uninvolved without major long-term consequences, an infant's permanent brain development is shaped by the level of attentiveness she receives from her "first loves."

(moderated by our own genetic slants). The initial availability of responsive care and the pursuant level of bonding with consistent caregivers determine to what degree responsible social beings will develop. While an adult may be able to be romantically neglected, deceived, or totally uninvolved without major long-term consequences, an infant's permanent brain development is shaped by the level of attentiveness she receives from her "first loves."

While many clues have been found along the way, over the last decade research has described the chemical bases of bonding reactions, confirming many people's suspicions that attentiveness and touching enhance a child's development. Recent advances in measuring stress hormones have spurred a deluge of research into infant responses to stresses such as maternal separation. Amazingly, or perhaps not, these findings tie in very well with earlier psychological findings. By becoming familiar with baby's biochemistry, one can clearly understand how parents' actions can affect their children's psychological health. Moreover, parents can better recognize their parenting instincts, plan their parenting choices, and understand the feelings of their spouse and child.

Oxytocin: A Bonding Hormone

Oxytocin is a chemical messenger released in the brain. It is very important for developing bonding between mothers and their infants, and between mother and involved father. To a lesser extent, oxytocin is elicited by friendships and general social contact, even by relationships with pets. The most common stimulus for its release in both men and women, in adults as well as in children (and mammals in general) is social contact — especially physical contact, being most pronounced with skin-to-skin contact. After it is released, oxytocin promotes the desire for further social interaction. Therefore, frequent close proximity develops a continuous drive to maintain a given relationship, and physical touch heightens this drive. Over time, the sight, sound (especially a cry), or even thought of the individual can cause oxytocin release.

Oxytocin calms and relaxes and reduces stress responses, playing a likely role in the health benefits reportedly seen with long marriages and social relationships,[1] or when the elderly keep pets. By promoting lower blood pressure and reduced heart rate as well as certain kinds of artery repair, long-term social interactions that increase oxytocin levels actually reduce heart disease.[2] In fact, adults who display the symptoms of poor childhood attachment, such as bouts of depression or anxiety, face a tripled risk of dying from heart disease.[3] Oxytocin lowers pain sensitivity, which is why a parent's kiss is effective treatment for a scraped knee. It also helps to regulate bodily functions such as digestion and hormone secretion, promoting absorption of nutrients and growth in the well-attended baby.

Oxytocin & the Mother

When the process is uninterrupted, oxytocin is one of nature's chief tools for creating a mother. Roused by the high levels of estrogen ("female hormone") during pregnancy, the number of oxytocin receptors in the expecting mother's brain increases dramatically near the end of her pregnancy. This makes the new mother highly responsive to the presence of oxytocin. These receptors increase in the part of her brain that promotes maternal behaviors.[4]

Oxytocin's first important surge is during labor, when labor is allowed naturally, that is. Serving to encourage uterine contractions for the passage of the infant from the uterus to the birth canal, this is the beginning of highly elevated oxytocin levels that assist the initial bonding after birth. Beyond this stage, further release of oxytocin is stimulated by the infant's passage through the birth canal.

When all goes well, the oxytocin level is very high in a mother at the moment her infant is born. It continues to rise until 45 minutes after birth, returning to its pre-labor level at the end of 1 hour,[5] if no nursing has occurred. This high level is one of several factors that create the imprinting opportunity during the first hour after birth. Initially high levels of oxytocin and the mother's high receptivity to its presence help mother imprint strongly onto her new infant. High oxytocin levels promote mother's maternal feelings and behaviors, as well as her tendency to bond. Oxytocin also causes mother to become familiar with the odor of her infant and attracted to it, preferring it above all others.[6] By influencing maternal behavior and stimulating milk "let down" (allowing milk to flow) during nursing, oxytocin helps make the first attempts at breastfeeding feel entirely natural. High levels after birth also help reduce mother's pain recognition. The first nursing attempts after birth then cause further oxytocin release, which not only continues the bonding process, but serves to help shrink the uterus, preventing hemorrhage.

Much higher levels of oxytocin are found in a mother after a vaginal delivery than after an elective C-section.[7] A cesarean section after labor produces oxytocin levels somewhere in between. It has been found that the oxytocin levels secreted during nursing remain low even two days following a C-section, with a notable negative impact on mother's anxiety level[8,9] and her success in breastfeeding. Furthermore, the infant is receiving less of this comforting and bonding hormone from mother's milk.

After the first hour following labor and birth, mother continues to produce elevated levels of oxytocin as a consequence of nursing and holding her infant. She may be aware of helpful uterine contractions during breastfeeding for days or weeks. Her increased level of oxytocin receptors also remains high for a long time, for more than several months. This hormonal condition provides calm, pain tolerance, reduced blood pressure, and a sense of well-being for her, and also promotes bonding and maternal behaviors that help her to fall in love with her baby.

Oxytocin causes mother to be more caring, to be more eager to please others, to become more sensitive to others' feelings, and to recognize nonverbal cues more readily. Under the early influence of oxytocin, certain nerve junctions in certain areas of her brain actually undergo reorganization, thereby making her maternal behaviors rather permanent. High oxytocin in the female has also been shown to promote preference for whatever male is present during its surges[10] (one good reason for dad to hang around during and after the birth).

Elevated levels of oxytocin also promote what is referred to as social memory — developing increased memory for people's faces, odors (subconsciously), and impressions, although the highest doses of oxytocin create an amnesia-like effect[11] that helps the mother forget some of the trauma of childbirth and makes her a bit forgetful at other times during the first months spent close to her infant. Oxytocin levels create increased social behavior as well. Having spent much time at home nesting during pregnancy, new mothers now seek the company of other family members and other mothers. We see her comparing baby's teething schedules, forming play groups, attending parenting classes and support groups, or just cruising the malls. But this attached mother may not be buying many fancy clothes and accessories for herself because her brain receptors have been reorganized by oxytocin (and prolactin). Her priorities have been altered and her brain no longer signals her to groom and adorn in order to obtain a mate, and thus a pregnancy. Now that the child has already been created, mom's grooming habits are directed toward baby.

Even though estrogen helps oxytocin secretion in the non-mother, estrogen levels in the mother gradually decrease in the days after an infant's birth in order to sustain lactation (breastmilk development). At this point it is safe for the body to do this because a strong and lasting imprinting and neural reorganization should have already taken place, and mother still has more oxytocin receptors than usual, thanks to the high estrogen of pregnancy. Estrogen stays low for about the first year of nursing, then gradually increases to normal levels, even when lactation continues.[12] Even though estrogen levels drop, oxytocin levels are not necessarily depleted in a nursing mother. The reduced estrogen can be more than made up for with a lot of physical contact during nursing, holding, and sharing sleep (parents and children in the same bed). Oxytocin levels are higher in mothers who exclusively breastfeed than in those who use supplementary bottles.[13]

Oxytocin & the Infant

Just like his mother, an infant is born with highly elevated oxy-tocin levels, but the first attempts at nursing during the initial hour of bonding will cause these levels to surge even more. The initial bonding of an infant to its parents appears to be mostly, but not entirely, inspired by odors (pheromones). When the infant is born, he is already imprinted on the odor of his amniotic fluid.[14,15] This imprinting occurs shortly before birth with the help of oxytocin, and this imprinting is then heightened during the high oxytocin window just after birth. In the days following birth, the infant can be comforted by this odor — babies who remain exposed to these odors cry far less than those who do not.[16] Gradually over the next days, baby starts to prefer the odor of his mother's breast. A newborn can quickly find mother's nipple even on his first couple of tries because mother's breast odor resembles that of the amniotic fluid. While this pre-birth imprinting must have a partial role in helping a newborn find his food, continued imprinting upon his mother is not food related. In fact, formula-fed infants are more attracted (in laboratory tests) to their mother's breast odor than to that of their formula, even two weeks after birth.[17] Elevated oxytocin levels cre-ated by body contact and nursing help the infant continue to develop odor preferences, especially in the first weeks of life. To me this suggests that father has a very good chance of having baby imprint on him in the early days after birth if the newborn learns his father's odors, even though father is not feeding the baby. I also imagine some infants having an unusual attraction to a certain bottle of perfume or bar of deodorant soap. Mates can imprint on each other's odors throughout adulthood, but the early abilities of the infant are much stronger.

Although baby makes her own oxytocin in response to nursing, mother also transfers oxytocin to the infant in her milk.[18] This oxy-tocin serves to promote continuous relaxation and closeness for both mother and baby, over and above the oxytocin-induced expe-riences of breastfeeding. A more variable release of oxytocin is seen in bottle-fed infants, but is definitely higher in an infant who is "bottle-nursed" tightly in the arms (causing oxytocin release in the feeder as well), rather than with a propped bottle.

Often the calming granted an infant during nursing helps her to drift off to sleep naturally, with mother joining in on occasion. Although whole cow's milk contains some factors that sooth humans, such as tryptophan, the author could not find data on whether there is oxytocin in infant formulas. Since the dairy industry vigorously attempts to convince the public that certain cow hormones are not active in humans, although many are, and with less than desirable results (*see the chapter on cow's milk*), one wonders whether they have found it unwise to explore oxytocin effects in formulas.

Oxytocin also provides some relief from hunger, helping the infant to end nutritive nursing (taking in milk), even though she may continue non-nutritive nursing (taking no milk) for many more minutes for its calming and bonding effects.

Regular body contact and other nurturing acts by parents produce a constant, elevated level of oxytocin in the infant, which in turn provides a valuable reduction in the infant's stress hormone responses. It has been demonstrated that, *depending on the practices of the parents, the resulting high or low level of oxytocin will control the permanent organization of the stress-handling portion of the baby's brain* — promoting lasting securely attached or insecure characteristics in the adolescent and adult. Psychiatrist Michael Commons suggests that the now-common poor stress regulation is responsible for the proliferation of post-traumatic stress disorder (PTSD) seen today in Americans.[19] Others liken it to type A behavior.

Oxytocin & the Father

It has been shown in various mammals that a live-in father's oxytocin levels rise toward the end of his mate's pregnancy.[20] In humans, an involved father can discriminate between the odor of his newborn's amniotic fluid and that of others, and can associate it with his infant and his late-pregnancy wife.[21] Apparently, nature means for father to bond with his infant, and at the same time develop heightened bonding with his mate.

When the father spends significant amounts of time in contact with his infant, oxytocin encourages him to become more involved in the ongoing care in a self-perpetuating cycle.

When the father spends significant amounts of time in contact with his infant, oxytocin encourages him to become more involved in the ongoing care in a self-perpetuating cycle. Oxytocin in the father also increases his interest in physical contact with the mother, but not for sexual contact.[22] After a birth some fathers have a long wait before their mates have much sexual interest (or their babies allow the time), but just as sexual drive is a hormonal event, nature now provides a hormonal boost for father to become more interested in being a devoted and satisfied part of the family picture through his involvement with the baby. Just as with the hormonal effects on mother, this design is primarily for baby's benefit, to provide another caretaker and a protector for him and his mother. The parents certainly benefit too; in fact, the health benefits they receive help keep them around for baby.

Oxytocin: Love & the Heart

The existence of oxytocin in humans and its elevated presence in parents and in infants at birth in no way guarantees bonding, nurturing, and growing love. Only by acting on your instinctive desires to enjoy close contact will your oxytocin levels continue to surge, thereby continuously stimulating your desire to be physically close. Once the initial imprinting has occurred in the first days of the infant's life, it will persist, but it can fade over time without continued involvement. If you provide sensitive responsive care to your infant through breastfeeding and prolonged body contact, high levels of oxytocin in you and your baby will continue to promote strong long-term bonding, assuring each of reciprocal love. In addi-

tion your infant's brain will be organized so that stress responses are minimal and well-handled, thereby improving future behavior and relationships and reducing later risk of heart disease to one third that of an insecurely attached child. Bonding creates a happier individual who can form strong adult bonds with a mate.

The father who is physically involved with his infant will become more and more attracted to the child, enjoying strong paternal feelings and becoming more in tune with the mother as well. Everyone benefits from his enhanced role as father and husband. He will reap heart and health rewards as well as a better future relationship with his child. High oxytocin levels in mother prevent her from feeling like she is a beast of burden at times. Instead, she will beam with love and will be happy to continue to nurse and cling to what feels like her bundle of joy. She will feel much desire to nurture and to be more socially responsive, and she'll feel good and will remain calmer, which allows her to handle her busy new job with composure and joy, then pass that joy on to her baby and those around her. She too reaps heart benefits from the long-term effects of oxytocin. Incidentally, alcohol reduces oxytocin levels.[23] Regular consumption can reduce one's ties to the family, replacing that rewarding sensation with the rewards of the bottle. (Wonder where this bottle attachment started?)

> *High oxytocin levels in mother prevent her from feeling like she is a beast of burden at times. Instead, she will beam with love and will be happy to continue to nurse and cling to what feels like her bundle of joy.*

With all of its powers, oxytocin is but one of a list of many chemicals that nature uses to ensure that baby finds the love and care he needs.

Vasopressin & Protection

Although present and active during bonding in the mother and infant, vasopressin plays a bigger role in the father. Vasopressin is largely dependent on testosterone ("male hormone"), and in a male it modifies testosterone's effects. Animal studies have found that vasopressin causes some reorganization in the male brain, but not in the female's.[24] Although these studies report that this starts after mating, mating generally leads to pregnancy in animals, so mating and pregnancy effects cannot easily be separated in these studies. Other studies indicate that, in humans, brain reorganization is stronger when males are living with a partner, and strongest when cohabiting with a pregnant mate. After this has occurred, the male is more dedicated to his mate and expresses paternal behaviors of protection and maintaining nearness. Virgin male prairie voles (a small mammal) injected with vasopressin were found to begin touching, grooming, and huddling over nearby pups, where normally they would have avoided them.[25] While evidence indirectly suggests that touch elevates vasopressin (as with oxytocin), it seems to develop from close proximity alone.

Like oxytocin, vasopressin promotes bonding between the father and the mother,[26] helps the father recognize and bond to his baby, and makes him want to be part of the family, rather than alone. It has gained a reputation as the "monogamy hormone." Dr. Theresa Crenshaw, author of *The Alchemy of Love and Lust*, says, "Testosterone wants to prowl, vasopressin wants to stay home."[27] She also describes vasopressin as tempering the man's sexual drive.

Vasopressin reinforces the father's testosterone-promoted protective inclination regarding his mate and child, but tempers his aggression, making him more reasonable and less extreme. By promoting more rational and less capricious thinking, this hormone induces a sensible paternal role, providing stability as well as vigilance.

Vasopressin helps to control stress responses[28] in baby, mother, and father, thus providing calm, but also encouraging positive social interaction and behavior. It also improves learning and memory.[29] Although it has a weaker effect than oxytocin, vasopressin plays a role in odor attachment, at least in infants, as well as the onset of maternal behaviors.[30]

Prolactin & Behavior

Prolactin is released in all healthy people during sleep, helping to maintain reproductive organs and immune function. In an expecting mother prolactin levels are elevated throughout pregnancy, preparing the breasts for milk production and speeding the onset of maternal behavior after birth. Then, after a woman gives birth, her prolactin promotes milk production for lactation as well as maternal behavior. But prolactin production is not stimulated by baby's hunger cries, as is oxytocin. It is produced in response to suckling during nursing. While some milk is produced and stored between nursing sessions, most is made during nursing. Prolactin also relaxes mother, and in the early months, creates a bit of fatigue during a nursing session so she has no strong desire to hop up and do other things.

Prolactin promotes caregiving behaviors and over time directs brain reorganization to favor these behaviors.[31] Father's prolactin levels begin to elevate during mother's pregnancy, but most of the rise in the male occurs after many days of cohabitation with the infant.[32]

As a result of hormonally orchestrated brain reorganization during parenthood, prolactin release patterns are altered. Fathers release prolactin in response to intruder threats, whereas childless males do not,[33] thus indicating that prolactin plays a role in creating protective paternal behavior. On the other hand, nursing mothers do not release prolactin in response to loud noise, whereas childless females do.[34] In children and non-parents, prolactin surges are related to stress levels, so it is generally considered a stress hormone. In parents, it serves as a parenting hormone; in others, it behaves as a stress hormone. Research indicates that the brain uses different pathways during acute stress responses and during parental care, and parental care in the attached parent does not cause the release of other stress hormones.[35]

Prolactin not only promotes maternal and paternal behaviors in parents but also reduces their sex drive. In childless adults, prolonged elevations are associated with the fatigue and infertility that often accompany long periods of stress, and with depression and other emotional difficulties as well.[36] Just as an infant's early attachment levels will permanently affect its stress responses, adults who had less-attached infancies will typically experience more stress-like prolactin elevations, actions, and responses. A common link between elevated prolactin levels and mood disorders provides one explanation for the psychological difficulties that are more prevalent in insecurely attached adults.

In a child, prolactin is a stress hormone, not a parenting hormone. Pediatrician Betsy Lozoff found that children with high prolactin levels were described as hesitant and unhappy during stressful test situations.[37] She noted that different children had different levels of stress response (measured here by prolactin release). Other studies (*discussed in the previous chapter*) have strongly correlated these differences with the levels of early maternal responsiveness. One researcher suggests that prolonged periods of elevated prolactin in poorly bonded infant males (reducing testosterone levels during a sensitive brain organization period) could influence their sexual orientation.[38]

Elevated prolactin levels in both the nursing mother and the involved father cause some reduction in their testosterone levels, which in turn reduces their libidos (but not their sexual functioning).[39,40] Their fertility can be reduced for a time as well.[41] This reduction in sexual activity and fertility is entirely by design for the benefit of the infant. First, it focuses parental time and affection on the baby, which will ultimately lead to the highest degree of behavioral development and bonding. More important, by preventing another child from entering the picture for at least a couple years, the infant is assured ample breastfeeding and holding time, ample parental attention and energy, and the parents' resources for his use. The infant is also more likely to have a consistently low-key, level-headed mother who is not subjected to the mood swings and energy drops of premenstrual syndrome (PMS) or pregnancy. When the father is intimately involved with the infant along with the mother, there should be some accord between the desires of the two, and oxytocin and other chemicals provide for heightened bonding and non-sexual interest in each other, which serves to retain a second devoted caretaker for the infant.

Opioids & Rewards

Opioids are natural morphine-like chemicals created in our bodies (endorphins and enkephalins). They reduce pain awareness and create feelings of elation. Social contacts, especially those between parent and child, and most especially touch, induce opioid release, creating good feelings that will enhance bonding. Play, including rough and tumble play, also causes opioid release,[42] as does smiling. Some of the most special smiles are those intently shared between parent and child. Odor, taste, activity, and even place preferences can develop as the result of opioid release during pleasant social contacts, and certainly the sight of a loved one's face stimulates surges. Opioid released in a child's brain as a conditioned response to a parent's warm hugs and kisses can be effective for helping reduce the pain from a tumble or a disappointment.

Parents "learn" to enjoy beneficial activities such as breastfeeding and holding, and infants "learn" to enjoy contact such as being held, carried, and rocked, all as a response to opioid release. Babies need milk, and opioids are nature's reward to them for obtaining it, especially during the initial attempts. The first few episodes of sucking organize nerve pathways in the newborn's brain, conditioning her to continue this activity.[43] This can create a problem for an infant who is given bottles in the newborn nursery. Any incidental sensations experienced during rocking, touching, and eating that aren't noxious can become part of a child's attachment and will provide comfort. It could be the warmth of mother's body, father's furry chest, grandma's gentle lullaby, the background aroma of grandpa's cooking, a blanket, the wood-slatted side of a crib — or a bottle. Psychologist Jaak Panksepp has extensively researched the relationship between opioids and infant bonding. He believes that those stimuli that are encountered prior to weaning, in particular, can cause opioid releases in both the child and adult.[44]

Opioids initially suppress the young infant's curiosity for his environment during nursing so that he can focus on obtaining milk and the more immediate cues of his mother's face and voice. Later, opioids can enhance learning during nursing, as the reward of obtaining milk connects the

> *Prolonged elevation of prolactin in the attached parent stimulates the opioid system, heightening the rewards for intimate, loving family relationships, possibly above all else.*

infant to other experiences at the nipple such as the specific patterns of mother's speech or her comments on surrounding objects and sounds.[45] Opioids also reduce appetite and help the nursing infant know when he has obtained enough breastmilk.

Prolonged elevation of prolactin in the attached parent stimulates the opioid system,[46] heightening the rewards for intimate, loving family relationships, possibly above all else. Just as with codeine and morphine, tolerance to natural opioids can occur, which will reduce the reward level for various opioid-releasing activities over time. But this is not a problem for infants and parents, because the desired learning will have already taken place. Furthermore, higher levels of oxytocin, especially when created through frequent or prolonged body contact, actually inhibit opioid tolerance,[47] protecting the rewards for maintaining close family relationships. On the other hand, consuming artificial opioid drugs replaces the brain's need for maintaining family contacts.

Once a strong opioid bonding has occurred, separation can become emotionally upsetting, and in the infant possibly even physically uncomfortable when opioid levels decrease in the brain, much like the withdrawal symptoms from cocaine or heroin. When opioid levels become low, one might feel like going home to hold the baby, or like crying for a parent's warm embrace, depending on your point of view. Sometimes alternate behaviors are helpful. For instance, thumb-sucking can provide some relief from partial or total withdrawal from a human or rubber nipple and can even provide opioid-produced reminiscences for a while.

Norepinephrine & Learning

Breastfeeding also causes dopamine and its product, norepinephrine (adrenaline), to be produced, which help maintain some of the effects of the early bonding. They enhance energy and alertness along with some of the pleasure of attachment.[48] Norepinephrine helps organize the infant's stress control system, as well as other important hormonal controls in accordance with the nature of the early rearing experiences.[49] It is elevated in mother and infant just after birth and is a factor that helps create the initial window for imprinting, including odor imprinting.[50] Beyond birth, norepinephrine promotes learning — especially learning by memorization that is carried out by oxytocin, opioids, and other chemical influences.

Pheromones & Basic Instincts

How does the man's body know to initiate hormonal changes when he is living with a pregnant female? Of course, he may consciously know that his mate is pregnant (sometimes not at first), but it is not the conscious mind that causes prolactin and vasopressin production. Also, how can an infant accurately interpret mother's "odors" that adults often can barely detect? The answer is pheromones. Very recently, proof of their role in human perception has become quite conclusive.[51] Between 1 and 2% of our DNA (genetic information) is devoted to sensors inside the nasal cavity — a rather large amount in light of our limited sense of smell, but we now know there is another set of receptors in our nose besides those for smelling. Vomero-nasal organs are chemosensory receptors situated along our nasal septum[52] that are sensitive to the pheromones released by other humans. Among other things, pheromones are hormones, such as estrogen and testosterone, that are made in our skin.[53] Our bodies are instinctually programmed to react accordingly when we detect these pheromones around us.[54]

Newborns are much more sensitive to pheromones than adults. Unable to respond to verbal or many other cues, they apparently depend on this primitive sense that controls much of the behavior of lower animals. Most likely the initial imprinting of baby to odors and pheromones is not just a matter of preferring the parents' odors, but is a way nature controls brain organization and hormonal releases to best adapt baby to its environment. Baby's earliest, most primitive experiences are then linked to higher abilities such as facial and emotional recognition. Through these, baby most likely learns how to perceive the level of stress in the caretakers around her, such as when mother is experiencing fear or joy. Part of an infant's distress over separation may be caused by the lost parental cues about the safety of her environment. Of course the other basic sensation an infant responds to well is touch, and coincidentally, body odors and pheromones can only be sensed when people are physically very near each other.

The powerful effects olfactory and chemical sensations have on infants' hormone levels and brain development, as well as those of the parents, lead one to wonder what future research will uncover regarding the effects of close contacts with infants.

Other Chemical Bonding

Growth hormone is increased by touch and by good sleep, and is decreased by separation from the mother.[55] Melatonin is increased by good sleep, only in the dark, and in turn enhances prolactin and growth hormone. Cholecystokinin, diazepam, GABA, serotonin, somatostatin, progesterone, androgens, and other biochemical systems, including the immune system, all affect the parent–infant attachment process, and most are likely influenced in some way by our caregiving choices as parents.

Chronically elevated cortisol in infants and the hormonal and functional adjustments that go along with it are shown to be associated with permanent brain changes that lead to elevated responses to stress throughout life, such as higher blood pressure and heart rate.

Cortisol & Stress

The HPA (hypothalamic–pituitary–adrenocortical) axis, a relationship between specific brain organs and the adrenal glands, is the chief regulator of stress reactions. While several hormones direct stress reactions, often in concert with each other and with some playing more than one role, cortisol is probably the most typical of the stress hormones. It is the subject of many recent reports. During stress, stress hormones are released under control of the HPA axis to help the body cope. Cortisol can elevate the blood pressure and the heart rate, increase blood sugar, and interrupt digestive and kidney functions.

Norepinephrine responses and cortisol responses are connected. Both are released in reaction to excitement, exercise, and stress. Both cause increased heart rate, blood sugar, and brain activity. I have discussed how surges of norepinephrine during affection and play can promote learning in infants (you may remember how you occasionally learned better under the stress and excitement of last-minute studying), as well as bonding (since bonding occurs in children and adults when they share exciting activity). However, chronic exposure to negative stress causes *chronic* elevations of cortisol, instead of *surges* that have a positive effect. Chronically elevated cortisol in infants and the hormonal and functional adjustments that go along with it are shown to be associated with permanent brain changes that lead to elevated responses to stress throughout life, such as higher blood pressure and heart rate.[56] This elevated response begins quite early. Even infants regularly exposed to stress already demonstrate higher cortisol releases and more sustained elevations of cortisol in response to stressful situations.[57]

Occasional surges of cortisol throughout the day can be beneficial, but continuously elevated stress hormone levels in infancy from a stressful environment are associated with permanent negative effects on brain development. Some evolutionary theories even go so far as to suggest that the heightened stress responses that apparently lead to aggressive behavior and early puberty serve a purpose, aiding survival of the species during drought, war, or other hardships.

Studies have shown that infants who receive frequent physical affection have lower overall cortisol levels,[58] while psychological attachment studies reveal higher levels in insecurely attached children.[59,60] Women who breastfeed also produce significantly less stress hormone than those who bottle-feed.[61]

Stress in Infancy

What causes stress during infancy? Laboratory and psychology research on animal and human infants gives us many clues. Certainly,

> Studies have shown
>
> that infants who receive
>
> frequent physical affection
>
> have lower overall
>
> cortisol levels.

pain from unfortunate medical conditions can create stress. So would pain from sensitivity reactions to formula or to foods passed along in breastmilk. Physical abuse and extreme neglect provide a very high degree of stress, but the effects of these severe cases are not the point of this text. Even short-term separation from mother leads to elevated cortisol in infants, indicating stress.[62,63] In fact, after one full day of separation, infant rats already show altered brain organization of chemical receptors.[64] A similar rat study revealed that *one day without mother actually doubled the number of normal brain cell deaths*.[65]

Animal findings demonstrate that isolation from mother, decreased skin stimulation, and withholding of breastmilk have biochemical and permanent brain consequences. Correlating these findings with human behavioral research suggests which events lead to chronic stress and its permanent consequences:

- allowing a child to "cry it out" without parental attention and affection
- not feeding the child when hungry
- not offering comfort when the child is disturbed or distressed
- limiting body contact during feeding, throughout the day, and during stressful parts of the night
- low levels of human attention, stimulation, "conversation," and play

When these occur regularly, they can lead to early chronic releases of high levels of stress hormones, as well as low expression of favorable hormones, as previously discussed. All these practices have been promoted during the last century in the form of scheduled feedings, "don't spoil the child," bottle feedings, which lead to propped bottles, and physical separation during the day and night.

While it is evident that genetic makeup and life experiences influence behavior, it has been demonstrated that experiences during infancy have the strongest and most persistent effect on adult hormone regulation, stress responses, and behavior.[66] Research has demonstrated that high levels of early physical contact and maternal responsiveness can even mitigate genetic predisposition for more extreme stress reactions.[67]

Biological psychology researcher Megan Gunnar and her colleagues did infant studies that confirmed animal research findings. In their work, infants three months of age who received consistent responsive care produced less cortisol. Also, eighteen-month-olds classified as insecurely attached (who had received lower levels of responsiveness) revealed elevated levels of stress hormone.[68] These same children at age 2 continued to show elevated levels of cortisol and appeared more fearful and inhibited. Again, these children were those who had been classified as having lower levels of maternal responsiveness.[69] Other investigations have confirmed these findings.[70] Dr. Gunnar reports that the level of stress experienced in infancy permanently shapes the stress responses in the brain, which then affect memory, attention, and emotion.[71]

Results of Infant Stress

Without regular closeness to a caregiver, an infant not only suffers from elevated stress hormones, but also receives less benefit from oxytocin surges and other positive biochemical influences. The biochemical environment imposed on an infant's brain during critical development stages affects the anatomy and functioning of the brain permanently.[72] A poor biochemical environment results in less desirable emotional, behavioral, and intellectual abilities for the rest of a child's life.

As previously described, a brain developed in a stressful environment overreacts to stressful events and controls stress hormones poorly throughout life. Levels of cortisol and other stress hormones are regularly elevated in these individuals. As adults they may demonstrate type A behavior, which is associated with a high risk of heart disease and adult-onset diabetes. Interestingly, one psychiatrist found that the poor health consequences for adults who received restricted mothering during childhood — high blood pressure and high levels of cortisol — closely resemble those in adults who lost a parent as a child.[73] The effects, however, go way beyond one's blood pressure and ability to deal with stress.

The hippocampus, a structure important in learning and memory, is one brain site where development is affected by stress and bonding hormone levels. The level of the stress hormones circulating in an infant affects the number and types of receptors here.[74] It has also been demonstrated that nerve cells in the hippocampus are destroyed as a result of chronic stress and elevated stress hormone levels, producing intellectual deficits as a consequence.[75] Memory and spatial learning deficits have been demonstrated in rats that suffered prolonged stress in infancy.[76] Similarly, children with the lowest scores on mental and motor ability tests have been shown to be the ones with the highest cortisol levels in their blood.[77]

Premature development of puberty has also been associated with significantly higher levels of cortisol and other stress indicators.[78] This study additionally reports that these children have more depression, more behavior problems, and lower intelligence scores. *Here again, the laboratory studies fully confirm psychological attachment studies.* Furthermore, premature puberty increases one's risk of developing cancer.

In individuals who suffer from anxiety disorders, anorexia nervosa, and depression, excess production of cortisol is a very consistent finding.[79] Oversecretion of stress hormones has also recently been implicated in obesity, Alzheimer's disease,[80] and accelerated aging symptoms.[81] Animal studies have demonstrated decreased immune system functioning in infants subjected to the stresses of prolonged separation from mother,[82,83] which coincides with the increased incidence of illness shown in less-attached children.

Beginnings

Much has been written about the first moments after a child is born. The infant, if not entirely intoxicated by drugs used in labor, has been primed by hormones during the birth process to be born wide awake and alert for a short while. During this time the initial imprinting takes place. Already familiar with the voices of his parents, the baby, who can distinguish faces from other objects and body parts, gazes intently into the eyes of his parents, as if to record their images for life. He recognizes the odor of the amniotic fluid, which is chiefly his own, but is also that of his mother. His important early programming guides his mouth to seek and find a new physical method of maternal nourishment, and he is immediately attracted to the specific odor of the nursing vessels that will now replace his umbilical cord. The newborn, barely able to maintain his body temperature, finds comfort and ideal temperature regulation in contact with mom's warm body. Having known only the firm secure confinement of his womb, he feels comfortable against a warm body or in secure arms, and he will cry loudly, uncomfortable and anxious, if left to flail on a cold, hard surface. With his first taste of concentrated nutrition and immunity-providing colostrum, and hearing the familiar beating and gurgling sounds of mother's body, he soon falls into a peaceful sleep — even his heartbeat and breathing are regulated by mother's rhythms. As he sleeps, his first breaths and tastes of his mother establish normal, healthy flora in his digestive tract, providing defense against the less friendly microbes all around him.

However, the greatest lesson from these studies is that while nature has a very good plan, failure to follow it may lead to less desirable results.

Although all is not lost if an infant's life did not begin this way, this is the first chance for attachment and the first choice made regarding baby's health. There is a long life ahead for parents and child, and there are many directions a family can take. While a child is born seeded with specific potential (nature), the parenting style (nurture) will greatly influence the likelihood these latent abilities will come to fruition, much to the benefit or detriment of the child, family, and society.

Bonding Matters

Research on the biochemical factors influenced by child care methods demonstrates that with responsive parenting the body produces substances to help generate effective, loving, and lasting parents for an infant, as well as infants who are strongly bonded to their parents. Over time these bonds mature into love and respect. Without a doubt these chemicals permanently organize an infant's brain toward positive behaviors and later development of strong, lasting attachments. However, the greatest lesson from these studies is that while nature has a very good plan, failure to follow it may lead to less desirable results. In other words, when parents heed instinctive desires to enjoy a great deal of closeness with their infants, by feeding them naturally and responding quickly to their needs and desires (which in the infant are truly one and the same), nature is designed to develop sensitive, responsible adults. Withholding attention from an infant allows the vital chemical messengers to quickly diminish, and as a result, weak bonds are formed, and parenting becomes more arduous and less successful. At the same time, the infant manifests the effects of stress. Moreover, stress reactions and other behaviors in a child and the adult he will become are permanently altered in unfortunate ways. Aspects of the intellect and health may suffer as well.

The incredible, extensive, innate human system of hormonal rewards for consistent, close, and loving physical and social contact between parent and infant, and the just as incredible consequences, combined with the psychological research findings about attachment, provide overwhelming evidence for the intended plan for infant care, at least for me.

I once heard an older pediatrician say to a mother, strongly disapproving of the way her toddler clung to her and demanded that she hold him while his blood was drawn, "It all starts the first day you pick him up when he cries."

My only answer to this is, "Yes, it does."

(rying & (aring

"Contrary to earlier belief, the genetic constitution of each cell of the body
(nature) is subject to modulation by environmental factors (nurture)...
The effects begin during early development..."
— Bruce S. McEwen, M.D., Rockefeller University, 1988[1]

"Major brain pathways are specified in the genome; detailed connections
are fashioned by, and consequently reflect, socially mediated experience in
the world."
— Leon Eisenberg, M.D., Harvard Medical School, 1995[2]

WE HAVE SEEN THAT RESEARCHERS HAVE LEARNED A GREAT DEAL
about how early parental care affects the development of an infant.
We have also seen that many elements of infant care can profoundly
impact a child's behavior into adolescence and shape his mental and

physical health and his bonding abilities through adulthood. Now let's consider some specific caring and nurturing patterns.

Whether to allow children to cry it out is one key issue, emblematic of many others. Many old school child care advisors promoted the idea that children should be left alone to cry without consoling. As a rationale, they suggested that long bouts of crying were needed to develop the lungs. This lung theory has since been disproved, but many of today's popular authorities continue to come up with (unproven) reasons why an infant should be left to cry it out, particularly when they are learning to sleep alone. In fact, crying is a result of much of the advice given by those who are considered experts in child rearing.

> *As many cultures are proudly imitating the affluent Western picture of artificial infant feeding, separate bedrooms, and fancy baby containers, Western-style ill health is increasing along with their use.*

The Western world's familiar crying baby is far different from what is seen in cultures where parental responsiveness and affection are the unquestioned norm. It is disturbing that health problems in Western adult populations tend to coincide with the history of detached child-rearing practices — the West being plagued by eating disorders, high blood pressure, heart disease, diabetes, ulcers, colitis, depression and anxiety disorders, as well as a fear of intimacy. The prevalence of these problems in the non-nurturing world is in stark contrast to their limited occurrence in traditionally more nurturing cultures — at least until lately. As many cultures are proudly imitating the affluent Western picture of artificial infant feeding, separate bedrooms, and fancy baby containers, Western-style ill health is increasing along with their use. As you will see, a discussion of these practices and their consequences must also lead to a discussion of sudden infant death syndrome or SIDS, which frightens all parents.

Crying Babies

A newborn child cannot speak. He is helpless, unable to mobilize or feed himself. He can't even lift his head. He is trapped inside a mysterious existence where unusual and often painful sensations come frequently, where sights and sounds buzz around him, some frightening and some comforting. Having spent his prenatal life connected to his mother, he is driven by instincts to remain connected to her until his brain and motor development grow, gradually giving him independence and the ability to be a contributing member of the family and village. He begins with only one chief communication tool — crying. Crying has evolved into a highly successful means for youngsters to communicate. Any parent flooded with parenting hormones or past experience is biologically predisposed to be deeply affected by the sight and sound of an infant crying. Unless parents have rehearsed away their natural reactions (their innate intelligence), they strongly desire to respond to crying — and quickly!

If baby's communication works and his discomfort is relieved, he will develop an intimate relationship with the caretakers who provide comfort and companionship. Baby will then gradually learn that when a caretaker is nearby, other gestures can often be just as effective. A smile can lead to eye-to-eye contact and friendly facial "conversation." A grunt, whimper, or mouth gesture can successfully express hunger. Eventually, an infant won't always need to cry when other cues are well responded to. More advanced communication develops. Still, there is not always going to be someone looking directly at him for such communication to work, and in an infant, pain and fear lend themselves to crying. Stress strongly lends itself to crying unless an infant or child is encouraged to hold the stress inside, releasing it in other less healthy ways. In fact, infants with responsive mothers quickly develop the ability to create different cries, to indicate different levels of distress. Their communicative intelligence grows naturally through maternal interaction. This ability cannot manifest and flourish in infants whose cries are regularly ignored.[3]

For Crying Out Loud

While crying is intended to be purposeful, it can also be stressful. Extended crying is physically exhausting for an infant, consuming large amounts of precious energy. The digestive system is impaired and tensed during crying. Cortisol, the damaging stress hormone, is released into the bloodstream and persists at least 20 minutes after a crying bout has stopped.[4,5] During crying, an infant's blood pressure rises dramatically and blood oxygenation falls. The return of oxygen to the brain is hindered; thus, oxygenation of the brain is diminished.[6] Crying also suppresses the body's immune system, decreasing its ability to fight infections and weakening its infant defenses. Moreover, prolonged crying continues to perpetuate the sensation of sadness that initiated it.[7,8]

It is normal for infants to cry in response to fear, stress, sleepiness, or pain, or when they wish to request food, entertainment, or comfort. Yet, such cries, when frequently unanswered, are responsible for much of the stress that interferes with the attachment process and causes brain cell death, stress control disorganization, adolescent behavior problems, and physical and psychological difficulties in adults. Since crying is exhausting to the infant and mother, both mentally and physically, it is understandable that mothers feel the urge to answer crying quickly. A mother attempting to ignore crying also becomes quickly exhausted because she is being helplessly exposed to prolonged and annoying wails. She also becomes flooded with cortisol. Responsive parenting is best for an infant in terms of immediate safety, health, and comfort, as well as for long-term development. It is healthier and generally more comfortable for mother too.

"Normal" Crying

We have long been conditioned to think of the normal newborn as red-faced and loudly crying. However, when a newborn is treated with affection and comfort, this is not the case. In fact, one study found that responsive treatment led to 2 minutes of crying during the first 3 hours of life, compared to over 18 times that amount in infants treated by the culturally accepted hospital routine.[9] Thus, it is reasonable to conclude that the "normal" newborn American infant is crying from sudden abandonment. Another study found infants who received peaceful warm physical contact during their first hours actually cried much less during their one-year physical examinations,[10] suggesting a profound and lasting effect probably on the parenting behaviors as well as those of the infant.

U.S. child care experts provide descriptions of what they refer to as "normal" amounts of crying in infants, generally suggesting that 2 to 3 hours per 24-hour period is normal. Yet, these "normal"

> Quite consistently they have found that when frequent natural feeding, close contact, and quick responsiveness are the norm, the average amount of infant crying is far below that seen in the U.S., and furthermore, colic is generally unknown.

crying measurements are made in hospital nurseries where newborns are severed from their mothers, and in traditional homes where the practice of ignoring crying is commonplace. Crying beyond this amount is then defined as "colic." In the absence of obvious medical disorder, the diagnosis of colic is intended as an explanation that will provide some sort of relief to parents. At a certain point crying goes beyond what is classified as normal; then long crying is termed "colic"; the problem is now "explained," thus no further investigation or action may be suggested. Often, parents are offered assurances that "this time will pass." Many researchers have made detailed observations of child care practices in cultures around the world. Quite consistently they have found that when frequent natural feeding, close contact, and quick responsiveness are the norm, the average amount of infant crying is far below that seen in the U.S., and furthermore, colic is generally unknown.[11-13] Since these cultures represent by far a greater portion of the world population, *their* infant crying behaviors should more accurately be considered the norm.

Studies show that in U.S. families with long-crying infants, when parents are taught how to quickly respond to their infant's cries and learn how to understand their cues, the amount of crying drops dramatically.[14] Also, when American mothers in La Leche League (an organization that promotes breastfeeding, whose members generally feed their infants on cue and are otherwise responsive to their infants) were compared to American mothers using typical care techniques, far less crying was measured.[15] Both frequent feeding and regular responsiveness, measures that reduce infant stress, were found to be independently responsible for decreased crying.

If children are left alone in bed and start to cry, responding to that crying greatly reduces it. Also, breastfed infants cry less in the night,[16] in part because bottle-fed infants have to wait for their formulas to be mixed and warmed, in part because breastfed infants experience fewer digestive problems and illnesses, and in part because of the calming, soothing effects of nursing. Yet night waking and night crying are two very different things. A healthy, cosleeping (sleeping with mom), breastfed infant seldom finds need to cry during the night, but may feed frequently as a result of some degree of arousal several times through the night. This natural stirring can be very helpful in preventing SIDS.

To Respond or Not: "Spoiling" Myths

The stress of isolation and infrequent feeding can cause infants to cry a great deal, which in turn causes more physical and emotional stress. Infants who have succumbed to the idea that crying for desired feeding and attention is futile suffer possibly even more stress, having no outlet for their ongoing frustrations. As seen in the last two chapters, the consequences of regular stress for an infant are far-reaching. Some parents believe that little they do before the age of 3 to 5 matters, since there are no memories before this time. Quite to the contrary, early brain organization is a very powerful memory. *While the specifics may be lost, unconscious memories are developed neurologically and biochemically from birth.* Just as the tiny body needs to grow, the brain needs to discover what kind of environment it exists in, so it can develop accordingly.

Yet, many advisors suggest that delaying or avoiding response to infants and allowing them to cry over easily resolvable stresses is in their best interest. Some suggest that "giving in" to their "controlling demands" will cause them to become more demanding. But the extensive amount of research performed on this subject has shown that about half the children whose needs were neglected actually became more demanding, fussier infants. The other half became withdrawn, learning to suppress their emotions and not trusting their parents to be there for them, often making no attempts to engage their mothers at all. Some of the latter are what many call "good babies." Desmond Morris refers to these kinds of infants as those who have been truly "spoiled," in the sense of spoiled fruit. Their potential is being wasted.

Infants' reactions to unresponsive caregivers is like to that of patients in a busy hospital ward: When patients' call button requests are not answered for very long periods of time, nurses know well that some patients will begin to signal over and over, eventually crying out frequently for assistance. Others simply stop trying, resolving to bear their pain, thirst, or other discomfort until help arrives on its own. For a telling comparison, let's translate today's prevalent baby care advice into marital advice: From the very start, withhold affection from your mate or he may come to expect it, or even worse, ask for it. Ignore his wishes for comfort so he does not become spoiled. Do not validate his feelings, and refuse to console him when he is sad or lonely so he will not bother you with those feelings. Forbid him to eat unless your watch says it's time for him to eat... Needless to say, strong marital bonds could not be developed this way. Nor would you care for your helpless bedridden mother in this fashion.

Twentieth-century Western culture has stressed independence. Many experts assert that if an infant doesn't learn to be independent quickly, it never will learn. Yet, attachment studies have shown that infants who receive strong responses from caregivers request holding less often and appear to enjoy holding more. *Attached children also become more responsive to parental requests, a kind of "dependence" that is preferable.* Lozoff studied a sample of contemporary hunter–gatherer cultures around the world to observe the relationship between the kind of infant care provided and the outcome in the children. She found that the mothers were the chief nurturers of infants, providing lots of body contact throughout the day and night, prolonged breastfeeding, and quick, affectionate response to crying. The children in these cultures achieved independence by 2 to 4 years of age, spending more than half their days away from their mothers.[18] Apparently, infants are able to develop confidence in themselves and their environment when they are able to obtain what they need through their communication attempts. By contrast, delayed response creates a sense of helplessness.

One common bit of advice has been to respond to a baby only when she is being "good." That is, when she is not expressing fear or sadness, or any desire for food or help. Psychologists have found that this kind of behavioral conditioning is very effective for creating individuals who hold their feelings in and can't ask for what they need. These same individuals possibly also spend too much of their time trying to please others (this was termed "codependency" for some time, but the term has gone out of vogue). This kind of behavior can lead to inappropriate acting out in children and adolescents, and ulcers and other health conditions in adulthood. Similarly, a child who receives affectionate responsiveness only when he is ill may become skilled at developing illness and may practice this skill throughout life, even if it stops serving the initial purpose. Babies fed on schedules are left frustrated by their hunger between feedings, and as a result, they experience feeding as a way to relieve frustration. This could possibly be linked to eating disorders later on.

Eating disorders such as anorexia and bulimia are predominantly Western society disorders,[20] although they are now penetrating sectors of other countries where Western child care practices have become popular.[19] In France, responsiveness and other forms of affection are very high. Some point out that even though the French may worry about their appearance as much as Americans do, their eating disorder rates are much lower than ours, as are other psychological disorders.[20] A Minnesota survey of 30,000 adolescents found that eating disorders are related to "low family connectedness," as well as other insecure attachment signs.[21]

Nighttime is important too, comprising nearly half of an infant's life. Babies don't turn off at night, no matter how much we sometimes wish they would. They continue to have hunger, to grow, and to consolidate brain pathways. Their minds, feelings, and needs continue, and they continue to learn during their nighttime experiences, as much as at any other time. For babies, just as with mates, nighttime is a valuable time for catching up on the warmth and comfort of togetherness — this reassurance is available each time baby stirs. And when baby is close, little effort to wake up is required on the parents' part for providing protection, comfort, feeding, and support throughout the night.

Colic

Still, babies cry. It is normal. And some cry more than others. Sometimes parents who provide the very best response will have infants who frequently cry for long periods. So a decision needs to be made whether an infant is in physical pain. Certainly, when an infant's inconsolable cries are signals of pain or disorder, parents should have their baby examined medically and should often get second opinions. For a large portion of these infants, no diagnosis can be made, other than calling the problem "colic."

Studies comparing the acoustic values of cries during long bouts in "colicky" infants, versus their "normal" cries and the cries of "normal" infants, find higher acoustic frequency and other sharper acoustic measures during colic.[22,23] Yet, connected parents don't need much experience under their belts to detect these differences without fancy equipment. There is a different look and sound of pain or great distress. Intensive care nurses use the following scale to measure pain, listed in decreasing order: "fussiness, restlessness, grimacing, crying, increasing heart rate, increasing respiration, wiggling, rapid state changes, wrinkling of forehead, and clenching of fists."[24]

When an infant appears to be frequently in pain, and no diagnosis besides colic is made, there is in fact another diagnosis that will help the great majority of these infants. Doctors whose chief education about feeding difficulties comes from formula companies usually miss this simple solution. *Intestinal intolerance to cow's milk protein (not lactose) and other foods in mother's milk or in formula is the major cause of undiagnosed pain, usually called "colic."* Often other signs such as sleeplessness, waking with screams, abnormal stools, or rashes are part of this picture. This topic is covered extensively in the last few chapters of this book. Interestingly, cultures where colic is not a familiar condition are the same ones where infants do not receive cow's milk formulas and the mothers have very little dairy in their diets, if any at all. (Those studied include rural Japanese and Chinese, the Kenyans and !Kung San of Africa, the Balinese, the Samoans, and the Fore of New Guinea.)

I Hear Ya

When infants cry from physical pain, certainly we all wish to do anything we can to comfort them, just as we would wish to be comforted ourselves. Holding infants is very valuable. Rocking, providing something to suck on, or pacing the floors with them may provide additional comfort and pain relief.

Long periods of crying not related to pain also occur, frequently in some children. Who knows? Frightening thoughts or memories, confusion or bewilderment over their busy surroundings, recollection of frustrations, some say birth traumas — there are certainly many possibilities beyond pain or hunger that could cause an infant to cry, even in the arms of a responsive parent. Many caretakers observe that accumulated stimulation of random sights and noises and unfamiliar voices throughout the day may be a major factor in unappeasable crying, often referring to this as hyperstimulation. Crying may be a kind of emotional release from this accumulated stress, described well by psychologist Aletha Solter.[25] We must remember that infants may simply be crying to be heard — to express their feelings — even though they may not be able to reveal the source for their upset. It is advised that not all crying needs to be "fixed." When a child is apparently not hungry or in pain, but can not be mollified with simple comforting, what they may need is simply an empathetic "I hear ya." Be there for them, meet their eyes if they look to you, tell them you understand they are hurting, and let them get it out. Children benefit from gentle comforting, mostly from empathy, but not from distraction or attempts to quiet them. Such attempts only invalidate their feelings. The goal is not to stop the crying; it is to let a child know that someone cares, to give him an outlet and a sounding board. The benefits from natural parental comforting are numerous.

> *And, just as crying causes certain physical stresses, forced suppression of crying has been shown to cause undesirable increases in heart rate and blood pressure as well.*

According to psychologists, it is very important to acknowledge one's feelings. There may be damaging potential in telling a baby verbally or otherwise not to cry. "Stop crying," "don't cry," "it's not that bad," "you're all right," "that's enough," are ways of telling an infant his feelings are not valid. And, just as crying causes certain physical stresses, forced suppression of crying has been shown to cause undesirable increases in heart rate and blood pressure as well.[26] When adding the research findings on the damaging effects of prolonged crying to what psychologists say about healthy release of emotion, it appears likely that unanswered frustrated crying would be very detrimental to health, but crying out your emotions, then knowing you are being validated, loved, and received, would be very beneficial, at least psychologically.

When children have a startle or a tumble, it is also best to hold, acknowledge, and comfort them, providing a safe place for empathy and protection. An exception to this, however, may be the child who experiences bouts of physical pain regularly; in this case it may be kind to attempt to distract them from their pain, which does not mean shushing them or plugging them. Distraction techniques are often taught in pain centers for adults who suffer chronic pain.

Of course, as parents we can only do so much, tolerate so much, and be there so much. When a child is occasionally left hungry for a time, or left to cry on his own, no major damage is done. The brain organization comes from the adding up of the many, many responses from the child's caretakers. We must also remember that sometimes it gets to the point where it is the parents who need to cry.

Infant Attention

Even in his latest (1998) book, Dr. Spock advised parents to be "hardhearted" toward their infants, because infants do not know what is good for them. If a mother has difficulty ignoring her infant, he suggests she make a schedule for herself that will keep her busy during most of the child's waking hours. When the infant becomes bored with his crib in the afternoon, she may move him to a playpen, and when bored with that, to a bouncing chair. He suggests the infant be hugged every hour or so, and mom should "play with him a bit at the end of the afternoon."[27]

In stark contrast to this kind of advice, it has been shown that a high level of attention to the infant creates good bonding, physical health, and social development. The stimulation of regular interaction leads to heightened brain and motor development, which will be discussed in the next chapter. Regular smiles, conversation, and play all constitute very important parts of nurturing. For this reason, infants have been designed so that it is difficult to take your eyes off them; the mere sight of them begs for illuminated facial responses, physical affection, and verbal engagement. On the one hand, Oxford researchers found that low levels of maternal play interaction are an important factor in development of behavior problems in a child;[28] on the other hand, it has been shown that laughter stimulates the disease-fighting immune system in adults and infants.[29] At the same time, regular contact with the child helps stimulate mother's maternal behavior.[30]

In Touch

Ashley Montagu wrote a venerable and timeless tome nearly 500 pages long, referencing over 900 studies, entirely devoted to the effects of touch between mother and infant and how this affects an infant's development.[31] He reminds us that "When a baby is born, a mother is also born." According to Dr. Montagu, it is a tragedy when "the two people who need each other at this time, more than they ever will at any other time in their lives," are separated from each other in their first days. He reminds us of simple lessons such as how the friendliness of pets depends upon the physical affection provided them during their infancy, and how many newborn animals die if they do not receive licking. He also recites some very early animal studies that demonstrated how young animals, given a choice between physical contact and obtaining milk, will prefer the close contact. Since his text was first published in 1971, research has rediscovered and confirmed his findings, repeatedly revealing the great value of contact for infants and the sad consequences when frequent affection is lacking.

Much of the human research into the effects of touch and other kinds of soothing and stimulation occurs with premature infants, for several reasons. First, these infants are in the hospital, available for study in a controlled environment; second, the effects of many stimuli may be greater in the youngest babies, or the differences produced more easily measured. Chiefly, however, typical preemie care is in such stark contrast to natural infant care that any positive intervention reveals its benefits readily. Even though these studies are performed on hospitalized premature infants, they provide a great deal of insight valuable for understanding all infants. A pair of Duke University researchers demonstrated that limited touching in infant rats leads to a decrease in the production of an important growth enzyme, reduced DNA replication, abnormal hormonal secretion patterns, and reduced response to growth hormone, prolactin, and to insulin (the hormone that regulates blood sugar). Their work led them to test the effects of touch on premature human infants in the U.S., who are usually touch deprived. Their application of massage to these babies produced dramatic weight gains, enhanced behavioral development, and marked maturing of their hormonal regulation.[32] A similar trial using limb movements and gentle stroking produced 47% more weight gain each day along with other motor and behavioral benefits.[33] Preemie care nurses will tell you that these tiny beings consistently wriggle their way across their incubators to be in touch with a wall or at least have a foot against one side, instinctively seeking any kind of touch.

An investigation into "failure to thrive" infants discovered that the mothers of these infants provided much less touch and other kinds of stimulation to their infants than those of the normally growing infants in the study.

Massaging of preterm babies decreases the level of the stress hormone cortisol[34] and has also been shown to enhance the functioning of the immune system.[35] An investigation into "failure to thrive" infants discovered that the mothers of these infants provided much less touch and other kinds of stimulation to their infants than those of the normally growing infants in the study.[36]

And an investigation into infants' attachment behaviors found the highest attachment rates in those with the most physical contact with their mothers.[37] German researchers, comparing maternal behaviors, reported that "experience of a direct sensual and physical contact was most important" for the continued loving relationship between mother and child.[38]

As with many other facets of child care, animal studies are valuable for studying the effects of touch and touch deprivation in infants, and they correlate strongly with human studies. One rat study found that the amount of physical affection received in infancy was a major determinant of adult stress control: the more licking and grooming received as an infant, the better stress control exhibited, both behaviorally and chemically.[40] These Canadian researchers also found *those who received the most affection displayed the highest levels of independence as adults.* They also demonstrated increased numbers of brain receptors for calming biochemicals. Interestingly, they noted that when mother rats needed to leave for short times to obtain food, they would groom the pups with enhanced vigor for a time after their return, as though they were making up for the reduction in affection. Another rat study found that depriving pups of physical sensory input leads to permanent deficits in the brain's ability to interpret touch sensations, in spite of months of training.[40]

> *The U.S. children displayed aggression toward their peers 29% of the time compared to 1% in the French youngsters.*

Untouched infants also become children and adults who don't touch. Compared to U.S. preschoolers, French preschoolers were not only touched much more by mothers and teachers, but they showed much physical affection toward their peers. The U.S. children displayed aggression toward their peers 29% of the time compared to 1% in the French youngsters. American children, who receive far less attention than most others around the world, displayed 3 times more attention-seeking behavior when compared to cultures that provide high infant contact such as those in Japan and Mexico.[41]

Caring by Carrying

Infants around the world are carried much of the day, either in the arms, in variously fashioned slings, or wrapped closely to the back as mother works in the field. Carrying provides stimulation through motion, known as "vestibular" stimulation, and allows babies and children to observe mother's activities and converse with her. Infant carrying also renders soothing through exposure to mother's odor, close body contact, body warmth, and body sounds, as well as with the motion.

When U.S. mothers in an experiment were given baby slings and instructed to increase infant carrying time, it was found that their infants were more securely attached to their mothers at 13 months of age than those who were simply given baby seats.[42] In another study that induced increased carrying for infants, the babies cried 43% less, fussed less, and ate more contently.[43] Yet, it has been shown that increased carrying may not reduce the crying in infants who have colic.[44] This refers to the colic with cries related to pain, as opposed to extended crying due to other reasons. If a food reaction or other disorder is occurring, carrying may provide support, but it does not make a painful problem go away.

Kangaroo Care

After studying 186 non-industrial societies, Lozoff reported that 98% of newborns rest with their mothers after being bathed, but actually only 14% initially receive the kind of skin-to-skin contact that is promoted below.[45]

Standard care for Western newborns, for premature as well as full-term babies, is separation from mother. Full-term newborns remain in bassinet carts for most of the day. Preemies generally remain in incubators for their first weeks of extra-uterine life. Self-regulation of body temperature is weak in term newborns and very inadequate in preemies. Temperature, oxygen, and infection regulation are the chief purposes of incubators. Of course, breastmilk regulates infection too. It has been found that for all newborns, even very premature infants, placing them skin to skin on the chest of the mother or father provides superior temperature regulation to that of an incubator. Measures of important energy conservation (oxygen consumption) in these infants are excellent as well.[46,47]

The concept of kangaroo care was introduced in Colombia in 1978. Designed especially for small and preterm babies, the infant wears only a diaper and is placed upright inside the mother's clothing, in between her breasts. Here he can feed at will and can enjoy the comfort and gentle stimulation of continued contact with mother — her warmth, sounds, and odor. Almost no crying is heard this way, compared to the long pulses of "separation distress calls"[48] normally found in the nursery. This method of care has become standard in Scandinavian countries (where the infant death rate is half that of the U.S.) and has been adopted in other European countries for several hours per day. In the U.S., in 1979, researchers demonstrated significant improvement in the recovery of newborns when affectionate treatment was given to them on cue. Not yet ready for allowing the mother in, this treatment was provided by nurses. Newborns were rocked, cuddled, and provided with verbal and visual stimulation, and they were allowed to suck on a pacifier as much as desired. In comparison with standard care infants, these babies demonstrated superior temperature regulation and respiratory rate, and far fewer heart murmurs were detected, fewer sucking and swallowing difficulties were seen, and almost no crying was found.[49] Over twenty years later, some in the U.S. are starting to seriously consider this kind of care.

> *Kangaroo care decreases newborn deaths, and these infants gain twice as much weight per day as incubator babies.*

Kangaroo care decreases newborn deaths, and these infants gain twice as much weight per day as incubator babies.[50,51] Kangaroo care also results in more sleep, good oxygen saturation, less agitation, many fewer episodes of apnea (no breathing), and more stable heart rates.[52] A 1999 U.S. school of nursing study confirmed all these findings and reported that kangaroo care would be beneficial for newborns, beginning in the delivery room.[53] This care can also be used with preterm infants who require tube feeding; it even accelerates production of a hormone that stimulates secretion of digestive enzymes.[54] Even those on respirators can benefit from kangaroo care.[55] Hospital stays are much shorter for preemies who receive this kind of attention. This early skin-to-skin care has also been shown to significantly improve mother's milk volume, a common challenge with preterm births,[56] and it improves mother's attachment and maternal behaviors.[57,58] Certainly all the advantages of close contact and responsive care in newborns apply to older infants as well. Although it is difficult to study the individual effects of contact at different ages, the cumulative effects are apparent in attachment studies.

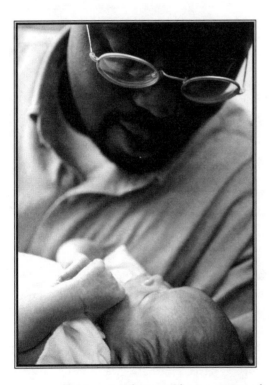

The Rock of Ages

In an infant all six senses are developed by regular stimulation (yes, there are six senses). Vestibular information (the sense of position) is controlled by the semicircular canals in the inner ears that sense our position. Stimulating this sensory system helps develop the infant's balance and motor control, while also providing much soothing. Rocking an infant in a chair or while standing is a very popular form of vestibular, or kinesthetic, stimulation. The instinctive light bouncing commonly seen around the world, carrying, and playful "tossing" are all means of providing such input to the baby. Children love to swing and various fashions of swings are found all around the world. Adults find rock-ing very soothing as well. Many rock themselves in their office chairs or during embraces. Grandma knew that soothing, pain relief, and brain stimulation could be found in her treasured rocker.

Although infants in Western societies were no longer carried much or slept with by the early twentieth century, they were com-forted and stimulated with rocking in cradles for a few more decades, at least until twentieth-century advisors recommended that these comforting measures should also be thrown by the wayside. Today, many child experts still advise against anything that might provide comfort to an infant, for fear they may come to expect comfort, but they seem to have overlooked the new electric baby swings. These swings have found their way into most new Western families' homes. They are clearly beneficial in the absence of more natural means. Many people even take them along on family visits or vacations, or rent them, finding life with baby to be difficult without them.

Some authorities have suggested that rocking an infant can cause a self-rocking disorder; however, one study on self-rocking in (not retarded) youngsters found that self-rocking children displayed symptoms similar to those classified as poorly attached: hyperactiv-ity or attention-deficit disorder.[59] This is not to suggest that children displaying such behavior are not well attached, but only to point out that the rocking of infants is not a likely cause of a psychologi-cal dysfunction. In fact, a study on developmentally delayed infants who exhibited self-rocking movements found that providing regular vestibular stimulation to them reduced this behavior and improved motor control.[60] Rocking has even been found to reduce spells of apnea in premature infants.[61]

A study of older infants who had life-threatening moments of apnea were found to have less than half as many episodes when they were rocked during sleep.[62] Infants also regulate their breath-ing more rhythmically with rocking,[63] and rocking relaxes infants' heart rates.[64] These studies suggest that sleeping in an electroni-cally rocked cradle could be beneficial. These benefits are similar to the heart and breathing control benefits an infant receives by sleeping next to mother or father's body, another form of providing

Brain cell deaths occur in

brain areas that the body

deems unnecessary.

A SIDS study found such

brain cell deaths in the

brain areas for vestibular

control (and for facial

sensation) in 76% of SIDS

infants and none in infants

who had died from other

causes.

constant stimulation. However, these are not the only benefits of rocking.

Vestibular stimulation such as rocking has been shown to improve the development of the cerebellum, which is in charge of motor control (coordination) and is still developing in the first six months of life.[65] Premature infants rocked for 15 minutes, 3 times per day for 2 weeks, demonstrated significant gains in motor control and muscle development as well as matured responses to auditory and visual stimuli. They also were more alert and had better defensive reflexes when compared to infants who were not rocked.[66] In another study, this same daytime rocking led to an improvement in preemies' sleep patterns.[67] One more similar study found improved neurological development and much higher scores on mental development tests.[68] A waterbed flotation study reported the same kind of benefits.[69]

In earlier chapters we noted that brain cell deaths occur in brain areas that the body deems unnecessary, in response to the parenting environment of the infant. A SIDS study found such brain cell deaths in the brain areas for vestibular control (and for facial sensation) in 76% of SIDS infants and none in infants who had died from other causes.[70] This suggests to me a great necessity for vestibular stimulation in infancy — that which is not stimulated in the brain is lost, in this case posing a threat to life.

Nursing & Nurturing

To all who know infants, it is apparent that infants are designed to nurse for the purpose of being soothed and for other benefits besides nutrition. Still, this form of comfort (called non-nutritive sucking) is discouraged by many once the meal is done, and parents are often encouraged to end all forms of sucking when their infants reach the age of 12 months.

Sucking at the breast increases EEG activity in areas of the brain that govern alertness and attention, as well as in areas that control the cycle of sleeping and waking. Bottle-feeding produces similar but lesser changes in brain patterns. Pacifier sucking has little effect,[71] but pacifier sucking has been shown to produce a valuable reduction in the heart rates of newborns, even much more than rocking.[72] Heart rates are lower still in breastfed infants compared to bottle-fed,[73] and this reduction continues during sleep.[74] Moreover, breastfeeding with skin-to-skin contact leads to far superior blood oxygenation in premature infants over standard breastfeeding (and the mothers were far more successful in continuing breastfeeding).[75] The dangerous reduction of oxygenation produced by crying in newborns who do not receive unrestricted breastfeeding can be prevented with pacifiers — the amount of crying is reduced and the oxygenation after crying is better than in those who do not receive non-nutritive sucking.[76]

Premature infants feed much better during inactive awake states, as opposed to excessive fatigue or fretful flailing. These calm states are associated with lower heart rates. It has been shown that pacifier sucking in preemies who are tube fed increases these beneficial behavioral states. When combined with rocking, significant improvement in feeding is found.[77]

In Holland, a country with low rates of nursing, it was found that babies who slept sucking on pacifiers had one twentieth the chance of dying of SIDS.[78] In New Zealand infants who did not have the benefit of night nursing, a very significant reduction in SIDS rates correlated with pacifier use during sleep.[79]

Although sucking easily promotes sleep, many of those who make a living by treating infant sleep difficulties warn against allowing the infant to fall asleep through this natural means. Pediatrician Donald Shifrin of the University of Washington states that "Good sleepers are made, not born."[80] He advises that if an infant begins to look sleepy during feeding, you should stop and place the infant, now more awake, into his crib. This reverses all soothing, bonding, and brain and heart benefits, and leads to crying and the release of wakening stress hormones, which surely makes falling asleep much more difficult. He warns against any other natural soothing measures such as rocking, and he is against pacifier sucking as well. It's no wonder these babies now need harsh training and "expert" advice in order to sleep. Yet, nature has a wonderful plan that helps infants easily fall asleep. Breastfeeding, and to a lesser extent, bottle-feeding, lead naturally to sleep in an infant when sleep is needed. This is partly due to the natural comfort provided by sucking, partly due to hormone releases in the mother and infant due to sucking and body contact, and partly due to other factors in mother's milk. Even pacifier sucking can provide drowsiness. While Shifrin suggests promoting a bond with a stuffed animal containing mother's scent, the benefits to baby of bonding with real caretakers and receiving frequent comforting are far superior.

> It's no wonder these babies now need harsh training and "expert" advice in order to sleep. Yet, nature has a wonderful plan that helps infants easily fall asleep. Breastfeeding is a time for nursing, a time to provide comfort and nurturing.

Breastfeeding is meant to be much more than just feeding — it is a time for nursing, a time to provide comfort and nurturing. This time is allotted for studying and memorizing each other's faces, for speaking or singing to the baby, and for developing nonverbal communications. When allowed, comfort nursing often continues long after nutrition needs have been satiated, deepening the soothing, bonding, and educational relationship between parent and child. Bottle-fed babies can certainly be "nursed" as well.

The Downside of Pacifiers

Clearly, sucking a pacifier or a thumb helps infants when unrestricted breastfeeding is not available. Frequent sucking is very important to infants for many reasons, from reducing heart rate, stress, and SIDS, to increasing oxygenation and intelligence. While sucking on artificial nipples approximates some of the benefits of natural nursing, there are downsides to artificial sucking as well. The use of a thumb or pacifier after two years contributes to the development of crossbite,[81] whereas breastfeeding actually improves proper jaw development.[82] Pacifier use also increases the amount of bacteria and yeast in the mouth, which in turn increases the susceptibility to dental cavities. Using a bottle during the night, especially after age 2, causes a significant, but smaller increase in tooth decay.[83] Using pacifiers or bottles during the first months of breastfeeding teaches improper sucking that can cause pain and infection in the mother and difficult nursing for the infant, reducing the chance of continued successful breastfeeding by half.[84,85] Thumb or pacifier use is high in those weaned prematurely from the bottle or the breast, and is generally minimal when there is extended on-cue breastfeeding.[86]

Safe Sleep & SIDS

Unlike most adults, when infants are tired, they often become increasingly active, displaying restlessness, irritability, and crying. Also unlike adults, who sleep more deeply when stress is low, infants sleep more deeply when stressed. Stress is so fatiguing for the tiny energy-dependent body that nature uses deep sleep as a healing response. Infants delivered surgically, who miss out on many of the hormonal and other natural benefits of passing through the birth canal, and who often meet their

We are now discovering that the once-coveted deep sleep in infants has led to countless sudden infant deaths.

mothers much later than those who are vaginally delivered, fall into longer sleep states for days after birth.[87] Although it was once thought that this deep sleep was desirable because it reduced an infant's requests for the comfort of his parents at night, and for food when his stomach was empty, we are now discovering that this once-coveted deep sleep has led to countless sudden infant deaths.

When bottle-feeding was successfully imposed on the majority of families early last century, the malady of severely sleep-deprived parents suddenly became commonplace. Babies had to sleep separately so that breastfeeding was not encouraged, although this was not the reason given. Other comforting measures were being taken away as well, one at a time. As a result, long and loud bouts of crying occurred throughout the night, and child care advisors had to search for measures that would promote long phases of deep sleep in infants to help parents get some rest. Because the unnatural position of sleeping prone (on the stomach) was found to deepen infant sleep states, it was promoted with vigor as a solution. Lying prone is unnatural for a baby, in the sense that nursing is very difficult in this position, and it does not occur when mother and infant sleep together naturally — except when baby lies tummy-down on mom or dad's chest where the neck is less strained and a parent's heartbeat and respiration regulate baby's. Another motivation for the prone positioning was the unusual patterns of baldness developed by many highly frustrated and long-crying infants who flailed their heads left and right on their backs. Prone positioning in the crib also provided a solution for isolated infants who became withdrawn and developed flat spots on the back of their skulls from spending so much time lying motionless on their backs.

It is now known that a baby lying prone has pressure on the brain stem (where sleep is controlled), partially occluding it. This is the likely reason such positioning produces deeper sleep, as well as

> A large New Zealand investigation found that sharing a room with a non-smoking adult reduced the risk of SIDS by 81%.

why it is a factor in the escalation of SIDS. A gradual build-up of cell deaths in this region seems to occur, rendering the infant very fragile. Cellular destruction has been found in portions of the hippocampus that are very sensitive to reduced oxygen. In studies, this was seen in 44% of SIDS babies and in none of the controls, suggesting that *any additional reduction of oxygenation, such as from prolonged crying, would exacerbate the problem of infant deaths.*[88]

Now that prone sleeping has become greatly reduced, other statistical associations with SIDS are more easily found. For instance, a Dutch study demonstrated that breastfeeding reduces the incidence of SIDS.[89] An English study revealed that separate bedrooms raises the risk of sudden infant death.[90] A large New Zealand investigation found that sharing a room with a non-smoking adult reduced the risk of SIDS by 81%.[91] This study came out only after another huge factor leading to SIDS had been revealed and adjusted for — smoking. A different New Zealand report had found that 26% of SIDS cases could be explained by the fact that babies were sharing beds with smoking mothers[92] (so they banned all infant bed-sharing for a time), while a Scottish report had demonstrated that *infants were more than 5 times as likely to die of SIDS when sleeping with a smoking parent.*[93] Even if a parent does not actually smoke in the bed or even in the bedroom, the particulate released from the smoker's lungs is released into the air and the nearby baby breathes it for hours. This ongoing release of tobacco combustion products from the lungs of smokers is well known in industry by those who work in clean rooms with semiconductors. After adjusting for smoking,

After adjusting for smoking, researchers in England uncovered a tripled risk of SIDS for bottle-fed babies, a University of California study has reported the same results, and a German study suggested nearly 8 times the risk for babies who are not breastfed.

researchers in England uncovered *a tripled risk of SIDS for bottle-fed babies*,[94] a University of California study has reported the same results,[95] and a German study suggested nearly 8 times the risk for babies who are not breastfed.[96] Because sharing the bed promotes breastfeeding, and breastfeeding promotes sharing the bed, these two factors are intertwined in the protection against SIDS.[97]

Now that crib-sleeping babies are being placed on their backs, new concerns over flattened skulls, called "positional plagiocephaly," are arising. Large numbers of infants are now having to wear corrective helmets, and some are undergoing unnecessary tests and even operations. A cosleeping infant who nurses during the night spends much of its time on its side, and this position changes several times during the night as baby feeds and mother switches baby from one side to the other. This natural changing of back and side-lying positions creates a naturally, properly formed skull.

The circadian rhythms (daily cycle) for heart rate and blood pressure in the young infant are poorly developed.[98] Doctors at Baylor College of Medicine report that half the SIDS victims they studied had heartbeat irregularities a little beyond the norm.[99] Although only 1.5% of babies with such an irregularity will succumb to SIDS (compared to .037% without it), these researchers suggest all infants be screened and placed on beta-blocker drugs (which are not without serious side effects) when such an irregularity is found. Yet, numerous studies have shown that an infant in close contact with an adult has significantly better heart rhythms.

Significantly, *victims of SIDS spend longer intervals in deeper sleep and have very few arousal periods during the night (like those exhausted from crying or who are sleeping prone).*[100] This effect is most pronounced in the early morning hours when SIDS deaths most often occur.[101] On the other hand, cosleeping breastfed infants nurse most frequently during the early morning hours, thereby reducing the danger. Poor control of respiration rates, respiration reflexes, and poor arousal were also reported by Berkeley researchers looking into unexplained cases of infant deaths.[102] Remember that most of the infants studied were solitary sleeping infants because this has been the norm in the U.S. during the twentieth century. Ironically, for a time it was customary for some to instantly blame infant death in a cosleeping infant on parental suffocation. This notion is contradicted by research. James McKenna, Ph.D. and colleagues found that infants sleeping next to their mothers tend to synchronize their arousal from deeper to lighter stages of sleep on a minute-to-minute

"SIDS Risk," a brief article in *Time* magazine reported that "Babies who died from SIDS were found to have a much higher rate of *H. pylori* infection than other children." Manchester "researchers theorize that the bug could be passed on to infants by parents' kissing them…" was the explanation recounted in the story, but the picture unwittingly attached to the blurb tells the actual tale. Babies either partly or fully bottle-fed lack intestinal protection from dangerous microbes. *H. pylori* (the "ulcer" bacteria) is one of them. The chronic irritation that formula causes in many infant intestines leads to immune breakdown that allows this bacteria to take hold. Unless raised in a very sterile (and cold) environment, most babies (and most people) will be exposed to this common bacteria many times in their lives. With a healthy immune system, which during infancy requires mother's milk, exposure should help babies develop their normal balance of flora and their own protective mechanisms. While the researchers may suggest never kissing your baby, I suggest smothering her with love, and providing her with the natural defenses of mother's milk.

basis throughout the night.[103] Much sensory information is being exchanged between the two during the night. Additionally, such infants experience reductions in the deeper states of sleep (stages 3 and 4).[104] Their number of arousals (stages 1 and 2) is greatly increased, although actual wakefulness is not. The amount of REM (rapid eye movement) sleep was not affected.[105] English researchers have also suspected that prolonged periods of lone quiet sleep are a factor in SIDS.[106]

Infants sleeping close to a parent are physiologically regulated much like they are during rocking, tactile stimulation, and kangaroo care. They also do not suffer from the effects of crying and cortisol releases. Generally, they will frequently be nursing as well, therefore obtaining the sucking benefits as previously described. Heart rate and rhythm, respiration, and blood oxygenation are all improved in cosleeping babies, and apnea is reduced, thereby mitigating the influence of these harmful factors strongly associated with SIDS in Western families where babies sleep alone. In addition, when an infant has anxious or unusual moments, they are rapidly noticed by a nearby parent, who can respond to difficulties that might have otherwise been missed. Some of these same benefits are experienced by infants who sleep in a bed near their parents. The odor and pheromones of at least the mother apparently play a regulatory role in ending spells of apnea.[107]

In cultures where infants sharing the bed and nursing are the norm, SIDS rates have always been quite low. In England this cultural difference was found to be responsible for the greatly lower sudden infant death rates among their Asian populations,[108] and a Japanese study found sleeping alone to be a significant SIDS risk factor.[109] African Americans, who more often bottle-feed, have high SIDS rates compared to the already high general American population,[110] yet Africans from the highly breastfeeding and cosleeping peoples of Zimbabwe have a very low degree of SIDS,[111] one fifth the rate of the U.S. Taiwan is a nation that has been rapidly Westernized over the last two decades. During the period from 1984 to 1993, their SIDS rates more than doubled.[112]

Historically, in Europe, "overlying" on baby during the night was used as an excuse for "accidental" infant death in very poor families when another baby meant too many mouths to feed (and when in reality, the mother purposely suffocated it). For this reason, bed-sharing was actually outlawed in some areas, giving cosleeping a dangerous reputation that still permeates the thinking of some today.[113] Such events still occur occasionally, and rumors of accidental suffocation due to cosleeping continue to circulate. There *is* a danger in cosleeping with a parent whose natural reflexes and awareness are greatly altered by drugs or alcohol, or with a neurologically compromised infant whose reflexes may be greatly impaired, who may not naturally turn his head, whimper, or move away if his air supply becomes compromised.

The U.S. Consumer Product Safety Commission reported in 1999 that there were 515 deaths of children up to age 2 sleeping in their parents' bed, over an 8-year period (about 64 per year).[114] Compare this to 7,000 U.S. SIDS deaths overall per year measured up to age 1. One quarter of these adult-bed deaths were reported as overlying of the child by a parent. I have addressed the factors associated with this verdict. The rest were reported as due to some kind of entrapment in the bed structure or bedding. Such entrapment deaths were extremely high in cribs for decades, in comparison to this amount. In response to the recent CPSC report, the American Academy of Pediatrics released an advisory against children being placed in adult beds. In contrast, when such dangers were found in cribs, recommendations were made to make cribs safer. Even with stringent efforts, strangulation and suffocation still occur in infant furniture to this day. At the same time, countless infant lives are certainly being saved in numerous ways through sharing parental beds. Many more would be saved if more were not sleeping stressfully isolated from important comfort, bodily regulation, vigilance, and night nursing. In addition to the factors mentioned previously, waterbeds, soft bedding, and overt parental obesity are suggested risk factors in the parental bed, as is wedging between the mattress and headboard. For the greatest infant survival, the answer is to make the parental bed safe, not to throw out the baby.

It appears that a combination of various factors comes into play in most cases of SIDS. In summary, these are some of the twentieth-century experiments in Western cultures that have led to the escalation of SIDS:

- Promoting artificial feeding
- Promoting isolated sleep
- Allowing babies to cry themselves to sleep
- Promoting the prone position in bed (seldom naturally seen in cosleeping, breastfeeding infants) to induce deeper sleep
- Discouraging pacifier use during sleep for those not nursing

There is a correlation between pertussis vaccinations and SIDS as well, as discussed in a later chapter, but one must consider that pertussis itself can occasionally cause episodes of oxygen deficit.[115] In either case, the safest place for a baby is in bed with or at least very near his parents where he can be monitored, his oxygenation can be regulated by his parents' rhythms, and he will spend less time in the deepest sleep states.

In addition, although about 7,000 U.S. infants die each year of SIDS, another 1,000 young children die each year in home fires and other disasters (mostly at night), who may have been saved if they had been sleeping near their parents rather than in another part of the house.[116]

Nurturing Sleep for Everyone

In the great majority of families around the world, throughout the millennia, and throughout most of the animal kingdom, babies sleep warmly and safely next to their mothers or a close family member. These cultures experience far fewer psychiatric problems, lower infant mortality rates, and much less SIDS. The same effects are found in the animal kingdom, when the health and survival of baby animals separated from their mothers is compared to that of those who are not. Among Westerners unfamiliar with this kind of sleeping arrangement, many often have some fear of "squishing" the baby. In fact, babies have strong instinctual protective reflexes that assure head turning, creeping (even in newborns), or whimpering if air availability becomes impaired. Adults also have a strong sense of orientation during the night, evidenced by the fact that few fall out of bed or even fall off their pillows. The roaming hormones of those affected by parenthood help to increase nighttime awareness. New mothers have practiced increased awareness during the night for many months because they have been arousing themselves to turn their large pregnant bodies during sleep.

> *Forced isolation at bedtime is very stressful for infants. We know this from the almost universal fretful crying pleas against this abandonment.*

Dr. Richard Ferber and others have demonstrated that allowing a child to cry alone at bedtime helps the child realize that its parents will not be there for them at night. Some children, however, will continue to cry themselves to sleep and will also cry during the night. Parents are encouraged to accept this situation as normal, not as a signal that baby needs something. Tine Thevenin, author of *The Family Bed,* put the possible consequences of such actions quite well: "Unfortunately, a suppressed need is not erased, although it may lie dormant within the person for many, many years."[117] Forced isolation at bedtime is very stressful for infants. We know this from the almost universal fretful crying pleas against this abandonment. Some suggest that a person will never know how to fall asleep if not put through this traumatic nighttime ritual during infancy. However, throughout the cosleeping majority of the world, children, adolescents, and adults actually experience fewer sleeping difficulties than we do. Some studies suggest that cosleeping infants experience greater sleeping difficulties, but this is due to a definition of sleep difficulty that condemns the natural, more frequent (and possibly lifesaving) arousal to lighter stages of sleep, which are part of the infants' obvious enjoyment of having their parents near. We are told that forced isolation develops the autonomy that a child supposedly wants and needs; however, as soon as a child is able to climb out of the crib, she instinctively and most deliberately seeks out a warm cuddly spot in her parents' bed.

While cosleeping babies enjoy increased safety, bonding, and comfort, cosleeping parents get much more sleep as well, especially when nursing. Gone are the startling, adrenaline-pumping awakenings to loud baby cries, the preparing of bottles, and the feeding in a chair, trying to stay awake, followed by trying to sneak away from the infant, now sleepy again, who hits the cold mattress and cries once more. Baby can have an open bar all night, with mother and child barely waking, and father often being entirely undisturbed. Since mothers' and infants' sleep levels tend to coincide, baby will nudge mother for nursing generally during mother's lighter sleep states. Then the hormones released from breastfeeding easily send mother and baby back to sleep. Neither parent need lie awake wondering whether the baby is all right, or spend the night peeking into the nursery for reassurance. Simply placing a hand on the baby's side reassures the parent that he is breathing. Many find that sharing the bed also helps make up for lost contact during a day spent away at work. Parents notice that baby finds a way to keep at least one foot in contact with at least one adult at all times during the night — revealing the child's constant innate need for security throughout the night and his constant awareness of his parents' presence. Nightmares and night terrors, common childhood dilemmas in today's society, are almost unknown in the bed-sharing youngster[118] (except for some special cases, such as with food allergies). Babies' daytime naps, if not on mother's back or in a sling, benefit from just being in the midst of daily activities — in the living room or somewhere close by — rather than stowed away in isolation. In fact, the sound of mother's voice produces healthy reductions in the infant's heart rate during sleep.[119] Lozoff has reported that when children fall asleep, the mere presence of an adult makes them less likely to suck their thumbs or use a regular attachment object — suggesting possibly more secure attachment to the parents.[120] When insomnia is present, even in a non-isolated infant, pain may be a component.[121] Intolerance of cow's milk proteins is, again, a major cause.[122,123]

What the World needs now...

Today there seems to be a race to get babies separated, off the bottle, toilet trained — to make "grown-ups" of them. But even under ideal conditions, being an infant is often painful and difficult, and babies grow up soon enough without any pushing at all. Possibly, many do not grow up in certain ways or to certain degrees because they have not fulfilled various stages or needs during the developmental years. While babies are designed to survive in the face of adversity, it may not be wise to intentionally create it. We should instead honor babyhood, rejoice in all the special cozy comforts parents are designed to provide, and smother our babies with unrestrained love.

5

Brighter Babies, Not Super Babies

As with many other aspects of a child's development, IQ can be greatly influenced by parenting choices and practices. Children and adults can be bright in many different ways — from artistic creativity, to a gift for reading human emotions, to physical or musical talent, to being able to achieve a high level of education. IQ tests try to measure how easily one can grasp or think through problems or concepts. While by no means the best measurement of success, IQ is often discussed instead of some other talents because it can be quantified and is therefore more easily researched. It's used here to compare brain development with regard to various environmental situations, such as diet and child care. But all the methods described below for enhancing IQ development are just as valuable for promoting any talent or potential brightness in a baby, so baby has the best chance of becoming a shining star in whatever direction calls her. These methods also promote healthier individuals who can build strong, lasting relationships and can lead honest and less stressful lives.

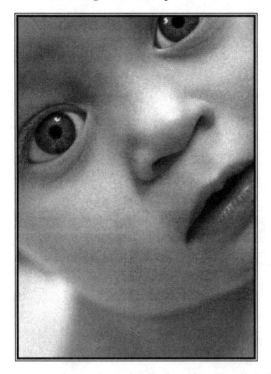

To many, these skills may be the best measurement of success. Research into IQ development is designed to assist parents who desire to help their children achieve deeper educational experiences to expand their future possibilities.

For a time there was a huge fad concerned with developing "super babies." Little intellectual development can take place when baby spends the waking hours in a pale-colored room staring at a white ceiling and the same little mobile day after day, so trendsetters became enthralled with providing higher and higher levels of stimulation, then waited for the results. Fetuses were bathed with loud music and infants were bludgeoned with flash cards all day long. This was a valuable experiment for researching the limits of intellectual development, although it may have produced some highly frustrated individuals as well. Soon researchers found that only a portion of the infants' great gains persisted throughout the school years, while other developmental elements may have been inadvertently ignored during all the enthusiasm. In other children, the efforts didn't seem to work at all, and in some, they backfired.

We now know that regular stimulation throughout the day is valuable for baby's intellectual development, but there must be a wide variety of stimuli, and they must be within the limits of a child's attention and interest. We also know that breastmilk is important for brain development, and that without it, baby's IQ can fall well below his potential. Baby's brain does 80% of its (postnatal) growing during the first 2 years after birth, and during this time the body decides how big the brain should be and how many nerve cells will be retained in its various regions. Beyond genetics, the child's early environment may affect his intellectual potential by 15% or more.

Breastmilk for Brain Power

EEG activity in an infant's brain increases significantly during breastfeeding, but not during pacifier sucking. This increased activity leads to improved brain function.[1] As we will see later, only breastmilk contains the ultimate nutrition for the brain and body. Additionally, the neurological stimulation and emotional confidence gained through the ongoing breastfeeding relationship can provide an intellectual edge. A Spanish study showed that brain development in 2-year-olds was higher in breastfed than bottle-fed babies,[2] and an English investigation reported a "robust" statistical elevation of later intelligence in breastfed youngsters.[3] Recently, additional studies in the U.S. attempted to control for as many variables as possible, including maternal intelligence and environmental factors, and found 5 points higher average IQ in 3-year-olds who had had any breastfeeding.[4] A more extensive U.K. study tested children at 8 years of age and found significantly higher IQs in those who had received human milk as premature

Consistently, the longer the duration of breastfeeding, the greater the IQ advantage. Little benefit was found in those who received both formula and breast feeds.

infants.[5] This advantage was the same for infants who were fed with tubes and those who were nursed. Additionally, preemies whose mothers chose to provide breastmilk, but failed, shared the same lower IQ as formula-fed infants, removing many confounding variables from the results and giving the credit to the breastmilk. British follow-up studies at 10 years of age revealed much higher vocabulary and intelligence in children who had been exclusively breastfed.[6] A Dutch investigation reported similar findings, after adjusting for social and other factors.[7] Most recently, a New Zealand study of over 1,000 children aged 8 to 18 years concluded that consistently, the longer the duration of breastfeeding, the greater the IQ advantage, as well as better reading comprehension, improved math and other scholastic abilities, and higher examination scores on national tests.[8]

We can see that children who are allowed their natural diet for a more natural length of time are able to achieve what is likely their fullest potential, reaping the rewards throughout their maturation. Vision and neurological functioning benefit from breastmilk as well. Interestingly, pasteurized breastmilk from milk banks does not have this IQ-promoting effect.[9] A British study of 1,000 adults born in the 1920s found higher IQs in those who had been exclusively breastfed. As with most studies, little benefit was found in those who received both formula and breast feeds.[10] This same investigation found pacifier use to be associated with lower IQ — most probably an indirect effect of other factors usually associated with prolonged pacifier use, specifically, the absence or reduction of breastfeeding. A Brazilian study discovered 40% fewer developmental delays in 1-year-olds nursed for over 9 months than in those nursed for less than 1 month.[11] Other studies have reported more activity in breastfed babies, especially arm movement[12] and greater "fluency of movement" in preschoolers who were breastfed as infants,[13] both indicating greater brain development.

Iron deficiency anemia is very common in infants who are not breastfed or are weaned early. Caused by cow's milk or cow's milk formulas, this anemia is associated with lower IQs in children, regardless of oral iron supplementation upon diagnosis.[14] A rare cause of developmental mental retardation in children (1 in 12,000) is a genetic error in protein handling known as phenylketonuria. When diagnosed, this condition can be treated through dietary measures for nursing mother and baby. It has been found that phenylketonuric children who had been breastfed as babies score 14 points higher on IQ tests.[15] Those who had been breastfed before diagnosis fared far better than those on formula. These findings suggest that the protein levels in human milk are more appropriate for infants, thereby reducing brain damage before diagnosis; furthermore, other factors in breastmilk enhance intelligence after treatment has begun.

Caring for Cognition

Studies show that the sensitivity with which parents care for an infant, such as frequent affection and interaction and quick response to cries, is strongly correlated with intellectual development[16] and is the best predictor of school performance.[17] On the other hand, harsh discipline and low motherly warmth are associated with a 12-point lowering of IQ.[18] Also, high levels of stress hormones in infancy — seen in those often separated from mother, frequently left to cry, and comforted less — are associated with nerve cell alterations that are linked to reduced intellect and memory.[19,20] There is a linear relationship: Those with the most cortisol have the lowest scores on mental and motor ability tests.[21]

In addition to high levels of parental response, other "more appropriate" forms of child management have been found to powerfully promote intellect, language, and problem-solving development in children. Psychologists suggest that more dialog and presentation of consequences, and less authoritarian control of behavior may be beneficial. These parental behaviors have twice the impact on a child's intellectual development as mother's education level and birth problems combined.[22] Another group of researchers focused on the mother's ability to accurately understand her small infant's cues, an ability developed through strong bonding practices. They found a significant correlation between this and positive language and intellectual measures at 18 months of age.[23]

Mother's frequent stimulation of her infant is a key factor. In an early study, Belsky confirmed a relationship between mother's attention-focusing conversations with baby and the growing baby's attention span and exploratory interests.[24] Fortunately, after some time, Tufts University researchers decided to focus on father's contribution as well. Their recent, large study of low-birth-weight babies found that infant IQs averaged 6 points higher in those with highly involved fathers compared to those with detached fathers.[25] Many studies have shown that increased social interaction with caregivers during infancy significantly improves mental development later on.[26]

An infant's interest in novel stimuli, the eagerness to continually embrace the unknown, strongly predicts later intelligence.[27] In those who are not so self-motivated (hence demanding less attention), other research indicates that frequent introduction to novel situations will likely produce a similar end result (or else clutter the mind of a potential Plato). According to professors Todd Risley and Betty Hart, the amount of speech a baby hears will strongly determine future intellectual development and social success.[28]

Others have found that maternal attention has especially significant effects on preterm infants.[29] Apparently, preterm babies have a broader range of possible outcomes than full-term infants. Those with highly stimulating environments seem to be able to catch up and overcome delayed intellectual development while those without much stimulation seem to decline further below their potential.[30] Researchers found a specific pattern in many preemie EEG tracings, referred to as "407-Trace Alternant," that was strongly correlated with later IQ levels.[31] Low levels of this particular trace were linked to lower IQs that persisted through the end of their study, which was to age 8. They noted an exception to this pattern, however, in babies who were raised in "consistently attentive, responsive environments." By age 2, these children had higher IQs, equal to those who initially had more promising EEG tracings. On the average, preterm infants and low-birth-weight babies demonstrate an average IQ that is 5 points lower. Yet, studies on preemies show that high language involvement from mother can raise this by

8 points, a positive, warm home environment by 5 points more, and preschool attendance by 5 more points.[32] As mentioned in the previous chapter, preterm infants are often more available or more interesting to study. Most findings on their brain development in response to various environments should certainly provide insight pertinent to all babies.

At 2 years of age, preterm infants who were regularly exposed to rocking and heartbeat sounds (a synthetic comforting mother of sorts) during their hospital stays scored significantly higher on mental development tests.[33] Another similar experiment using rocking alone found increased auditory and visual interpretation and increased alertness.[34] Also, increased cognitive abilities result from massage therapy.[35] One study even demonstrated that vaginal delivery can provide an edge for developing a higher IQ. Compared to surgically delivered babies, these infants had preferable lower respiration rates during sleep, even at 6 months. Lower respiration correlates with higher mental scores at 1 year of age.[36]

From all these studies one can see that, while IQ may be largely determined genetically, parental practices can influence it; some studies suggest by as much as 10 to 15%, or approximately 10 to 15 points on the IQ scale. As found in the above study and others, premature infant IQs can be influenced even more — nearly 20% — with institutionalized babies showing even greater variations, at least with regard to ability to function intellectually.[37]

Animal Models

Psychology researchers P. A. Ferchmin and V. A. Eterovic first reported on the effects of genetics and early environment on rat brain development in 1970. Then in 1980, they reported on experiments with rats bred to be genetically learning deficient (low IQ). They found that providing highly stimulating environments to these rats, including increased physical, visual, auditory, and tactile stimuli, produced animals that could outperform genetically superior rats that were left in normal environments during early development.[38] Fourteen years later, these same researchers measured the brain's uptake of a specific sugar used in the laboratory to reflect brain activity, suggesting development. They found evidence of significantly higher levels of brain growth in rats raised in "enriching" environments compared to those raised in "impoverished" ones similar to the environment of infants left in their cribs for much of the day.[39]

Womb Lessons

There was a time in my life when I was extremely aware of a physical condition I had — I was pregnant. I was also assured by everyone that one day I was going to have a baby. I took care of myself in this condition, taking proper measures not to pollute the tiny group of cells growing inside me. At the same time, I made preparations for the eventual arrival of a child. After meeting some tiny preemies one day, when my own infant was a few weeks old, I suddenly realized that I already had "had" a baby for quite some time: There had been a thinking, feeling human being inside of me. Somehow, the reality of this never quite sank in very far until I got to know him on the outside. As we struggled through his 8 P.M. crying and fussing session every evening, I realized that the kicking tummy we had reacted to each evening by poking, calling to, and shining in flashlights was actually this little tiny person feeling some kind of distress.

Just as the super baby movement correctly declared a while back, a child's intellectual development begins inside the womb, and parental behaviors impact the fetal brain. Researchers have found that the emotions and stress levels of pregnant mothers have significant effects on the brain development of the fetus.[40] Lower blood flow to the fetal brain is found in women with higher anxiety levels,[41] and increased levels of stress hormones in the mother will alter the development of the fetal brain.[42]

The fetus begins to produce detectable responses to sound by 23 to 28 weeks of gestation.[43] The noises that reach him are those that are louder than his background environment of heartbeat, respiration, and digestion. Mother's voice is most prominently available to him, both as sound and vibration. Investigations have found that mother's voice and low sounds are actually enhanced by the uterine environment, but outside voices (which have a higher pitch) are somewhat subdued.[44] Many classical and behavioral conditioning experiments have demonstrated that fetuses can learn. Now that playing classical music to fetuses has gone out of vogue, researchers found that rats exposed to Mozart's complex Sonata no. 448 performed significantly better in mazes than those exposed to simple music or no music.[45] (Hmm, did Mozart have bright children?) In response to linguistic and neuroscience studies, psychologist Mark Seidenberg and others are convinced that language acquisition begins in the womb.[46]

Electronic Teachers

A variety of stimulation provides enhanced brain development and education to youngsters. Our new age has brought many declines in the stimulation of infants. They have much less exposure to bugs and butterflies, gibbering squirrels, rustling leaves, and falling rain. Moreover, most do not have the ever-present neighbors and extended family members conversing, working, and playing about them, and paying attention to them.

In the place of this, we have electronics. While human interactions are the best, we unfortunately live highly isolated lives (partly as a result of television). I have seen households where adults or other children are seldom available to stimulate baby, yet television shows or battery operated toys are felt to be stunting, so baby's exposure to these are limited. Instead these youngsters lie or sit alone with a few bland toys and four pale walls around them, their brains wasting away. While the occasional Waldorf school provides wonderful natural environments to nurture youngsters, our electronics are not all bad. Growing up in this country, children will constantly use and depend on computer technology and other electronic devices. Teaching is one way we introduce the young to society's collective knowledge and belief systems: morals, daily living skills, culture, arts, language, science, and trade skills. Computers and other electronics are intimately entwined with many of these.

Our education needs to go beyond growing or catching our food and contending with the elements — a vast amount of brain training and knowledge is needed to obtain an average college degree today or even just to enjoy some of what our technology has to offer. The incredible amount of stimulation and education available through educational television cannot be discounted.[47] Neither can the significant brain developing effects of some video and computer games and electronic toys. Psychologist Patricia Greenfield of UCLA describes how playing video games can quickly improve scores on tests of spatial relations.[48] Others tout the improved concentration, social development, and imagination children get from watching good preschool television shows.[49] In moderate amounts, media can be used in controlled contexts for intellectual and other benefits to children of all ages.

> Our society finds weapon-toting warriors an important theme for children's shows and baby toys, but the sight of life-providing vessels of baby nourishment (breasts) is vehemently guarded.

However, there is little doubt about several negative qualities of the media. The extreme amount of violence that can be seen on TV when it is not vigilantly monitored is often associated with violent acts in children and adolescents.[50] In fact, introducing television broadcasts to previously remote areas has resulted in a more than 50% increase in murder rates 10 to 15 years later.[51] Even cartoons, Disney movies, and other shows designed for our youngest children parade large amounts of weaponry, violent acts, and cruelty toward innocents — as if this were acceptable in everyday life (possibly helping to make it a reality). TV viewing ratings do not help to screen this either. Our society finds weapon-toting warriors an important theme for children's shows and baby toys, but the sight of life-providing vessels of baby nourishment (breasts) is vehemently guarded. Another drawback of television is the language level. While the fifth-grade vocabulary is highly stimulating for younger children, it provides no language advantage to children after that. The other important objection is that time spent with other valuable activities is reduced when much time is spent with television and other electronic entertainment.

Got Fatty Acids??

Visual function as well as many other brain functions are improved in breastfed infants compared to formula-fed babies, and in direct correlation to the duration of breastfeeding.[52] Various fatty acids are responsible for some of the brain development attributed to breastmilk, and they are not found in formulas. DHA is thought to be one of the important factors. The fact that more of it is found in the brains of breastfed than formula-fed infants, and that it is found in human milk but not in formulas, suggests that it must be introduced from the diet. Recently it has been confirmed that infants can convert certain fatty acids in their diet into other important fatty acids that are building blocks of the brain. It is for this reason that infants survived with formulas at all. Yet this research also demonstrates that fatty acid availability in formula is not complete enough for the optimal development seen with breastmilk — especially DHA. These researchers' attempts to fortify formulas with fatty acids, however, did not lead to any hoped-for benefits.[53] Another investigation attempted fortification with DHA as well as another fatty acid, AA, but this effort did not produce breastfeeding standards of development either.[54] Others tested four different concentrations of fatty acids hoping to raise DHA and AA levels. They were successful in raising DHA levels in infants, but AA disappointingly decreased and the sought-after visual improvement did not occur. Also, infant growth was reduced below desirable levels.[55] Still more attempts yielded similar results.[56] As with many other efforts to make formula "behave" like breastmilk, so far, all efforts to fortify formulas with various combinations of fatty acids have failed to produce the level of eye and brain development that breastfeeding and only breastfeeding can provide.

Fatty Acid Content of Various Baby Feeds

Fatty Acids	Breastmilk	Carnation Good Start	Ross Similac	Wyeth Babysoy
Saturated Total	.619	.448	.376	.486
8:0 Caprylic	Not measured	.015	.033	.027
10:0 Capric	.019	.012	.024	.021
12:0 Lauric	.079	.104	.148	.146
14:0 Myristic	.099	.043	.056	.070
16:0 Palmitic	.283	.238	.078	.143
18:0 Stearic	.090	.037	.035	.076
Monosaturated Total	.511	.329	.399	.426
16:1 Palmitoeic	.040	0	.001	.012
18:1 Oleic	.454	.329	.397	.407
20:1	.012	0	.002	.003
Polyunsaturated Total	.153	.226	.244	.152
18:2 Linoleic	.155	.207	.220	.137
18:3 Linolenic	.016	.018	.023	.015
20:4 Omega-6 AA	.008	0	0	0
22:6 Omega-3 DHA	.009	0	0	0
Cholesterol	.0043	.0018	.0006	.0005

Figure 5-1 Values of fatty acids, in grams per 1 fluid ounce, found in human milk and popular formulas (ready-made). (Collected from USDA Nutrient Database for Standard Reference, 1998 and cited fatty acid studies.)

Figure 5-1 compares the fatty acid levels in human milk with a few popular formulas. The importance of each fatty acid is not important to us here; rather, it is interesting to see the comparisons, which reveal the subtle effectiveness of natural breastmilk. Even when human levels or ratios of certain fatty acids are well matched by a formula, results are not as desired. Why? First, there seem to be too many fatty acids in human milk to attempt to match them all. Second, other brain factors are missing in formula as well. Third, hundreds of components of human milk, as well as the hormones and other factors connected with the act of nursing, all operate in concert, in ways we will likely never be able to synthesize or even understand. We are only beginning to learn the many implications of these crude imitations.

Since there is no correlation between fetal and maternal blood levels of fatty acids or other lipids,[57] and since fetuses strongly resemble each other in their lipid levels, it is clear that the placenta delivers a finely tuned supply of just the right amounts to a fetus. In the same way, breastmilk is finely tuned to bring just the right amounts of each to the developing baby. Additionally, colostrum, premature breastmilk, newborn breastmilk, mature baby milk, and toddler age breastmilk all differ in their lipid concentrations as well — providing exactly what is right for each stage of development.

Brighter Times

The quest for super babies is no different than many other sincerely motivated but somewhat misguided attempts to control our children's behavior and destiny. Some important research was initiated by this fad, but in the long run, what we really learned was that good attentiveness, warmth, and natural feeding makes for the healthiest children. The evidence is overwhelming that breastfeeding gives a child the best opportunity for success, and the longer the better. At this point in time, research is showing us in bits and pieces that following your instincts and holding dearly to Mother Nature's course is usually the first choice in child care. True super babies are those with high self-esteem and high bonding ability; everything else follows from the parenting techniques that create these — including higher IQ, good health, and better just about any other talent you would like your child to have.

6

Immune Protection Matters

INFANTS ARE BORN WITH ACTIVE IMMUNE SYSTEMS, BUT THESE SYSTEMS are not mature, so babies are very vulnerable to illness and infection. Luckily, babies receive a lasting immune boost from mom during labor, if labor is allowed. Then, mother's milk, if it is available, adds the remaining protection that is needed. Still, a child's health is often challenged, and the parents' behavior can either help or hinder the child's immune battles. As with many other facets of baby's well-being, parenting choices influence to what extent a child develops infection and illness. Every day more and more information comes to light that calls into question many of the practices followed during the previous decades. I feel that the only way for an individual family to truly make the informed choices best for them is to understand the most debatable issues and the current research findings about them. First, however, it is necessary to have some background about how babies function and know some details about the role of human milk in baby development.

Without Protection

Studies from various parts of the world report that the infant death rate in artificially fed infants is anywhere from 1.4 to 2.7 times that in exclusively breastfed babies, even after controlling for many confounding factors — the larger studies weighing in on the higher side.[1-6] Such studies are only performed in developing nations, chiefly because their mortality rates are of more concern, with problems of poverty and poor sanitation affecting all babies, no matter how they are fed. I am quite interested in one such study, performed in Malaysia, because the overall infant death rate there is barely above our own. This study reports a doubled infant death rate for formula-fed infants.[7] Studies in industrialized nations, including our own, reveal that, for formula-fed children, the rates for most illnesses are doubled, there are much higher rates for some predominant diseases, and illnesses are prolonged. It follows that deaths from these maladies would be proportional to their occurrence (perhaps higher). Therefore, we can conclude that even in industrialized countries, even in the U.S., death in formula-fed infants is twice that of breastfed babies. Since the U.S. has an infant death rate of 7.2 per 1000, and a breastfeeding rate that drops quickly from under 70% to 30% in the first 3 months, one could deduce that *there are at least 2 extra infant deaths per 1,000 due to the absence of breastmilk*. Statistically, the longer the breastfeeding, the better the protection; hence a larger portion of breastfed babies who die are most likely those who were weaned very early. As already noted in the previous chapter, SIDS is less often a problem in naturally fed babies. Breathing and heart regulation provided by mother's proximity accounts for part of the protection. At the same time, the stress of infant separation can contribute to SIDS. Undetected infections resulting from reduced immune protection in those not receiving mother's milk contribute to SIDS as well. Nutrition, brain development, and allergy factors are also responsible for some of the difference in survival rates.

Beyond the elusive SIDS deaths, infections account for most of the difference in mortality rates between those who receive mother's milk and those who do not. The greatest danger is death from intestinal infections and diarrhea. While the risk of death from diarrhea in developing nations may be 14 times higher or more without exclusive mother's milk,[8] the risk in industrial nations is much more than double overall. One predominant form is up to 20 times more frequent.[9] As usual, those who receive a mixture of human milk and formula fall somewhere in between, but much closer to formula-fed rates.

The increased threat to the lives of artificially fed children persists beyond the age of formula and nursing. A significantly higher risk of childhood cancer exists for those who never received human milk, compared to those who nursed exclusively and for extended periods.[10,11] Clearly, breastmilk should be considered an important part of the child's immune system.[12]

> A significantly higher risk of childhood cancer exists for those who never received human milk, compared to those who nursed exclusively and for extended periods.

Infection Protection

Not only does formula feeding increase infant and child mortality, but the number of infant illnesses such as respiratory infections, ear infections, intestinal infections, pneumonia, and influenza doubles (on the average), as does the need for health care.[13-18] The duration of most illness is significantly longer as well. While mixing breastmilk with formula partially protects children from mortality and some non-fatal illnesses, the largest study to date, performed by the University of Michigan School of Nursing,

> While mixing breastmilk with formula partially protects children, this protection is minimal for common illnesses when compared to exclusive breastfeeding.

suggests this protection is minimal for common illnesses when compared to exclusive breastfeeding.[19] However, a positive relationship between the increased duration of breastfeeding and reduced illness remains strong in all studies.[20]

Lasting Protection

In 1998, in light of a few very recent research studies, Dr. M.K. Davis of the CDC (Centers for Disease Control and Prevention) confirmed that *breastmilk plays a role in the long-term development of the immune system and the prevention of disease, well beyond the time of breastfeeding.*[21] At the same time others reached similar conclusions,[22,23] and for the first time suggested the chemical pathways[24] for breastmilk's apparent role in encouraging heightened immune system development in the child.

Baby's First Defenses

An infant is generally born "sterile," meaning without any bacteria or other germs in his body. Never having been exposed to any kind of microorganism, newborns haven't built up any antibodies to resist the germs that are all around us. Without any defenses, newborns would have to develop hundreds of different antibodies to fend off hundreds of infections in the first days of life. The energy consumption for this battle would be trying for a young infant who already has so much growing and neurological development to orchestrate. But, by design, a baby doesn't have to fend for itself. In addition to its own immature immune system, there are two other key sources of immunity for defense against disease — antibodies from mother's placenta *and* the antibodies and other immune factors in mother's milk.

In the immune system, antibodies are created specifically for each invading microorganism (bacteria, virus, or fungus) or foreign protein that threatens the body — each specific invader causes the creation of one or more specific antibodies. The body can then copy these by the millions to mount a counterattack. Creating a tailor-made antibody can take from a day to over a week. The cells that create these antibodies are not fully mature until a few weeks after a full-term birth,[25] and the reliable development of antibodies does not occur for many more months to a year.

Another immune system action includes the gobbling up of invaders and damaged cells by immune cells called "phagocytes." A newborn has a limited ability to develop new phagocytes, and as a result, large or prolonged battles are difficult for him to wage. Additionally, immature phagocytes have reduced ability to go to the part of the body where they are needed.[26] But baby's immune system may be somewhat limited by design. During the huge influx of microbes in the first hours and days of life, the newborn could be overwhelmed with inflammation resulting from immune battles. Filling in for baby's limitations, mother's milk also supplies anti-inflammatory agents while it provides less-damaging ways to fight infection.

Placental Transfer

Baby receives certain antibodies from mother during the last weeks in the womb, especially during labor. These help fight the thousands of microorganisms that mother has already developed resistance to, including polio, measles, and pertussis. Although I say "thousands" of microbes, this does not mean that mother has been ill thousands of times in her life. Only 1% of all bacteria causes disease in a normally healthy human being. A weakened immune system may be susceptible to double this amount. In general, immunity is acquired to many or most of the microbes that lead to the well-known diseases without noticeable illness. Most of the antibodies obtained from mother while in the womb remain abundant in the infant's body for about 6 months after birth, with

> The transfer of antibodies is greatly reduced when a baby is born without labor (planned C-section), which reduces his infection-fighting abilities over the next several months.

some lingering on several months more. This provides for a gradual withdrawal from the initial support, but this immunity should be bolstered with mother's milk.

The transfer of antibodies is greatly reduced when a baby is born without labor (planned C-section),[27] which reduces his infection-fighting abilities over the next several months. Premature infants are born with many fewer of mother's antibodies — the earlier, the fewer. Also, the earlier the birth, the less mature baby's immune system is. Thus, the protection provided in mother's milk is all the more valuable for premature babies.

Some antibodies seem to transfer to the fetus better than others. Furthermore, when mother's immunity to a disease such as measles is from vaccination rather than through natural exposure, the immunity passed on is often very slight or absent.[28] As a result, now that most mothers have received vaccinations before they developed natural immunity to many diseases, vaccinating infants at more and more delicate ages is deemed necessary. All these vaccines need to be repeated at the usual intervals as well, because the young infant is unable to develop an adequate amount of antibodies after early vaccination to build any significant resistance. Moreover, the levels of antibodies from mother are unknown at the time of vaccination, and any existing antibodies from mother will prevent the infant from developing immunity upon vaccination.

Breastmilk Completes Baby's Protection

While the placenta provides many antibodies, breastmilk contains more kinds of antibodies, plus a multitude of other infection-fighting, healing, and growth factors. These not only provide multiple means to fight disease, but these antibodies and other factors also fight infections for which few or no antibodies are received before birth. Few if any cow's milk antibodies are pertinent to the human infant since different animal species are susceptible to different microbes. A large portion of the immune factors in human milk are not found in cow's milk at all. Some factors do exist in fresh cow's milk, but these are only minimally found in formulas. Certain antibodies in cow's milk (and cow's milk formula) actually pose problems for human infants, sometimes leading to disease.

Unlike placental antibodies, mother's milk is most helpful in the gastrointestinal tract from the mouth to the end of the intestines, where it is introduced and travels. Most microbes enter the body this way as well. Even microbes that enter through the nose meet mother's milk defenses in the back of the throat. Yet, milk antibodies and presumably other factors also pass through the walls of the intestine to aid other areas of the body. This can occur because of the special properties of milk and the young intestines.

Breastmilk antibodies offer a broader spectrum of protection than those from the placenta. In addition, antibodies to new organisms that mother and child are both exposed to can be developed by mother and furnished to baby through mother's milk. Beneficially, mother's milk provides protection without causing inflammation.[29] Breastmilk can also be provided long after placental antibodies are gone. Along with protection for bacterial, viral, fungal, and parasitic invasion, mother's antibodies provide some protection against food proteins that may occur in mother's milk as well as in baby's other foods.

Protective Factors in Mother's Milk

One unique quality of the antibodies in mother's milk is that they interfere with many microorganisms' ability to attach to the mucous membranes lining the throat and intestines, including those that can cause middle ear infections.[30] Factors associated with the fat globules of breastmilk also augment this protection. For instance, one factor protects against a dangerous form of E. coli, at least in the mouth,[31] and another limits an E. coli that causes bloody diarrhea.[32] Still another binds with an intestinal virus, rotavirus, to prevent infection.[33] Rotavirus and E. coli are responsible for most cases of infectious diarrhea in infants. One million and five million infant deaths, respectively, are attributed to these worldwide.[34] Another factor, called "90K," stimulates maturation of the infant's immune system, reducing respiratory and other infections.[35]

Oligosaccharides are complex carbohydrates with immune properties found in abundance in human milk (1/3 of the solids), but almost never found in the milk of other animals — none in cow's milk. The levels of these important factors in mother's milk vary with the maturity of the newborn at the time of birth and with the age of the child, in concordance with need. These are known to act against dangerous E. coli, Streptococcus pneumoniae, and many other invaders. There are 130 different oligosaccharides, and many have been found to act against specific microbes.[36] Similar complex carbohydrates that act against infection include one that blocks the first step in HIV infection (the AIDS virus).[37] Chondroitin sulphate has antibacterial and antiviral activities.[38]

The whey proteins of human milk consist mostly of lactalbumin and lactoferrin, important components of immune protection. The chief whey protein of cow's milk is betalactoglobulin, which is actually a problem protein for humans in terms of digestion and allergy. Lactoferrin provides antibacterial, antiviral, and antifungal protection in several ways,[39] but *infant formula actually encourages the growth of many dangerous bacteria, including* E. coli, *salmonella, and* shigella.[40,41] A human curd protein, kappacasein, acts against *Helicobacter pylori,* a factor in ulcer formation.[42]

Necrotizing enterocolitis is a serious inflammation of the intestines that involves destruction of the cells used for nutritional absorption. It generally occurs during the first days after birth, although it is seen at up to 3 months of age. Five to ten percent of premature infants are affected, as are over 1% of full-term infants. One quarter of those affected die. Over 90% of those who contract this disease have been formula fed.[43,44] One could almost say that formula feeding "causes" this deadly disease. Of those breastmilk-fed infants who are affected, most are in hospital care units where babies develop less natural early protective intestinal flora, due to lack of exposure to mother's breast or the environment. While imbalance of flora contributes to this disease,[45] human milk contains an enzyme that prevents the tissue destruction. This enzyme is more prevalent in breastmilk when an infant is born prematurely, and its level continues to rise over the next weeks to protect against necrotizing enterocolitis.[46]

These are only a few of the disease-fighting factors in mother's milk; to cover them all would require a book in itself. Nearly all the important factors are absent or poorly functional in formulas, including the following:

- White blood cells (immune system cells), including neutrophils, macrophages (phagocytes), and lymphocytes (including B cells and T cells) are known to be active and mobile within the infant's system.
- Prostaglandin E2, plasminogin activator, and complement, all produced by the macrophages, help to orchestrate immune reactions.[47]
- Many different cytokines, including several chemokines and colony-stimulating factors, stimulate immune functions.[48]
- Products of human milk fat digestion have antiviral and antiprotozoan action.

- Bile-salt-dependent lipase and peroxidase kill bacteria.
- Antiproteases protect valuable immune proteins of mother's milk from digestion.[49]
- Neuraminic acid and linoleic acid, with antibacterial actions, are in higher concentrations in human milk than in cow's.[50]
- Superior levels of iron, zinc, and selenium absorption aid the fight against disease.
- Higher levels of arginine, glutamine, and nucleotides assist intestinal adaptation.
- Interferon has powerful antiviral properties.
- Lysozyme degrades undesirable microbes.
- Probiotics are friendly bacteria for protective colonization of the intestines, and prebiotics, including many of the complex carbohydrates, feed and foster beneficial flora. Formula-fed infants have entirely different intestinal floral environments offering little or no protection.[51]
- Growth factors, including nucleotides,[52] polyamines,[53] and hormones, encourage maturation of the various immune defenses in the intestines.
- Antioxidants, including multiple forms of vitamins C, E, and A, along with cysteine, protect against oxidation damage of the immature immune system.[54]
- Tumor necrosis factor receptors and interleukin receptors have anti-inflammatory consequences.[55]

Around 6 months of age, just as the effects of the original IgG antibodies from mother's placenta are wearing off, infants become less able to pass mother's antibodies and immune blood cells into their bloodstream. As solid foods are introduced, other immune factors are becoming somewhat less effective as well. Luckily, by this time, the lysozyme in mother's milk has increased to 10 times its 2-week level, in a sense to make up the difference. Other immune factors in her milk change with the increasing age of the child as well.

Interestingly, various studies compare the amount of infection in infants to the levels of 90K, lactadherin, and other components found in their mothers' milk. Reduced numbers of certain infections are seen in infants when higher levels of certain components are in their mother's milk. We can only hope that future research will investigate how a mother can influence the levels of immune factors in her milk, although it is already known that the levels of most of these do not reflect the levels in mother's blood.[56]

We also know that when mothers stay close to baby and are exposed to baby's saliva via kisses and stools during diaper changes, this helps mother provide appropriate immune factors to baby through her milk. The "enteromammary pathway" is the name given to the process by which mother supplies specific immune factors in her milk according to what she has been exposed to. When premature infants receive mother's milk in neonatal centers, they receive much better immune assistance when mother is in intimate contact with the infant.[57] *High levels of sanitation between the nursing mother and her infant can prevent this valuable transaction from occurring.*[58]

> We also know that when mothers stay close to baby and are exposed to baby's saliva via kisses and stools during diaper changes, this helps mother provide appropriate immune factors to baby through her milk.

Colostrum, the name for mother's first milk, is especially high in antibodies, immune cells, lactoferrin, and other factors, but levels drop off over a few weeks' time. Lysozyme levels are also high and drop significantly in the first weeks; however, they rise again by a factor of 10 around 6 months of age,[59] just when placental antibodies are wearing off.

While the breastfed infant has less need for vaccinations, her immune response to them is superior to those who do not receive mother's milk, creating better and longer-lasting immunities.[60]

A few papers suggest that the immune-protective benefits of breastfeeding outweigh the risk of an HIV positive mother transmitting HIV to her infant through her milk, especially in third-world countries.[61,62] It seems that antibodies against HIV are also passed along if mother was infected well before nursing began. When mother becomes infected during the nursing period, this is not the case, and transmission to the infant is more likely. In either case, some risk of transmission does exist, via cracked nipples for instance.

The thymus gland in the upper chest is an immune system organ that typically shrinks during puberty and then shrinks more with advanced age, leaving the elderly system low on defenses. It is important for fighting disease, especially for creating T cells to fight viruses. Recently, *researchers found that starting from birth the thymus gland shrinks much more in formula-fed infants compared to breastfed babies.*[63] At the age of 4 months, the thymus of the artificially fed infant is only half the size of a breastfed baby's gland, most likely accounting for some of the increased susceptibility to disease that accompanies formula feeding. The breastfed baby's thymus gradually reduces in size after weaning. Apparently, breastmilk provides some unknown stimulant that maintains a large thymus capable of supplying more T cells during the first years of life, when these cells are immature and slow to respond, or the stress of formula feeding causes the thymus to shrink. Stress-related cortisol releases cause this gland to shrink, but this can be reversed by relieving stress.[64] We have already discussed the fact that infants who frequently suffer from separation and inattentiveness have higher cortisol levels throughout much of their lives, and that these infants may develop reduced

> *Fever should not be routinely reduced; in fact, it has been shown that in most infections illness and death increase when fevers are reduced.*

health and may succumb to early aging. The thymus gland's sensitivity to stress is certainly one source of these reported results.

Other Immune System Defenses

Besides the many direct ways the body's immune system fights microbes, developing a fever is a powerful disease-fighting tool. Fever is not only valuable for indicating the presence of infection, but is highly effective for fighting infection; in fact, that is its purpose. Today parents have been programmed by advertisers as well as the medical community to reduce fever whenever present, even in light of the side effects of fever-reducing medications. Fever should not be routinely reduced;[65] in fact, it has been shown that *in most infections illness and death increase when fevers are reduced.*[66,67] Many even believe that recovery from infection is swifter when a fever is raised with warm baths, warm fluids, covering warmly, or raising the house temperature. Fevers are dangerously high however somewhere beyond 103°F,[68] at which point reduction through medication or a cool bath should be considered to prevent possible brain damage (thought to occur around 106° in children, possibly 104° in adults). A child under 3 months of age with high fever must be medically examined. By blocking certain elements of the immune system, common fever-reducing drugs such as aspirin and ibuprofen (Motrin) interfere with disease fighting, and healing as well. Using ibuprofen with chicken pox greatly increases the chance of developing necrotizing fasciitis (flesh-eating bacteria) infection,[69] since it reduces a child's immune defenses. Aspirin use with influenza or chicken pox can lead to dangerous Reye's syndrome. Acetaminophen (Tylenol) prolongs chicken pox illness,[70] among others, and poses liver risks.

Other symptoms in ill children can generally be respected as well. If they are tired, they should rest, if they are energetic, they can probably play. If they have no appetite, this may be the body's way to concentrate on the infection. Food should be in sight, but not forced, although one may wish to provide vitamin supplements. On the other hand, fluid intake is always important and should usually include electrolytes (Infalyte, Pedialyte) when no other nutrition is being consumed. Infant formula can be irritating when diarrhea is present, but breastmilk is helpful. It is rare for an ill child to stop nursing.

Other Issues of Immunity & Health

The human immune system is far more complicated and powerful than anything man will ever develop to fight disease. For this reason, protecting and boosting the immune system often makes the most sense in the face of illness. Antibiotics are wonder drugs that can kill dangerous, life-threatening bacterial infections. Many are borrowed from the chemical defenses of fungi that must fight against bacterial foes just as we do. But our bodies are able to discriminate between friend and foe when they attack bacteria, where antibiotics are only partly specific. This often creates imbalances in the normal flora, creating susceptibility to other normally unexpected infections. Vaccines also come to mind in the saga of science versus disease. They do not in themselves prevent disease; they are intended to encourage the body's own immune system to develop antibodies against the introduced, weakened version of the disease (a form of facilitating the body's ability to develop immunity). In theory, this seems ideal.

The infant's strong desire to orally sample everything in the environment, starting tentatively with more familiar objects such as the parents' fingers and furniture, then gradually graduating to small and then greater amounts of dirt and other matter, *is an important facet of developing the child's immune system.* This is a natural vaccination practice whereby the youngster slowly ingests tiny samples of the environment, subsequently developing antibodies to introduced microbes. This occurs while the thymus gland is large and additional infection fighting power is supplied via mother's milk. Another function of the thymus gland is to catalog which proteins and other elements are "self," and therefore should not be attacked by antibodies, and what is foreign matter. The environmental sampling aids this endeavor while the thymus is at its peak. In children where this practice has been strongly prevented, far fewer antibodies are developed to protect against infection from large exposures to microbes. The safety of this sampling process has a limit, however. When large populations of people live closely together, increased exposure to dangerous microbes becomes a problem, especially due to sewage exposures, rat exposures, and some other major issues, hence the value of modern sanitation.

The Vaccination Question

With major sanitation problems resolved in most industrialized nations, many epidemic diseases were subdued even before the advent of vaccines. Likewise, in regions of the world where sewage sanitation is not adequate, new epidemics occur frequently, even though polio and other diseases may be controlled through vaccination programs. Interestingly, when polio was epidemic in the U.S. in the mid 1900s, it was not those from impoverished areas who were affected the most, but those from affluent urban locales. Most likely, people in these areas acquired less immunity during infancy from natural environmental exposure. It has been suggested that improvements in water treatment and sewage handling in the late 1800s and increased sanitation in the early 1900s may have caused the polio epidemic. As exposure to human waste diminished, so did natural immunities, leaving vulnerable communities.[71] As outbreaks occurred, community immunities again grew, and the epidemic naturally subsided, as most do. Now, rightfully reluctant to reverse sanitation practices, only one other option exists to prevent further epidemic cycles of this paralyzing disease — developing immunity through vaccination, which is a more controlled means as well. There is hope, and it seems likely, that the strains of poliovirus for which widespread vaccination occurs will entirely disappear from the planet, as smallpox has.

Vietnam still suffers from inadequate sewage handling in most of its communities. This nation also frequently suffers from epidemics. Formula feeding is quite uncommon in this country, but solid foods are introduced at a very early age, so the ratio of solid food to breastmilk quickly becomes very high, even though some nursing generally occurs for extended periods.[72] Hence, in addition to poor sanitation, the infants here are generally not receiving the exclusive breastfeeding that is most important for early disease protection and extended immune system development. Most likely both of these factors contribute to the continuing suffering from disease in Vietnam.

As the rates of serious infectious disease drop in the industrialized nations, and the memories of these maladies fade, the occasional, unfortunate adverse effects of vaccinations become a clear target of criticism. However, some real questions do exist, and there is a real potential for future difficulties. It is best for the public to remain informed in order to keep vaccine manufacturers and policy makers vigilant.

In light of many issues surrounding vaccination programs, many now question immunization of their children. Those wishing to find true information come across some highly sensational anti-vaccination literature, as well as much pro-vaccination literature that tends to wear rose-colored glasses. Without digging deeply into volumes of literature, there is no way to make an educated choice.

A review of the literature shows that while many claims in anti-vaccination books are inflated, and some prove to be untraceable, there is still valid information presented. Fortunately, concern over some of the issues has led to further studies, such as a 1988 vaccine trial that suggested an increased rate of bacterial infections in vaccinated children compared to placebo children.[73] A 1992 report reviewed nearly 65,000 vaccinated children and found no such correlation.[74]

Without a doubt, vaccination programs have been scarred by many unfortunate errors, but we need to look at today and the future, not at the past. The most valid popular questions and objections about vaccinations, a few new issues, and what seems to be the most reliable information about these are listed below. Many more valid issues exist, but most are similar to these:

- Antibiotic therapy reduces the risk of death from many diseases.

  True, but antibiotics are already being overused, causing the development of more serious microbes and more serious diseases. Antibiotics are also not without side effects. Yet, the availability of antibiotics does tremendously reduce the death rate of all currently vaccinated-for diseases — either directly or by reducing dangerous secondary infections.

• Many epidemics are already prevented through sanitation in industrialized nations.

Yes, but as described above, regions eventually lose their natural immunities and become vulnerable to rapid spread of disease, especially in the face of today's high-speed world travel.

• There is a high correlation between many epidemics and malnutrition from blights, droughts, and high grain prices.

Yes, the above factors of sanitation and malnutrition play definite roles in epidemic cycles — both prior to the introduction of vaccinations as well as during immunization programs. Both need to continuously improve in all populations. Still, significant drops in disease correlate with introducing or improving vaccination programs. As other factors change only gradually, rates of previously ameliorated disease often increase sharply where vaccinations wane or are discontinued.[75]

• New epidemics from microbes for which there is no vaccination persist and grow in the absence of sanitation,[76-79] *including 3,333 strains of polio-like viruses,*[80] leading one to wonder whether vaccine money could be better spent elsewhere.

Japanese encephalitis virus has recently dropped to near eradication in Japan due to sanitary control measures,[81] although it continues to be bothersome in other nations. Unfortunately, not all diseases can be controlled like encephalitis; it depends on the disease's mode of transmission.

• Minimal efforts are made to prevent the continuing formula promotions in all nations and the immense concurrent increases in infant disease and mortality. At the same time birthrates are harder to control because breastfeeding's contraceptive effects are missing, often resulting in poorly afforded and poorly surviving children.

On top of formula's reduced nutrition, its high cost often causes feeding of diluted formula in poor regions where free samples have usurped mother's ability to nurse. By robbing the infant of mother's immune support, in conjunction with formula mixed with unsafe water and the high potential for iron loss and diarrhea,[82] formulas have certainly caused many lives to be needlessly taken, as have epidemic diseases from unrelated causes.

• Many sometimes devastating accidents of vaccination programs have occurred, including the probable introduction of HIV into the human population through the use of infected monkey serum in an African polio vaccine.[83,84] This is an important issue, although this was apparently not the first introduction of HIV to mankind.

Many of the same techniques that have caused such accidents continue to be used today.[85] In fact, polio vaccine was very recently recalled by Britain's Medical Control Agency due to suspected mad cow disease contamination, where fetal calf serum was being used. So-called stealth viruses are being found today in some chronic fatigue and brain-disordered patients, the likely result of other monkey viruses obtained through polio vaccines.[86] These monkey viruses have shown the ability to spread from human to human, as seen in a current burst of neurological illnesses in the Mohave Valley,[87] with the potential to create a brand-new epidemic.

In addition to the stealth viruses, well-known evidence reveals that genetic mutation and recombination of vaccine-acquired polio viruses cause a wide spectrum of neurological symptoms.[88] Known strains are rare, but one must remember that polio strains are seldom looked for in patients with neurological disease.

• Questions often arise about the legality of the absolute immunity from lawsuit that the U.S. has granted vaccine companies.

The logic seems to be that, while unfortunate effects are expected, more damage may be expected without the vaccines, and vaccine companies could not afford to do their research if constantly sued. This is a radically different approach to the Hippocratic "First do no harm."

• The most difficult situation to draw conclusions about is that of the occasional neurological damage found to have statistically significant correlation to pertussis vaccines[89-91] and less provable questions about a possible link to SIDS. Pertussis itself can cause the episodes of stopped breathing (apnea) that are associated with SIDS.[92] SIDS rates increased in response to increases in pertussis rates in Sweden after pertussis vaccination ceased.[93]

Although pertussis immunity is not permanent — either from vaccination or natural exposure[94] — well over 99% of pertussis exposures probably go unnoticed in adults, leaving many with ongoing protective antibodies.[95] However, more than half of the young children in Sweden contracted pertussis after vaccination was terminated in 1979.[96] Dangerous complications of this respiratory disease include pneumonia and brain involvement.

A Swedish study compared an acellular form of pertussis vaccine (used often in Europe) to the whole cell form (used in the U.S.) and to DT vaccination with no pertussis serum, for control, in nearly 10,000 infants. The study found "significantly higher" rates of adverse effects in those receiving the whole cell vaccine compared to either of the other two.[97]

Fever and local pain at the sight of the injection are expected from many vaccines, the fever resulting from the body's efforts to build immunity to the introduced germs. Seizures, shock, cyanosis (turning blue due to lack of oxygen, a precursor to SIDS), encephalitis (inflammation of the brain), and persistent high-pitched crying are more serious consequences consistently associated with whole cell pertussis vaccines. The most disconcerting question is whether these events occasionally signify some degree of permanent brain damage. While some have suggested that prolonged crying is simply injection discomfort, this effect is reported by parents at a very high rate only after pertussis vaccinations, even though some others are surely just as painful. A German study compared whole cell to acellular vaccine in over 10,000 infants and found this type of crying in response to 1 in every 113 doses of whole cell vaccine, as well as in 1 in 500 acellular injections.[98] Four doses are typically provided to a child. While most children appear normal a few days after this phenomenon, the characteristic piercing cry leads many to wonder just what is happening inside the brain, and how many seemingly incidental later events can be correlated with it. The same study reported convulsions in 1 in 4,000 receiving whole cell vaccine, 4 times the number in those receiving acellular.

> A large multidisciplinary workshop in the U.S. reviewed all available data and concluded that these seizures following pertussis vaccination were not simply a result of vaccine-related fevers, and are therefore a cause for concern.

A large multidisciplinary workshop in the U.S. reviewed all available data and concluded that these seizures following pertussis vaccination were not simply a result of vaccine-related fevers, and are therefore a cause for concern.[99] Brain damage is observed in a significant, although small, number of children after this crying. When these reactions do occur, the very low rate of reporting of these incidents by MDs prevents good statistical analysis, which could reveal whether there is real causation or just coincidence. Also, brain damage related to birth defects often becomes apparent around vaccination age, confusing the issue. This workshop was able to ascertain that seizures occur in 2% of pertussis cases, brain involvement (encephalitis) in .3%, and death in 2 to 3 out of 1,000 reported cases — significant numbers for a parent to consider should they risk allowing their child to contract the disease. More often, it is the weaker who are seriously injured from the disease, such as those missing immune protection from mother's milk, those who are malnourished, or those who live with poor care and sanitation.

A University of California experiment was designed to establish the accuracy of determining vaccine efficiency rates through reporting. Here, it was concluded that observer bias probably plays a large role in efficacy trials, and that actual infection most likely occurs in considerably more (even twice as many) vaccinated individuals than reported, leading to inflated accounts of vaccine effectiveness.[100] From this trial and a Swedish report, one may conclude that the efficacy of pertussis vaccines may be only 40 to 50%.[101] Many reports in the medical literature suggest that the whole cell vaccine is superior while other reports applaud the acellular vaccine. Physicians' assumptions and mindset lead to far greater underreporting of adverse results after vaccination than so-called controlled trials suggest. The tragedy is that inaccurate and greatly limited reporting of adverse reactions makes it impossible to calculate the statistical advantage of vaccinations, especially in the case of the pertussis. Where vaccination coverage is as low as 23% in some areas such as some U.S. inner cities,[102] combined with a possible 50% efficacy for pertussis vaccines, one has to wonder whether pertussis is controlled by vaccination in this country at all. The other question is why the more profitable whole cell version continues to be used here when Europe and Australia have abandoned its use due to the higher rate of dangerous side effects. Although again the minimal reporting efforts prevent accurate conclusions, it seems apparent that while the already immune-compromised are the ones susceptible to serious complications of disease, vaccination damages seem to hit even the healthiest of children. One final mention about the wisdom of pertussis vaccination efforts is that pertussis is not a disease that can be eradicated through vaccinations as smallpox was, because it is spread by respiratory means.[103]

• There is increasing risk of Guillain-Barré Syndrome (a nervous system disorder) resulting from any vaccinations as the number of vaccines provided per child escalate.[104]

This real but slight risk is lower than the risk of serious disease to the unvaccinated.[105,106]

• Correlation has been found between measles vaccination and inflammatory bowel diseases.[107]

There is other evidence suggesting this link is at most very weak.[108]

• There are human rights issues about mandatory introduction of foreign proteins into one's body.

On the other hand, the first few known AIDS victims were not quarantined, leading to countless suffering and deaths, due to human rights issues.

• Risks of allergic response to vaccines exist.

These risks are reportedly slight, and known allergic individuals can avoid vaccinations and still possibly obtain protection to some diseases through "herd" immunity, the exposure from vaccinated individuals. On the other hand, many food allergy sufferers report that their symptoms began or increased with a vaccination — many vaccines do contain dairy, corn, egg, and other potentially allergy-causing residues not intended for direct entry into the bloodstream.

• Acquiring multiple sclerosis is associated with contracting childhood diseases later in life (as opposed to during early childhood).[109]

Infant vaccination programs cause such late-life occurrences of disease when their weak, unnatural immunity wanes later in life (although adolescent and adult boosters would prevent this).

Vaccinations create reduced immunity compared to the immunity developed through natural exposure (whether illness occurs with such exposure or not). As a result, one must consider the substantial danger of diseases such as measles and mumps that can be far more devastating when they infect adults.

• Less immunity is passed on to infants from vaccinated mothers than from those who were naturally exposed to a disease.

Older adults with reduced immunity due to vaccination develop diseases and then pass them on to the very young who have not yet been vaccinated.[110] The very young exposed to these adults also have less protection of their own because their mothers had childhood vaccinations. Increased disease, including measles and pertussis, are now being seen in these two most-delicate groups.

Because of the weaker immunity that results from vaccines, the danger of contracting diseases in adulthood, and the danger that these adults will then infect infants before vaccination, an immense increase in the number of vaccinations is suggested: vaccination right after birth, revaccination according to today's childhood schedules, revaccination in adolescence, and then once or more for each vaccine type during later adulthood. Additionally, there are suggestions about vaccinating before birth through vaccination of pregnant mothers. Nearly all vaccines need boosters throughout life to remain preventive. Unfortunately, the risk of serious side effects from a vaccine multiplies as the number of vaccinations goes up (and as new vaccines continue to emerge).

Rotavirus is responsible for fewer than 100 (mostly formula-fed) deaths in the U.S. each year, but the Advisory Committee on Immunization Practices recently suggested

I just saw a vaccine-promoting ad that said, "40 children died this year from chicken pox." Consider that the death rate from chicken pox is much lower in nations where breastfeeding is the norm, so this disease only causes about 1,000 deaths worldwide per year. On the very next page was a formula ad, which did not mention that 1.5 million deaths worldwide could likely be prevented each year by exclusive breastfeeding.

that every child in the U.S. should receive a high-dose vaccination for this diarrheal disease,[111] which is mostly preventable through breastfeeding. Only four months later, this recommendation was then rescinded by the CDC based on reports of dangerous bowel obstructions occurring after vaccinations.[112] Currently, chicken pox vaccination is being introduced. A five-year study in France from 1991 to 1995 revealed that no deaths due to chicken pox occurred in that nation, even though no vaccination was used there.[113] Complications occurred in 2% of cases, all with complete recovery. These numbers are far better than the numbers of complications, permanent injuries, and deaths that likely result from some immunizations such as vaccines for measles, a similar disease.[114] (Measles has a death or disability rate of 1 per million in industrialized nations without vaccination.[115]) The consequences of chicken pox vaccination will not be known until it has had widespread use over a period of time, although there have already been thousands of reports of serious reactions, including several deaths. While these are only reports, and many could be coincidence or other errors, the FDA advises that typically fewer than 10% of serious adverse reactions to vaccines are actually reported.

It used to be expected that every child would obtain chicken pox infection, as well as mumps and measles, and then have lifetime immunity to these diseases. Chiefly, children who are poorly fed, highly medicated, overly tired, lacking mother's antibodies, or otherwise immune-compromised have possibly serious complications from these diseases, and even here, mortality rates are incredibly low. Yet, since the introduction of a vaccine for chicken pox, articles and advertisements suddenly abound about the serious dangers of chicken pox. I just saw a vaccine-promoting ad that said, "40 children died this year from chicken pox." Consider that the death rate from chicken pox is much lower in nations where breastfeeding is the norm, so this disease only causes about 1,000 deaths worldwide per year. On the very next page was a formula ad, which did not mention that 1.5 million deaths worldwide could likely be prevented each year by exclusive breastfeeding.[116] One must weigh the risk of serious complication from multiple vaccinations for a disease versus the risk from childhood illness. These ads also refer to the economic burden of treating ill children — in other words, the "economic profit from selling vaccinations." Chicken pox is a very serious disease in teens or adults. Since vaccination wears off by this time, our adult population is now at risk. The same is true for measles.

Most vaccinations, if the decision is made to give them, should be repeated throughout teen and adult years. This poses a new danger, as in the case of chicken pox. Children with the chicken pox are kept at home, but people freshly vaccinated go on about their days in public. As a result, chicken pox viruses are being shed around the elderly, who are susceptible to development of shingles upon exposure to the virus as their natural immunity finally wanes sometime late in life. Certainly, with an active vaccination program for this illness, there is a strong possibility that many younger adults will soon be developing shingles from exposure to newly vaccinated individuals and their own waning immunity. Finally, this scenario puts our youngest infants at the greatest risk. With their mothers now passing on weak or no immunity during birth because they were vaccinated, and with tiny infants barely able to mount any defenses on their own in response to either vaccination or infection, many more dire cases of this disease will develop in our most vulnerable population.

Hepatitis B vaccination, which is not without complications, is now provided regularly to tiny infants, even though disease risk occurs only after needle sharing, receiving blood, or sexual promiscuity. Vaccines for TB, pneumonia, and other maladies are on the horizon for compulsory use in this nation as well.

Many parents question the wisdom of vaccinating their children, and there are valid concerns. Some feel most comfortable in at least delaying vaccination until an infant is older and stronger, as long as they know he has obtained good antibodies during labor and receives ongoing protection from exclusive breastfeeding, and even then being selective about which they feel to be most appropriate. The hope of vaccine supporters, and all of us, is that the level of suffering, disease, and mortality caused by immunization is outweighed by the reduction of the same due to disease itself. It should be recognized that this equation will be different in different regions of the world as well as in different individual situations.

Antibiotics

In cases where the immune response lags behind a bacterial infection that is dangerously decimating the body, the advent of antibiotic medications (introduced 1950 to 1960) has miraculously saved the lives of millions of people who would have otherwise succumbed. However, the massive overzealous use of these wonder drugs has now created a new realm of powerful diseases we are unable to fight with existing antibiotics.[117] Once a resistant bacteria has been created in response to antibiotic therapy, it has the power to transfer its resistance to other microbes, developing new resistant

strains.[118] This has been an especially significant issue for the young, who have
been chief targets for antibiotic misuse,
because they are more susceptible to infections, and infections are more worrisome
in them. It is now recognized that these
powerful resistant strains spread easily
around day care centers.

The excitement over antibiotics has led
to reduced hygiene in hospitals. Sanitation
peaked decades ago when its importance
was first widely recognized. Now 10% of the
patients in hospitals acquire infections; a
large portion of these infections are resistant to antibiotic treatment due to its expan-
sive use in hospitals. Three percent of these
cases die from their infections.[119] TB and pneumonia were once con-
quered with antibiotics, but we are now threatened again by tubercu-
losis epidemics and increased pneumonia deaths.

In addition to the burgeoning strains resistant to antibiotics,
more invasive forms of bacteria are also being created by widespread
antibiotic therapy.[120] Some strep strains have recently become more
aggressive and can produce infections that rapidly destroy skin.
These often fatal "flesh-eating" strep (chiefly) infections occur especially in people who have previously been on antibiotics or other
therapies that alter the immune balance. Even scarlet fever, another
strain of strep, seems to be reemerging.[121]

Antibiotics have many possible side effects. Diarrhea, malabsorption, cramping, yeast infection, agitation, rashes, and blood disorders are a few of these. By wiping out much of the normal flora
throughout the body, they leave the child, especially, far more vulnerable to other infection such as thrush (oral candida) or dangerous
intestinal microbes that cause diarrhea. Infectious diarrhea follows
most antibiotics at a rate of 5 to 39%, depending on the drug.[122] The
most common intestinal infection caused by antibiotics is colitis
from clostridium infection, which has a 3.5% mortality rate.[123]

> A recent controlled study of antibiotic therapy for sinus infections showed that antibiotics had no influence on recovery or on the occurrence of relapse.

With all of this in mind, much evidence suggests that the common everyday antibiotic use in children is ineffective. A recent controlled study of antibiotic therapy for sinus infections showed that antibiotics had no influence on recovery or on the occurrence of relapse (and that X rays were not useful in treatment decisions).[124] Significantly, antibiotics are generally inappropriate for treating ear infections as well. They have no effect on viruses and are certainly inappropriate for colds and flus, where they can cause secondary infection. Yet, the majority of children visiting physicians with these complaints will receive antibiotic prescriptions. This is unfortunate because, most of the time, children are better off left to fight illness with their own immune systems, while the parents and physician provide careful monitoring.

Delaying antibiotic treatment of strep throat for 2 days after the child is seen by the doctor greatly reduces the number of recurrences,[125] probably because the body is allowed to develop its own defenses. This delay also allows time to obtain laboratory culture results, leading to more accurate treatment as well. Valid concerns about heart disease (rheumatic fever) lead most to recommend antibiotics in the case of strep infection. Preventing this disease is one of the blessings of antibiotic development.

The medical community is not entirely to blame for overuse of medications. Many parents bring their children in to their doctors at the first sign of a cold and demand medication. For many doctors, antibiotics and fever reducers have become an obligatory prescription. Moreover, excessive antibiotic therapy in humans is not the only source of new, dangerous, resistant strains. Regular prophylactic treating of animals creates resistant strains that can pose problems to humans. As we are increasingly exposed to antibiotics in meat, poultry, and cow's milk, we may often be developing resistant strains inside our bodies.

Ear Infections

The now highly prevalent middle ear infections in children illustrate the parameters of wise antibiotic use and its abuse, while at the same time revealing the effects of breastfeeding and formula. Middle ear infections (otitis media) have been on the rise throughout the twentieth century, increasing 150% between 1975 to 1990 alone.[126]

The major source of these infections is threefold: the withholding of protective mother's milk, antibiotic treatment for mild, non-bacterial ear conditions, and the inflammatory reactions to certain foods, particularly cow's milk, as covered in the last chapters of this book.

Permanent hearing damage does not occur from acute or chronic otitis.

The middle ear is the part of the ear that is enclosed behind the eardrum. There is a tiny tube, called the Eustachian tube, intended to drain any fluids from the middle ear into the throat. Colds and episodes of allergic runny nose, due to airborne allergens or cow's milk or other food allergens, block this Eustachian tube with mucus and inflammation. When this tiny mucous-membrane-lined canal is closed off, inflammatory fluids build up in the middle ear cavity (serous otitis media), sometimes referred to as effusion. Over time, passage of nasal and throat bacteria into this tube, especially when a child is lying on his back, can seed the middle ear; then the bacteria can multiply to large numbers in the friendly fluid-filled middle ear environment, creating painful infection and fever (acute otitis media).

The occurrence of otitis media was found to be 19% lower in breastfed infants, with 80% fewer prolonged episodes.[127] The risk of otitis remains at this reduced level for 4 months after weaning, but by 12 months after weaning, the risk is the same as in those who were never breastfed.[128] In addition to general immunities afforded the infant through breastmilk, there are specific antibodies that prevent otitis-causing bacteria from attaching to the mucous walls of the middle ear.

The presence of fluid in the middle ear from chronic or acute conditions reduces the child's capacity to hear. This fluid muffles sounds, but does not cause damage to the hearing mechanism, so hearing returns once the fluid is gone. *While permanent hearing damage does not occur from acute or chronic otitis,* chronic interference with hearing can delay language development.

In some cases of acute infection, treated or not, the eardrum may rupture, allowing the pus to drain, most likely resolving the infection. The eardrum will then heal with some scar tissue, just as it would have after tube insertion. Hearing is affected very minimally or not at all by this scar tissue found in many an eardrum. (Drainage from an ear can also be an outer ear infection. This is common after swimming and responds to ear drops. Drainage from the ear for more than 2 days, especially associated with hearing loss, requires prompt medical attention.)

> There is a higher rate of returning acute ear infection seen in those who receive antibiotic therapy, and the return of serous otitis is 2 to 6 times higher in those treated with antibiotics.

The major concern with ear infections is that infection will develop in the mastoid air cells behind the ear. This is called mastoiditis and is of concern because of the proximity to the brain. Mastoiditis, seen as redness behind the ear and protrusion of the outer ear, can occasionally lead to brain damage as well as to permanent hearing loss. Although claims are made that the incidence of mastoiditis has been greatly reduced since the introduction of antibiotics, this is not clear from a review of the literature. After the advent of antibiotics and CT scans, however, it is apparent that serious complications of acute mastoiditis have been reduced, and that the number of mastoid removals (mastoidectomies) has been reduced as well. In fact, antibiotic therapy for cases of mastoiditis appears to be valuable for preventing surgery in 86% of cases.[129]

Just over half of all mastoiditis cases occur following bouts of acute otitis media; other cases appear due to other causes, but less than 4% of the rare deaths from mastoiditis complications occur in cases that originated as ear infections.[130] Some mastoiditis is blamed on poor antibiotic treatment of ear infections; however, some is blamed on antibiotic therapy itself. At the 1998 American Academy of Otolaryngology meeting, it was reported that serious cases of mastoiditis are currently on the rise as a direct result of strongly resistant bacteria developed through the common use of antibiotic therapy for ear infections.[131] Additionally, "masked mastoiditis" is a highly worrisome, occasionally seen condition that is directly caused by antibiotic treatment of ear infections. The behavior of the bacteria that promote this condition makes it very difficult to discover, and it has a high rate of dangerous complications.[132]

Standard treatment for acute middle ear infections is antibiotic therapy. Antibiotics are also prescribed very often when fluid buildup is present by itself, without infection, although the parent is generally told infection exists, chiefly because it is often impossible to know for sure without puncturing the eardrum and taking a sample. At times the eardrum can appear very red just from crying or fever of other origin or allergies, causing suspicion of infection and prescription of drugs. One third of ear infections are viral and the distinction cannot be made upon examination.[133] Antibiotics do not kill viruses, but can make viral infections worse by wiping out competing bacterial flora and encouraging secondary bacterial infections of resistant strains. Although seldom recognized, a number of chronic ear infections are actually fungal (candida), produced when multiple courses of antibiotics disrupt the normal floral balance and encourage fungal growth.[134] Many large studies have shown that antibiotic treatment provides only a small benefit over no treatment for short-term resolution of ear infections. A 1994 analysis reviewed 33 studies, covering 5,400 cases of acute otitis, and found that spontaneous recovery without medical treatment occurred in 81% of acute cases, and that short-term recovery with antibiotics occurred 95% of the time.[135] Side effects are experienced by at least one third of the children on antibiotics. Although short-term resolution is slightly improved, long-term benefit from antibiotic therapy is not seen: Medicated children demonstrate no less otitis four weeks after treatment than those on placebos.[136] In fact, there is a higher rate of returning acute ear infection seen in those who receive antibiotic therapy, and the return of serous otitis is 2 to 6 times higher in those treated with antibiotics.[137]

There is much discussion as to the value of surgical insertion of tubes through the eardrum as there are risks involved, and there is a much greater return of infection once tubes are removed.[138] However, when language development is retarded due to prolonged middle ear fluid, tubes may be worth the risks in order to allow for temporary hearing improvement.

The most sensible modern recommendation regarding ear infection treatment is to use antibiotic therapy only in acute infections that do not resolve on their own within a few days.[139] This regimen is currently followed in several European countries with positive results; it also reduces the development of bacterial strains resistant to antibiotics. A heating pad over the ear affords some relief, as does acetaminophen, if needed. Fever should not be reduced unless it is very high.

In conclusion, medical treatments not only complicate the picture of middle ear infections, but they also don't provide long-term benefits. Removing the chief causes of middle ear infections should be the preferred goal, which can be achieved by providing breastmilk, avoiding overuse of antibiotics, and recognizing, treating, and avoiding exposure to allergens, especially food allergens.

Natural Immune Assistance

Herbal remedies have been used in health care as far back as we can trace man's history. There is no question about their power — a large portion of today's modern medications are made of or fashioned after natural extracts from plants, molds, and fungi, including aspirin, antibiotics, migraine medicines, and heart medications. While a great advantage to herbals is their easy availability, the frustrating factor of these remedies not developed under the auspices of pharmaceutical companies is that little formal research exists for many, making them sometimes difficult to trust or compare. But this does not reduce their power, and the collective knowledge of those who have used these throughout the ages seems to be very strong. Formal medicine sometimes refuses these remedies because "we don't know how they work." Yet, medicine did not understand the chemical actions of aspirin during the first decades of its medical use, and many pharmaceuticals are used today whose mechanisms are poorly understood. We also need to remember that just because something is "natural," this does not necessarily mean it is without harmful long-term side effects. It merely means that "medicine," where all the research money is, has not yet decided to incorporate them into practice.

Of late, "alternative" health practices have made large inroads into the medical community's profits. Thus, we have recently seen more money and interest pouring into research of common natural remedies, including herbs and nutritional supplements. Among the most popular natural remedies for fighting infection are echinacea, vitamin C, and zinc, which have all recently undergone good clinical trials with positive results.[140–143]

A Road Less Traveled

Medical intervention sometimes interferes with the body's natural and powerful processes of fighting infection and developing immunity. Unfortunately, at this point in time, the long-term benefit-to-harm ratio of interventions such as vaccination and antibiotic therapy is less than certain. By the same token there are strident critics of this medical care who apparently are more aware of the dangers of treatment than of the harrowing consequences of some diseases.

Advances in sanitation and wonder drugs have miraculously all but eliminated many diseases of horrific consequence that many of parenting age know little about. The wise parent will keep this in mind when they search for middle ground that does not blindly apply therapies when there may be contraindications. Pertussis vaccination is questionable in benefit versus risk. Further doses of pertussis vaccine should be seriously questioned if any dose leads to piercing cries. Chicken pox vaccines are of questionable benefit because the disease is mild in children, and vaccinated immunity likely wanes during adulthood, leading to more dangerous adult disease. The prevention of shingles, a lasting and painful possible result to infection with the chicken pox virus sometimes suffered in advanced age, is a potentially great benefit of chicken pox vaccination that is yet to be proven.

In cases of apparent infection, antibiotics should be withheld a few days instead of routinely applied, to allow some natural immunity to develop and to confirm bacterial infection. After confirmation, antibiotic use may be beneficial when bacterial infection causes great illness for days. Sometimes antibiotics can be lifesaving, as in the case of rheumatic fever. On the other hand, for ear and sinus infections antibiotic use is often misguided, especially in light of the effectiveness of proper diet.

Make decisions cautiously; the body is wise, but it is not all-powerful. Treatment can be dangerous, but disease can be even more so. Above all, remember that many fewer difficult decisions have to be made by parents who choose to give their children all the advantages of breastfeeding, a more natural birth, appropriate hygiene, and a nutritious diet free of allergenic foods.

7

Digestion Matters

NATURALLY, PARENTS WILL TAKE MEASURES TO PROTECT THEIR BABIES from disease, and they will seek the best possible nutrition for their development. Furthermore, parents will take measures to prevent future disease, to promote life-long health for their children. But, in order to do this, they must have the correct information. Unfortunately, misinformed parents with the best intentions can unintentionally have a negative impact on their children's health.

As we go on, we will see, as we have seen so far, that what is natural is usually best for baby. In order to understand the significance of intestinal symptoms such as colic, diarrhea, and gas, and have a better grasp of infant nutrition and immunity, a good understanding of the unique mechanisms of infant and childhood digestion is necessary. Only then can we understand the ramifications of feeding cow's milk and formulas to young children, instead of human milk.

Several attempts to improve the survival of prematurely born infants and questions about the early introduction of solid foods have spurred new research about how the digestive system develops from birth throughout childhood. It is apparent that although many digestive functions are intact at birth, the maturation of numerous digestive processes goes on for years. In addition, the immunological workings of the newly formed digestive tract are unlike the adult system and differ considerably between breastfed and bottle-fed babies.

In many countries, people are keenly aware of how valuable good digestive functioning is to overall health and energy. They monitor the appearance and characteristics of each stool passed for clues about their state of health and the adequacy of their diet. Even in the U.S., parents of a newborn often adopt this practice for their baby and will have many a conversation on the subject.

Baby's Digestive System

The villi of formula-fed infants are slightly shortened, and multiple large "holes" are found.

The digestive tract begins with the mouth. Food or liquid is swallowed and travels down a tube (the esophagus) to the stomach. Here, some acids are released and some initial digestion occurs. From the stomach, materials pass through the small intestine for more digestion and for absorption of nutrients. Eventually the rest goes on into the large intestine, the colon, for a little more work, until it is finally eliminated. The average length of the small intestine in a fetus at 20 weeks of gestation is 4 feet. At 30 weeks it has grown considerably to 6.5 feet long. A full-term (40-week) infant has approximately 9 feet of small intestine.[1] This rapid growth rate toward the end of gestation creates some of the nutritional difficulties faced by preterm infants, because their short intestines have little surface area for digestion and absorption. The inside walls of the digestive tract are lined with mucous membrane, like in your mouth. In the intestines, the walls are covered with small finger-like projections called "villi" that are the surfaces that absorb nutrition.

In the newborn, these villi are relatively undeveloped. They grow rapidly over the next several months with the aid of an insulin-like human growth factor from mother's milk, and other factors such as nucleotides and polyamines from breastmilk.[2-5] Lacking these growth factors, the villi of formula-fed infants are slightly shortened, and multiple large "holes" are found.[6] It has been shown in formula-fed rabbits that these holes allow bacteria to be transported directly into the bloodstream, a process that can lead to illness.[7]

The Digestive Process

Hunger starts the digestive process going, and enzymes are released in the stomach and small intestine. If one eats or is fed when not hungry, these enzymes are not present, and indigestion can occur. Therefore, when infants are fed on a schedule rather than when hunger is expressed, poor digestion and painful indigestion might be the result.

Stomach enzymes continue to work on food until it enters the small intestine. Then, in this intestine, enzymes perform most of the digestion. Most nutrients are absorbed through the small intestine walls into the bloodstream so they are available to the body. The unabsorbed portions are then passed on to the colon. Bacteria living in the first portions of the colon further degrade waste, using it for their own nutrition, while also manufacturing some vitamins. Water is absorbed along the entire intestinal tract.

Unique to Infants

The digestive system of the newborn infant is not at all equipped to handle solid foods or digest anything but mother's milk. Human infants, like all other mammals, are designed to survive on nutrition made by the mammary glands of the mother, just as they were previously supported by her placenta. This arrangement provides many survival advantages because it ensures parental protection, loving social contact, and controlled, optimal nutrition.

Whereas digestion in the older child or adult begins in the mouth, *the infant is wisely born with a protective tongue-thrust reflex that pushes foods not obtained through nursing out of the mouth.* Likewise, infants are born without teeth and without coordinated tongue and swallowing movements to help keep out foods they cannot handle. These reflexes make it obvious that young infants should not be fed solid foods, yet various forms are frequently promoted and encouraged for babies only weeks or months old. Compared to the mature digestive system, infants' systems produce only a very small amount of the digestive enzymes. This helps allow them to use important components of mother's milk. By design, breastmilk is so easily digestible that few digestive enzymes are needed. Notably, lactase, the enzyme for lactose digestion, is quite plentiful. The infant's large intestine is rather "leaky" to larger molecules, which allows valuable immune factors from mother's milk to pass through its membrane into the bloodstream and causes problems when foreign proteins from cow's milk or soy are introduced. The immune functioning of the digestive system is also diminished in several ways. For instance, baby's own immune cells meant to protect against allergic reactions to foreign foods are not highly present until around 7 months of age and increase throughout the first several years of life. This is another important reason to take caution with solid food or formula for babies. Not only is the newborn system not yet fully equipped with adult levels of digestive enzymes, but newborns have some unique digestive mechanisms that they will lose later on.

The infant's nourishment system is designed to achieve maximum benefit with minimal work. This savings of energy and effort is possible because mother's system is expending extra energy to create a special food, which is why this ideal arrangement (for baby) cannot go on indefinitely. Luckily, mother's milk makes up for all the shortcomings of the infant's system. The composition of her milk even changes as the infant grows.

Lactose: the Mommy Sugar

The amount of sugar (or carbohydrate), mostly in the form of lactose, in the milk of any given mammal is generally directly proportional to the size of that creature's adult forebrain, humans therefore having the greatest proportion of sugar in their milk.[8] (An exception to this rule is the sea lion, whose pups rely solely on fat and protein to grow.) The access to sugar, as well as a great number of other nutrients in proper proportions, is essential for proper brain development in infants. Infant sugar (carbohydrate) digestion is designed mainly for the unique sugar of mother's milk, lactose. Lactose is also found in cow and all other mammal milks (except for sea lions) and exists in most milk-based formulas. In order to be utilized, lactose must be broken down by lactase, an enzyme found in infants and young children. This enzyme *normally* begins to diminish around the age of two and disappears somewhere between the ages of 6 and 15.[9,10]

Descendants of northern Europeans are an evolutionary exception to this situation.[11] Left with little to eat in the winters, early people migrating to colder northern climates learned how to raise cows for milk. Initially, very few of these people would have stayed healthy on this winter diet long enough to reproduce. Those who did were the ones who retained the lactase enzyme for longer periods. (Eskimos are cold climate people who did not depend on lactase persistence; instead, they survived on the meat and blubber of seals.) As these lactase-persistent adults reproduced, and as their lactase-persistent offspring did so as well, a huge population of adults developed who could digest milk at later and later ages. These European descendants account for a significant percentage of US citizens today, but are a small segment of the world population.

Nearly all infants are born with the lactase enzyme. From an evolutionary standpoint, we realize that an infant without lactase couldn't survive on mother's milk; therefore this genetic condition would never be passed on. Such an infant would quickly suffer brain retardation from lack of sugar in the system, and would die of diarrhea within weeks. Interestingly, there is a small pocket of this recessive gene disorder in Finland.[12]

> Many infants sensitive to cow's milk proteins are incorrectly labeled as lactase deficient.

One would assume this kind of persistent gene mutation would have been a rather recent phenomenon, because an infant couldn't survive unless the problem was understood within a few days of birth and a formidable nutritional substitute for milk was supplied. Of course, today we have lactose-free formulas with an alternate sugar for this extremely rare situation (most likely much rarer than the 1 in 23,000 fructose intolerant British mentioned below). Many infants sensitive to cow's milk proteins are incorrectly labeled as lactase deficient. Although many with diarrhea may be diagnosed as lactose intolerant with lactose intolerance tests, they will continue to have difficulties with lactose-free formulas based on cow's milk. By contrast, even though mother's milk is full of lactose, these infants will have no difficulty tolerating human milk after a couple days of recovery — if the breastmilk comes from a mother who doesn't drink cow's milk, that is!

Digestion of Other Sugars

Oligosaccharides are complex sugars in human milk that are not digested in the small intestine. The body preserves these so they can provide immune functions and nutrition specifically for *Lactobacillus bifidus*, friendly bacteria found in high quantities in the large intestines of breastfed infants.

Corn syrup, fructose, and sucrose, commonly found in formulas, are fairly well digested in infants, even though they are not considered ideal sugars for brain development and calcium absorption.

Occasionally, one hears of sugar intolerance in children. Just as a very few children are born without the lactase enzyme, in rare instances some other enzyme is deficient. Intolerance of fructose, a fruit and corn syrup sugar, is thought to occur in 1 in 23,000 children in the United Kingdom.[13] This can be a problem for a formula-fed infant. There is also a small pocket of sucrose intolerant individuals in Greenland.[14] This and other sugar intolerance seem to become less problematic with age. While there could be several thousand such sugar intolerant children in the U.S., after quizzing parents in my own practice who said they had a sugar intolerant child because their children had stomach or behavior problems after consuming sweets, I found these children could eat natural fruits without problems, but could not tolerate candies and other sweets. In the U.S., 99.9% of all candy and other sweets are sweetened with corn syrup or other sugars that have been derived from corn such as fructose, glucose, dextrose, dextrin, maltose, maltitol, sorbitol, and "hydrolyzed starch"; therefore, it is most likely these children cannot tolerate corn, instead of natural sugars. (I ask about popcorn and generally learn that it also bothers these children.) Still, a few children are apparently allergic to cane (in the grass family) or beets, and thus react specifically to cane or beet sugars (common table sugars).

Indigestible and unabsorbed carbohydrates are broken down by normal bacterial flora in the large intestine; this occurs more efficiently in the breastfed infant and is important for taking advantage of certain nutrients in mother's milk. When in excess, the fermentation of undigested and unabsorbed materials in the large intestine can create uncomfortable gas. Some of the very rare sugar intolerance disorders in infants lead to extreme abdominal pain and diarrhea due to excessive fermentation, and undiagnosed, may lead to brain damage from these sugars reaching the brain.

Protein Digestion

In adults, protein digestion begins with enzymes in the stomach, which is very acidic. The infant stomach maintains a much less acid state and digestion occurs here only minimally. This protective mechanism ensures that immune factors,[15] live immune cells, and beneficial bacteria from mother's milk survive to be used in the infant intestines. Undesirable components of cow's milk are also protected by the infant's lack of stomach acid. In infants, protein

> *This reduced ability to metabolize protein in infants will leave many of the larger cow's milk proteins undigested, whether they come from formula or from a mother who drinks cow's milk.*

digestion occurs predominantly in the small intestine, and even here, infant digestion is weak compared to adults. Unfortunately, this reduced ability to metabolize protein in infants will leave many of the larger cow's milk proteins undigested, whether they come from formula or from a mother who drinks cow's milk. Other undesirable components of cow's milk (formula) are protected in this way, and cow's milk itself has factors that protect its bovine hormones and other substances from early destruction. As a result, these are able to pass through the unusually leaky colon walls of infants, allowing allergic sensitization and other possible consequences.[16]

In the small intestines of adults, the acidic contents from the stomach are quickly neutralized until they become alkaline. The intestinal environment of the breastfed infant stays closer to neutral (neither acidic or alkaline) than a formula-fed infant's (who is alkaline).[17] The neutral state in breastfed infants better resists colonization by some unwanted bacteria and prevents the destruction of the lysozyme from mother's milk,[18] which helps the infant destroy unwanted bacteria.

Fat Digestion

Lipase is the key enzyme for breaking down fats into important elements that are used for brain and body nourishment. For the first several months, stomach lipase is twice as effective for breaking down the fat in breastmilk as the fats of formula.[19] As a result, breastfed infants are likely receiving superior brain food. Mother's milk also contains a form of lipase (found only in humans and gorillas[20]) that is activated in the small intestine. This makes up for the normally low amounts of lipase available in infant intestines, so that breastmilk fats completely break down and the resulting fatty acids are readily available for optimum brain development. Formula manufacturers are currently researching and improving the fatty acid contents in some formulas, although they are not yet able to approach the quality of breastmilk.

Closure

Compared to adult absorption, whole proteins pass easily across the newborn's colon membrane and into the bloodstream. This is by design, so that (IgG and IgA) antibodies in mother's colostrum and milk can leak into the infant's bloodstream and provide immune protection throughout the infant's entire system, most noticeable in the first few weeks after birth.

Eventually, the membrane barrier of the large intestine becomes more adult-like, disallowing most protein leaking. This process, called "closure," is pronounced by around 3 months of age, but may not be complete until around 5 years.[21] Closure occurs more slowly in artificially fed infants than in breastfed.[22] In addition to the gradual closure, many of the newborn's low or absent enzymes begin appearing in higher quantities around 5 or 6 months of age. Some doctors recommend breastfeeding to at least the age of 6 months to achieve a good level of closure, as well as more adequate levels of digestive enzymes and the infant's own antibodies, before formula is introduced.

Calcium Absorption

Calcium absorption is promoted by vitamins C and D, among other factors. While breastmilk is low in vitamin D and contains much less calcium than formulas, the calcium in mother's milk is extremely available for absorption in the small intestine. Lactose greatly increases calcium absorption; it is prevalent in mother's milk and is often less present in artificial feeds. The sugars such as sucrose and corn syrup that are commonly added to formula do not aid calcium absorption. Formulas also contain 2 to 4 times the amount of phosphorous as mother's milk (and cow's milk has 8 times the amount). This is not good because phosphorous competes with calcium for absorption. Therefore, when there is too much phosphorus, calcium isn't used to build bones. Phosphorus also binds to calcium, forming salts that can't be used by the body in the presence of the alkaline milk, thereby further reducing the amount of available calcium and hardening the stool. However, by adding extra calcium and vitamin D and by altering some other factors, formula manufacturers have created formulas that prevent the rickets that was rampant when feeds based on cow's milk became popular in the early 1900s.[23] This leg-bowing disorder, a result of calcium deficiency, is no longer a risk in modern formula-fed infants.

Beyond the differences in available calcium between breastmilk and formula, calcium is less a concern for those who do not consume large quantities of cow's milk. Epidemiological studies demonstrate sufficient or improved calcium bone density in nations with lower milk and calcium intake, in general, than the U.S. Vegetables apparently prevent osteoporosis (insufficient bone strength) better than cow's milk, because vegetarians who don't drink milk (vegans)

have lower intakes of calcium, but have higher bone density than the average American.[24] It is now known that the reduced bone density prevalent in the U.S. and some other industrialized nations is not so much the result of inadequate calcium intake, but rather is the result of high calcium loss into the urine associated with high animal protein intake (meat consumption and high dairy intake),[25,26] as well as insufficient intake of magnesium (the high dairy diet is magnesium deficient), other bone-building nutrients, and possibly other factors. (*This is covered more completely in Chapter 11.*)

Iron Absorption

Iron behaves differently than most vitamins or minerals in that it is used over and over again in the body. Generally, only a very small amount of ingested iron is absorbed. The need for added iron is greater when there is growth, as is the case with all children.

Lactoferrin, a human milk protein, aids iron absorption in the infant intestine. Lactoferrin is also found in very small amounts in cow's milk, but is inactive in formulas. Attempts to fortify formulas with added lactoferrin have not yet successfully increased formula-fed infant blood iron levels to those of the breastfed, until after 90 days of life.[27]

Extra iron is also needed when there is blood loss, as with the *common intestinal blood loss in infants fed formulas based on cow's milk,* which is any formula with added whey or casein, or cow's milk itself.[28] For this reason, iron is added to formulas at values that are very high when compared to human milk, enough to prevent anemia in most infants. Various other factors in breastmilk besides the lactoferrin also help to make its iron highly absorbable. Generally, infants absorb 50% of the iron in human milk, but only about 4% of that in formula. When there is intestinal reaction to cow's milk derivatives, as most eczema, and often diarrhea or constipation suggest in infants, the cells at the tips of the villi, where the iron is being slowly absorbed, become destroyed, and consequently iron is lost. Beyond this stage, *dark tarry stools are a sign of significant blood loss — often labeled as a normal infant reaction to milk products, but in my opinion, this is a signal to change the infant's formula.* Just because this occurrence is somewhat common does not mean it is healthy.

Copper is 5 times more concentrated in human milk than in cow's milk and helps make iron available to the blood after absorption. Formulas generally add copper to nearly human levels. Vitamin C is also important for absorption of iron. While the C in cow's milk is only one fifth that in human milk, formulas are supplemented to human levels of this vitamin.

Living with Bugs

Although newborn infants are born sterile, within hours they are inhabited by vast numbers of bacteria. Within days, infants not on antibiotic therapy will develop large colonies of friendly normal flora in the mouth, stomach, and small and large intestines. Normal flora assist digestion and form certain vitamins. They compete with undesirable microbes to help prevent colonization that could lead to illness. The normal flora in infants is quite different from that of adults, becoming more and more adult-like as solid foods start to predominate in the diet. Eventually, there are over 500 different bacterial species in the normal intestine, including *E. coli*, enterococci, and lactobacillus. Also, the flora of formula-fed infants is very different from that of breastfed babies. Where do these bacteria come from? This necessary invasion of flora comes primarily from the food in our diet. The very first infestations come from mother's milk, formula, the normal flora on the skin of mother's nipples, kisses from mom and dad, sucked-on fingers, and the air. Remember, the stomach and intestines in newborns are rather neutral (neither very acidic or alkaline) allowing these bacteria to survive and flourish. No, you do not want to prevent this from occurring. This is a necessary part of life and good health, unless you wish your child to live in a sterile plastic bubble, untouched by human hands.

Remember, only 1% of all bacterial species cause disease in humans. The natural defense systems developing in the infant, the temporary immunity gained from mother's placenta during labor, and the broad and continuous immunity derived from mother's milk all help to vanquish incompatible microbes, preferentially allowing compatible ones to flourish. The sooner infants can go through this process, the sooner their natural immunity to undesirable organisms will develop, making them less susceptible to infection and illness. The infant cared for in a highly sterile fashion will have less immunity. The flora double in number once to twice every day and make up one third the weight of eliminated stools.

Establishing flora has been shown to occur more quickly in infants who "room-in" with their mothers after birth, thereby reducing their early rates of infectious diarrhea and other diseases.[29]

Normal Flora

The colon of a breastfed infant is almost entirely inhabited by odorless bifidobacteria. This helps protect the young system from infection and illness caused by more potent bacteria, many of which will eventually, but gradually, become a part of the flora as solid foods are gradually introduced at an older age, when the immune system is stronger. Lysozyme from mother's milk helps to break bifidobacteria down in order to release usable proteins for the colon flora and for absorption.[30] Also seen in the colon of the breastfed infant are some lactobacilli and some friendly staphylococci (staph). In contrast, the formula-fed infant is colonized chiefly by bacteroides and (foul-smelling) *Escherichia coli*, better known as *E. coli*, which predominate in adult systems. *E. coli* can cause diarrhea in the very young infant whose immune system is not yet strong enough to tolerate it, as can some strains of bacteroides. Certain strains of *E. coli* are more dangerous than others. Some of these are the ones heard about in the news. While many strains are tolerated around us and in us, the news stories are related chiefly to *E. coli* from the intestines of cows (contaminated meat or apples fallen on the ground where cow's manure has been used). Children and adults can also become ill from strains of *E. coli* from other parts of the world, because people only maintain immunity to the strains from the region where they live.

Significant numbers of other potentially dangerous bacteria are found in the artificially fed infant. Diarrhea or antibiotics can wipe out much of the weaker flora, allowing some mighty nasty bugs to grow in abundance. Once they reach a critical density, these microbes release their harmful toxins, causing diarrhea, abdominal cramping, and fever. Clostridium infection has been indicated in a "modest proportion" of crib deaths in formula-fed babies.[31]

Some good news is that many studies are demonstrating good immune and digestive benefits to formula-fed infants, or infants on frequent antibiotic therapy, through the oral supplementation of high doses of friendly bifidus and lactobacilli.[32] These can be found in health food stores in various forms.

Vitamins in the Colon

In formula-fed infants, *E. coli* and streptococcus are 10 times more prevalent than in breastfed infants. These bacteria produce B vitamins[33] and vitamin K (a factor in blood clotting), and possibly some others. Much higher amounts of vitamins K_1 and K_2 are found in the colons of formula-fed infants, and their blood concentrations of K_1 are higher, meaning their absorption of this nutrient is good. However, K_2 is found only in the blood of breastfed babies.[34] Apparently some factor in human milk provides for its absorption. We do not yet know what the effects of insufficient K_2 may be. Children beyond formula and exclusive breastmilk feeding are at risk for vitamin K deficiency when on prolonged antibiotics, because *E. coli* are destroyed by many antibiotics.

More Bugs

Candida albicans normally cannot grow inside the intestine with well-established natural flora because they cannot compete with these bacteria. Found everywhere in our food and environment, external candida overgrowth is responsible for many diaper rashes. It colonizes in the intestine as a result of other infection, antibiotic use, or intestine-damaging food sensitivity reactions (or does its colonization cause some sensitivities to develop?). Commonly known as "yeast," candida can become established in the intestines, and harmful changes in digestive functioning will result.

Streptococcus mutans in the mouth is the chief bug involved in childhood cavities. It lives on sugars, such as those in fruit juices, sweetened beverages, and sweetened treats, as well as any sweeteners added to formulas other than lactose. Generally this bacteria is not found in an infant's mouth until there are teeth to live on and these sweet foods have entered the diet.[35] Cavities are significantly less frequent in children breastfed for more than 3 months.[36]

Lactoferrin

Lactoferrin, the breastmilk protein that aids iron absorption, acts somewhat selectively against undesirable bacteria in the infant's digestive tract, killing them by binding with their iron. In the laboratory, lactoferrin derived from cow's milk will kill bacteria also, but attempts to supplement formulas with this ingredient have failed to achieve this benefit inside the human infant.[37] In breastfed babies, the infant's own lactotransferrin apparently can attack strains of *E. coli* that mother's milk does not. This ability to inhibit *E. coli* is not seen in bottle-fed babies or even in bottle-supplemented breastfed babies.[38] This is one of the many poorly understood deficiencies of formula feeding.

If a breastfed infant is injected with iron at birth, or his diet is supplemented with high-iron formulas, this iron will bind

> If a breastfed infant is injected with iron at birth, or his diet is supplemented with high-iron formulas, this iron will bind with the lactoferrin in mother's milk and prevent it from providing important immune protection.

with the lactoferrin in mother's milk and prevent it from providing important immune protection. For this reason, low-iron formulas and cereals are better choices if supplementation for the breastfeeding infant is desired. When possible, providing no supplementation is the healthier answer.

Abdominal Pain

Studies on the sources of pain in the intestines have suggested that pain is caused chiefly by distension of the bowel, from the bloating associated with gas, infection, and diarrhea, or from the build-up of material with constipation. Pain may also arise from spasms in the stomach and intestinal wall muscles. In general, the rhythmic waves of normal intestinal contractions that flow regularly along the intestines (peristaltic waves) are not felt, although they may be associated with hunger pangs. "Colicky pain" is the name given to abdominal pains that build and diminish rather cyclically with the on-and-off nature of peristaltic waves, most likely secondary to bloating. The term "colic," when associated with infants, describes this condition, but the frequency and duration of the infant's crying is generally the reason for using this term, whether or not the crying spells are colicky, and whether or not the condition is associated with abdominal difficulties.

Gas

Gas is normally created in every intestine every day, much of it by bacterial fermentation of underdigested or unabsorbed foods. Generally, most gas created in the intestines is absorbed into the bloodstream; then part of it is filtered out by the liver, and part is expelled through the lungs. Excess gas that is not absorbed will be passed. Prior to solid foods, the breastfed infant who is not reacting to any foods in his mother's diet should pass very little gas. More gas is produced when a child is fed when not hungry, when the child is fed harder-to-digest infant formulas or early solid foods, when digestion and absorption are reduced by food sensitivity reactions, and when undigested milk lactose is passed into the large intestine in older children whose lactase enzymes are no longer sufficient. Also certain foods, especially beans, are rich in undigestible complex carbohydrates that can create great increases in gas production. Excess gas trapped inside stools is generally the cause of floating stools.

Diarrhea

When certain elements such as undigested lactose become very highly concentrated in the colon, relative to their concentrations in the colon blood circulation, this difference can cause fluids to flow into the colon from the bloodstream, causing loose or watery stools. High concentrations of acids produced by fermentation of undigested materials cause diarrhea as well, as can chemicals released by intestinal allergic reactions to milk proteins or toxins released by overgrowing, unfriendly microorganisms. Sometimes parents' complaints of diarrhea in their infant are only answered with the suggestion that they misunderstand the term. Strictly defined, diarrhea is the frequent passage of loose or watery stools. Since a normal infant can pass several stools per day, or one every three days, the term "frequent" is relative. The consistency of the stool is truly the more important factor. No matter the definition, one must recognize that there is a reason for any change in stool habits. Minor changes can result from variations in diet. Generally, however, if an infant normally has one stool of medium firmness per day, but then has a couple loose stools in a day, or even just one watery stool, this is significant. An infant can even withhold stool for several days, followed by an explosion of loose stool. Rightfully, this should be recognized as a bout of constipation followed by a bout of diarrhea.

It is customary for hospitals to advise that breastfeeding should be discontinued for two days when there is diarrhea or dehydration, but this advice is quite contrary to what is best for the infant, and only follows from what is best for bottle-fed babies.

Diarrhea causes digestive enzymes to be flushed through the system too quickly to be used well. The irritation sometimes leads to reduced production of enzymes as well, including lactase. These two factors lead to positive lactose intolerance tests when an infant has diarrhea, often leading to the improper diagnosis of lactose intolerance. Normal flora can be flushed out also. Clearly the child can quickly become nutritionally deficient. Bifidobacteria and lactobacillus supplements are often beneficial in reestablishing normal flora and normal intestinal function in infants with diarrhea.

It is customary for hospitals to advise that breastfeeding should be discontinued for two days when there is diarrhea or dehydration, but this advice is quite contrary to what is best for the infant, and only follows from what is best for bottle-fed babies. Breastfed infants with diarrhea of any cause should continue to nurse to their desire. On the other hand, formula is difficult for any infant to handle, and diarrhea reduces the child's digestive enzymes, making it more difficult to handle formula. Additionally, the breaks in the defenses of the mucosal walls can allow undigested proteins to enter the child's system to a much greater degree. If large quantities of foreign milk or soy proteins enter the bloodstream, allergic immune reactions can develop. Even the child with no previous intolerance to formula can now become intolerant. Bottle-fed infants with diarrhea, even when caused by antibiotic use, often do better with only electrolyte solution such as Infalyte (which contains no corn products) for a couple of days. Alternatively, an elemental formula, such as Vivonex, should be well tolerated and provides good nutrition as well.

> *Studies have found that 78% of infant and child constipation cases resolve with the removal of cow's milk proteins from their diets.*

Constipation

As with diarrhea, many definitions of constipation may meet with resistance from some quarters. There are doctors and baby books that state that an infant who moves her bowels once a week is normal. This may be common, just as food sensitivity reactions are common, but it certainly is not a sign of health. By the same token, one movement in one or two days is suspicious in an infant who normally moves her bowels five times a day. Regardless of frequency, a movement that is unusually prolonged, hard, painful, difficult to pass, or causes rectal bleeding should cause concern and should be considered constipation. Constipation is more common in formula-fed infants.

The exclusively breastfed infant has little waste from her diet and will have fewer and smaller bowel movements than those fed formula or solid foods. There is a considerable amount of indigestible or unabsorbable matter in formula. The usual stools of formula-fed infants are much firmer than breastfed. Bottle-fed infants have very high amounts of minerals and fats lost in their stools. These form calcium–fatty acid soaps and mineral salts that cause their stools to be harder. These soaps are responsible for the frequent intestinal obstructions seen in formula-fed preterm babies.[39]

Studies have found that 78% of infant and child constipation cases resolve with the removal of cow's milk proteins from their diets.[40,41] Often other food allergy symptoms exist in these children, helping to confirm the suspicion of allergy. It was long thought that negative symptoms associated with constipation arose from the toxins absorbed during the long stay of material in the colon. It is now generally accepted that potential toxins released in the colon are generally dealt with by the liver before they can reach the blood circulation. Sluggish symptoms sometimes associated with constipation are thought to be caused simply by the distention and irritation of the bowel. They may also be associated with a food allergy reaction that is causing the constipation.

What Does It All Mean?

Baby's system is designed to take advantage of mother's milk in many ways. Mother's milk meets all of babies' nutritional and immunity needs so they can conserve energy and have time to develop their own digestive systems and immune defenses after birth. During the transition period from placenta feeding, tiny infants are not at all equipped to handle solid foods. Formula falls into this solid food category: It is difficult to digest and obtain nutrients from, it causes allergic immune reactions, and it allows dangerous flora to develop.

It takes years for the immune system to become fully developed. Digestive enzymes appear only very gradually with maturation. The lactase enzyme is normally lost in the middle of the first decade of life, and intestinal closure occurs in this same time frame. A child's drive for sucking, when allowed, will last for years, whether on a bottle, nipple, thumb, pacifier, or sippy cup; therefore, it could be surmised that the human system is designed to benefit from breast-milk for several years. Further support for this contention will be presented in later chapters.

8

In the Womb & the First Few Days

A CHILD IS AT GREATEST RISK WHILE DEVELOPING INSIDE MOTHER, during delivery, and during the first days outside the uterus. During this time the parents' actions can impact the likelihood they will have a healthy baby. We must remember that the pregnant mother's world, including her diet, is the fetus's world as well, and that her behavior can definitely affect the developing little person. Infants born too early or too tiny are most in need of their parents' care and must be given very special consideration. Often parents of preemies need to be proactive to achieve the best results. Health care providers are learning how to help parents in most of these areas, but educated parents can help to speed this positive progression along.

Stressed Before Birth

When mom is under stress during pregnancy, her stress hormone levels become elevated even though pregnancy hormones are designed to have a calming effect on the mother-to-be. Stress hormones disrupt some of the protection induced by the hormonal state of maternity. Increased levels of these stress hormones increase the chances of a preterm delivery.[1] The stress regulation systems of a fetus subjected to this hormonal environment are disrupted as well,[2] just as the hormonal balance is altered in infants living in stressful home environments. Exposure to loud noise during uterine life, such as a mother working in noisy surroundings, has been shown to reduce the newborn's protective immune system,[3] possibly due to stress.

And After Birth

We have already discussed the physical and psychological stress a newborn experiences when separated from mother. This separation has a tremendous impact, reducing the chances for prolonged breastfeeding, mother–child attachment, health, and survival. There is evidence that intense noise surrounding newborns in the hospital after birth may be stressful to the newborn as well. Tiny nervous systems are much more sensitive to various sources of stress than adult systems, and noise levels safe for infants' hearing may be well below those considered safe for adults.[4] Abrupt noises such as rapidly closing incubator doors are potentially worse than background noises such as the hum of the incubator motor. When it comes to nursing, some infants do not seem to mind a flood of loving attention from friends, relatives, and lactation nurses, while others need quiet peace and solitude and the familiar sound of mother's heartbeat if they are to nurse comfortably in the beginning.

Dangerous Foods for the Fetus

Many new potential dangers to a developing fetus have been recognized in the last decade, but this information has barely made its way into maternity care. Over 15,000 (of a total of over 70,000) manmade chemicals are used in significant quantities in our environment today, most of them introduced within the last 50 years. More than half of these have not been tested for their toxicity,[5] and many may mimic or block the action of reproductive hormones (estrogens and androgens). When they have the potential to disrupt the normal functioning of hormones inside the body, they are called "endocrine disrupters" and are a focus of concern. The young newborn and more so the developing fetus are most vulnerable to possible adverse effects from these environmental pollutants.

These chemicals include PCBs, dioxins, pesticides, and plasticizers. We have not yet witnessed the effects of these on an entire generation exposed to them from conception to death, but medical studies are already uncovering evidence suggesting significant reductions in fetal development and increased malformation. We also know that each successive generation of men has a lower sperm count than the one before, and we suspect that manmade chemicals are at least part of the problem. These environmental pollutants are suspect with regard to increased cancer rates as well.

Chemicals make their way into our food chain when air and water pollutants come into contact with fruits and vegetables (even organic vegetables), as well as when pesticides are used directly on crops. Non-organic apples have the highest levels of added pesticides,[6] but the level on most fruits and vegetables is low compared to the levels in foodstuffs further up the chain. Livestock are fed on these crops and are also exposed to chemicals in the air and water. Additionally, they are fed other overmedicated livestock deemed unfit for human consumption. Drug-tainted milk unfit for commercial sale is fed to calves, adding further to their lifetime toxic buildup. As a result, toxins are concentrated into the fat tissues of livestock until a lifetime of toxins is contained in a few servings of meat. These chemicals are also concentrated into the fat portions of cow's milk. Thus, eating meat and dairy fats introduces significantly higher quantities of endocrine-mimicking toxins, and humans concentrate these accumulated chemicals into their own tissues. Milk fats make up an especially large portion of the typical American diet (cheese, ice cream, butter, sour cream, whole and low-fat milk), and dairy consumption has the most impact on statistical risk estimates of potential harmful effects.[7] It is believed that endocrine disrupters have mild effects on all ages of people, as well as on many animals, but the greatest potential danger by far is to the developing fetus. Young children and the sperm-producing tissues of males of any age have the next highest risk.

Incidence of hypospadias, a defect in the placement of the penile urethra, or urinary outlet of males, has doubled during the 70s and 80s[8] and has likely continued to increase since then. The severity of these cases has risen considerably as well. Most agree that fetal exposure to chemicals that disrupt the sex hormones appears to be the chief cause. In 1993, this defect alone was seen in 1 out of every 100 newborn boys. The rise in various cancers, especially testicular and breast cancer, lymphatic cancers, and leukemia, is being linked to hormone mimics in the environment, and partial responsibility is being assessed. Subtle, generally permanent effects that can only be measured by large population studies also include mild reductions in brain and motor function, reduced sperm quality, and reduced immune function. Apparently, vitamin K deficiencies can result from these toxins as well. Subtle birth abnormalities are now found in 10% of newborns in the high meat- and dairy-consuming Netherlands.[9]

Several key problems plague attempts to correlate endocrine disrupters to birth defects. First, few of these chemicals leave detectable fingerprints at their low levels. Second, there is a huge variety of chemicals and modes of exposure in the environment. Also, many are thought to have an additive effect on each other, increasing the impact through accumulated exposure. As far as anyone can tell, there is no threshold quantity for endocrine mimics to be dangerous, below which they could be considered safe.[10] It appears that even very tiny amounts of various chemicals can accumulate or complement each other to produce small effects (such as reduced sperm counts). Hence, setting government controls is difficult, and it is now clear that the Environmental Protection Agency's (EPA) guidelines for testing chemicals prior to 1998 were inadequate. Now, safety testing for all chemicals, such as multigenerational reproduction studies on animals, needs to be performed again under the recent new guidelines.[11]

Animal studies can reveal the potentially toxic consequences of these chemicals. Suspicions are then confirmed by epidemiological studies such as reviews of infants born to agricultural workers. The rates of nervous system abnormalities, oral clefts such as a cleft lip and cleft palate, male genital malformations, and other anomalies are considerably higher in children born to mothers (but not fathers) who work in gardening or farming occupations, where exposure to many endocrine disrupters is high.[12,13]

Although studies suggest that many chemicals accumulate in the mother's body over many years, they also suggest that the rate of occupational exposure during and just before pregnancy is highly important. Hence, while women planning to have children should reduce their exposures to manmade environmental chemicals many years before conception, mothers-to-be can make some difference in the risk of malformation or miscarriage through preventive measures during the pregnancy as well. Reducing animal fat consumption, especially dairy fats (organic non-fat milk can be consumed), as well as fish and liver, consuming filtered water and washed organic fruits and vegetables (non-organic grains are fairly safe), and avoiding solvents such as fingernail polish remover and paint thinner or foods heated in plastics may be reasonable measures to take.

BPA, or bisphenol A, is an estrogen-mimicking chemical that leaches from plastics such as those we store foods in, those in dental sealants, plastics that line food cans, those that create that "new car" smell, and from new furnishings made with particle board (which contains formaldehyde) or covered with fabric guards. The longer food is in contact with plastic, or when it is heated in plastic, the greater the absorption of BPA. When doses of BPA estimated to be similar to human exposure levels are fed to pregnant mice, the males demonstrate mild alterations of their reproductive organs, and the young mice grow larger and enter puberty earlier.[14,15]

DEHP is another chemical recently raising serious concern, especially for high exposure to the early fetus. Found in soft vinyl plastics such as IV bags, toys, and respiratory care products, only a few pregnant mothers may have enough exposure to pose a risk of reproductive organ abnormalities or other birth defects.

Dioxins come into our air and onto our foods from burning of municipal waste, factory pesticide production, industrial paper production, chlorinating processes, and steel mills. They have an elimination half-life of 7 to 11 years inside humans,[16] which means that after about a decade, only half the amount of a consumed chemical remains in the body. Infants can be exposed to these during their critical development periods inside mother's womb. Dioxins also concentrate in mother's milk, and the breastfed child is exposed to these during nursing. Most formulas have the cow's milk fat removed, reducing dioxin levels, but many are stored in plastic-lined cans or packages, which would cause BPA leaching. When milk or formula is stored or warmed in plastic bottles, significant levels of BPAs can leach into the formula as well.

Dairy products contribute nearly 50% of the accumulated PCB and dioxin found in toddlers. Breastfeeding for 6 months contributes 13% to the levels accumulated in one's body by age 25.[17] (Tripling the breastfeeding time however, increases, but does not triple, the levels attributable to breastfeeding. Typically a child who is weaned early consumes meats and dairy fats so their continued exposure is the same or higher than from breastfeeding.) Intrauterine exposures to these environmental toxins lowers the IQ several points in those with higher exposures, while breastfeeding has shown no such correlation.[18] By avoiding animal fats and eating organic, mother can reduce the amount of toxins she passes to her fetus, and later to her baby through her milk.

One More

Another reason for pregnant mothers to avoid dairy is a finding that pregnant women who drink 3 or more glasses of milk a day are found to have a doubled risk of developing preeclampsia,[19] a dangerous pregnancy disorder that includes high blood pressure and risks to the mother and fetus. While these researchers did not compare whole milk intake to non-fat, they suspect the milk fat may be the culprit. Yet, it is now known that high levels of milk protein intake reduce one's calcium retention, and calcium is known to reduce high blood pressure. In fact, calcium supplementation (of non-dairy sources) during pregnancy actually reduces blood pressure and incidence of preeclampsia.[20] I suspect that the milk protein or hormones may be part of the problem in preeclampsia.

Dangerous Fumes for the Fetus

The connection between maternal smoking and underweight newborns, which reduces survival, has been known for some time. Blood flow to the infant becomes constricted as a result of nicotine, thereby limiting nutrition. A 1997 review estimated that 46,000 cases of low birth weight and 2,800 cases of miscarriage and newborn deaths per year can be attributed to parental smoking.[21] In fact, infants of smoking mothers are born abnormally small nearly twice as often as those of non-smoking mothers.[22] Connections between maternal exposure to cigarette smoke and childhood cancers are only being proven recently.

Researchers investigated samples of cord blood that had been passed from mother to fetus in mothers who were exposed to passive cigarette smoke only. When compared to those not so exposed, they found a significant number of genetic mutations in blood cells: the type that generally are associated with blood cancers such as leukemia or lymphatic cancers.[23] It has also been discovered recently that some smoke, from mother or anyone smoking around the mother, gets to the fetus directly through the birth canal, giving him direct exposure to the carcinogens of tobacco smoke. This passage of toxins to the developing fetus carries a much higher risk for cancer than was previously thought possible.[24] While secondhand smoke from father can damage a developing fetus, smoking by the father prior to conception of an infant, even with a non-smoking mother, has been shown to more than quadruple the child's chance for leukemia or lymphatic cancer.[25] It is expected that this may be due to tobacco-induced genetic damage to the sperm.

In addition to cancer risks and reduced birth weight, significant alterations in prolactin and growth hormones have been discovered in pregnant smoking mothers. These same alterations are found in their newborns.[26] This demonstrates that cigarette exposure disturbs an infant's hormonal balance, including those for dealing with stress. This may explain another researcher's finding that most newborns will be calm and peaceful if laid upon their mother right after birth, but those born to heavily smoking mothers continue to cry and behave anxiously.[27]

Vitamin K: To Inject or Not

> It has recently been shown that this tight regulation of vitamin K levels helps control the rate of rapid cell division during fetal development. Apparently, high levels of vitamin K can allow cell division to get out of hand, leading to cancer.

Newborn infants routinely receive an injection of vitamin K after birth in order to prevent (or slow) a rare problem of bleeding into the brain weeks after birth. Vitamin K promotes blood clotting. The fetus has low levels of vitamin K as well as other factors needed in clotting. The body maintains these levels very precisely.[28] Supplementation of vitamin K to the pregnant mother does not change the K status of the fetus, confirming the importance of its specific levels. Toward the end of gestation, the fetus begins developing some of the other clotting factors, developing two key factors just before term birth.[29] It has recently been shown that this tight regulation of vitamin K levels helps control the rate of rapid cell division during fetal development. Apparently, high levels of vitamin K can allow cell division to get out of hand, leading to cancer.

The problem of bleeding into the brain occurs mainly from 3 to 7 weeks after birth in just over 5 out of 100,000 births (without vitamin K injections); 90% of those cases are breastfed infants,[30] because formulas are supplemented with unnaturally high levels of vitamin K. Forty percent of these infants suffer permanent brain damage or death. The cause of this bleeding trauma is generally liver disease that has not been detected until the bleeding occurs. Several liver problems can reduce the liver's ability to make blood-clotting factors out of vitamin K; therefore extra K helps this situation. Infants exposed to drugs or alcohol through any means are especially at risk, and those from mothers on anti-epileptic medications are at very high risk and need special attention. Such complications reduce the effectiveness of vitamin K, and in these cases, a higher level of available K could prevent the tragic intracranial bleeding. This rare bleeding disorder has been found to be highly preventable by a large-dose injection of vitamin K at birth. *The downside of this practice however is an 80% increased risk of developing childhood leukemia.* While a few studies have refuted this suggestion, several tightly controlled studies have shown this correlation to be most likely.[31,32] Apparently the cell division that continues to be quite rapid after birth continues to depend on precise amounts of vitamin K to proceed at the proper rate. Introduction of levels that are 20,000 times the newborn level, the amount usually injected, can have devastating consequences.

Nursing raises the infant's vitamin K levels very gradually after birth so that no disregulation occurs that would encourage leukemia development. Additionally, the clotting system of the healthy newborn is well planned, and healthy breastfed infants do not suffer bleeding complications, even without any supplementation.[33] While breastfed infants demonstrate lower blood levels of vitamin K than the "recommended" amount, they show no signs of vitamin K deficiency (leading one to wonder where the "recommended" level for infants came from). But with vitamin K injections at birth, harmful consequences of some rare disorders can be averted.

Infant formulas are supplemented with high levels of vitamin K, generally sufficient to prevent intracranial bleeding in the case of a liver disorder and in some other rare bleeding disorders. Although formula feeding increases overall childhood cancer rates by 80%, this is likely not related to the added vitamin K.

Extracting data from available literature reveals that there are 1.5 extra cases of leukemia per 100,000 children due to vitamin K injections, and 1.8 more permanent injuries or deaths per 100,000 due to brain bleeding without injections. Adding the risk of infection or damage from the injections, including a local skin disease called "scleroderma" that is seen rarely with K injections,[34] and even adding the low possibility of healthy survival from leukemia, the scales remain tipped toward breastfed infants receiving a prophylactic vitamin K supplementation. However, there are better options than the .5 or 1 milligram injections typically given to newborns.

The breastfed infant can be supplemented with several low oral doses[35] (possibly 200 micrograms per week for 5 weeks, totaling 1 milligram, even more gradual introduction may be better). Alternatively, the nursing mother can take vitamin K supplements daily or twice weekly for 10 weeks. (Supplementation of the pregnant mother does not alter fetal levels but supplementation of the nursing mother does increase breastmilk and infant levels.) Either of these provides a much safer rate of vitamin K supplementation. Maternal supplementation of 2.5 mg per day, recommended by one author, provides a higher level of vitamin K through breastmilk than does formula,[36] and may be much more than necessary. Formula provides 10 times the U.S. recommended daily allowance," and this RDA is about 2 times the level in unsupplemented human milk. One milligram per day for 10 weeks for mother provides a cumulative extra 1 milligram to her infant over the important period and seems reasonable. Neither mother nor infant require supplementation if the infant is injected at birth.[37]

There is no overwhelming reason to discontinue this routine prophylactic injection for breastfed infants. Providing information about alternatives to allow informed parents to refuse would be reasonable. These parents may then decide to provide some gradual supplementation, or, for an entirely healthy term infant, they may simply provide diligent watchfulness for any signs of jaundice (yellowing of eyes or skin) or easy bleeding. There appears to be no harm in supplementing this vitamin in a gradual manner however. Currently, injections are provided to infants intended for formula feeding as well, although there appears to be no need as formula provides good gradual supplementation. Discontinuing routine injections for this group alone could reduce cases of leukemia.

One more curious look at childhood leukemia is the finding that when any nation lowers its rate of infant deaths, their rate of childhood leukemia increases.[38] Vitamin K injections may be responsible for some part of this number, but other factors are surely involved, about which we can only speculate.

The Unkind Cut

Once considered a cure for maladies from diphtheria to insanity to paralysis, male circumcision is chiefly a phenomenon in the U.S., practiced very rarely in Western Europe and most of the rest of the world.[39] Even among European Jews it is only considered necessary among those who are Orthodox. By the turn of the twentieth century, circumcision became a symbol of social class, of being delivered by a doctor in a hospital.

There is no medical reason for routine painful and damaging circumcision of male newborns. Many reasons are given for this surgical removal of a large, sexually sensitive portion of the male genitalia. It has been shown that circumcised male infants experience about two thirds fewer urinary tract infections,[40] although these are generally easily treatable and without complications. These are also reduced with bathing and timely diaper changing. In fact, greater complications arise from the surgical procedure itself, up to 10%, including infections (rather common), excess scar tissue formation, granuloma (precancer) formation, frequent removal of the most sensitive fornix portion, narrowing of the urinary outlet, hemorrhage, accidental partial amputation, need for total amputation after death of penile tissues, denudation (falling off of the skin), childhood penile cancer, and rarely death.[41-49] The cruelty of the great pain imposed upon newborn males by this surgery has recently been recognized; still, less than half of all U.S. doctors use anesthesia,[50] which has some occasional complications as well. Researchers from the University of Toronto performed an experiment on a hunch about the reason male infants seemed to respond more painfully to vaccinations than females. They found that circumcised males showed significantly greater pain responses than intact males, representing, in their eyes, a memory of the pain of circumcision.[51]

It has also been argued by some that penile cancers are reduced by circumcisions. This rare disease has actually been shown to occur up to 3 times more often in intact males.[52] This disease of the elderly has a high long-term survival rate of over 70%. In Finland, a nation where circumcisions are uncommon, 1 in 1,000,000 men die of penile cancer each year.[53] Possibly more than twice the number of cancers occur in similar female genitalia,[54] with similar survival rates,[55] suggesting utility in female circumcision by the same token. Female circumcision is widely considered dangerous by those in industrialized nations, yet the chief complications of this procedure arise from uncleanly techniques, and uncleanly male circumcisions pose similar risks.[56] Incidentally, cancers of female external genitalia occur at the lowest rates by far in Asia and Africa,[57] where female circumcisions are chiefly performed. The much more common disease of breast cancer would likely be nearly eliminated by removal of "unnecessary" breast tissue at birth. It has been suggested that female cervical cancers are increased in spouses of intact males, yet this assertion has not been proven.[58,59]

One of the unspoken forces behind routine circumcision (especially by certain Gentile religions) is that it reduces masturbation. It is true that it is made more difficult. Since it is no longer believed that this normal practice leads to blindness, hysteria, or deviance, it appears to no longer be a concern. Beauty is another reason for male circumcisions. Of course this is only an acquired taste, and it has a negative effect on the supposed reasons for the assumed advantage. The absence of protection for the otherwise sensitive glans at the end of the penis causes callusing and reduced sensitivity. This is likely the reason that one circumcision study reports "a more elaborated set of sexual practices" in circumcised males[60] — apparently a need exists to find increased stimulation.

Since the complications of male circumcision appear to be approximately equal to any that are prevented, there may be no reason to prevent this practice for religious or traditional reasons, except that the infant is too young to consent, and the argument of tradition is sexually and racially biased. This practice on girls is referred to as "mutilation" by American and European nations (male circumcision is regarded as mutilation by some Europeans as well). On girls, circumcision is prohibited by law in North America and Europe, preventing immigrants from receiving sterile hospital procedures and forcing them to use more dangerous techniques. Millions of these procedures are performed every year, revealing the great level of customary, religious, and other significance attributed to female circumcision in large portions of the world. Still, those immigrants practicing this traditional procedure on their female infants in France and other nations are being imprisoned.[61] While a portion of female circumcisions are much more severe than typical male circumcisions, clearly I am only showing the weakness in the arguments of health benefits and tradition for American male circumcisions.

The American Cancer Society stated that they wished the AAP would stop promoting routine circumcision as a prevention of cancer, calling it a mistaken belief.

The newest argument for the often strongly defended practice of circumcision is a reduced rate of acquiring HIV disease. One new study suggested the risk was cut in half by this cut on infant boys.[62] Yet, this suggestion is very new and not entirely defended, and there are other means of preventing this disease that provide other health benefits as well.[63] Circumcision does not reduce other sexually transmitted diseases.[64, 65]

The Canadian Pediatric Society, the British Medical Association, and the Australian College of Pediatrics all hold firm that routine male circumcision should not be practiced. The American Academy of Pediatrics fluctuates in their opinion from year to year, but their 1999 policy statement does not recommend routine circumcision,[66] especially since the American Cancer Society stated that they wished the AAP would stop promoting routine circumcision as a prevention of cancer, calling it a mistaken belief.[67] Still, circumcision is performed on 80% of white non-Hispanic males in the U.S., and a large portion of other U.S. citizens.[68]

Feeding the Premature Infant

The premature infant, as well as a term infant born too small, presents a very special and delicate case nutritionally. They are designed to be fed totally digested nutrients in mother's blood through the umbilical cord; their digestive systems are not well developed, and some may be too weak to suck. Many are given various feeds through tubes, bottles, or through needles directly into their veins, even though in other countries all but the tiniest of these infants have been successfully fed by using mother's milk exclusively.[69] When the infant is too tiny or weak for breastfeeding, mother can express her milk for spoon or cup feeding, or for tube feeding if necessary. Artificial nipple (bottle) feeding should not be used in an infant intended for breastfeeding because it has been shown to reduce the success of an infant's continued breastfeeding by nearly two thirds (known as nipple confusion).[70] Not only does the opioid reward of food intake and sucking help to bond the infant to the artificial nipple instead of to mother's, but the latching technique, sucking pattern, and the use of tongue and mouth muscles are very different for bottle nipples and real nipples. The tiniest infants are generally fed intravenous sugar, fats, and protein pieces, but can take breastmilk by mouth even on day one. Although seldom practiced in the U.S., these infants should be fed on nothing but breastmilk as soon as possible, within a few weeks at most.

Nearly all kinds of infections are significantly elevated when premature infants are fed artificial formulas instead of breastmilk, including urinary tract infections and diarrheal diseases.[71] Among the tiniest preemies, there are 45% more serious infections in those exclusively fed formula.[72] While the difference in mortality between low-birth-weight infants fed breastmilk versus formula is not as great as the difference seen between term infant feedings, those not receiving breastmilk still have a 26 to 37% greater death rate.[73,74] The statistical benefits of breastmilk in these studies are reduced by some of the various types of breastmilk used (stored, pasteurized, term milk) and the various forms of supplementation or fortification of breastmilk.

It has been found that the breakdown of fats in the diet of the preemie fed mother's milk is twice as efficient as in formula-fed, making the appropriate fat products more accessible for use.[75] Of course, other nutrients are more available in mother's milk as well. Many studies on breastfeeding preterm and low-birth-weight babies complain that the nutrients in breastmilk are lower than in chemically derived milks, and breastfed preemies sometimes gain weight more slowly during their stay in the hospital. However, follow-up studies to age 2 or 3 show there is no difference in the size between naturally or artificially fed babies.[76] Additionally, studies suggest the breastfed preemie's growth rate is similar to that inside the uterus.[77] In fact, the bone mineral content is greater in childhood follow-ups in direct proportion to the amount of human milk received.[78] The growth of head circumference, an indicator of brain development, is not lower during premature hospitalization in infants fed human milk, even when the breastfed infant weighs less.[79] Preterm infants who are fed breastmilk grow up with higher intelligence scores, and other neurological development parameters are better as well.[80] Also remember that permanent long-

> *Breastmilk-fed preterm and low-weight infants have higher survival rates, lower illness rates, stronger bones (eventually), greater intelligence, and superior neurological development; hence, weight gain comparisons are not highly relevant.*

term immune development is superior in those who receive breast-milk. Breastmilk-fed preterm and low-weight infants have higher survival rates, lower illness rates, stronger bones (eventually), greater intelligence, and superior neurological development; hence, weight gain comparisons are not highly relevant.

A big difference in the health of tiny hospitalized infants can be induced by caring for them via kangaroo care and other nurturing measures, as presented earlier. Oxygenation, temperature control, and respiration are all superior when these infants are directly breast-fed. Additionally, they have fewer sucking and swallowing problems, they tolerate their oral feedings earlier, and their breastmilk feedings are greater when received directly at the breast or in another nurtur-ing manner. When these measures are added, weight gain is faster than for those in standard care. Thus, although a small infant fed breastmilk through a tube will have a higher chance of healthy sur-vival than one fed formula by tube, any infant who is fed directly at the breast or who is otherwise fed breastmilk with warm body con-tact and affectionate care will have the best chance for success.

Unfortunately, kangaroo care and exclusive breastfeeding are almost never seen in U.S. neonatal intensive care units (NICU). Breastfeeding at any level is not always encouraged, and sometimes not even allowed. I heard of a mother who was laughed out of the NICU when carrying in one or two tiny ounces of her first colostrum, which is actually liquid gold. I must reiterate that infant mortality rates (up to age 1 year) in the U.S. are higher than in 22 other industrialized and developing nations who record and report statistics.[81] The restricted availability of premature feeding formu-las and supplies, incubators, and other equipment in less affluent nations cause premature infants to be more often held and breast-fed — hence, they more often survive. Additionally, it has been shown that early discharge of low-weight infants (at 4 pounds or less), leads to faster weight increases as well as longer breastfeeding with no decline in health or survival rates.[82] In the Philippines, where an infant born at home will generally stay at home regard-less of birth weight, low-birth-weight infants were breastfed far longer when born at home than when born in hospitals.[83]

Mothers of underdeveloped infants need to be proactive in order to improve the outcome for their children. Mother has to be as close as possible to her preemie from the very start to encourage her milk development. Just hearing the infant cry will help to promote milk production.[84] When some kind of breastfeeding attempt is made within the first 6 hours after birth, prolactin levels are much higher than when the first attempts are 3 days later.[85] Mother needs to take measures to maintain elevated prolactin levels. If breastfeeding attempts are infrequent or weak, the possibilities include kangaroo care, maintaining nearness to the infant, hearing and responding emotionally to baby's cries, having the infant attempt to suck or at least nuzzle, and regularly attempting to manually express or pump milk (which is beneficial even though only drops may come the first days). Every time the infant receives food other than mother's milk, mother's milk production is impaired. Thus she should express milk each time such a feeding occurs.

As mentioned before, many kinds of breastmilk are fed to low-weight infants. Pooled donor milk, which is a collection of stored milk from multiple donor mothers, can be of two types: from mothers of term infants, or from mothers of premature infants. Mother's milk after premature birth is much higher in nutrients and studies show superior growth and head circumference in low-weight infants fed milk from preterm baby mothers.[86] Important fat absorption is greater when pooled milk is not sterilized.[87] Growth is shown to be even better when mother's own milk is used, rather than pooled milk,[88] likely because it is fresher and unprocessed, naturally customized to the maturity of the infant, and because mother's exposure to the infant allows her to create customized antibodies in response to the microbes in the infant's body and environment.

Researchers have just discovered (to their admitted surprise) that when preemies are being bottle-fed or spoon fed, these infants, when allowed, quickly become able to self-regulate their caloric intake when fed in response to hunger and to satisfaction.[89] As suggested in earlier chapters, there are many advantages to on-cue feeding, especially less frustration and better digestion. In all likelihood baby knows best, yet scheduled feeding of prescribed doses continues to be the norm in hospitals, likely because they are easier to monitor in this kind of setting.

Fortify Mother's Milk?

Attempts to fortify human milk for preemies are very common. Calcium and phosphorous are often added to improve early bone mineralization.[90] Protein is added in an attempt to increase growth rate. Other vitamins and minerals are often added as well. It all sounds great, but there are many problems associated with fortification.

One study analyzed the feeding of a high-protein formula that contained 3 times the protein of human milk, comparing this feed to mother's milk in low-weight babies.[91] The growth rates were similar, but the high-protein infants had high levels of toxins from protein breakdown in their blood (urea and creatinine). Additionally, two amino acids (components of protein), phenylalanine and tyrosine, were found to be too high in the formula-fed infants' blood. In excessive amounts, these hinder nervous system development. Another study reviewed protein utilization in a formula with extra cow's milk protein added, compared with human milk with extra human milk protein added.[92] The human protein fortified infants gained more weight and had better protein balance.

> A higher rate of infection is seen in infants fed fortified breastmilk versus those fed only human milk.

Most breastmilk fortification contains cow's milk proteins. These are not desirable with breastmilk or in preemie formulas (although they are in nearly all formulas). A few of the problems with these dairy proteins are the high incidence of bovine protein intolerance associated with intestinal inflammation, bleeding, and diarrhea; the slow breakdown of these large proteins in the tiny system, preventing additional formula feedings as early as they are needed for proper caloric intake; and the increased risk of developing childhood diabetes — the risk being greater the earlier cow's milk proteins are introduced (*all of these are addressed elsewhere in this book*).

It has been shown that breastmilk fortified with any cow's milk products, which includes nearly any preemie or infant formula or milk fortification powder, reduces the immune protective properties of mother's milk. A higher rate of infection is seen in infants fed fortified breastmilk versus those fed only human milk.[93,94] The immune protection from mother can be reduced by fortification in part because *E. Coli* bacterial growth in the intestine increases, which mother's milk alone hinders. This bacterial flora sets the stage for many diarrheal illnesses. Soy derived products do not promote *E. Coli* and lead to a lesser increase in infection overall; however, soy can also cause allergic intolerance.

Various researchers are interested in supplementing elements such as sodium, phosphorous, calcium, and vitamins to the breastfed preemie. These can all be provided without dairy products. Iron supplements will block much of breastmilk's infection protection and is not needed in most cases. Vitamins shouldn't be harmful in low quantities according to the research to date, and vitamin D may enhance bone building when neither mother nor infant is obtaining much sun exposure.

In a German study, half of the preterm infants receiving medium or high levels of calcium supplementation were found to have dangerous calcification in their kidneys, and many suffered abdominal distension as well.[95] We have already seen that breastfed preemies eventually show very good bone mineralization with no supplementation. Another study suggests that bone mineralization in breastfed preemies is as high as in formula-fed preemies by just a few months after birth,[96] but the concern continues about the light bone mineral content early on for breastfed low-birthweight infants. While it seems a little backwards to use formula-fed infants as the gold standard, comparisons to intrauterine growth are used as well. Breastfed preemies' bones may lag behind formula-fed preemies in this arena. Possibly a very low level of calcium and phosphorous supplementation to the breastfed preemie is a good choice. If protein fortification is desired, it should come from a human or possibly soy source. Much more research is needed in this area.

IV Feeding of Preemies

There has been a dangerous but preventable finding in regards to the tiny newborn who is receiving nutrition parenterally, that is, not by mouth but directly into the bloodstream. This feeding is known as TPN for "total parenteral nutrition." It seems that vitamin E, which is typically a beneficial antioxidant, can actually become a harmful oxidant, a pro-oxidant, when exposed to light, especially phototherapy lights, throughout the day.[97] This causes the fats in the parenteral formula to quickly become rancid. This infusion of rancid fats into the bloodstream of preemies, which are toxic and can even be cancer causing, may add to the many difficulties encountered in these tiny infants. This oxidization can be prevented by covering the liquid with aluminum foil or by adding vitamin C to the solution at time of use, although this is not always practiced.

TPN solutions can be lifesaving when they are truly needed, but these formulas are far from perfect nutrition and are not yet truly safe. Liver damage is very common in tiny infants receiving TPN.[98] Although this damage is generally reversible in adults, it can be more permanent in infants and can lead to lifelong illness or early death.[99] Finally, this liquid sits for long periods in plastic bags and tubing, allowing dangerous leaching of BPA (if PC plastic) or DEHP (if PVC plastic) into the IV fluid.

Oral feeding of breastmilk is tolerated much sooner than formula by mouth.[100] Moreover, early introduction of formula increases the chance an infant will develop life-threatening necrotizing enterocolitis.[101] This condition is rarely seen in infants receiving no formula by mouth even if they received parenteral nutrition. Human milk proteins and lipids are more easily absorbed than formula components, and human milk speeds the maturation of the digestive system. Hence, feeding of breastmilk to the infant who is on intravenous feeding will reduce the total amount of parenteral solution needed, reducing the possible negative consequences.

Robbing Antioxidants

Oxygen therapy, direct or through an incubator, causes many harmful oxidizing reactions in infants.[102] This creates toxicity and predisposes them to cancer. Furthermore, this oxidation uses up the infant's supply of antioxidants, including selenium and vitamin E. Low levels of selenium and vitamin E predispose an infant to more infections. Supplementing these elements as well as vitamins A and C may help to reduce this, but the infant's ability to absorb these is limited. When these supplements are added to mother's milk, they are absorbed more readily than with formula. In addition, kangaroo care can provide superior oxygenation, reducing the need for artificial oxygen supplementation.

Regardless of oxygen therapy, parenteral nutrition preemies develop very low selenium levels within weeks.[103] Selenium levels decline in formula-fed infants as well. This decline is likely due to oxidative breakdown in these feeds as well as other stresses caused by the feeds and feeding methods. Supplementation does not adequately compensate. On the other hand, those fed mainly breastmilk maintain healthy selenium levels (except with the highest levels of oxygen therapy).

Feeding the Term Infant

The newborn should feed at mother's breast within the first hour after birth. Those who feed early and stay close to their mothers in the

hospital have a doubled chance of continuing to breastfeed exclusively.[104] Spinal anesthesia (which keeps mother awake) for cesarean
birth aids early initiation of breastfeeding. Breastfeeding in the first
weeks, and especially in the first hour, also helps to contract
mother's uterus to expel the placenta and allow the uterus to return
to normal size. When the newborn is given sugar water during the
first days, as continues to be common practice in some hospitals,
breastfeeding for mother and infant is disrupted. As a result the
infant will be less likely to receive exclusive breastfeeding after-
wards and statistically will lose her breastfeeding opportunities
entirely at a younger age. Infants who do not receive sugar water do
not display hypoglycemic (low sugar) symptoms,[105] which reveals
that there is no justification for this practice.

A Kinder, Gentler Relationship

Rooming in with mother is where the newborn belongs, if at all
possible. If not, the parents can room in with the baby as nearly as
possible. This way the infant's protective natural flora develop more
quickly, breastfeeding becomes more successful, and establishing an
early connection between mother and infant generally leads to a
longer duration of healthy practices overall. Reducing medical procedures applied to the delicate newborn, increasing intimacy, reducing noise, and providing natural feeding lead to more survivals as
well as to healthier, less-stressed babies. The birth of a child should
not be viewed as a medical procedure, but as the beginning of a
family. The parents and the dynamics of the family unit will benefit from staying together from the start.

9

Baby's Nutritional Beginnings

WE CAN BE IMMENSELY GRATEFUL THAT RESEARCH HAS DEVELOPED AN artificial substitute for mother's milk that can keep most infants alive when mother's milk is unavailable for some reason. Although wet-nursing was likely commonplace for millennia, feeding with the milk of mother goats, cows, and other animals has largely usurped this practice in recent centuries. The younger the infant, the lower their chance of survival on these animal milks, with none likely to survive if this is implemented exclusively at birth. Today's infant formulas generally begin with cow's milk, but an enormous amount of processing, extracting, and supplementing is done to make it adequate for consumption by infants.

Many like to point out that formulas have higher levels of many nutrients than mother's milk, thereby implying that natural human milk is deficient by comparison. But it is the poor digestion, absorption, and availability of nutrients in formula that necessitate these higher levels — and nutrients are still deficient in formula feeds. A more important distinction is the large array of immune factors, enzymes, human hormones, and human growth factors found in breastmilk, which are not found in formulas. Some nutrients such as DHA and certain nucleotides are missing from formula as well. Because the interplay between all the elements within any food is extremely delicate, attempts to provide the correct balance of many factors in formula usually fall short.

It is known that when birth mothers are given ample assistance, at least 99% of those who so desire can breastfeed their infants. Yet, as a result of an extremely successful worldwide marketing campaign, this does not happen. In fact, by only 3 months of age, fewer than 30% of U.S. babies receive any breastmilk at all. Sometimes the choice is not so much whether or not to breastfeed, but whether and when to supplement with formula, when to provide solid foods, or how soon to wean from the breast. A good understanding of the nutritional dynamics of both formula and breastmilk should help parents make the decisions best for their family situation.

Fat Intake & Fat Soluble Vitamins

Milk fat is removed from cow's milk as it's being adapted for infant feeds. This is just as well since it contains the most residue from pesticides, drugs, and other contaminants. Unfortunately, fat soluble vitamins, A, D, E, and K are removed along with it. There is an inadequate supply of these fat-soluble vitamins in cow's milk for formula anyway, so they are added as supplements. Only one form of each of these vitamins is added back, even though we now know that there are at least 4 kinds of vitamin E and 5 kinds of vitamin A, all having slightly different benefits, and all found in mother's milk.

It has been customary to use the least expensive oils in place of the milk fat. Today, oils from industry excesses continue to be used, such as palm and coconut oils, but many formulas are now using some higher quality oils in addition. Beef tallow (often listed as "oleo") is still occasionally seen, and it is reasonable to assume it contains toxic residues as high as those in butter. The ratios of the various kinds of fats in formula are very different from those in human milk. Each formula is very different from the others as well, depending on the combination of fats chosen. One commonly used oil of concern is palm oil. The palmitic acid in this oil is very different from the palmitic acid beneficially found in breastmilk. It is largely unusable. This fat combines with available calcium to form soaps that are passed in the stool. Thus, both fat absorption and calcium absorption by the infant are decreased when this palm oil is present.[1]

Human milk has a broader spectrum of monounsaturated and polyunsaturated fats and mono-, di-, and triglycerides than butter fat or any of the oil combinations used in formulas (*see Figure 5-1, Chapter 5*). Possibly the most important of these are the long-chain polyunsaturated fatty acids, which are considered heart protective. One of these missing in formulas is DHA, recently found to be very important in brain development. Even more recently it has been decided that other fats missing in formulas are important as well.

As mentioned previously, attempts to more closely match the ratios of fats, especially fatty acids, to those in human milk have not led to successful absorption of the correct ratios by the infant. It is assumed that an infant can manufacture the non-essential fatty acids, but with formula feeding this ability relies on an ample supply of the essential fatty acids, linoleic, linolenic, and arachidonic, as well as other nutrients such as the vitamin E needed to alter them. It appears that this manufacture of fatty acids by the formula-fed infant does not occur to the optimal extent. Additionally, many fats in human milk considered non-essential confer many special benefits. Their variety

> *Many difficult-to-use fatty acids contained in infant formulas bind with the formula's calcium, forming soaps and making the stools hard.*

and ratios appear to aid absorption of other nutrients. On the other hand, the poor digestibility and improper ratios of fatty acids in formulas cause competition that decreases their utilization by the body. Debate continues among researchers about which fats and what ratios of these should be in formulas.

Since there is no longer animal fat in most formulas, there is little to no cholesterol. (Small amounts remain in the non-fat milk.) In ample supply in mother's milk, cholesterol is an important building block for many hormones. The level of cholesterol in the mother's diet does not impact the cholesterol level in her milk, indicating that the body maintains a close watch over the level of this ingredient supplied to the baby. It is likely that a formula-fed infant without liver impairment is able to manufacture sufficient cholesterol however.

> Iron deficiency is a common problem in formula-fed infants. The chief causes are the frequently seen intestinal bleeding caused by cow's milk formulas, and the very poor absorption of iron from infant formulas.

Breastfed infants have higher levels of long-chain fatty acids in their blood and tissues, including DHA. Their muscles have higher percentages of them as well. The impact on muscles is not well known, but researchers have found that children who incorporate these lipids in their early muscle development maintain lower blood-sugar levels and may be less prone to developing diseases such as diabetes.[2]

Calcium

Many difficult-to-use fatty acids contained in infant formulas bind with the formula's calcium, forming soaps and making the stools hard.[3] Because this reduces the amount of calcium available, formulas need to have extra calcium. Manufacturers need to be careful how much they add, however, as calcium can compete with iron for absorption, and iron absorption is already a problem.

Adequate Iron

Iron deficiency is a common problem in formula-fed infants. The chief causes are the frequently seen intestinal bleeding caused by cow's milk formulas,[4] and the very poor absorption of iron from infant formulas, despite the high levels of this mineral in these formulas. Feeding whole cow's milk instead of formula before many other high iron foods are in an infant's diet leads to the worst iron deficiency of any diet. Cautions against this practice are commonly heeded in most parts of this country. The pale appearance of anemia is not observable until iron deficiency is rather pronounced. The earlier signs of irritability, weight loss, and poor appetite are difficult to recognize. In addition to low energy and slow growth, the chief concerns associated with iron deficiency anemia in infants are reduced neurological development of mental and motor capacities,[5] and increased incidence of mild and moderate mental retardation.[6] The proteins from both cow's milk and formula bind quickly with iron and most iron (96%) is passed unused into the diaper.[7] Soy protein also inhibits iron absorption.

When an infant is formula-fed, his stores of iron received from mother prior to birth help maintain adequate iron until 4 to 6 months of age. After this time, those not receiving high-iron cereals or other iron-containing solid foods often become anemic. Those receiving cow's milk as part of their diets usually become anemic. In fact, research suggests the milk in a non-breastfed infant's diet should be formula rather than cow's milk for at least 18 months. Higher mental and motor functioning has been found in inner city infants fed this way; moreover, 2% of these infants were anemic compared to 33% of those consuming cow's milk.[8]

As stated, most infant formulas are supplemented with very high levels of iron compared to the level in mother's milk. This is to compensate for blood loss and poor absorption. Although iron supplementation definitely reduces anemia in formula-fed infants, there are downsides to this supplementation as well. The more iron an infant receives in his formula, the higher the level and the greater the variety of potential illness-causing bacteria in his intestines.[9] Also, the more iron there is in infant formula, the harder the infant's stools are, sometimes leading to constipation and to local blood loss where this hard stool passes. Low-iron infant formulas were chiefly introduced because of perceptions that high iron sometimes causes diarrhea. Higher levels of undesirable bacteria suggest that these infants should be more susceptible to infectious diarrhea, and a small difference has been found, but it is very slight compared to the high diarrhea rates from formula feeding in general, as compared to exclusive breastmilk feeding. Iron in great excess can potentially become an oxidizing agent as well, which increases susceptibility to cancer. Also, the more iron supplemented, the lower the infant's absorption of copper and selenium[10] and possibly other trace minerals.

The so-called low-iron formulas on shelves in the U.S. are still supplemented with iron. In fact, the levels of iron in some of these (Mead Johnson: .7 mg per 100 cal, which is equivalent to .14 mg/ounce) are comparable to levels found to be quite acceptable as standard iron levels in formula in other countries,[11] while others are lower (such as Wyeth and Ross brands). There is a very delicate balance to be sought to achieve optimal iron supplementation in infant formulas. European iron-fortified formulas contain half the iron of those in the United States. Infants drinking iron-fortified formulas in the U.S. take in (but do not absorb) nearly 100 times more iron each day than breastfed infants do. Some suggest an iron level between our high-iron and low-iron formulas may be the best choice.[12] University of California, Davis researchers suggest that .6 mg per 100 calories is ample.[13]

Mother's milk contains lactoferrin, which carries iron directly into the infant's system, providing a very high percentage of absorption. Efforts to supplement formulas with lactoferrin concentrated from cow's milk found higher iron absorption in infants only occurred after a few months, for an unknown reason. Since iron-fortified solid foods can be started soon after that, it has been decided that it is not worth the cost to add this ingredient to formulas.

Children who are exclusively breastfed for long periods sometimes demonstrate little or no extra iron *storage* on blood testing, allowing formula promoters to label them iron deficient even though they are robust and do not display iron-deficiency anemia (read their precisely worded ads very carefully).[14,15] In fact, breastfed babies' chief blood iron indicators are more often than not superior to formula-fed infants' (red blood cells have very good iron levels). Nonetheless, doctors often insist on providing these infants with iron supplements because of low stores. When a breastfed infant is supplemented with iron, this binds up the remaining lactoferrin and prevents it from performing its other chief duty — providing immune protection. When a nursing mother is given high iron supplements, the level of iron in her milk does not change,[16] indicating that the body tries to precisely control iron levels for optimum infant health.

> *The longer the infants were exclusively breastfed, the better their iron status was.*

Just as formula-fed infants develop more undesirable intestinal flora with increasing doses of iron in their formula, when a breastfed infant is given iron supplementation or iron-supplemented formula, he develops more dangerous fecal flora as well. The Centers for Disease Control found that breastfed infants receiving higher-iron-fortified formula supplements developed diarrhea 6% more often than those receiving low-iron formula, who develop it much more often than those receiving no supplemental formula.[17] Why supplement for iron, however, when even those feeding exclusively on mother's milk until 9 months of age do not demonstrate anemia.[18]

Some infants receiving mother's milk as well as formula become more iron-deficient than those fed exclusively on either. Adding formula or baby food to a breastfed infant's diet significantly decreases the absorption of iron from mother's milk.[19] While the formula prevents mother's iron from being absorbed, and its own iron is poorly absorbed, it also may introduce some bleeding that reduces iron stores. *Twenty-eight percent of breastfed infants beginning iron-fortified solid foods at 6 months become anemic by 9 months of age.*[20] One study found no difference in the infant iron status between breastfed infants who received high-iron foods or those given more usual solid foods,[21] suggesting that any dietary additions disrupt mother's well-designed mechanisms. Another study of breastfed infants of various ages who began receiving foods not fortified with iron (and no cow's milk) showed that the longer the infants were exclusively breastfed, the better their iron status was. Forty-three percent of these infants whose exclusive breastfeeding lasted less than half a year became anemic (consistent with the 28% reported by other researchers after 6 months of exclusive nursing), while none whose breastfeeding was exclusive for 7 months showed anemia at either 7, 12, or 24 months.[22]

Zinc & Selenium Concerns

Although infant formulas are supplemented with triple the amount of zinc found in human milk, formula-fed infants have blood zinc levels that are half the level found in breastfed infants, when measured at 3 months of age.[24] One cause for poor zinc absorption in formula-fed infants is the high levels of competing iron in formulas. Women who consume double the recommended level of iron during pregnancy and lactation have significantly lower zinc levels in their milk, due to this same competition.[25] Balanced nutrients are just as important as ample nutrients.

Only as recently as 1980 did formula companies decide that some formula-fed infants were not obtaining enough zinc, leading to supplementation of this mineral. Then, it wasn't until about 1990

Figure 9-1 Quantities of *nutrients per liquid ounce* in mother's mature milk, two milk-based formulas, a soy-based formula, and whole cow's milk. Human milk is 21 calories per ounce, formulas are 20 calories per liquid ounce. Nutrients in human milk are in highly absorbable forms, and other human milk factors promote absorption as well. Formulas are supplemented with high levels of nutrients in an attempt to achieve adequate absorption. By comparison, it can be seen that the nutrient makeup of whole cow's milk is quite inappropriate for a young infant, or for a total diet in even an older infant or toddler. (Extracted From USDA Nutrient Database for Standard Reference, 1998)

Nutrients in Infant Feeds[23]

Nutrient	Human (Mature)	Carnation Good Start	Ross Similac	Wyeth Babysoy	Whole Cow's Milk
in grams					
Proteins	.32	.49	.41	.54	1.003
Total Fat	1.35	1.04	1.08	1.06	1.019
Carbohydrates	2.12	2.23	2.16	2.04	1.42
Fiber	present	0	0	0	0
Minerals in milligrams					
Calcium	9.9	12.8	15.8	17.9	36.4
Iron	.009	.302	.359	.359	.015
Magnesium	1.05	1.22	1.22	2.13	4.10
Manganese	.008	.001	.001	.001	.001
Phosphorus	4.22	7.32	8.51	12.46	28.49
Potassium	15.77	19.82	20.98	20.98	46.20
Zinc	.05	.15	.15	.16	.12
Vitamins in micrograms					
B-1	4	12	20	21	12
B-2	11	27	30	30	49
B-3	55	149	209	149	26
B-6	3	15	12	12	13
B-12	.014	.043	.049	.061	.109
A	20	18	18	14	9
E	278	296	402	281	31
Fats in grams					
Saturated	.62	.45	.38	.48	.63
Monosaturated	.51	.33	.40	.43	.29
Polysaturated	.15	.23	.24	.15	.04
Cholesterol	.0043	.0018	.0006	.0005	.0041

that researchers suggested some formulas needed more selenium, a mineral that was highly variable in formula. Selenium levels vary in human milks also, depending on mother's intake, and can be low when mother lives in a region with low selenium soils (although more foods come from distant regions today) or selects a selenium-poor diet. Zinc is important for good vision and fighting infection. Selenium is important for blood vessel integrity and immunity, and it is an antioxidant.

Fluoride, Teeth & Bones

Fluoride, like selenium, is a trace element that varies in its availability in the soil and water in different areas of the world. Dental researchers have found that higher levels of fluoride reduce the incidence of cavities in children's baby teeth. For this reason, many public water systems around the country and around the world have added fluoride to the drinking water in an attempt to reduce dental caries. Fluoride is added to most toothpaste and is applied in some dental treatments as well. Believing breastmilk to be low in fluoride, many pediatricians and dentists are recommending fluoride supplements to breastfed babies. However, since the installation of water fluoridation and other measures beginning around 1950, the results of excess fluoride have revealed themselves.

> *Nearly a quarter of all our children are showing some signs of excess fluoride, or fluorosis.*

Today, fluoridation is all around us, in 50% of U.S. drinking water, in 50% of bottled drinks, and it gets into cows and soy and thus infant formulas. Although human milk appears unaffected by the amount of fluoride ingested, concentrations of fluoride in cow's milk can be 20 to 70 times the level found in breastmilk, depending on the level of fluoride contamination from fertilizers and pesticides a cow is exposed to.[26] This fluoride is concentrated in the milk for formulas as a result of dehydration, and then more is added with the water used for rehydration. Now nearly a quarter of all our children are showing some signs of excess fluoride, or fluorosis.[27,28] An early sign is altered formation and discoloration of teeth. Fluorosis is marked in 5% of these children and very great in some of those.

It is becoming increasingly apparent that high fluoride levels damage bones.[29] In Morocco, a nation with rich fluoride levels in their soil and water, fluorosis is common. Skeletal defects, such as knock knees, and joint pains and teeth abnormalities are commonly seen.[30] This damage can include a wearing down of the teeth, as well as deviation of teeth and eventually cavities.

Moderate fluorosis, seen in some heavy drinkers of fluoridated water, juice, or soda is associated with mild teeth and bone malformations, possible nervous system alterations, osteoporosis, and eventually kyphosis, the humped upper back. Gastrointestinal pain and damage can occur with established fluorosis as well.[31] Severe fluorosis leads to misshapen major bones and other bony defects, along with neurological problems. Development of severe fluorosis is not likely except in children who especially like to swallow toothpaste and have other high fluoride sources as well.

Excess fluoride, at the level considered beneficial to teeth, causes detrimental changes in the mineralization of bones. Bones become hard, in the sense of brittle, and at the same time there is deficient bone calcium (osteoporosis).

Excess fluoride, at the level considered beneficial to teeth, causes detrimental changes in the mineralization of bones.[32] Fluoride replaces magnesium in bones, making them harder. This hardness is partly desirable in teeth, giving them extra defense against destructive cavity-causing bacteria. But excess fluoride combines with available calcium, and they leave the body together, leaving less calcium for bone strength and density. Thus, bones become hard in the sense of brittle, and at the same time there is deficient bone calcium (osteoporosis), which leads to easy fractures.

The latest studies are suggesting the benefit to children's teeth from ingested fluoride (water or supplements) is very small.[33] The greatest benefits seem to be when fluoride comes into direct contact with teeth, suggesting that small amounts of fluoridated toothpaste, without swallowing it, would be the best choice for cavity reduction.

Fluoride supplementation for children is strongly associated with increased risk of fluorosis.[34] *Beyond supplementation, the major risk factors for fluorosis are formula feeding, weaning before 9 months of age, and swallowing toothpaste.*[35] Breastfeeding to at least 6 months may even protect against fluorosis in the permanent teeth.[36] Breastfed infants are not drinking fluoridated water, and mother's milk provides a very consistent level of fluoride regardless of the amount the mother ingests.[37] A large body of evidence suggests that one should not supplement fluoride for breastfed or other babies or older children, and it is no longer recommended by researchers, even when levels in water are low.[38] Unfortunately, some doctors continue to recommend it for breastfed kids.

Vitamin D

Vitamin D deficiency rarely occurs in breastfed children — only when a child and mother get little sun and the mother's stores are low. This can happen when one child quickly follows another, taxing mother's stores, with darker skin pigmentation (of either), and in northern latitudes. Vitamin D is manufactured by the skin when exposed to sunlight, and is then stored. So, preventing vitamin D shortage in an infant requires either the breastfeeding mother or the infant to be exposed to some sun each week. The further north, the closer to December, or the darker the skin, the longer this exposure needs to be. Supplementing vitamin D to mother or child (as in infant formulas) is a fine alternative to sun exposure for breastfed babies.[39] Except for these very rare and easily preventable cases, breastfed infants show excellent bone mineralization, which depends in part on vitamin D, even though typical mother's milk has been labeled as low in vitamin D.[40]

Nucleotides

Free nucleotides (building blocks of RNA) are highly beneficial factors in mother's milk that promote iron absorption, fatty acid digestion, the presence of healthy flora, and intestinal and possibly liver growth.[41] Any benefits from supplementing formula with nucleotides appear limited so far. In some cases supplementation helps growth-retarded newborns catch up in their growth.[42] At least two U.S. manufacturers are now adding these to their formulas.

Protein Ratios are Important

Free amino acids (protein building blocks) are abundant in human milk at four times the level found in cow's milk.[43] Levels vary during lactation in a predictable pattern, independent of mother's diet, and glutamate remains the predominant amino acid.[44] Attempts to match the average human milk amino acid levels in formula have not produced breastfed baby blood levels in formula-fed infants.[45] Even with high glutamate in formula, phenylalanine is found to be high in the blood of formula-fed infants. This is the amino acid that causes mental retardation when in very high levels due to the rare disorder called phenylketonuria (PKU).

Milk proteins are divided into casein proteins and whey proteins. The casein in bovine milk comes in large units that are difficult for humans to digest. The chief whey of cow's milk is another large protein that is not found in human milk at all. Mother's whey is predominantly lactoferrin, good for providing immunity. Forty percent of mother's whey is alpha-lactalbumin. Only 3% of bovine protein is similar to this.[46] Bovine milk is 20% whey and 80% casein. The ratio of whey to casein in formula significantly affects the availability of other nutrients and the digestibility of the formula. Both bovine whey and casein interfere with iron absorption in humans. Many formulas add whey to achieve a 60:40 whey to casein ratio, which is the average found in mother's milk. However both portions are very different from their human counterparts, both are problematic, and each interferes with absorption of various nutrients. Hence, there are advantages and disadvantages to any ratio found in a formula. Formulas vary this ratio considerably in either direction. Human milk starts out with an 80:20 ratio of these protein fractions (the opposite of cow's milk) and gradually moves to 60:40 whey to casein over several months. A 50:50 ratio is found in milk of mothers who nurse for extended periods.[47]

Tolerance of Formula & Mother's Milk

Intolerance of formula made from cow's milk is very common in infants. This intolerance is to the unusual bovine proteins, not to lactose (*see Chapters 7 and 10*). Colic, frequent fussiness, poor sleep, waking with screams, frequent spitting-up, vomiting, diarrhea, constipation, yellow or green stools, eczema and other rashes, including many diaper rashes, ear infections, chronically stuffy nose, and failure to thrive are among the most common reactions. These same symptoms often occur in breastfed infants who are reacting to foods in their mother's diet, especially dairy. Continuing to allow a child to experience these symptoms means continuing to allow damaging inflammatory reactions to go on inside their growing intestines, as well as decreased absorption of nutrients. For breastfed infants, mother simply changes her diet. Initial relief may be found for artificially fed infants through use of soy formula, although many infants eventually develop sensitivity to the corn or soy in these. Hydrolyzed milk protein formula works for many, but a small amount of intact bovine protein remains, often enough to continue to aggravate a sensitive child. Solutions to these symptoms and problems are presented in the last chapters of this book.

Soy Formulas

The decision to use soy for an alternative formula was not based on research over what would provide the best alternative in the case of milk formula intolerance, rather, the idea came from the overabundance of soybeans. Soy, in fact, is among the most commonly reported allergens (as is corn, which is added to many formulas in the form of cornstarch, corn syrup solids, corn-derived dextrose, or corn oil). Actually formula based on lamb meat (some have existed in Europe), sheep's milk, or possibly rice would likely be better alternatives.

Phytate (or phytic acid) is a plant acid found in high concentration in soy formulas. Unfortunately, this ingredient causes greatly reduced absorption of zinc, copper, iron, and other minerals from the formula.[48] The high fraction of protein in soy formula adds to reduced mineral absorption.[49] Additionally, the protein of soy formula is difficult to digest, and the available amino acids are in the wrong proportions, thus requiring twice as much protein to be put into soy formula than is in mother's milk, in an attempt to compensate. Researchers suggest that reduction of the phytate and partial hydrolysis (chemical breakdown to aid digestion) of the soy protein could reduce the problems of poor absorption and digestibility.[50] Hopefully, these alterations will be found on grocery shelves in the future.

Soy formula also contains high levels of phytoestrogens, estrogen mimics that behave as mild estrogens in a woman low in them (reducing symptoms of menopause), but compete with natural estrogens when they are prevalent (reducing chances of breast cancer for instance). The effect of these is not known when an infant receives them as the sole source of nutrition. An infant fed soy formula receives more than 7,000 times the amount of phytoestrogens as the infant fed mother's milk does. In their blood, the level of these is 13,000 to 22,000 times that of their own natural estrogens.[51] Some researchers predict these may provide powerful cancer prevention to those who begin life on soy formula;[52] others express concern over possible toxicity from this tremendous dose.[53]

Soy formula does not naturally contain the milk sugar lactose. I have found none with this ingredient added, although it should be. Lactose, in the milk of almost all mammals, greatly augments calcium absorption. Hence, soy formulas need to add more calcium than do milk formulas. The galactose produced from lactose digestion and barely found in any other food in the diet makes valuable contributions to rapid brain development.[54]

In all probability, lactose, which is truly baby sugar, is not added to soy formulas since they are designed for those who cannot tolerate bovine formulas, and the misconception that lactose intolerance causes this sensitivity is promulgated by many.

Dynamic Mother's Milk

In contrast to the nutritional constraints of formulas, breastmilk is dynamic in its nutritional makeup. Mother's earliest milk is exceptionally dense in certain nutrients and many immune factors. When comparing mature milk at various stages of lactation, protein levels are highest early on when the infant is growing most rapidly. Protein levels drop 30% by 6 months and remain around this level during the rest of lactation.[55] Lactose levels increase somewhat over the first months; but oligosaccharides, the immune and fiber-providing complex carbohydrates, begin higher and decrease slightly over this same time.[56] Immune-providing zinc levels are also higher in the first months, dropping to a new level by 6 months. Magnesium levels plateau at 3 months. Calcium levels increase over the first month and remain high during the next 4 months, during the time of greatest bone growth.[57] After this time, calcium levels gradually decrease by 25% to a level at 12 months that remains steady throughout the rest of lactation.[58] Vitamin K levels increase gradually over the first weeks after delivery,[59] matching a newborn's need for tight control over K levels. Overall, fat levels and calories do not change over time.

There can be nutritional variances in each successive child. On one hand, the second fetus and breastfed child receives fewer toxins from mother's body than does the first. On the other hand, mother's stores of iron, vitamin D, B_{12} and other elements can become reduced through her first pregnancy and nursing, and a second child can be born with lower stores of certain vitamins and minerals than the first, more so with each successive child. Of course, good diet and supplementation on behalf of the mother will prevent this.

While many studies reveal that supplementing mother's diet with various nutrients does not affect the levels in her milk, this is not exactly the case for severely starving mothers. And for some nutrients, especially the B vitamins, mother's intake does affect her milk levels. This suggests that all nursing mothers, as well as pregnant mothers, need to maintain their own health in order to provide the best nutrition to their infants. Many pregnant mothers take multivitamin and mineral supplements, beneficially. Mega-dosing of any nutrients can cause imbalances. Certainly, in the same way, maternal supplements can be beneficial to mother and infant during breastfeeding as well, although it does not appear to be highly necessary in a mother who eats well. Any supplements given directly to a breastfed infant should first be researched and well thought through.

A Weighty Issue

Breastfed infants gain weight more slowly than do formula-fed babies, especially after the third month. Their head circumferences and lengths are the same however,[60] and health, activity, and brain and motor development are superior in breastfed infants. All indications show that the weight difference between breastfed and formula-fed infants is fat.[61] This excess fat in formula-fed babies is an artificially developed characteristic, and fat infants are nearly twice as likely to become obese adults.[62] Although adults who gained excess weight only during adulthood are able to control high blood pressure with diet, large adults who were obese in early childhood are not able to reduce high blood pressure in this way.[63] Excess fat provides no health advantage for the infant except in the case of starvation, as occurs during prolonged bouts of formula-induced diarrhea. Hence, we should more accurately say that *formula-fed infants generally become overweight after 3 months of age*.

Formula-drinking infants consume 20% more formula each day than the amount of milk a breastfeeding infant drinks, although these milks have similar calories per ounce.[64] Even though most formulas have less fat than mother's milk, formula-fed infants still put on more fat weight than do breastfed ones. The protein in formula is harder to absorb, and certain unusable fatty acids combine with calcium to form soaps that are lost in the stool. Well-absorbed carbohydrates (sugars) are converted and stored as body fat in formula-fed infants, which causes the unnecessary weight gain. Their bodies know how much protein, fat, and certain nutrients they need, and they have to consume more calories in order to acquire them.

At least two other factors play a role in the disproportionate weight gain in formula-fed infants. Breastmilk becomes higher in fat the longer an infant nurses on a breast,[65] providing greater satiation of hunger and preventing the nursing infant from overfeeding. Breastmilk also contains leptin, which signals fullness and may help prevent overeating.[66]

Formula researchers recently tested a formula made with reduced protein to match the same protein-to-calories ratio as human milk, wondering whether this more "natural" concoction would be beneficial. They found that infants consumed considerably more calories, most likely in an attempt to acquire enough usable protein for their bodies.[67] While their length was not different, they gained considerably more weight in the form of fat. The conclusion was that this formula is not safe. But more importantly, this study is another indication that

> This study is another indication that the higher weights of formula-fed infants is not a good sign, but rather a sign of malnutrition. Reducing the available nutrition increases total consumption. Excess fat is the result.

the higher weights of formula-fed infants is not a good sign, but rather a sign of malnutrition. Reducing the available nutrition increases total consumption. Excess fat is the result.

While some have suggested that breastfed infants are lighter because of "low" protein intake (compared to cow's milk), researchers have shown that supplementing breastfed infants' diets with added concentrated protein (and vitamins and minerals) does not increase their weight gain compared to non-supplemented infants.[68] Nor does the amount of fat or calories in individual mothers' breastmilk have any impact on the weight gain of their infants.[69] Neither the weight of the mother nor her nutritional status (beyond severe malnutrition) impacts the growth rate of a breastfed baby,[70] nor does the size of her breasts.

Formula companies developed weight charts in the early 1900s based on the weight gain of formula-fed infants. They provided these in baby-weighing stations they set up around the world in order to sell their products. With these, they could often convince breastfeeding mothers that they were suffering from insufficient milk, and that their "malnourished" infants needed supplements of their new "scientific" milk formulas.[71] Of course, formula only replaces mother's milk so mother makes less and less milk until the child eventually becomes totally formula-fed. As medical doctors were invited to attend these weigh-ins, these weigh stations gradually evolved into well-baby medical office visits, and the pediatrician was born. Formula companies continue to provide these charts to pediatricians today and encourage them to advise formula supplementation for infants whose growth is "faltering." These charts now reflect the average of all U.S. babies. Most of the statistics for these were gathered in 1979 when a very tiny percentage of U.S. infants were exclusively breastfed beyond a few months, even fewer than today. Hence these charts simply portray formula-fed patterns. By definition, nearly half of all breastfed infants will fall below this so-called average weight even during the first two months when their weights are similar to those who are bottle-fed. Then after the second month, many more will fall into the "below average" range on these charts.

Weight gain *is* an issue. One needs to know that an infant is growing in order to know that they have no serious digestive disorders or other problems. But just because grandma likes fat babies doesn't mean parents should attempt to alter a very lean and active baby. Should they try, the desired result is unlikely. By the same token, of course, plump babies should not be dieting. In many cases you would simply find that one or both parents were pudgy-cheeked babies themselves. What is important is that an infant continues to gain weight (after the natural initial drop in the first week). Do not be concerned about the rate or the weight. These are greatly governed by heredity (especially in the naturally fed infant), as is their final height.

Babies exclusively breastfed for 3 to 5 months have been shown to have only half the chance of being obese as children. Those breastfed for more than 1 year develop childhood obesity only 17% as often as formula-fed babies.[72] Other studies show a very high correlation between childhood obesity and adult obesity.

Much more important than weight is neurological development, which is evidenced by reaching various developmental milestones. Although these vary widely even in very healthy children, one might wish to look for some milestones being reached a littler early, while others are normally reached late. Slower rates are expected for prematurely born infants. The intuition of experienced parents and doctors goes a long way here and is usually far more valuable than any growth chart. Among breastfed infants, even those with the slowest growth rates show no differences in their average rates of neurological development or of illness.[73] Dozens of studies have suggested that separate growth charts need to be made for naturally fed infants. Still, few exist, and no one is distributing these. Interestingly, a London psychologists' study on the impact of growth rate versus intellectual and motor development suggested that the first few months pose a "sensitive period," beyond which there is no relation between growth rate and mental development. One third of the differences in intellectual and motor development of 15-month-olds could be explained by growth rates that occurred between birth and 3 months of age.[74] These researchers did not discriminate between those who were formula-fed or breastfed. Since the slightly brighter infants, on the average, would eventually be the smaller infants for the most part (breastfed), it is not surprising that this 3-month critical period showed up in their study, and that a slight negative relationship between weight and intelligence eventually revealed itself beyond that age.

Beginning Solid Foods

It is very important to supply formula-fed infants with the appropriate weaning foods at 4 to 6 months of age in order to provide relief from many of the negative effects of formula, one of those being iron loss. At the same time, formula feeding should be continued in lieu of straight cow's milk. The growth rate of formula-fed infants does not vary whether solid foods are introduced at 3 months or at 6 months of age.[75] The majority of formula-fed infants tend to lose their excess fat by 15 months. The formula-fed infant starting on solids experiences catch-up growth from nutritional deficiencies at about the same rate that they lose fat. Solid food introduction at 4 to 6 months is not for faltering physical growth, but for improving nutrition. Formula-fed infants who are smaller due to intolerance of bovine milk proteins will gain weight faster only after most of these are removed from their diets.

> While there is no need to restrict solid food intake in breastfed infants after 7 months, neither is there reason to strongly encourage it at or before this time, regardless of advertising or common pediatrician and family pressures.

In contrast, for naturally fed infants, based on iron studies, as well as on bone density, immunity, allergy, intelligence, motor development, cancer, and other studies presented throughout this book, it is apparent that *the longer the duration of exclusive breastfeeding (no supplements or solid foods), the better* — with at least 7 to 9 months being a good goal (not counting little tastes and nibbles). Most nutritional studies on exclusive breastfeeding have gone as far as nine months, finding that these infants have no nutritional deficiencies by that age.[76]

Breastfed infants who received complementary foods by 2 to 3 months were shown to have "significantly lower" *length* for their age within weeks, as well as lower weight for length.[77] They then continued with steady growth rates from this lower level. *Breastfed babies begun on solids at 4 to 5 months showed drop-offs in their weight gains as well.* Thus, early attempts to plump up breastfed infants are counterproductive. Those complemented at 6 to 7 months showed no difference in growth from those continuing to be predominantly breastfed. The World Bank reports problems in breastfed infants if supplements or solids are not started by 3 months (formula companies are part of the World Bank support), based on their studies of African women. But independent studies in Zimbabwe find quite the opposite,[78] as have other studies.[79]

While there is no need to restrict solid food intake in breastfed infants after 7 months, neither is there reason to strongly encourage it at or before this time, regardless of advertising or common pediatrician and family pressures. Scientific evidence does not support this early feeding practice. Detailed studies reveal a gradual diminishing of the benefits of exclusive breastfeeding over partial breastfeeding beginning between 8 and 12 months of age.[80] After 1 year of age, the advantage of feeding solid foods increases gradually until it is significant enough to suggest that solids should certainly begin by 2 years of age. Basically, introducing solid foods to breastfed infants under age 1 only replaces the more nutritious and otherwise highly beneficial mother's milk with inferior calories. Baby likely knows best, and each will vary in his own natural timing of ingesting solid foods, based on the readiness of his digestive system and his motor interests in straying from mother, as

> *Potentially allergy-causing high carbohydrate cereals from refined grains may not be an optimal choice for starting foods.*

well as genetic and other factors. Infants with food sensitivities naturally tend to want fewer solid foods, especially after reacting to a few.

Most infants will show interest in foods around 4 to 6 months of age, but observation usually reveals that this is chiefly curiosity and a search for teething comfort. It generally takes effort to get much down a baby at this age, unless the food happens to bring them some physical relief from an all dairy diet. While the age of curiosity presents a beneficial window for important solid food introduction in those who are formula fed, it may be best to keep it to a play-and-taste level for breastfed infants. Urges to chew and swallow (different than teething on anything available) come a few months later. Potentially allergy-causing high carbohydrate cereals from refined grains may not be an optimal choice for starting foods. Neither are the nutritionally poor puddings, fruit sauces, and pale overcooked squashes with added starch often given as first foods.

When any infant stubbornly avoids certain foods (especially dairy, wheat, corn, tomatoes, or citrus), he is probably sensitive to these and his cues to this fact should be heeded. Keeping foods in the diet that cause diarrhea, fussing, rashes, or other symptoms only reduces nutritional absorption in the intestines. In the last chapters of this book, information is provided about how to recognize the symptoms of food allergy and intolerance, and how to diagnose, avoid, and treat these. These steps should be initiated in nearly all infants starting on solid food.

A New Fat Deceit

As more and more breastfeeding mothers are becoming wise to the fallacies of formula supplementation and the early introduction of solid foods, a new practice has become popular. If a mother cannot be convinced she should feed formula to her infant, many doctors are now suggesting that these mothers should feed their youngsters an extra tablespoon or more of butter each day. I have not tracked down the source of this advice, but I can guess. Actually, fat is very satiating. It is believed to satisfy hunger more than proteins or carbohydrates, for the same caloric intake. This unhealthy fat not only replaces healthy nutritious calories, but it may actually reduce the child's total caloric intake and weight gain, causing a perceived increased need for butter supplements. It may also combine with the infant's calcium to form soaps in the stool, reducing calcium status, not to mention setting the child up for life-long preference of concentrated fats in her diet. It is already known through studies that higher fat in mother's milk does not produce a fatter child, nor does higher fat in infant formulas. There is no scientific basis for this practice of feeding butter.

Babies are born with mechanisms to control their nutrient consumption and regulate their weight gain so they can meet their genetic targets throughout life. While attempts at force-feeding infants and young children seldom have much impact on weight initially, these practices do serve to disrupt natural controls. Avoid encouraging children to eat before they are hungry, and don't encourage continued consumption after they are full. Children can learn, as many of us have, to consume calories for reasons other than hunger, such as pleasing others and enjoying calorie-dense rewards. Once natural weight control is gone, obesity is a possibility.[81]

No Cigar

Since the end of the nineteenth century, child rearing in the Western world has been characterized by attempts to improve on Mother Nature's fine-tuned, million-year plan for developing healthy babies. Many of these attempts have been characterized as "scientific," although I believe that the information in this book shows that much of it was not scientific at all, but rather the product of culturally expedient programs promoted by doctors and others. Out of this melee, however, the groundwork was laid for true scientific investigation and debate.

Formula sustains the lives of many infants and is a valuable substitute when breastmilk is not available (although banked milk is still a better alternative). It has taken a huge effort to convince the public that breast and bottle-feeding are similar choices, but this is not even close to being true.

10

Baby Feeding: Facts & Fallacies

*"To ensure that all segments of society, in particular parents and children,
are informed, have access to education and are supported in the use of basic
knowledge of child health and nutrition, the advantages of breastfeeding..."*
— United Nations Convention on the Rights of the Child

THE UNITED STATES AND SOMALIA ARE THE ONLY NATIONS IN THE
world that have not ratified the Convention on the Rights of the
Child, which was enacted in 1990. Books provide access to information, but the only prominent advice in the U.S. promoting the
advantages of breastfeeding is the little required statement for TV
formula ads, "Breast is Best," which is not very informative. As for
education about the advantages of breastfeeding, I had no pamphlets given me, no statements from my obstetrician, no suggestions by hospital staff, I saw no posters or TV public service

announcements. I did receive formula samples and coupons from my obstetrician's office, from the hospital, and in the mail.

Insufficient Milk Syndrome: A Fallacy Becomes Reality

One of the biggest fallacies surrounding breastfeeding is that it can provide insufficient milk. This fallacy was purposely created by formula manufacturers. The fact is, mother's breasts are designed to produce as much milk as baby desires, whenever natural feeding is allowed. Careful studies demonstrate that mothers who initially complain of insufficient milk are in fact producing adequate quantities, and their babies are growing normally.[1] The faulty perception of insufficiency can be made a reality, however, with scheduled feedings and with formula supplementation,[2] especially in the beginning.

Regular, frequent stimulation of oxytocin and prolactin by the act of breastfeeding is required to keep milk levels flowing. When a baby cries with hunger, but a schedule prevents feeding, mother's body still responds to the cries with oxytocin release. But when the milk is not taken, prolactin is not produced; thus, there is no milk production when suckling does not occur. Just as a dog will stop responding to your call when no reward is given, hormone and milk production decrease when the body perceives that the need is less. Then when formula supplements are provided to an infant, the amount it takes from the breast is further reduced, again decreasing the amount the breast believes it should produce.

If milk production is suspected to be inadequate, the last thing to do is to provide a supplement to baby. The first thing to do is to increase nursing time and frequency and make sure the mother is not dehydrated. The milk supply can be quickly renewed within a few days in this way if supplementation or infrequent feedings have caused decreased production.

In addition to self-serving marketing, poor medical advice, and misinformed family advisors, another reason many mothers feel they have inadequate milk is that a few days after birth, and then for several weeks more, there is a sensation of engorgement.

This sensation is natural in the beginning and is probably designed to guide mother's behavior to get breastfeeding established. After a while, as the breasts "figure out" the milk levels required, and hormone levels adjust, this engorged sensation lessens or disappears and breasts remain less full, producing most milk only on demand. As this breast filling reduces, some mothers wait for prolonged intervals to feed until they feel their breasts are engorged. Every time this happens, the breasts fill more and more slowly and produce milk with less fervor. Hence, a natural process turns into a true problem. Trying to maintain an engorged sensation can also lead to mastitis, an inflammation of breast ducts due to pooling of bacteria or candida. At this point, certain ducts do not produce normally. Slower but not inadequate milk production is the result.

The production of any notable quantity of milk does not occur for 2 to 4 days after birth. This too is by design. If formula supplements are given during the period when there should be frequent suckling and taking of colostrum, the stimulation of milk production will be inadequate. In fact, the likelihood of breastfeeding is dangerously impaired by early formula supplementation.[3] The first few days of colostrum provide a high degree of important immune protection during this most vulnerable period. At the same time, with minimal fluid intake and little to digest, the infant's system rids itself of excess fluid and develops balanced kidney control, clears intestine-clogging meconium, and ramps up for its first attempts at digestion, with the help of some initial growth-promoting factors received from the colostrum. At birth the system is not instantly ready to begin full digestive and elimination duties, but needs a few days of "priming." This is well known for premature infants but not always remembered in term newborns.

Any time mother's milk production has diminished or disappears, which occurs during restricted access to a preterm baby in intensive care (which should not occur), re-lactation can be induced with frequent pumping and suckling, and sometimes with hormonal supplements. By this same means, adopted babies can be breastfed as well.[4]

Sleep Aids

The belief that feeding cereal to infants before bedtime will prolong their sleep has been perpetuated for a long time. It is interesting that this practice is recommended at the ages of 4 weeks and 4 months, ages when most infants adopt less fussy, longer sleeping on their own. Controlled studies do not confirm increased sleeping with cereal feedings,[5] although one study did find an undesirable reduction in the infants' calcium levels.[6] Another study found no increase in sleep or decrease in crying with thickened bedtime formula, but reported a dangerous seven-fold increase in the bacteria level in the stools, which were harder as well.[7] Conversely, infants who had significant problems at bedtime with spitting-up, crying, and poor sleep, who were diagnosed with gastric reflux, did demonstrate improvement in all these symptoms when fed thickened formula (a little rice starch thickens the mixture just as corn starch thickens gravy).[8] Reflux is a common cause of colic seen especially when baby is in a reclined position. Merely reducing the liquid in the stomach reduces the amount returned to the esophagus. Either a weak gastroesophageal sphincter or an allergy to formula causes this reflux. Success in bedtime thickened feedings with these infants probably helps promote the idea that increased sleep could be induced by such feedings in any infant. Actually, young infants are designed to fall asleep nursing, and the desire to feed during the night is natural for tiny, rapidly growing infants who can consume, digest, absorb, and assimilate only so much food at a time.

The Lactose Fallacy, the Protein Reality

Mother's milk is full of lactose. Lactose is a sugar designed especially for mammal babies. This sugar aids calcium absorption, ensures sugar is released at the proper time, and supplies carbohydrates important for infant brain development. Lactose-intolerance has become a household term, representing an inadequate presence

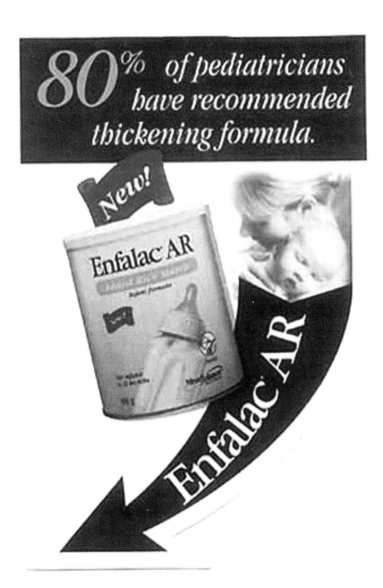

Figure 10-1 Apparently 80% of pediatricians have not read the research. This formula contains non-fat milk solids, rice starch for thickening, which is added carbohydrate, and lactose. In all, it has a little more carbohydrate and protein and a little less fat than standard formula. Taken from *INFACT Canada,* "Enfalac ARGGG..." www.infactcanada, summer 1998 newsletter.

of lactase, the enzyme needed to digest lactose. As mentioned before, babies unable to digest lactose would quickly suffer brain damage and die unless there was quick and appropriate substitute feeding. The loss of the lactase enzyme is a natural part of growing older, but a deficiency of this lactose-digesting enzyme at birth could never have persisted during our evolutionary history, because lactase-deficient babies would never have lived to pass on their genes. Lactose-free formulas have only been available for a few decades. Other animals' milks contain lactose as well and would not sustain a lactase-deficient infant. Genetic mutation or rare genes can produce such an infant today, but quite rarely.

Still, lactose-free formulas are highly promoted. Why? Because many babies have difficulty digesting cow's milk proteins in formulas or have allergic reactions to these proteins. Additionally, formula-fed infants have frequent problems with diarrhea: both infectious diarrhea due to a lack of immune protection from mother and non-infectious diarrhea from digestive and allergic intolerance to cow's milk proteins. When these illnesses and reactions occur, the resultant inflammatory process and the rapid transit of intestinal contents cause many digestive enzymes to become depleted in the infant digestive tract, including lactase enzyme. Formula manufacturers advertise to the public and educate pediatricians about recommending lactose-free formulas when babies appear to have digestive problems from their milk formulas. Lactose digestion tests are sometimes performed and serve to confirm this recommendation. These tests will often suggest lactase enzyme deficiency, but this is not the source of the problem. Lactose-free formula will likely provide little improvement in the infant unless it contains partially hydrolyzed milk proteins, which some do, hoping these proteins will be better tolerated.

The dairy industry appears to be very careful to prevent widespread recognition of dairy protein intolerance. Instead, the public's awareness is focused on lactose intolerance. Milk, formula, and dairy products with the lactose removed or with added lactase enzyme (for predigesting lactose, the milk sugar) can be easily sold, with little added expense. The positive reputation of dairy products is strongly based on their protein content, so it is in the dairy industry's best interest to keep this reputation intact. Predigested (hydrolyzed) protein products are expensive and very poor tasting. Even infants don't accept the taste of hydrolyzed milk formulas very well.

When are lactose-free formulas appropriate? When an infant has had diarrhea due to an infection or a cause other than protein allergy, they will have decreased lactase enzyme, as just described. At this time, infants will produce less gas due to undigested lactose if they are given lactose-free formula. In this situation, however, the infant is very vulnerable to developing an allergic reaction to cow's milk proteins, because it is easy for these poorly digested proteins to leak through the damaged intestinal walls. Hydrolyzed formula or elemental formula (both are lactose-free) is the appropriate formula after diarrhea or for formula intolerance.

feeding & Cavities

Breastfed children have far fewer dental cavities than those who are bottle-fed.[9-11] This includes nursing caries as well as other cavities. The unfortunate term "nursing caries" refers to a typical pattern of dental decay seen when juice, formula, or breastmilk sits in the mouth frequently for extended periods. Nighttime snacks are highly cavity causing because saliva is not very mobile during sleep, leaving baby without its rinsing and antibacterial qualities. Juice bottles by far promote the greatest number of nursing caries.[12] Both breastfed and bottle-fed infants have a need for comfort nursing. The only way bottle-fed infants can find this comfort is to "nurse" their bottles very slowly when allowed to lie and hold their own bottle, causing formula to sit against their teeth for long periods. Nursing caries are more common in bottle-fed infants, especially in those who have nighttime bottles at older ages. Among breastfed infants who develop nursing caries, most are those who comfort nurse for long periods during the night after teeth have developed.[13] And among these, most are those who have frequent snacking and sugary foods or juices in their diets.[14,15]

In cavity-prone families, or when any evidence of decay has been detected in an infant, night nursing and bottle practices can be gently reduced (not necessarily eliminated) once several teeth are present. A squirt of water into the mouth or stirring the child enough to cause some extra swallowing after nursing will help to clear the mouth of milk. Juice bottles should never be given at night. Still, there will be genetic tendencies or other unknown factors that will make some children more susceptible to bacterial presence and destruction in their mouths no matter what measures are taken.[16] Although damage to baby teeth does not affect adult teeth, a strong tendency for decay will likely carry over to adult teeth. Caries in baby teeth can serve as a warning that good preventive measures must be taken with permanent teeth.

While dental treatments on infants are certainly traumatic, the mere possibility of infant caries (about a 14% chance) is not enough of a worry that I would withhold or withdraw important feeding and comforting from any infant, especially before any such symptoms have occurred.

Mother's milk has immune factors that reduce the presence of unfriendly bacteria, and laboratory tests show human milk does not encourage cavities.[17] On the other hand, formula is definitely cavity promoting.[18] Formulas with sugars other than lactose are the worst.[19] Although *Streptococcus mutans* bacteria is generally thought to be the chief cause of dental decay, the candida yeast that builds up on pacifiers has been found to promote cavity formation to a great degree.[20] Because of this candida and the high incidence of nursing caries from bottles or nighttime breastfeeding, dentists, and thus pediatricians, commonly recommend throwing out bottles and pacifiers at 12 months of age and weaning breastfed infants prematurely. But we must remember that permanent teeth are not harmed by baby teeth cavities.

Babies naturally experience hunger and need comforting during the night. Withholding response to these needs can possibly be more harmful to a child than any risk of damage to temporary teeth, although your dentist may feel that teeth are the primary concern. While dental treatments on infants are certainly traumatic, the mere possibility of infant caries (about a 14% chance) is not enough of a worry that I would withhold or withdraw important feeding and comforting from any infant, especially before any such symptoms have occurred. Feeding and comforting practices can be modified when needed to protect teeth, without blunt, drastic weaning measures.

Nursing mothers may be prone to cavities related to nursing (maybe these are the true "nursing caries"). Especially during the first months of breastfeeding, nursing mothers often find a need for midnight snacks. This food sitting against the teeth in a sleeping mom may cause some cavities in her teeth, which have mildly reduced calcium content (no matter how much calcium she supplements) until after the end of lactation. Preventive measures should be taken in a cavity-prone mom.

More on Teeth

"Did you know that according to the American Association of Orthodontists, two out of three children need braces?" cants an orthodontic ad in my local paper. As mentioned in the chapter entitled "Crying and Caring," prolonged bottle-feeding, pacifier use, or thumb-sucking (found chiefly in bottle-fed, schedule fed, or prematurely weaned children) cause dental malocclusion and crossbite (buckteeth) that lead to the recommendation of correction with dental braces. Breastfeeding does not.

A Breastfeeding Effect in Mother

Breastfeeding mothers often experience about a 5% reduction in bone density. This is not rightfully referred to as osteoporosis because this level of reduction does not lead to bone fractures. This effect is seemingly harmless for mom (except possibly to teeth), and this bone loss is not prevented or reduced by calcium supplements[21] or by exercise.[22] Bone density returns to normal after weaning, with some return beginning during lactation at around 9 months.[23] The return of density after weaning is only slightly augmented by calcium supplementation. Reduced estrogen is most likely responsible for the reduced retention of calcium in mother's bone, just as it is after menopause. This period of low estrogen is also responsible for the reduction in breast and ovarian cancers in women who breastfeed. This period of lower bone calcium should cause no concern about osteoporosis since it has been shown that women who have breastfed suffer fewer hip fractures in old age (indicating less osteoporosis).[24]

The amount of calcium available to baby through mother's milk is just right and is also unaffected by calcium supplementation to mother (including cow's milk). Incidentally, research suggests that vitamin A, not calcium, may be the most important supplement for increasing baby's bone growth when there is an undernourished mother.[25]

Breast & Nipple Pain: The Unrecognized Reality

Painful breasts, itching or painful nipples, cracking, bleeding, and scabbing of nipples, and mastitis are problems seen in some breast-feeding women. In general, little help or information is available. Nipple pain and sometimes scabbing may be common in the first two weeks of nursing. When latch-on is correct and the problem persists beyond that time, candida is generally the cause. Will you hear this from your doctor? Probably not. Medical practitioners receive little or no breastfeeding education; in fact, this information has only begun to penetrate La Leche League and the realms of other lactation specialists within the last several years. The earliest medical reference to this problem I found was 1990, with one 1980 citation coming close to an understanding. Although the source of the problem is not that difficult to ascertain with a little research, it apparently was not a matter of concern in the once male-dominated medical field (just as PMS and other female maladies were often written off).

Candida is normal flora. This may be recited to you when complaining to your doctor. Trust me, painful overgrowth of candida is not normal. When "alternative health" proponents began diagnosing, and then way over-diagnosing, some yeast problems that medicine was ignoring, the issue of yeast overgrowth, especially when it is chronic and other than vaginal, became a bit of a joke in the medical community. This has led them to ignore these complaints even today. Secondary overgrowth of common bacteria often compounds this candida nipple problem, especially when there is cracking or fissuring.[26] Why would nature do this to us? Nature did not. Candida cannot grow if nipples aren't frequently confined in a warm moist environment. In addition, antibiotic use will encourage candida growth in many parts of the body. Any antibiotic use or yeast infection in the months before birth or during lactation can lead to chronic "nipple thrush," as it is often called.[27] The usual recommended care for episiotomies and tears also provides an excellent environment for yeast to become established in the body. On the other hand, exposure to UV radiation from the sun kills candida and other microbes. The answer? Certain climates and job situations preclude going topless, but growth of candida can be limited in other ways.

First, recognize the problem. Nipples that are bright red and persistently sore and possibly itchy are likely infected with candida. Candida has a way of changing its own environment to be more amenable to future habitation. Sometimes little white spots will be seen inside the mouth of the infant. Mother and infant often share a candida problem and pass it back and forth.

Painful let-down (filling with milk during nursing) or deep shooting or radiating pain is likely infection in the ducts, often termed "chronic mastitis." This might be candida, but it is more likely bacterial.[28] Frequent (and prolonged if the nipples are not too sore) nursing will reduce the pooling of flora in the ducts that encourages flora to establish and overgrow. Application of heat will help mobilize the microbes out of the area. Also determine the source of the microbes — from an infected nipple, baby's mouth, or associated with vaginal or even colon infection (mom gets a little "diaper rash" or itchy bottom) — and treat the source. When painful, hardened areas of the breast or bright red tree-branching over portions of the breast occur, eventually with fever, "acute mastitis" is the appropriate term. Pay quick attention to acute mastitis. Treat it immediately and regularly with heat and massage so that a need for antibiotics might be prevented. There are small microwaveable hot packs that will fit right into the bra, which can be pre-charged for use away from home. The baby is not harmed by any increased levels of bacteria in the milk. By design, normal flora are always present in mother's milk, helping maintain baby's normal flora balance. Breastmilk contains factors that prevent these from getting out of control. (Today's cow's milk has higher microbe counts, and not always the friendliest kinds — even after pasteurization.) If antibiotics are needed, only a very small percentage (generally much less than 1% of mother's dose) goes into baby, so minimal if any side effects result (possibly a bit of diarrhea, diaper rash, or thrush).[29] When antibiotics are prescribed, candida growth is encouraged due to lack of competition, and a twofold medical approach may be needed. Taking acidophilus or eating soy yogurt may help mom or baby deal with primary candida infections or reduce candida overgrowth associated with antibiotics.

For nipples, frequent washing with warm water and drying well, followed by applying moisturizing cream with some vitamin E, aloe, or other friendly ingredients is helpful, at least for starters. Yes, candida likes moist places to grow, but it establishes well in any skin that is irritated — not entirely intact. When even microscopic skin breaks occur, candida and bacteria find deeper and better homes. Hence, nipples need to be dry but moisturized, not dry and chapped, as with alcohol or some other preparations. Some mothers find help from applying over-the-counter anti-fungal creams (sold for vaginal yeast infections) to the nipples, while many others do better with Neosporin (helping when there is also bacterial growth). These should be applied right after nursing so they have time to soak in before nursing again. Used gingerly, there is no need to wash these off before nursing. Some suggest alcohol or gentian violet application (a messy fungus-killing dye), but they are terribly drying for the skin and will produce more cracking and irritation, thus creating the very environment where more candida and then bacteria can thrive. Treat baby too if mother's condition is stubborn. Treat any vaginal infection (or even suspected yeast overgrowth) quickly and re-treat mother if an infant has any oral thrush or candida-induced diaper rash.[30]

Breastfeeding Benefits to Mother

Breastfeeding for more than two years cuts a premenopausal woman's chances of breast cancer in half.[31] Recent reports suggest there is considerable postmenopausal benefit from prolonged breastfeeding.[32] Currently, nearly 4% of all women die of breast cancer, one quarter of these before the age of 55.[33] Ovarian cancer is reduced by breastfeeding as well.[34] Also, a breastfeeding mother's stress responses are significantly restrained by the associated hormonal changes, with healthy results.[35] Mothers who breastfeed exclusively have much greater levels of oxytocin and prolactin than those who provide supplements,[36] and certainly much higher than those who do not nurse at all. Sustained elevation of oxytocin provides for reduced blood pressure, a benefit that lasts long after breastfeeding ends.[37]

Breastfeeding is a wonderful way to lose the excess weight of pregnancy — which was gained to supply energy for making breastmilk — provided a woman eats according to her hunger and does not pad her diet for some reason (such as the unfortunate recommendation to consume 4 to 5 servings of dairy a day). When nursing on cue, menses generally do not return for a year or two, allowing mother to have more regular energy and the patience to care for a young infant without the stress of PMS.

> *Infant weighing stations were created around the world to promote the newly invented "problem" of breastfeeding: "insufficient milk syndrome."*

Formulation

Dr. Naomi Baumslag and Dia Michels present an in-depth history of formula in their enlightening book *Milk, Money, and Madness: The Culture and Politics of Breastfeeding*.[38] Boiled condensed milks were introduced in the late nineteenth century, eliminating some of the problems of contamination and spoilage associated with fresh cow's milk, and making milk suddenly highly available to many. Soon after came powdered milk. Even as infant deaths were declining as a result of public sanitation advances, infant death rates rose against this trend due to the new popularity of artificial feeds in the early twentieth century. It was later learned that many nutrients were destroyed during sterilization, leading to rickets, scurvy, blindness, anemia, and beri beri, and several contamination concerns continued. The sale of these products was so profitable, however, that large-scale advertising expanded worldwide. Occasional improvements or additions to the formulas were made. A large advertising campaign was also required to get the public to accept rubber nipples, which didn't become widely accepted until decades into the 1900s. Infant weighing stations were created around the world to promote the newly invented "problem" of breastfeeding: "insufficient milk syndrome." It became rampant. More and more babies were switched to the artificial concoctions, and infant death rates around the world soared from diarrhea, failure to thrive due to malnutrition and intolerance, and increases in many other illnesses due to lack of immune protection. Newborns could rarely survive on these early renditions. Every year another important missing element was discovered or some other improvement to the recipe was made. Only in the last several decades have young infants survived rather well on artificial formulas. Of course, reduced survival, health, and intelligence continue around the world from formula feedings today.

Without the natural birth spacing provided by breastfeeding, *birth rates around the world have climbed since artificial feeding became popular*, further reducing infant survival. Close spacing of children poses a high risk to their survival for multiple reasons, including shortened breastfeeding, decreased parental attention, limited food and parental resources, and decreased nutritional stores in the mother.[39,40] Mother's system can easily become depleted of nutrients when infants are born within 1 or 2 years of each other, especially after two children. The newborn's nutrient stores are then depleted as well.

Incidentally, pediatric medical schools and their continuing education seminars are highly funded by formula manufacturers and dairy associations. Even some of the vaccination literature (and research) that keeps babies coming in regularly is funded by these. Although the American Academy of Pediatrics (AAP) has broken some ties with the American Medical Association, due chiefly to cow's milk issues, most pediatric offices continue to push formula and dairy.

Promotional & Pediatric Practices & Policies

The World Health Organization (WHO) has long known that the marketing from formula companies has a big influence on mothers' breastfeeding decisions. In 1981, in an attempt to reduce the severe diarrhea, malnutrition, and deaths caused by formula use around the world, WHO/UNICEF developed a code to restrict the mass marketing campaigns of breastmilk substitutes. But many people now believe that formula companies attempt to influence choices without appearing to break the code by providing a wide array of breastfeeding pamphlets and videos that convey well-worded but misleading information with strong subliminal messages. Few if any of these meet the criteria of the code.[41] "Follow-up" formulas are another way to violate the code without appearing to do so. The marketing verbiage for these products proclaims that the breast is best, as is now required, but indirectly

> *Pediatric medical education on breastfeeding goes little beyond that provided by the formula companies.*

implies that several steps of breastmilk supplements or substitutes become appropriate to achieve adequate nutrition. Additionally, while the code bans using pictures of babies or glamorized formula bottles on "breastmilk substitutes," pictures of babies with sippy cups containing white liquid appear on follow-up formulas. The front of one such product says, rather unspecifically, "better than milk."

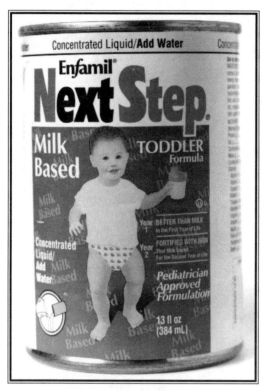

Figure 10-2 Skirting the WHO code.

In addition to the many methods used to skirt the code, direct violations are rampant around the world.[42] According to some sources, more than half of all new mothers in the U.S. illegally receive free formula samples, coupons, or gifts from formula manufacturers either through direct mail or through baby "welcome" packages passed out in hospitals, in return for generous gifts given to the health care workers. This occurs to varying degrees around the world as well. These have a proven negative impact on the duration of breastfeeding.[43] Posters, calendars, promotional booklets, and other supplies end up prominently used or displayed in hospitals. On the other hand, in my city, La Leche League brochures mysteriously disappear in the hospitals shortly after being put out. Women, Infants and Children (WIC) programs and food banks strongly (albeit indirectly) promote formula feeding with strong encouragement from formula companies, using funds from the government. Over 75% of users of these programs use bottle feeding from the start, and nearly all do within weeks.[44]

Impoverished mothers around the world are the chief targets of formula manufacturers and the dairy and baby food industries. As a result, these companies obtain much wealth from government and charity funds, the plight of the women is increased, and the future of their children is impaired. Nestlé is, and always has been, considered the biggest offender under this code, as well as earlier codes and rulings. For this reason, grass root efforts to boycott all Nestlé products have survived since 1974. Women from areas that are isolated from or highly resistant to formula promotions who come to the U.S. to find the American dream are often swayed by influences here, equating artificial feeding with an elite and superior lifestyle. For example, although 97% of the Indo-Chinese breastfeed in their native lands, in a recent survey only 4% of pregnant Indo-Chinese migrants from Cambodia and Laos living in the U.S. expressed the intention to breastfeed their babies.[45]

Pediatric medical education on breastfeeding goes little beyond that provided by the formula companies. A recent large (AAP) survey found that 35% of pediatricians do not promote exclusive breastfeeding for even the first month.[46] Only one third recommended that any nursing continue for 1 year. Most agreed with or had neutral feelings toward a survey statement that "breastfeeding and formula-feeding are equally acceptable methods for feeding infants." A survey was made comparing the knowledge of pediatric practitioners with 3 to 5 years of practice to that of pediatric students, in an attempt to reveal the amount of accurate breastfeeding information obtained in their education. The difference between these two groups was found to be quite small, indicating little education was provided. Sixty-four percent of practitioners versus 52% of residents were aware that providing supplements in the first weeks of life can lead to breastfeeding failure.[47] More than one fourth of both groups felt that exclusive breastfeeding was not the best feed for infants. Of course, this lack of education and abundance of misinformation percolates into the nursing staff as well. Breastfeeding failure is extremely common for premature infants being held in U.S. neonatal intensive care units (NICU), and most nurses seem to accept that this is the only possible outcome. But a

> Lack of extended
>
> breastfeeding in the U.S.
>
> may be partially
>
> responsible for our
>
> childhood death rate
>
> (under age 5) being higher
>
> than in 30 other nations.

breastfeeding intervention force recently concentrated efforts in a Chicago NICU with the result of no breastfeeding failures at all.[48] One investigator attempted to add up the cost of formula use in the U.S. She estimated that the health care costs of excess cases of diarrhea, middle ear infections, respiratory viruses, and diabetes totaled a billion dollars annually.[49] Of course neither the cost to society of widespread lowered intelligence nor the loss of lives can be measured in dollars. While formula companies have failed to gain any increase in the numbers of U.S. women who *initially* use formula over the last two decades (actually dropping from 50% to under 40%), their success is continuing to grow, as the average duration of breastfeeding is now even shorter than it was in the 80s.[50] While much of our low ranking as twenty-third among world nations for infant survival (under age 1) is certainly attributable to our low breastfeeding levels, lack of extended breastfeeding here may be partially responsible for our childhood death rate (under age 5) being higher than 30 other nations (rank according to UNICEF).

Convenience?

Where is the convenience of having to buy formula weekly at the store (and pay for it), carry it home, store it, wash, sterilize, and maintain bottles and nipples, crawl out of bed in the middle of the night to mix formula to the sound of hunger cries, warm it to just the right temperature, hold the bottle in the infant's mouth while trying not to fall asleep, try to figure out and keep track of how much the infant has had and will need, carry formula and all associated tools wherever you go, always have extra with you in case of emergency, keep formula cold while out and find ways to warm it away from home, and tote all the empty cans to the recycle station? A breast-feeding mother has warm, perfectly mixed, fresh milk available immediately upon request, anytime, anyplace, no spoilage, no fuss, no mess, no waste, she can even feed in her sleep — much cheaper too. With far less spitting-up from breastmilk than formula, clothes and carpets look better and last longer. Then there are the diapers. While breastfed stools have a familiar, almost sweet odor, and much less stool is passed due to highly absorbable breastmilk, formula-fed stools are full of unusable and undigested materials and offensive smelling bacteria; they are quite foul and frequent. Nothing cute or convenient about that, except for knowing quite well when it's time for a diaper change. Their urine is more odiferous as well.

Controlled?

Still, some assert ingrained propaganda such as "How can you know how much a breastfed infant is getting?" There is a simple way to find out, weigh before and after. However there is no need as long as the infant is being allowed to feed as much as desired. Infants have growth spurts and slow periods. While they know just the right amount of milk they need, how does a formula-feeder know when it is time to provide more formula for a spurt, or to stop pushing the bottle during a slow period?

Civilized?

Highly successful marketing has elevated the perception of an infant sucking on a rubber and plastic breast device, even in public, to that of adorable. To accomplish this, baby bottles were supplied early on to toy manufacturers to go with every doll and thus every doll ad. Billboards, posters, and magazine ads of babies with bottles were seen everywhere until the WHO developed the advertising code restricting this in connection with sales of artificial baby feeds. Soon these images had to be worked into TV shows in other ways. Then came wrapping paper, greeting cards, shower gifts, and sundry other items. In my state, where cigarette smoking has been outlawed

Shugrue Photography

in public places, the appearance of one sucking on such a smelly thing has lost much of its once enjoyed glamour and has become quite distasteful for many. Certainly the appearance of an infant discreetly and peacefully cozied up against her mother's breast could regain an image of civility or dignity, even of health and beauty. The sight of a pregnant mother in public was once considered very embarrassing and distasteful. The word could not even be used politely. It's all a matter of socially developed taste.

What Is Natural?

Several times, when people were trying to find a nice way to tell me that a, say, 7-month-old baby was too old to be nursing, I heard, "I think it's natural for a baby to wean when their teeth start coming in." Of course, since an infant, or even a toddler, is too young to chew, digest, and survive on solid foods alone, especially before food processors were invented (although pre-chewed food has been used), these people are actually suggesting that it is natural for babies to be weaned onto the artificially processed milk of another very different species, onto a plastic bottle with a rubber nipple — not exactly "natural" in my eyes. Most baby mammals nurse with their milk teeth in place (hence the name), and cross-species nursing is not observed in nature. The milk of each mammal is very specific to that species and few could likely survive on the milk of another. Human milk appears to be the most complicated and sophisticated of all milks, evolving along with the development of the most sophisticated species. Still, it is not appropriate for other young animals.

The appearance of certain enamel defects in first teeth has been found to correlate with stress on a developing child. On ancient finds, these are chiefly associated with the stress of weaning, which includes altered nutrition and increased infection. Anthropologists can "read" the dental records throughout history to surmise at what age weaning was begun, and when it was well under way or nearing completion. Anthropological reports on prehistoric populations from Illinois around A.D. 1000 reveal that weaning (meaning adding solid foods) was likely begun by the age of 2 years and was well under way by the age of 4.[51] Studies of children's teeth from Guatemala coming from 700 B.C. to A.D. 1500 similarly suggest that corn foods were started here before the age of 2, but nursing lasted for several more years.[52] Studies on nineteenth-century Americans found heightened peak stress levels between 2.5 and 4 years of age.[53] This researcher suggested that these samples revealed an earlier final weaning age compared to prehistoric finds that point to age 6. Evidence was also found that children in this industrial society had inferior health during this more abrupt weaning, compared to that of earlier agricultural societies. Researchers in Italy also reported 2 to 4 years as the peak stress in a nineteenth-century northern Italian village, suggesting this stress was greater and somewhat earlier than some other populations observed for the same time period.[54] Chimpanzees live much shorter lives than we do, but they nurse until nearly the age of 5.[55] One can find that children in remote areas around the world nurse until near this age or longer.

When not strictly prevented, most children have a desire to suck for several years, indicating an instinctual need to breastfeed. Pacifiers or thumbs are often seen in mouths to this age and beyond when not countered. Over 40% of U.S. children still receive bottles at 2 years and 8% are still using them at the age of 4.[56] These numbers would be much higher if this practice were not generally restricted for dental and social concerns. The passion for sippy cups demonstrates a continuance of this sucking desire as well.

Figure 10-3 This public breastfeeding device was invented in 1910 to be worn under the clothing, with a nipple attached to a tube that comes out from the bottom of the shirt, in order to "avoid unpleasant and embarrassing situations" of "exposure of the breast in suckling the child." No explanation was made in the patent as to how the milk was to be released from the breast.

All agree that children need milk for multiple nutritional reasons for at least 2 or 3 years. Children are born with a unique enzyme, lactase, to digest their unique milk baby-sugar, lactose. Normally this enzyme begins to reduce after age 2 and lasts in the child for 8 to 15 years, except in people of northern European descent where lactase persistence was evolutionarily selected over 2,000 years or so of cattle domestication. Maturation of the digestive system takes several years. Before this takes place, adequate nutrition can't be obtained without easy-to-digest, nutrient-packed mother's milk. Similarly, it takes many years before a child's immune system matures and can provide immune protection equal to that supplied by mother's milk. The immune system also depends on influences from mother's milk to maintain top functioning well beyond the nursing years. Baby's best motor, intellectual, visual, and other neurological development depends on extended breastfeeding, as does parental bonding and social security. Assuring adequate parental resources through child spacing also depends on prolonged nursing. Human infants are quite helpless and have ongoing needs to be close to mom for protection. This need gradually reduces after the age of 3 or so. *Clearly, it is natural to nurse for several years and highly beneficial to nurse for at least 2.* It is also natural for nursing practices to vary from pair to pair, according to the needs of mother and child.

> *When you decide to begin weaning foods, and then to totally wean your child, keep clearly in mind what your reasons are — who you are trying to appease or please, and who is important.*

The Bottom Line

When you decide to begin weaning foods, and then to totally wean your child, keep clearly in mind what your reasons are — who you are trying to appease or please, and who is important.

Some feel that we have become "scientific" and have evolved above the "animal behavior" of nursing. Any science or supposed evolution that precludes a parent's desire to provide the best nutrition, protection, bonding, and development for her child is no step forward to me. Even if we one day develop means to entirely replicate mother's milk, hormones, immune factors and all, there would be no reason for it to replace nursing. Of course, the womb is the next target. I heard a neighbor describe a medication they now give their dog to alleviate his separation anxiety. Already the widespread use of Ritalin and anti-depressants are substitutes for lost parenting and remedies for allergenic, mood-altering artificial feeding. I still personally lean toward the irreplaceable joys and rewards of total motherhood and sense that babies have an inalienable right to natural babyhood.

11

The Dangers of Cow's Milk

WE HAVE DISCUSSED THE MANY DOWNFALLS OF INFANT FORMULA. It reduces nutrition, bonding, immune protection, and intellectual development, and increases the death rate. The story does not stop here. We haven't even gotten to the meat of the dangers of dairy products. Cow's milk and formula consumption lead to increased risk of childhood diabetes, bowel disease, osteoporosis, heart disease, cataracts, and bowel and reproductive organ cancers. And that's not all. Intolerance reactions to bovine proteins in formula or breastmilk of moms who drink cow's milk leads to higher incidence of colic, ear infections, and attention-deficit disorder.

While there are literally thousands of research studies, each revealing at least one of milk's hazards, the dairy industry goes to great lengths to stifle any damaging rumors. Blanket statements, such as, "There is simply no scientific research to back up these claims," are easily made. With a long and successful history of dairy promotion, these are readily accepted by the public. *More people need to go to the real research and learn the truth for themselves.* They should be very suspicious of these foreign foods being pushed on their children. They should question motives as well as possible outcomes. Although some of the dangers of cow's milk consumption relate more to adults than to children, I touch on these topics since early childhood is when parents' actions form the basis for lifelong dairy-consuming habits in their children.

The harmful components of cow's milk include all the major parts of it, as well as some more minor elements. Lactose is a sugar meant for babies, but it's generally harmful to adults. The proteins in cow's milk are different from human milk proteins and cause problems of digestion, intolerance, impaired absorption of other nutrients, and autoimmune reactions. Few of the proteins meant for baby cows are found naturally in human mother's milk, and none are found in any "natural" adult human food. Even the high protein content in cow's milk creates problems. Human babies need the saturated fats and cholesterol in mother's milk even though there is not much health benefit from these fats after early childhood. Bovine milk fat is not appropriately composed for human babies and is only deleterious to the health of children and adults. Cow hormones are not meant for humans, and older children and adults are not meant to consume hormones. And, cows have been selectively bred over time to create high levels of these hormones — those being the cows that grow the fastest and produce the greatest amount of milk. As discussed earlier, cows also concentrate pesticides and pollutants into their milk fat, from their high dietary food and water requirements. The high amount of drugs now given to cows adds to this chemical soup. But we need milk to build strong bones, don't we? Sorry, heavy milk consumption leads to increased osteoporosis.

Milk Proteins & Diabetes

Although one highly promoted 1996 study contradicted the American Academy of Pediatrics (AAP) 1994 announcement of a link between cow's milk consumption in infants and development of diabetes,[1] many well-conducted studies have since left little doubt that the great increase seen in childhood diabetes mellitus is caused by early exposure to dairy products.[2-7]

A flaw in the methodology of the study that found no correlation between milk and diabetes is that it was based on the type of feed the infants reportedly received, breast-milk versus milk formula, without regard to whether the breastfeeding mothers were consuming cow's milk and passing it along to baby. A more recent study again denying links between diabetes and early milk consumption had the same design flaw.[8] Breastfed babies often receive significant exposure to cow's milk proteins when dairy is a part of their mothers' diets.[9,10] Both neg-ative studies were performed in nations with high dairy consumption (U.S. and Austria), so that the differ-ence in bovine protein exposure between the formula-fed and breast-fed groups was not significant enough to show up statistically. Studies performed on populations such as the Arizona Pima Indians and in a rural part of Chile, where adult dairy consumption was minimal at the time the studied children were born, did indeed find a higher incidence of diabetes in formula-fed versus breastfed children.[11,12]

> In fact, the rate of childhood diabetes in dairy-consuming, formula-using nations is up to 35 times that in non-dairy nations.

The first indications of a relationship between childhood dia-betes mellitus and dairy were discovered by correlating diabetes rates with the total dairy consumption by nation. A 95% correla-tion was found.[13] In fact, the rate of childhood diabetes in dairy-consuming, formula-using nations is up to 35 times that in non-dairy nations.[14] In the U.S., 2.6 children per 1,000 under the age of 19 develop diabetes, according to the AAP.

Diabetes associated with dairy exposure stems from infant hypersensitivity or allergic-like reactions to bovine proteins. Studies more accurately investigating the relationship between cow's milk proteins and childhood diabetes measure the amount of anti-bovine antibodies found in diabetic children's systems versus those found in healthy infants. Now, a firm relationship between cow's milk exposure and the development of diabetes has become quite clear.[15,16]

Large dairy proteins, which are quite foreign and difficult for young infants to handle, often lead to immune or allergic attacks in the infants' bodies, but not all infants are prone to these reactions. Whether they are sensitive to certain food proteins or not depends in part on heredity. However, one cannot determine in advance whether such a reaction will occur in any given newborn. The earlier the age of exposure, the greater the number of infants who react.

When an infant sensitive to cow's milk fills up with destructive immune antibodies in response to milk exposure, the islet cells of the pancreas become subject to destruction at the same time.

An infant vulnerable to problems with cow proteins will develop antibodies against these foreign proteins and direct them to destroy the invaders. The near neutral pH of an infant's stomach allows almost all milk proteins to travel undigested beyond the stomach and into the intestines where the assault takes place locally at the intestinal borders, or where they are absorbed intact into a baby's bloodstream. When the lining of a sensitive infant's intestines is irritated by the attack on these proteins (as revealed by the common intestinal bleeding, diarrhea, and colic in babies exposed to dairy), more proteins are able to cross into the bloodstream to cause heightened immune responses throughout the body, such as eczema and asthma (see Chapter 13).

Diabetes is a reduced ability to maintain proper sugar levels in the blood due to decreased sugar-clearing insulin, or reduced response to it, allowing blood sugar levels to become harmfully high. Insulin is manufactured in the islet cells of the pancreas beta cells. There seems to be a similarity between these beta cells and the beta-lactoglobulin or betacasein proteins in cow's milk. Thus, when an infant sensitive to cow's milk fills up with destructive immune antibodies in response to milk exposure, the islet cells of the pancreas become subject to destruction at the same time.[17]

Additionally, the bovine insulin in cow's milk is different from human insulin by only three amino acids. Some infants create antibodies against this foreign bovine insulin.[18] It is believed that regular consumption of the high amounts of insulin in cow's milk causes sensitive infants to become immune to the effects of their own insulin. Hence, we have at least two routes that can lead to diabetes. First, insulin production is reduced due to the destruction of insulin-producing cells. This creates what is known as childhood-onset or type 1 diabetes. Second, there is a diminished ability to respond to one's own insulin, having become "immune" to it. This is type 2 diabetes, which has traditionally been referred to as adult-onset diabetes, but this name is being dropped as the rate of insulin resistance has been seen in children at alarming rates over the past decades in formula and dairy-consuming regions.

> Not only is early exposure to cow's milk proteins a risk factor for childhood diabetes, but 3 or more glasses of milk per day during childhood leads to a quadrupled risk of diabetes.

A Swedish researcher suggests, based on twin and other epidemiological studies, that genetic risk factors play a role, but that environment (such as dairy exposure) interacts with this susceptibility to cause the disease.[19,20] The environmental factors she noted, in addition to early exposure to cow's milk proteins, were a cold environment, a fast growth rate, a higher rate of infections, preeclampsia, and stressful life events. Interestingly, all these other factors mentioned are associated with dairy consumption as well.

Dairy consumption in general is higher in northern climates. Formula feeding leads to a greater number of infections, faster weight gains, and possibly greater infant stress from receiving propped bottles rather than affectionate nursing. Preeclampsia, or toxemia in the mother, is associated with high dairy consumption during pregnancy. Not only is *early* exposure to cow's milk proteins a risk factor for childhood diabetes, but *3 or more glasses of milk per day during childhood leads to a quadrupled risk of diabetes.*[21]

Soy formula substitution may not be the ideal alternative to dairy formula. Early exposure to soy protein (and wheat protein) has been associated with some increased incidence of diabetes as well, thought to be another allergic mechanism.[22]

Not only does diabetes force a child to have blood and urine tests frequently, and to have insulin injections daily, but it can cause painful nerve irritations, sores that do not heal, loss of extremities, kidney and heart damage, and blindness. Additionally, diabetes is the seventh leading cause of death in the U.S. today. A few have pondered whether someone with early diabetes should eliminate dairy from their diet, since the pancreas should have regenerative powers like other organs in the body, and it may be possible that their insulin generation could gradually return to normal.

> It has been shown that 7-year-old children who were raised on formula have significantly higher blood pressure than those who were breastfed.

Multiple Sclerosis

Researchers have noticed a very strong correlation between milk consumption and multiple sclerosis.[23,24] Multiple sclerosis is a disorder where, for some reason, the body attacks the protective covering on nerves. Whether milk is truly a factor in MS, and a mechanism for its destructive action if it is, has yet to be resolved. When the body attacks part of itself, as in MS, it is called an autoimmune reaction. Milk protein antibodies attacking similar cells in the pancreas, causing diabetes, is an autoimmune reaction. The autoimmune process for MS could stem from a similar reaction.

Milk & Heart Disease

Elevated levels of oxytocin and reduced levels of cortisol from attachment behaviors such as nursing and nurturing responsiveness can cut heart disease risks for the nurturing parent, as well as for the adult who was nursed in such fashion as an infant (*see Chapter 3*). In fact, it has been shown that 7-year-old children who were raised on formula have significantly higher blood pressure than those who were breastfed.[25] The consumption of cow's milk at all ages has strong ties to heart disease. Although not all of the pieces have been put together for the ever-growing rates of heart disease (which probably involve more than one milk component or pathway), the common denominator in dietary studies is consistent: dairy consumption.

While it is currently understood that higher calcium intake reduces blood pressure and heart disease, this finding does not hold true when milk is the chief source of calcium.[26] A study from India found significantly higher rates of coronary artery disease with higher milk and butter intake.[27] Since dairy can be a large source of dietary fat consumption, and high fat intakes are linked to heart disease, some assume that milk fat is the chief assailant. An epidemiological study looking at Asian and Mediterranean countries suggested that high dairy fat (but not high "good" fat) consumption increased heart disease.[28] An earlier analysis of 21 countries reported that milk proteins and milk fats had strong statistical ties to coronary artery disease.[29] While milk fat is clearly a problem, a more recent 32-country study reported the strongest dietary connections with heart disease to be *non-fat* milk and lactose.[30] Such findings about links to bovine protein are consistent with findings (*see Chapter 13*) that antigen-antibody complexes formed through allergic reactions to cow's milk proteins can deposit in the artery walls, leading to plaque formation and heart disease. Other investigators are convinced today that some kind of chronic inflammation (of unknown source) going on inside the body is the chief cause for cholesterol plaques in arteries to develop into heart attacks and strokes. When these two groups of investigators get together, they will see that this chronic reaction to milk is the chronic inflammation they are looking for. Additionally, bovine growth hormone has been found to increase stress hormone levels in rats,[31] a condition known to damage the human heart over time.

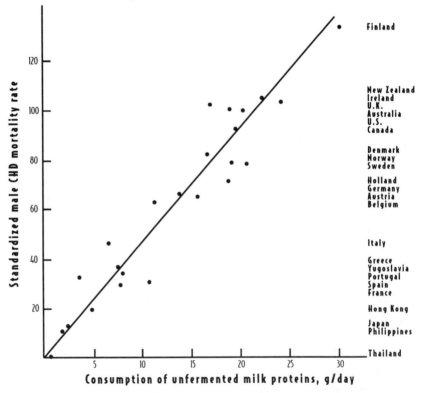

Figure 11-1 Rate of deaths from coronary heart disease (CHD) in relation to amount of milk consumption, for 24 countries.[32] Reproduced by permission of the publisher, Churchill Livingstone.

Lactose & Pain

There are two chief problems with post-childhood consumption of the baby sugar, lactose. One is that most adults around the world are unable to digest this sugar since the infant enzyme lactase

is normally lost after childhood. Many
Americans are of European descent, where
genes for lactase enzyme persistence developed over recent millennia, yet a growing
number of Americans come from the rest of
the world where lactase enzyme and therefore the ability to digest lactose is naturally
lost in late childhood: 80% of Native
Americans, 75% of African Americans,
100% of native Asians and Africans, and
50% of all Hispanics.[33] The result is fermentation of this sugar in the large intestine,

We will see that this trait, if it leads to avoiding dairy products, has provided health benefits such as reduced osteoporosis.

causing painful bloating and gas, and often diarrhea. Although
cheeses are well tolerated, and yogurt is partially tolerated, any significant amount of milk leads to misery. We will see that this trait,
if it leads to avoiding dairy products, has provided health benefits
such as reduced osteoporosis to those who are not lactase persistent.
Unfortunately, dairy is added and often hidden in more and more
prepared foods and restaurant meals, and free milk is given to school
children around the nation.

A report by the National Dairy Council (NDC) wants us all to
know that "many people erroneously believe they are lactose intolerant...psychological factors can contribute to gastrointestinal
symptoms that mimic lactose intolerance."[34] It is true that many
who have painful intestinal problems after dairy consumption are
not lactose intolerant; rather, they are bovine protein intolerant.
But the NDC won't tell you that. Many who *are* lactose intolerant
are protein intolerant as well. This is why many who eat cheese
(where lactose is consumed by the fungi) or who use lactase enzyme
additives still experience discomfort. Furthermore, protein intolerance reactions often lead to transiently reduced lactase enzyme. The
dairy council adds to its report that people with low levels of lactase
can consume "2 servings of milk per day in divided doses." They
include suggestions that "porous bones" and hypertension can result
if one does not do so. This report attempts to shame, embarrass, and
frighten people into continuing to consume dairy regularly, no

matter how much it hurts, while their supporting arguments are contrary to what science shows today.

Lactose & Cataracts

Lactose consumption produces more permanent, long-term effects in those who *are* able to break it down to its component sugars, glucose and galactose. When older adults drink milk, and *do* break down lactose into galactose, they can develop high levels of galactose in their blood. A high rate of cataract formation is seen in older adults who are lactose digesters (lactase-persistent), and galactose from milk is believed to be the cause.[35] Damage is caused by the elevated levels of galactose sugar circulating in the blood. Adults often gradually lose the enzyme that breaks down galactose. According to gynecologist Daniel Cramer, 10% of Americans are unable to digest galactose, and one does not know whether they are digesting galactose or not, since there are no noticeable immediate symptoms as there are with lactose.[36]

> By contrast, U.S. dairy farmers have noted that milk production goes up when a cow is infected with this leukemia virus, so they promote ways to take advantage of this situation.

In nature, this would not be a problem for adults, as just about the only source of galactose in the diet is from milk sugar — a baby food. An infant born with a rare inability to break down galactose (found in 1 in 18,000 infants) develops mental retardation and cataracts, which often become pronounced before a diagnosis can be made.[37] I am unable to find any comments about reduced brain function in the elderly related to elevated blood galactose, although a connection seems possible.

Milk & Leukemia

Bovine leukemia virus is widespread in commercial dairy herds.[38] This leukemia virus is a member of the human leukemia group of retroviruses and is known to infect human cells in the laboratory. Pasteurization kills this virus in cow's milk rather efficiently, although accidents certainly happen. Pasteurization errors are documented to have caused other diseases. Such incidents may be responsible for the occasional geographical pockets of leukemia cases. Raw milk is certainly dangerous to drink. It has been established that dairy farmers have higher leukemia rates.[39] In the late 70s it was also determined that geographic areas of high cow's milk protein consumption have high leukemia rates compared to areas of low consumption.[40] Iowa, a major dairy-producing state, has a high rate of leukemia, and these cases tend to concentrate around counties with the highest rates of leukemia in the cows.[41] Recent studies comparing the diets of leukemia patients with those of healthy patients in Italy and Poland both came up with heavy milk consumption as the strongest risk factor.[42,43]

The most worrisome aspect of this situation is the U.S. dairy farmer's attitude toward this possible danger. A Swedish study on this problem reported that their dairy industry was striving to eradicate this infection in their herds.[44] By contrast, U.S. dairy farmers have noted that milk production goes up when a cow is infected with this leukemia virus, so they promote ways to take advantage of this situation. While the "genetic potential for milk production was significantly greater in seropositive cows (those with the leukemia virus)…milk fat percentage was significantly reduced" when cows developed full-blown disease. The recommendation? — "These results suggest a need to reevaluate the economic impact of bovine leukemia virus infection on the dairy industry."[45] Yes, you heard right, the *economic* impact. It is also known that cows infected with leukemia virus actually live longer, that is those who do not become extremely ill.[46] University of Illinois researchers discovered a way to save the dairy industry an estimated $42 million dollars each year that was lost due to full-blown infection in these desirable leukemic cows. They found a gene that allows cows to maintain their infection without converting to the full-blown stage.[47] Unfortunately, a cow with the leukemia virus does not need to be in the full-blown stage in order to spread virus to other mammals, like humans. Another link between milk and leukemia will be discussed a bit later.

Lung Cancer

While the role of diet in highly fatal lung cancer is weak when compared to that of smoking, recent studies have looked for such links since smoking rates have decreased faster than lung cancer rates have, and non-smoker lung cancer cases are going up. A U.S. study found a dietary connection between saturated fat consumption (meaning dairy and meat) and increased lung cancer risk.[48] A Uruguay study found that the saturated fat effect that came from fried meats, which creates a different kind of carcinogen, only affected current smokers, but the common denominator for effects in current and past smokers was dairy products.[49] A Norwegian study reported that whole milk has twice the risk as skim milk, while no association was found for other saturated fats or cholesterol intake.[50] Two separate Swedish studies only mentioned milk for dietary risk, high intake leading to double the number of lung cancers as found in low dairy consumers.[51,52]

> A 1999 epidemiological study of 41 countries found the strongest association between diet and prostate cancer to be the non-fat portion of milk. Prostate cancers have climbed rapidly over each of the last 4 decades.

Milk & Prostate Cancer

A study of nearly 26,000 Norwegian men found non-fat milk to be the most significant dietary link to prostate cancer.[53] A smaller Italian study also reported milk, but not milk fat, to be a risk factor, and a strong factor with 2 or more glasses of milk per day.[54] Most recently, a 1999 epidemiological study of 41 countries found the strongest association between diet and prostate cancer to be the non-fat portion of milk.[55] Some continue to suggest that genetic race differences are the key to the wide variations in this disease rate around the world. However, when Asians and Africans from regions with very low prostate cancer rates migrate to the U.S., their rates rise dramatically with each generation or with the amount of time spent in this nation.[56] This cancer has traditionally been very rare in Japan, but their rates are now soaring since they adopted Western formula supplementing and adult dairy consumption.[57] Prostate cancers in the African nation of Nigeria, much of which was hit early and hard by milk formula campaigns, have climbed rapidly over each of the last 4 decades.[58] These cancers remain rare in African populations who continue to provide prolonged breastfeeding and have non-dairy diets.[59] Prostate cancer attacks U.S. men in their 50s and 60s and is the second leading cancer killer in U.S. men (now number 1 in Nigeria). The exact role of milk has yet to be determined.

> Female milk drinkers face three times the risk of developing ovarian cancer, and 8 in every 100,000 American women die of this cancer.

Milk & Ovarian Cancer

Female milk drinkers face three times the risk of developing ovarian cancer.[60] While dairy products contain much fat, and fat consumption is known to be linked with ovarian cancer, the milk connection proves to be much more powerful than just this. Traditionally, ovarian cancer has been considered a disease of societies with lactase enzyme persistence, and links to lactose have been hypothesized.[61,62] However, as dairy is pushed into more areas around the world, even where adults do not retain lactase, ovarian cancer rates increase parallel to per capita milk consumption. Increases are also being seen in U.S., England, and Canada in lactose intolerant subpopulations where it was once low, seemingly because lactose intolerant people have been encouraged to eat cheese, yogurt, and milk with Lactaid, increasing their dairy exposure. The five-year survival rate for ovarian cancer is less than 40% and 8 in every 100,000 American women die of this cancer.

Milk & Infertility

The harmful effects of dairy consumption on the ovaries have been also linked to increasingly younger infertility ages with increasing milk consumption per capita.[63]

Puberty & Breast Cancer

In some portions of the world, and in some peoples, puberty is arriving at earlier and earlier ages. These regions and peoples are the ones with the highest rates of formula feeding and childhood dairy consumption. These same children are also approaching their mature heights sooner. This phenomenon has been ascribed to improved nutrition. Dairy products are responsible for much of the perception that improved nutrition is being supplied, as well as for many of the consequences being recorded. In fact, regions that do not meet the accelerated growth expectations of large dairy-consuming populations are labeled deficient and malnourished, as are vegans (consume no dairy), even though dairy consumption and its effects are not natural. There is no basis for assuming the results are superior or desirable. The actual effects are shocking. Two percent of U.S. girls are beginning pubic hair growth or breast development at the age of 3! Faster growth may sound appealing, however, not only does early puberty lead to increased teen pregnancies and sexually transmitted diseases, but *accelerated growth means cancer*, and the statistics are bearing this out.

Ages of puberty among specific populations in the U.S. and around the world correlate with the history and volume of childhood dairy consumption. Early puberty is strongly associated with developing breast cancer.

In 1988, Japanese researchers noticed a high correlation between early puberty and higher milk consumption.[64] Milk is not the only factor associated with early onset of menstruation; higher consumption of animal fats is also linked,[65] but milk is a major contributor to the total animal fat in diets. We have already discussed the connection between low parental responsiveness, which is often connected with formula feeding, and early puberty. Another strong link to early puberty is a decreased response to insulin which leads to elevated blood insulin levels along with increases in an insulin-like growth factor. Remember, early and extensive dairy consumption is strongly linked to this pre-diabetic condition.

Ages of puberty among specific populations in the U.S. and around the world correlate with the history and volume of childhood dairy consumption. African-Americans receive formula from birth more often than the rest of the American population. At age 8, 15% of white girls and nearly 50% of African-American girls are showing pubic hair or breast development.[67] The average age of menstrual onset for U.S. black girls is just over 12 and for whites is just before 13. Compare this with girls studied in the African country of Cameroon who began menses after the age of 14 when living in highly breastfeeding rural areas,[68] but where the age of menarche dropped toward 13 the closer the children lived to the breastfeeding but formula-supplementing urban center of Yaounde. In nearby Senegal, with nearly universal breastfeeding and minimal dairy exposure, average menarche is at age 16. Mexico and Cuba are strong breastfeeding countries. But the breastfeeding rate for immigrants from these countries living in the U.S. drops for each successive generation. Recent measures show 45% of Hispanic-American girls, 42% of

> Breast cancer is the second leading cause of cancer deaths for U.S. women. Studies reveal that breast cancer rates correlate directly with levels of milk consumption in childhood and adulthood.

Caucasians, and 80% of African-Americans are developing breasts at 9 years of age.[69] In Mexico, the average age of menstrual onset was reported to be 14.25 years in rural areas in 1977, and 12.65 in urban centers where formula supplementing was widespread.[70] Japan has been seeing reductions in puberty ages following years of increased dairy consumption as well, along with the attendant accelerations in attaining mature height.[71] Norwegians, who have long been moderate dairy consumers and who have maintained high breastfeeding rates, have seen little change in their average puberty age over the last century.[72]

Early puberty is strongly associated with developing breast cancer.[73-76] The increased growth factors involved and the earlier estrogen surges are in large part responsible for the accelerated cellular reproduction in the breasts that is associated with cancer development.[77]

Breast cancer is the second leading cause of cancer deaths for U.S. women. This disease has risen by more than 50% from 1950 to 1990.[78] This corresponds with the rise in formula-feeding decades earlier when these women were infants. Many studies reveal that breast cancer rates correlate directly with levels of milk consumption in childhood and adulthood.[79-81] Two studies specifically point out that early bottle feeding correlates with a 26% increase in breast cancer risk.[82,83] Let's return for a moment to Cameroon. While formula supplements are infiltrating their urban regions, the nation's overall rate and duration of breastfeeding is much higher than that in the U.S., and adult dairy consumption is relatively new. Their overall breast cancer rate is estimated at 10 per 100,000 citizens (corrected for under-diagnosis),[84] while ours is 110 per 100,000[85] — 11 times higher. The French authors (from a very formula and dairy-oriented country) of the Cameroon puberty study suggest that the reduced age for menstrual initiation in the city girls demonstrates improved nutrition (which would mostly be from formula and milk). Another French study reflects this common conception again as they report on girls in another West African country. Peoples of rural Senegal have maintained nearly universal breastfeeding for long periods. Researchers report

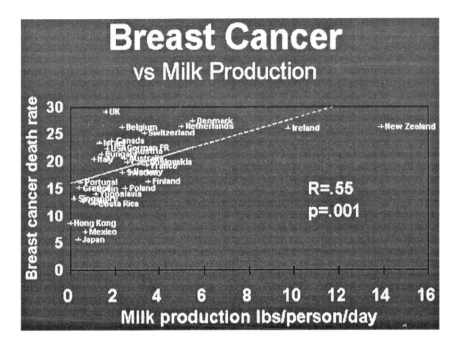

Figure 11-2   Breast cancer death rates versus milk production for various countries. Since some nations import much dairy, and others export much (such as New Zealand), the correlation may be even stronger.[88]

"stunted" growth before puberty, and menarche that is "delayed" to age 16.[86] Their studies then report that boys and girls experience "catch-up growth" after puberty. The final attained heights in adulthood in all such studies appear to be the same, with some conflicts in Asian reports.

By way of comparison, the "early growth stunted" people of Senegal suffer one fiftieth as much colon cancer as is seen in the U.S.[87] Overall cancer rates in Cameroon are one fifth that in the U.S., and Senegal's rates are even lower. As with early puberty (and diabetes, heart disease, bowel disease, osteoporosis, and several other cancers), breast cancer rates around the world correlate strongly with dairy consumption, trailing dairy increases by 2 or 3 decades.

Cow Hormones & Cancer

All cow's milk contains a protein called "bovine insulin-like growth factor-1." This factor is identical to human IGF-1.[89] This growth-promoting hormone is named for its structural similarity to insulin. Insulin also plays a role in growth regulation. We have already seen how cow's milk is connected to either too much insulin from decreased recognition of it by the body, or too little insulin, due to the body's autoimmune destruction of insulin-producing pancreatic cells. Human IGF-1 exists in mother's milk and is an important factor in the growth of infants. However, beyond childhood we have no reason to consume growth hormones. This growth hormone may be partly responsible for the accelerated growth seen in dairy-consuming children. Remember, rapid growth, especially when controls are out of balance, leads to cancer. Adults often harbor multiple benign tumors (cell overgrowths that are not out of control) in their bodies. Influenced by high doses or prolonged exposures to growth-accelerating factors, these can become malignant, meaning cancerous. Infants or young children should not have such precancerous growths in their bodies, and thus the growth hormones needed for rapid development don't promote cancer in them. As mentioned earlier, vitamin K injections at birth may be one source of loss of control over cell growth leading to early precancerous conditions in children, which could then be susceptible to the effects of growth hormones, leading to malignancies in children, such as leukemia. Human growth hormones naturally peak during puberty and drop gradually throughout maturity. There is a protective reason for this drop after growth is completed. Excess IGF-1 is strongly implicated in many kinds of cancers. Besides promoting cell division, IGF-1 protects cells from their normal preprogrammed cell deaths, creating a further cancer risk.[90]

A large percentage of the IGF-1 in dairy foods is protected from digestive enzymes by the casein protein and milk's buffering effects. Human, cow, and all mammal milks are designed this way in order to make important hormones, proteins, antibodies, and many other milk factors available to the baby. As shown in Chapter 13, infants and others who have intolerance reactions to bovine proteins suffer intermittent drops in digestive enzymes and develop "leaky guts" that allow even greater concentrations of various undigested bovine elements into the system.

Greek medical researchers studying childhood leukemia recently confirmed that excess quantities of IGF-1 might play an important role in developing this devastating cancer that has become increasingly prevalent throughout the twentieth century.[91] They also answered one of the common rebuttals to the IGF cancer reports. Dairy supporters suggest that the levels of IGF-1 in milk are infinitesimally small. However, the effective level of this growth hormone normally active in the human body, even in childhood, is also very small. Although the average level of IGF-1 in cow's milk is around 30 nanograms (.00000003 grams) per milliliter, growth promoting effects are seen in response to 1 ng per milliliter.[92] San Francisco researchers showed that addition of IGF-1 alone was enough to stimulate the kind of accelerated white blood cell growth connected with leukemia.[93]

Prostate cancer also has strong ties to high IGF-1 levels.[94,95] Breast cancer researchers from Baltimore reiterate that insulin-like growth factors are potent promoters of malignant cell production, and they specifically indict IGF-1.[96] Others have drawn the same conclusion.[97,98] Similarly, IGF-1 is implicated in ovarian cancer, which has risen in the U.S. by 18% in the last 20 years alone.[99-101] Brain tumors, gastrointestinal cancers, and childhood bone cancers are also associated with IGF-1.[102-104]

Other hormones and factors in cow's milk remain after pasteurization and have the potential to promote cancer as well. These include free estrogens, at a level similar to that in human milk,[105] and prostate-specific antigen, in high levels compared to that in male blood.[106] Other naturally occurring growth factors and hormones and estrogen mimics from concentrated pesticides and other environmental pollutants are suspected as well. Although the growth factor picture is very complicated and direct links to that from cow's milk are not entirely proven, IGF-1 attracts special attention for many reasons. One is the play of events to follow.

An Udder Conspiracy

As if cow's milk wasn't bad enough in and of itself, now one third of all U.S. cows are being injected with a synthetic bovine growth hormone (BST or rBGH). This hormone is used to increase milk production by about 15%. It also raises the IGF-1 levels in milk by 2 to 10 times.[107] This additional growth hormone is much more potent because much of it is "free," rather than bound to milk proteins. Additionally, it has been learned that pasteurization actually increases its potency, according to a 1990 Food and Drug Administration (FDA) report. Concerns have been raised by many scientists over rBGH use since 1985 when the FDA approved widespread experimentation with this hormone in commercial milk production. In 1993, they approved total commercial usage. Their approval was based on safety studies provided them by Monsanto, the manufacturer of the hormone.

Robert Cohen, in his highly revealing book, *Milk, The Deadly Poison*, presents a large amount of detailed documentation about how Monsanto's top scientist was hired by the FDA to review her own research.[108] Monsanto's attorney was hired by the FDA to write regulations for the rBGH approval. Using this hormone in cows causes a large increase in udder infections, and thus a large increase in the use of antibiotics. This attorney also helped make sure that the regulations for antibiotic levels in milk were revamped (i.e. reduced) at the same time. He then was hired by the USDA where he implemented related protocols. These ties go on and on. The Dairy Coalition conducted a large seminar on rBGH safety for medical doctors, then their doctor and a Monsanto-paid doctor wrote the key paper for the *Journal of the American Medical Association* expounding on the safety of rBGH and the need for milk to promote health. The AMA and American Dietician's Association received large sums of money from Monsanto as well. A U.S. Congress bill to mandate labeling of milk products with rBGH in them was never voted on; four congressmen on the committee received monetary gifts from Monsanto. Monsanto now tries to sue anyone who attempts to label any milk-based product as "rBGH free." Ben and Jerry's Ice Cream recently won the first lawsuit against them.

Monsanto's research paper presented to the FDA was never released for public or outside scientific review; instead, Monsanto provided the FDA with summaries of their own experiments. When it was brought before the Canadian government, however, the Canadian Health Protection Branch scrutinized the evidence and discovered that this hormone was absorbed into the bloodstream of 25% of the study rats, even though the conclusion claimed it was not. They also noticed that some rats developed dangerous indications in their thyroid and prostate glands in this short trial. Canadian scientists caused a serious setback for Monsanto when they revealed Monsanto's bribery attempts. Canada banned the use of this synthetic growth hormone, as have Europe, Australia, New Zealand, and Japan.

When an investigative reporter team for a Fox-owned TV station in Tampa, Florida tried to release the story, their report was stopped by Fox under pressure from Monsanto. They were asked to report a false rendition of the story, but they refused. Ensuing struggles by these reporters and their refusal to accept Fox's monetary offers finally led to their firing. The details of the lawsuit they recently won can be found on the Internet.[109]

There is no absolute proof of danger to humans from consuming this hormonally enhanced milk; no human studies have been done. Instead the research is going on today in your baby's body and your own. The results will not show up for two or three decades, but since the milks are not labeled, the evidence will be impossible to assemble.

Osteoporosis

But my child needs the calcium? While the National Osteoporosis Foundation tells us we need more calcium, especially from cow's milk, in order to build stronger bones, the scientific evidence does not support this.

The Chinese University of Hong Kong performed successive studies in the 90s analyzing milk and calcium intake as they relate to the growth of children. This was an ideal place and time for such an investigation because cow's milk was just making its way into popular use in that country, and the traditional diet was not high in calcium. The first study looked at children from birth to 5 years of age. With 90% of the study children drinking milk, their average calcium intake was 550 mg. At age 5, the current level of calcium intake for each child did not correlate with their bone mineral levels. The calcium intake during the second year of life proved to be the strongest predictor of bone "hardness" at age 5 (breastmilk would provide the same or more advantage as cow's milk or other source).[110] In the second study, 7-year-old children were given calcium supplements to bring their daily calcium intakes up to 800 mg. Over 18 months, no increases were seen in height or arm or leg bone density beyond those not supplemented, although some improvement in spinal bone density was seen.[111] At ages 12 to 13, calcium intake did not correlate to bone mineral content, except that the girls who consumed the higher levels of calcium had *lower* bone density in their arms.[112] In all these studies, higher weight and greater physical activity were strongly associated with higher bone mineral content. By adolescence, neither calcium intake nor physical activity had any more influence on bone mineral improvement.[113] A 14-year British study found that in young adults, their early teenage body weight and physical activity levels determined their bone mineral densities, with a slight effect from calcium intake.[114]

> The animal proteins of meat and dairy products cause calcium loss. Americans have among the highest osteoporosis rates in the world.

In a widely quoted study by a British hospital, researchers provided an extra glass of cow's milk to adolescent girls' diets, comparing their growth to those who drank an average of just over one half cup per day. Total daily calcium intake at the beginning of the study was 750 mg, the extra milk group increased to 1,100 mg. The researchers reported about 10% greater bone growth rate for those with the extra milk.[115] These children also gained a little more weight, but not height. The reported extra bone density could not be validated by any changes in the blood enzyme markers that typically reflect bone growth and bone reabsorption. Insulin-like growth factor was found to be higher in the extra milk group. Several experts wrote replies to this study, which had been paid for by the U.K. dairy industry. One suggested that *their* math found the milk group to actually have a slightly lower average total bone mineral content at the end of the study.[116] A U.S. study on child twins found some increases in bone density, at least in the arms and spine, with calcium supplements (not milk).[117] Once puberty began, however, calcium provided no benefits.

While dairy promotions include praise for the protein in milk, this protein may be more of a problem in osteoporosis than calcium could be a solution. The animal proteins of meat and dairy products cause calcium loss.[118] The level of calcium needed in the diet depends greatly on the animal protein intake.[119] For many of the high animal protein diets of Americans, it may not be possible to consume enough calcium in the diet to compensate for the amount lost to these high-acid proteins.[120] For this reason, Americans have among the highest osteoporosis rates in the world. Doubled animal protein causes 50% more calcium loss. Yet, when a high protein intake is soy based, a positive calcium balance can be maintained with only 450 mg of calcium per day.[121]

The chief concern over bone density is that bone density gradually reduces with maturity. At a certain point of bone loss, the term "osteoporosis" is used. This is a level where low-trauma bone fractures become more frequent. Spinal fractures are a problem, as are hip and arm fractures, which are easier to measure for research purposes. The highest level of bone density attained in

A recent study of 78,000 nurses found that women who drank more than one glass of milk per day had a 45% greater chance of hip fractures, compared to those who drank far less.

young adulthood correlates with the bone density maintained in later decades. What is not entirely understood is how much impact dietary factors have on these events. Some studies suggest that childhood calcium intake before puberty may have some slight positive effect. At the same time that diabetes, cancer, and other concerns may limit the amount of dairy that should be given a child, it also appears that bone protection is no reason to promote dairy consumption beyond childhood.

In 1986 a Harvard researcher produced the graph below which demonstrates a nearly inverse relationship between calcium intake and hip fractures.[122] A 1987 study of 106 adult women suggested that calcium intake between 500 and 1,400 mg per day led to no difference in bone mineral densities.[123] A larger Italian study found that in women who consumed between 440 and 1,025 mg of calcium per day, a slightly increased number of hip fractures occurred with higher milk intakes.[124] *A recent study of 78,000 nurses found that women who drank more than one glass of milk per day had a 45% greater chance of hip fractures*, compared to those who drank far less.[125] Those who took in the same amount of calcium from non-dairy sources saw no such increase, nor a decrease in fractures. Since many studies are performed on women only — they do suffer more osteoporosis — Harvard researchers decided to look at men. They found that those who drank 3 or more glasses of milk per day, compared to 1 or less per week, had very slightly fewer hip fractures, but these were balanced by slightly more arm fractures.[126] The highest calcium intakes from food and supplements together produced an increase in fractures overall.

The milk-drinking (and higher calcium intake) populations around the world are the ones who have osteoporosis as a major problem.

The rate of hip fractures in the U.S. for people of many races and ethnic origins is exactly inverse to their rates of lactose intolerance. In other words, those who are likely avoiding milk as adults have the fewest fractures. Non-

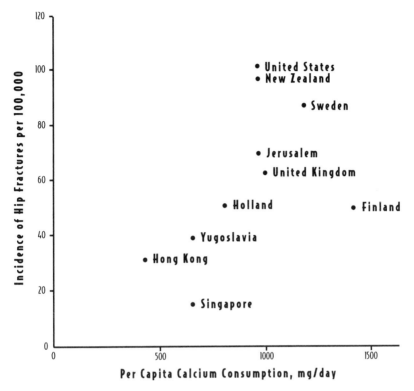

Figure 11-3 Rate of hip fractures occurring (signifying osteoporosis) in relation to the calcium consumption of several nations. Hegsted, 1986.[127]

Hispanic white women have 139 per 100,000, Mexican-Americans have 67 per 100,000, and African-Americans average 55 per 100,000.[128] The indigenous people of South Africa have not traditionally been dairy consumers. Their consumption is still very low, although formula is making great inroads. Those of osteoporosis age today however would not have been raised on formula. Typically, South Africans consume only 200 mg of calcium per day, but their rate of fractures is extremely low — fewer than 7 per 100,000 people per year.[129] Compare this to their dairy-exposed American counterparts. The milk-drinking (and higher calcium intake) populations around the world are the ones who have osteoporosis as a major problem.[130] These rates are increasing in typically low fracture areas around the world as these regions adopt Western practices. In Japan, as in many other non-Caucasian populations, dairy intake has traditionally been minimal and calcium intakes have been low — and hip fracture rates are low, but have been growing recently,[131] as is the portion of adults who were raised on dairy. While industrialization also brings reduced physical exercise, there is a much more consistent common denominator seen in the timing and geographic regions of these bone problems — cow's milk. While we feel our nutrition is superior today over centuries past, archeological research has shown that Caucasian post-menopausal bone loss in the eighteenth and nineteenth centuries was less than that seen today.[132] Clearly, high calcium intake, and certainly high dairy intake, are not the prevention for osteoporosis.

Milky Messages

Why the conflicts between the bulk of research findings and the recommendations of the National Osteoporosis Foundation (NOF)? It could be because much of NOF funding comes from corporations such as Kellogg's Cereal Company and Dairy Farmers of Maitland, Florida. Other funding comes from small and large private donations, with some from the federal government.[133] Another big supporter of the National Osteoporosis Foundation is Bozell Worldwide, the marketing firm that created the huge milk mustache campaign for the dairy industry. Only 2% of the NOF's funding has gone to osteoporosis research.

Good, Bad & Curious Solutions

Other common foods that are excellent sources of calcium, listed in order of highest amount per calorie, are molasses, dark salad greens, cabbage, broccoli, green beans, cucumber, peas, soybeans, squash, most types of beans (including cocoa), kiwi, real maple syrup, brown sugar, and tomatoes. In addition to this list is, of course, human milk. Calcium may also be added to corn tortillas and some orange juice, apple juice, and rice and soy milks. When these foods are the major source of calcium, and meat intake is not high, USRDA levels may be in excess of needs.

The World Health Organization suggests that 400 to 500 mg of calcium per day is appropriate for adults. The United States RDA for calcium is 800 mg for most people one year of age and over and 1,200 mg for teens and pregnant and lactating mothers. Ours is the highest recommendation in the world. Beyond these earlier set standards, the U.S. National Institutes of Health (NIH) has gradually raised their recommendations for calcium requirements: for children 6 to 10 years old, 800 to 1,200 mg; 11 to 24 years, pregnant, or nursing, 1,200 to 1,500 mg; over 65, 1,500 mg. They base their decisions chiefly on our increasing osteoporosis problems. At their Development Conference on Optimal Calcium Intake, they stated, "The preferred source of calcium is through calcium-rich foods such as dairy products."[134] They reinforce vitamin D intake too, which is added to milk, and naturally derived from sun exposure or eating fish.

Boron, copper, magnesium, manganese, zinc, vitamin C, and proper fluoride levels are just as important as calcium for optimal bone growth. None of these are high in cow's milk, so none of these are advertised as important for bones.

They do not, however, mention any of the other nutritional factors that are important for bone development — those that are inadequate in milk. At the same time, their report makes taking calcium supplements sound very complicated. Boron, copper, magnesium, manganese, zinc, vitamin C, and proper fluoride levels are just as important as calcium for optimal bone growth. None of these are high in cow's milk, so none of these are advertised as important for bones. Phosphorous is important for bone development as well, but cow's milk has too much of this, causing decreased calcium availability. This is apparently why phosphorous is not mentioned either. Nor does NIH mention that reduced animal protein consumption would help calcium levels. (Remember that the beef industry is the other end of the dairy industry.) Deep in the text they mention some other foods naturally high in calcium, but only in reference to vegans who do not drink milk. This list is rather inaccurate and exclusive, sounding a bit distasteful. They also emphasize that a little pain and gas should not prevent the lactose intolerant from having at least 2 servings of milk per day.

As more problems become apparent with milk, and people buy less, greater measures are taken to encourage milk drinking. The new motto for the government's Healthy People 2000 initiative is, "at least 3 cups of milk every day" for "every body." The NIH, whose initial intentions are often better than their final reported conclusions, funded half of the huge 1997 study that showed that nurses have more fractures when consuming more milk. To date, however, they have not changed their recommendations about milk consumption. All the while, the American Dietetic Association, with grants from the dairy industry, continues to publish reports such as "Many Asian American elderly consume an inadequate amount of dietary calcium."[135] Their conclusions were based on their milk consumption, not their bones. It's obvious what their recommended solution was. A recent dairy commercial shows young men playing basketball (exercising), while outside (soaking up vitamin D), two great ways to build stronger bones. A milk carton stands alongside urging them to go inside, sit down, and have some milk for their bones.

Dutch dairy researchers have come up with a new milk product designed to be better for bone health. They increased the calcium content and lowered the protein, phosphorus, and fat content — in other words, they lowered the dairy content. Not surprisingly, elderly people taking this new low-milk calcium supplement lost less calcium each day than those drinking normal milk.[136]

Deflating Dairy

The norms promoted as desirable for childhood growth rates and puberty are based on a comparison of those who consume bovine growth hormones early and regularly, to those who are raised on natural foods. While the same height is achieved in the end, with obesity more common on the side of dairy consumers,[137] those with the so-called superior nutrition experience a traumatic increase in cancer, heart disease, diabetes, and many other diseases.

The highly promoted idea that milk builds strong bones refers to the prevention of osteoporosis — this is the reason for strengthening bones. Decades of effort to demonstrate that high calcium diets chiefly derived from dairy products build strong bones have failed to prove any such correlation. In fact, the opposite seems to be true.[138] It appears that high calcium intake before puberty, and especially in young childhood, may have some slight positive effect on bones, but this diet is not the answer. A balanced intake of all the bone minerals, along with adequate vitamin A, C, and D, is what is truly needed. A balanced intake of minerals cannot occur when the diet emphasizes dairy. Dairy's high calcium causes relative deficiencies in magnesium and other bone-building minerals, and its high phosphorus and animal protein reduces calcium availability. Physical activity has the greatest benefit — the body efficiently uses what is available to build strong bones when it senses the need. Human milk and vegetable sources are superior to dairy for calcium and other nutrients in many ways. There are fewer nutritional or other health advantages to giving cow's milk to children than is generally believed, while there are certainly many risks.

If you pay attention to health research announcements in the news, you will notice that almost every day another finding is made about whole grains, soy, a serving of vegetables, two fruits per day, cashews, legumes, fish, or some other food, *other than milk that is,* and their connection to a reduced risk of heart disease, breast cancer, stroke, diabetes, or other disease. This is because cow's milk and its derivatives today make up one third of the adult diet and half to two thirds of caloric intake in children, thus replacing so much other important, nutritious food needed in the diet. This leads to insufficient intake of some important vitamins, several minerals, and of healthy fiber and vegetable oils. Cancer-preventing antioxidants in foods are missing in this milk diet as well. While one form of antioxidant vitamin A is added to milk (but not all dairy products), and likely counteracted by the pesticide and drug residues, the full complement of vitamin A and associated enzymes, found in vegetables and other foods, are required for cancer prevention. Many, many more kinds of antioxidants are found in vegetables, legumes, fruits, and grains.

No other animal in the animal kingdom drinks milk beyond childhood. No other animal suffers from osteoporosis, except the occasional pet raised on human meals.

If there remains a desire to provide milk to a child who has no diarrhea, rashes, or other intolerance reactions, organic (*organic — not raw*) non-fat milk would be the best choice. In raw (unpasteurized) milk there can be many potentially dangerous microorganisms, in addition to the leukemia virus. In organic milk there are fewer antibiotic residues, no *added* hormones, and cows are given better feeds. Non-fat means less chemical residue and no artery-damaging saturated fat — let them obtain their fat in the form of non-hydrogenated (especially monosaturated) vegetable oils, be it in potato chips or cashews. Goat's milk is considered by many to be superior in many ways, and today low-fat versions are available. Much less documented information is available about goat's milk. It appears that the proteins are less problematic for digestion, although allergic intolerance to these can also occur. Lactose and hormones would remain an issue although, to date, goats apparently are not injected with extra growth hormone.

Although it was apparent from day one that formula was a health risk for infants, back when it was first promoted, cow's milk for older children appeared to be a nutritional manna. And with one or two glasses a day from a healthy, range-fed animal, it likely nearly was. Since this time, however, the quality of dairy has drastically reduced while its consumption has exploded...with a little advertising help. The evidence suggesting that the early faith in milk was misplaced has been building up for decades. The dairy industry has had to take increasingly extreme efforts to keep this information out of public awareness.

I have only touched on the tip of the existing evidence against the health claims of the milk industry promoters. Since our childhood, the dairy industry has worked hard to have dairy products enshrined in a food group of their own. Even though they were given their own space in the new Eating Right food pyramid, they found themselves placed in a small upper portion and have lobbied to have the pyramid withdrawn.[139] Many nutrition experts such as Harvard's Dr. Walter Willett[140] suggest they should not be a featured group in the pyramid at all. The dairy industry has also successfully convinced many vegetarians that milk from cows, especially cheese, is a vegetarian food. Since few substantiated health claims can be made anymore, the milk industry's most recent promotion has been to simply show their product on the upper lip of celebrities of all kinds, even those who are dairy allergic (Bill Clinton), and even on those who are too young to be consuming whole milk (the Rugrats). Before this promo it was simply "got milk?" While an ever-growing preponderance of scientific information points to the dangers of cow's milk, favorable public and even mainstream medical opinion about dairy products has been very successfully maintained.

Figure 11-4 "Each year, LP&M (advertising agency) helps the American Dairy Association execute its national milk theme in elementary and junior high schools throughout the Northeast. The goal is to increase the consumption of milk by students during their school time meals."
— Latorra, Paul & McCann
        Advertising

12

Colic to Ear Infections, Behavior to Bedwetting

I FOUND THIS QUESTION TO A PEDIATRICIAN POSTED ON A PARENTING
Web site:

> My 21-month-old had no ear infections until he was 17
> months old. Upon taking him to the doctor due to a
> rash (diagnosed as eczema), we were surprised to hear
> he had an ear infection. He showed no symptoms at all.
> Since then, he has been declared "clear" only twice,
> and these only lasted three days and one week. Only
> once has it been obvious to me that he had an ear
> infection — he woke up screaming "Owwww" and
> grabbing his ear. He has been through the range of

antibiotics, and if it doesn't clear up this time, his pediatrician is referring us to an ENT, presumably for tubes. My mother insists that we take him off dairy to see if that stops the ear infections. I have resisted because I have seen nothing in the literature to indicate that milk causes ear infections in a toddler. To be honest, he doesn't drink much milk or eat much cheese anyway. Should I take Mom's advice?

I won't repeat the answer this mother received, except to say that I believe a simple dietary experiment has less potential for harm than a surgery under anesthesia.

The most likely cause of this child's problem is obvious; the mother provided multiple clues. First of all this child had eczema — a condition strongly correlated with food and airborne allergies. Secondly, at 17 months this child apparently had no symptoms of an ear infection — no pain, fever, ear tugging, complaining, or fussiness; therefore, in order for him to be diagnosed with an ear infection, his doctor must have seen fluid in the child's ear. Mucus production in the sinuses and inflammation of the mucous membrane tube leading to the middle ear (the Eustachian tube) prevents normal drainage, allowing fluids produced in the middle ear to build up. Acute blockage can occur with a cold or flu, but these were not mentioned, and the problem was quite chronic. Chronic inflammation of the Eustachian tube occurs as a result of food or airborne allergic reactions. In this case it appears that the normal balance of flora in the middle ear was disrupted by multiple courses of antibiotics, until the child finally developed a true, painful infection. The third clue is that the boy avoids dairy products. Finally, the grandmother must have made some observations of her own, based on her suggestion.

My recommendation to the inquirer: Follow your mother's advice.

Colic, fussiness, sleeplessness, waking with screams, "owie" tummies, constipation, diarrhea, red anal ring, pustules in the diaper area, eczema, asthma, tantrums, hyperactivity, malaise, ear infections, chronic stuffiness or nose picking, bedwetting, and more: These are many of the maladies of infancy and childhood that are frequently associated with allergies and food sensitivities, and thus are mostly avoidable. All of these symptoms have increased dramatically in our children over the better part of this century. Not only have we lost much of the wisdom of our fore-mothers and polluted our surroundings with countless chemicals, but we have drastically altered the diets of our babies and children — not always with the best results.

How Common Are Allergies & Sensitivities?

During the early twentieth century, the introduction of cow's milk formulas and the push for nursing mothers to drink cow's milk saw a concurrent rise in eczema, diarrhea,* colic, ear infections, behavior problems, and other complaints in children. Today, chiefly because of cow's milk, food reactions and other allergies are at an all-time high. For decades, the average number of allergic individuals in the U.S. was accepted to be 15% of the population. Studies after the 1920s started to report increasingly larger numbers.

In the U.S. estimates are that well over 50% of children suffer some kind of hypersensitivity to foods, additives, or the environment.

An allergy reaction is a set of symptoms resulting from the immune system's response to something that most healthy systems would not respond to. Chiefly, the mast cells that line tissues are the lookouts that alert the immune system that foreign substances such

---

* Infectious diarrhea increased greatly, due to formula feeding, before the popularity of refrigeration and sterile bottle measures. Even now with good sanitation, infectious diarrhea rates are much higher because fewer infants are gaining disease protection from mother's breastmilk. Non-infectious diarrhea, related to food sensitivity reactions — which is discussed here — also increased considerably with the popularization of dairy products.

as bacteria or some foods have invaded the body. Then, antibodies and chemicals such as histamine are released in response, creating havoc wherever they choose.

What is the rate of food sensitivity in children today? In 1993, Poland reported that 39% of its infants suffered from allergic disease.[1] A 1996 Health Survey for England reported 45% of children suffered from some form of allergy. As high as these numbers seem, they may not account for many delayed type reactions that are poorly understood by the mainstream medical community. Today in the U.S. estimates are that well over 50% of children suffer some kind of hypersensitivity to foods, additives, or their environment.[2]

How Often Is Food Sensitivity Found with Colic?

Colic, affecting at least 10 to 30% of babies,[3] is often one of the first signs of food sensitivities, characterized by inconsolable bouts of crying, gassiness, fussiness, poor sleep, and the appearance of being in pain. Removing cow's milk protein from the diets of these children (using soy formula) leads to substantial improvement in many cases. With soy removed from the diet as well (using hydrolyzed protein formulas), relief is seen in 68 to 95% of infants.[4-7]

Yet, even hydrolyzed milk protein formulas often contain corn, another strong allergen, and hydrolyzation is not total — leading to continued problems in highly sensitive infants. Sometimes a very expensive elemental diet (such as Vivonex), which is essentially a formula with all allergenic proteins broken into neutral pieces, is the only good solution for a very sensitive bottle-fed baby.

Breastfed babies have a somewhat lower incidence of colic and food sensitivities in general. If a colicky baby is eating by breastfeeding alone, he may exhibit sensitivities to foods in mom's diet. He's lucky to be nursing though. If he is sensitive to the small amounts of antigenic proteins in mom's milk, he would most likely be very much more sensitive to formulas. Colic will be discussed further in a moment.

How About Food Sensitivity with Other Symptoms?

According to the Centers for Disease Control, nearly 20 million acute ear infections occurred in U.S. children in 1994. Allergist Tala Nsouli found food allergies in 78% of children with chronic ear infections.[8]

In studies, food allergy has been found to be the cause in most cases of colitis in infants.[9-11] When milk and other allergy foods were removed from their diets, not only did symptoms disappear, but intestinal biopsies revealed great improvement in the damage that had occurred in the intestinal walls.

Gluten sensitivity, or celiac disease, generally beginning in infancy or childhood, is the only intestinal disease that has long been medically recognized as a food intolerance. In this case, the gluten protein found in wheat and other grains causes the destructive inflammatory reactions. The damage seen in this syndrome is very similar to that seen in milk sensitivity and other intestinal sensitivities.[12] It is well known that dietary management is the way to prevent the symptoms of celiac disease as well as the intestinal damage, and this has almost always been the recommended treatment.

Depending on the study, 80 to nearly 100% of Crohn's sufferers can maintain remission of symptoms and damage through food elimination diets.[13-15] The success of the study is usually dependent on the conscientiousness of the participants in following the diet. Significant elevations in (IgA, IgG, or IgM) antibodies to cow's milk particularly have been found in those diagnosed with Crohn's disease or ulcerative colitis.[16] These are diseases where inflammation and ulcers occur in the intestinal linings.

Elimination of cow's milk and other discovered allergens led to significant improvement in 73% of attention-deficit hyperactivity disordered (ADHD) children in a 1994 double-blind study.

Abdominal pain and diarrhea, sometimes bloody, are the chief symptoms. Eighty-seven percent of children suffering with the abdominal pain and diarrhea of irritable bowel syndrome recover through dietary management as well.[17]

In one study, migraine headaches may have been relieved in nearly 90% of children by eliminating the offending allergenic foods.[18] Other studies have found similar results. In this migraine study, half were found to have behavioral disorders, and 90% of those also showed improved behavior on non-allergenic diets.

Elimination of cow's milk and other discovered allergens led to significant improvement in 73% of attention-deficit hyperactivity disordered (ADHD) children in a 1994 double-blind study.[19] Another study of behavioral disorders showed relief in more than half of those studied with the elimination of cow's milk alone.[20] A study that mapped electrical brain activities during food trials supports these conclusions.[21] The behavior that is diagnosed as ADHD in school-age children may be the same thing as great fussiness and irritability in infants, and bouts of wild and contrary behavior in preschoolers.

A very high percentage of bedwetting children are found to be cured by eliminating allergenic foods.[22] Interestingly, a study of ADHD children found that they suffer day-wetting or bedwetting problems 4.5 times more often than other children.[23]

Food or other allergic reactions have been suggested as the cause for some cases of SIDS,[24] although the few small studies performed to date give weak, or absent, correlation.

Most cases of infant eczema are associated with food sensitivities. Skin rashes can be seen with the unaided eye, and thus, whether or not there are symptoms is less subject to interpretation (frequently, when complaints of abdominal pains are not easily understood, their validity is questioned). For this reason, infant eczema seems to have become the most highly investigated manifestation of food allergy. Although eczema in an infant may detract from her prettiness, skin rashes are the least of a mother's concerns when compared to the other problems a child could have. It is rather rare to have eczema without any other signs of food sensitivity though. The value of eczema observation is that it reveals to the unaided eye what may be occurring insidiously in more vital and more vulnerable organs inside the body — about which one should truly be concerned.

Combination & Progression of Symptoms

Generally, when more than one, especially more than two, symptoms are seen chronically without an obvious explanation, the chances that they are related to an allergy (and thus at least partially avoidable) are fairly high.

A very recent study by Italian doctors documented the evolution of allergic symptoms in some growing infants who couldn't tolerate cow's milk protein, the most common food sensitivity.[25] They found that the earliest symptoms were chiefly gastrointestinal, including colic, diarrhea or constipation, gas, abdominal pains, and vomiting. Around 5 years of age, the same children presented more wheezing (asthma), constipation (although I see diarrhea at this stage just as often), and their reactions were more delayed. More often, children with persistent cow's milk protein intolerance presented multiple food intolerances and had parents with allergic symptoms. Many of those with persistent intolerance also have what is called "atopic disease," which is asthma, eczema, and rhinitis (runny nose), while very few of the children with short-term intolerance demonstrated these conditions. Another 1998 study, this time performed in Spain, reported a natural progression from food sensitivity, to respiratory allergy, to (not so surprising at this point) medication allergies.[26] Food sensitivities are also retained into late childhood and adulthood by many, but often to a milder or at least less symptomatic degree than in infancy.

Abdominal Pain

Abdominal pain can arise from dozens of disorders that originate everywhere from the throat to the genitals. When any behavior in a child seems out of the ordinary to a parent, even when a child with frequent abdominal symptoms suddenly presents differently, more severely, or just arouses concern in any way, the parent may certainly wish to have the child examined for disease or disorder.

Usually, abdominal discomfort in children is related in some way to food. Infants can have abdominal distress when they are hungry or when they have overeaten. A child whose diet varies widely can also have indigestion when his digestive enzymes are not accustomed to certain kinds of foods. It has been shown that levels of certain digestive enzymes take a few days to adapt to the usual amounts of certain dietary constituents.

> One study found 42% of infants with gastric reflux were sensitive to cow's milk proteins.

In a small infant, abdominal pains can sometimes be suspected when crying is accompanied by arching backwards (often off the bed onto head and heels), refusing to lie on the stomach, or drawing the knees up over the abdomen. An infant in pain may kick, flail tight fists, and appear to be in despair. Parents learn to recognize their own infant's signs. All of these actions are certainly common in many infants. Possible allergic connections should be investigated when these behaviors occur frequently with no (or very slight) fever, when the parent derives a sense that the child is in frequent discomfort, and especially when other allergy symptoms are present as well.

As an infant gets older, this same kind of pain may elicit more fussiness and crabbiness than crying. It may be a long time before the child can recognize their pain and then ascertain what area of her body it is coming from. Sometime between the ages of one and two this will likely occur. One day a child confirms the parents' long-lived suspicions by verbalizing the presence of a "tummy owie." Of course, the verbal toddler or older child can fabricate a complaint for attention or avoidance reasons, however parents are bright enough to tell the difference, especially in a chronically complaining child.

Abdominal pain that occurs 10 to 40 minutes after eating, especially pain felt while lying down that is not generally associated with other digestive system symptoms, except for possible regurgitation, could be associated with hiatal hernia or gastric reflux — which may or may not have any association to food sensitivities. One study found 42% of infants with gastric reflux were sensitive to cow's milk proteins.[27] A hiatal hernia is a condition where the upper portion of the stomach is able to roll up through a weakened hole in the diaphragm. Gastric reflux is stomach acid spilling upwards out of a weak gastroesophageal sphincter at the junction of the esophagus and stomach. Both normal stomach acid and the excess acid produced by allergy-related histamine release can cause acid to regurgitate up through this sphincter into the esophagus. Some doctors suggest this sphincter is weak in many infants. Although adults experience this pain as a burning in the lower chest (heartburn), the young child may not discern the difference between this and abdominal pains. If either a hernia or reflux is the sole cause, avoid large feedings and avoid laying an infant down within 45 minutes after a meal, or at least lay her with the chest elevated so it is higher than the stomach; this should prevent or relieve the pain.

Hypersensitivity reactions to foods in the diet are the most common cause of abdominal symptoms. Unless the child is throwing up and starting to swell minutes after consuming a food, hypersensitivity is usually the more common but less recognized type of reaction, referred to as delayed reaction. Abdominal pain will begin anywhere from an hour to two days after the offending food has been ingested — most often beginning 2 to 12 hours after ingestion. The pain may then continue on and off for a couple of days. Most bouts of abdominal pain in food intolerant children usually coincide with other digestive symptoms such as passing gas, spitting-up, vomiting, diarrhea, constipation, and rather varied stool appearance, including signs of undigested materials.

"Allergy Ring" & Diaper Rash

Many food sensitive infants will display an "allergy ring" many hours or up to one or two days after allergenic food consumption, providing a clue to his parents that he is suffering. Allergy ring is the popular name for a round area of bright redness (1 or 2 inches in diameter) around the anus. This bright redness of the skin surrounding the anus indicates an inflammatory reaction going on deep inside — in the colon. Sometimes this ring appears just after a stool of allergic material is passed. Dr. Doris Rapp in *Is This Your Child?* describes this sign as an indication of yeast infection in the child. Certainly, if candida (a yeast) did colonize the colon, this could bring about such a reaction, but yeast is not always cultured from these rings. Still, it is quite common for yeast and food sensitivities to go hand in hand, although the reasons for this are not entirely understood. Personally I've been sensing that part of the phenomenon may be attributed to allergy reactions in the body to the yeast flora itself.

Often, diaper rash *is* candida. This yeast infection on the buttocks is often not symmetrical, may spread out from the reddest portions with red spots, and may favor the leg folds. It is a different phenomenon than the allergy ring. This kind of diaper rash could also indicate candida in the stool, and thus in the colon — a condition that may go along with food sensitivities, although yeast diaper rashes are very common in infants on antibiotics. To make matters more confusing, there is a larger, symmetrical, bright red buttocks condition, sometimes with small sores, called "scalded buttocks," which is likely a more severe form of the allergy ring that occurs when the buttocks have been in diaper contact with allergic material for some time.

Eczema of the diaper area will appear in irregular patches and resembles eczema rashes that appear on the face, hands, chest, and low back. This kind of "diaper rash" is likely associated with food sensitivities. A contact dermatitis rash can occur from a local skin allergy (as opposed to an internal food allergy) to detergent, softener, or other additive in the diaper itself, but would be seen only where the diaper is in direct contact with the skin. Other diaper rashes include some less common microbial infections, heat rash, and a chemical irritation rash that occurs when bacteria in the stool or the unsterilized cloth diaper gain long access to urea in the urine, causing ammonia formation and chemical burning of the skin.

Diaper rashes are much more common in formula-fed babies and in babies wearing cloth diapers covered with plastic pants.

Treatment of diaper rash with steroid creams may provide temporary remission, but if the *cause* of the rash is not treated, it will only continue to return. Desitin and eliminating the causes would be better choices than this drug with potentially serious side effects.

Child Avoids Certain Foods

As with other mammals, humans are born with an instinctive ability to avoid foods that have previously made them feel ill. This could be considered the first step in acquired immunity — we acquire the ability to avoid foods that will make us sick. These foods may be discerned by appearance, odor, taste, or even location. Besides simple dislike for the texture or flavor of a food, quite uncommon with dairy products, sensitivity is a common reason for a child to consistently attempt to avoid a food. Beyond the first year of life, foods may become so highly flavored and combined that it is more difficult for the subconscious brain to recognize the true culprit. This is why someone who suffered food poisoning from the potato salad at a big watermelon seed spitting contest will suddenly detest watermelon. This is also the reason why a child who usually refuses cheese or milk may quickly down a delightfully flavored chocolate shake. Of course, after one or two bad experiences with shakes, his intellect may assist his deeper instincts, and he'll avoid that food if possible. Other things that will override this keen ability are constant encouragement or attempts to disguise foods, and outright hunger.

If a child seems to avoid dairy products, tomatoes, or some other food, it is probably best to follow his lead — especially if he suffers abdominal symptoms, stool changes, asthma, eczema, painful diaper rashes, or uncontrollable mood swings. One mother told me she had to work very hard to sneak tomatoes into her infant son's meals. Yes, they would cause him diarrhea — but she wanted him to derive the nutritional benefits and learn to enjoy a variety of ethnic dishes. The problem with this logic is that allergenic foods are tagged by the immune system to be rushed through without digestion or absorption, and any excess untagged portions can ignite a cascade of immune reactions that lead to inflamed intestinal linings, making it impossible for many other nutrients to be absorbed. Most likely there were whole pieces of undigested tomato and other foods in her son's stools. Not only will he not derive nutrition from tomatoes eaten, but he'll lose other nutrition from such a meal as well, and he may eventually learn to distrust any fancy-looking meal.

Infants who are sensitive to something in a formula — when it's their only food — may just become regularly cranky or withdrawn, slow growing, frequently waking, fussy eaters. These same infants will quickly and happily consume any solid food that is offered to them, and they will probably sleep better, given some relief from the formula.

Breastfed infants will become fussy at the breast or frequently reluctant to nurse if they are sensitive to foods in their mothers' diets. Sometimes they may learn to tell by taste or odor whether or not the current milk will be a problem for them. But when the offending food is in the milk most of the time, or when they react to multiple foods, they may just remain fussy nursers. Some of these infants become quickie-nursers who frequently need to come back for more out of hunger, and some go on nursing strikes. Unable to solve their dilemma and being frequently in discomfort, they too become cranky or antisocial babies most of the time.

Bedwetting & Daytime Incontinence

The inability to be in full control of one's bladder (after appropriate toilet training at an appropriate age) is known as "enuresis." Reduced bladder control is more common at night when the mind is asleep. Children who seem willing but are unable to successfully remain potty trained could have histamine-induced bladder contractions and inflammation secondary to food sensitivities.[28] Mast cells, which are initiators of most allergic responses, are most abundant in the membranes of the respiratory tract, under the skin, and in the linings of the urinary and intestinal tracts. Histamine-1 receptors, also abundant in the bladder wall, can react to immune system histamine releases just as those in the bronchii of the lungs do. Consequential inflammation and muscle contractions can cause strong urges to empty the bladder, which will cause wetting if the child cannot override them.

One analysis included bedwetting along with asthma and chronic illness in terms of their affect on growth (*see the section on short stature, page 300*). Stunted growth was found to be even more pronounced for children suffering with bedwetting problems than for those with asthma.[29] Since no reduction in height was found in those with non-allergic chronic illnesses, allergic disease evidently plays a role in stunting.

Other factors often suggested as possible causes for bedwetting are hormonal imbalances, bladder immaturity, anatomical abnormalities, behavioral problems, chronic bladder infections, and dietary habits (such as drinking before bed). Bladder infections are more common in females; they are sometimes related to hygiene and often respond to cranberry juice. The issue of potty training is beyond the scope of this book, but I wish to caution against alarm over a child's toilet habits before kindergarten age. One would certainly want to eliminate the simpler or more likely causes of incontinence though (such as food reactions), before beginning expensive, frightening, or invasive diagnostic measures or deciding to medicate a child.

One should suspect that bedwetting is caused by allergy when other hypersensitivity symptoms are present in the child. Several studies have linked it to asthma, eczema, migraine, and hyperactivity, as well as to food intolerance. In a probe performed by Dr. Joseph Egger and his colleagues, three fourths of children who found relief through elimination diets from migraines, hyperactivity, or both, also found relief from bedwetting problems through the diet.[30] As previously noted, a study of children diagnosed with attention-deficit hyperactivity disorder (*discussed below*) found their bedwetting to be 4.5 times that in other children.[31]

Behavior

Food intolerance reactions and other allergies or chemical sensitivities often affect the moods and behavior of children. Part of this effect is certainly a result of their discomfort, but more is learned every day about how histamine, serotonin, and prostaglandins, which are released when the body discovers allergens, act as neurotransmitters in the brain and affect mood ("shorten the fuse"). Generally, the reactive infant will demonstrate long or frequent inconsolable crying, a need to be bounced and walked all the time (to help override pain signals), frequent waking from sleep, and general fussiness and crankiness. As the infant gets older, greater crankiness and contrariness replace much of the crying, eventually leading to the tantrum level. The ability to fall asleep is often poor. In younger children, fits will begin as the immune reaction begins and will rise and fall as intestinal conditions and chemical conditions vary through a couple of days of reactivity. As children get older, they may be more in control of their behavior at times, but they will also much more easily ignite into a mood they can no longer control.

The preschooler will continue with bouts of contrariness and tantrums, and may begin earning the label of "hyperactivity disorder." Once a child has grown too old to be labeled with "colic," and before he can be labeled with hyperactivity disorder, there is a void where the behavior is considered normal and labeled as "terrible twos," which in the allergic child can last from the "ones" through the "threes." Once this child enters school, the eventual label of attention-deficit hyperactivity disorder (ADHD) is very likely.

One recent investigation of 26 children diagnosed with ADHD found that 73% of these children improved on diets that eliminated common multiple allergenic foods, preservatives, and colorings.[32] The results were confirmed with double-blind, placebo-controlled challenges. An earlier but well-designed study found improvement in 82%, with full recovery in 21%, noting that concurrent symptoms such as headaches, abdominal pains, and tantrums improved as well.[33] They felt artificial colors and preservatives were big offenders although no child responded only to these. *In order to finally settle a long-time dispute between various branches of medicine and psychology, a very recent analysis provided a summary of all the well-designed studies reported over a decade and concluded that diet definitely can affect the moods of children*[34] (which their mothers already knew). At about the same time, another undertaking provided evidence of electrical (EEG) alterations in beta wave brain activity in children with food-induced ADHD after they consumed response-provoking foods.[35] A study that found significant improvement in over half of hyperactive preschool boys noted the strong connection to sleep problems and also mentioned halitosis (bad breath).[36] A German investigation supports the contention that allergic children have a much higher incidence of attention-deficit disorder,[37] and a 1990 national study of 7,000 English children found a very strong association between parental reports of irritability and parental reports of food intolerance in their children.[38]

So this is it — our new and ever-growing classroom image full of "hyperactivity," "bad" behavior, ADHD... and children on drugs such as Ritalin. First came the push for detached parenting, accompanied by formula feeding, both of which we have shown to have powerful influences on children's behavior. Now, over the last 50 years, children's dairy consumption has grown from 1, then 2 glasses of milk per day, to cheese sticks, cheese crackers, cheese burgers, cheese and butter covered vegetables, yogurt, pudding, ice cream, cream sauces, cream cheese, sour cream dressing, buttered bread, milk at every meal, plus dairy ingredients being added to almost every prepared food on the grocery shelf.

Colic

Colic, now present in about 20% of U.S. infants, is often the first symptom in a food sensitive child, eventually attended by other bowel symptoms and possibly eczema. Colic is generally defined as three or more hours per day of crying, for three or more days a week. The real distinction should be in the intensity of crying, and whether it is easy or impossible to console the child. Colicky infants often do not sleep well and will wake from sleep with screams. Studies have shown that "normal" crying in infants can be reduced by increased carrying[39] and increased attentiveness, bringing their level of crying down closer to that of healthy infants in less industrialized nations. However, another study showed that increased carrying time may not reduce the crying of a baby with colic[40] (although jiggling and bouncing

may help relieve some immediate pain). Herein lies the key: A so-called normal baby may cry from a lack of body contact and a need for stimulation or security, as well as from overstimulation. But there is another kind of cry, one that causes parents to instinctively feel concern. A colicky infant's cries are forceful, pleading, and inconsolable. The parents know the child is in pain and distress despite the comforting advice these parents may receive from well-meaning advisors.

Bovine protein found in milk-based formulas or in the milk of dairy-consuming mothers is by far the greatest cause of colic. Other foods can cause colic too, but in almost all cases, the multiple food intolerant infant will include cow's milk in her list of irritating foods. Certainly other hidden causes can make an infant uncomfortable enough to display colic as well (in 3 to 5% some other organic disease is found), but the percentage of infants who recover through dietary measures alone is very high.

Figure 12-1 summarizes eight investigations into the effects of diet on infant colic. Of course it's difficult to find funding for such

Colicky Infants Recovery[41–48]				
	Sample Size	No Cow's Milk Protein (Soy)	Hydrolysate	Medication
Formula-fed Studies				
Oggero 1994	120	66%	95%	53%
Iacono 1991	70	71%		
Merritt 1990	21		71%	
Campbell 1989	19	58%	68%	
Lothe 1989	27		89%	
Weissbluth 1984	24			62%
Lothe 1982	60		71%	
Breastfed Study: Mother Had No Cow's Milk Protein				
Jakobsson 1983	66	53%		

Figure 12-1 Percentage of colicky infants who recover with elimination of cow's milk protein, hypoallergenic formula, or medication.

investigations. It's even less likely to find the results advertised. Six of these studies involved infants with colic who were fed milk-based formula. In three studies, cow's milk proteins (CMP) were eliminated from these infants' diets by substituting soy-based formulas (which contain the strong allergens of soy and corn). The percentage of colicky infants who responded in each trial is listed in the table. In two studies, those who did not respond to soy formula were then placed on hypoallergenic formulas made from hydrolyzed milk proteins where most of the bovine proteins are broken down into non-antigenic pieces. The total number of infants who recovered or improved significantly on either soy or hypoallergenic formula is listed. Three more trials tested CMP hydrolysate alone. The weighted average of these trials demonstrates that the chief source of colic in 67% of infants is intolerance of cow's milk proteins (relieved by soy formula). Eliminating soy and probably corn as well (hydrolysate formula) suggests allergens are the source of colic in 84%.

> 90% of the infants who
>
> failed to improve with
>
> hydrolysate formula
>
> recovered on elemental
>
> formula. Thus, the number
>
> of cases of infant colic
>
> that can be reduced or
>
> relieved by removal of
>
> cow's milk proteins and
>
> other allergens may
>
> approach 100%.

Other investigations demonstrate that many infants who do not respond to the hydrolyzed-protein formulas, which still contain small amounts of intact proteins, will still recover on experimental highly hydrolyzed formulas, lamb-based formulas, or elemental diets (where proteins are totally broken down into amino acids). One trial found that 90% of the infants who failed to improve with hydrolysate formula recovered on elemental formula.[49] Thus, the number of cases of infant colic that can be reduced or relieved by removal of cow's milk proteins and other allergens may approach 100%. Some who initially improve with CMP hydrolysate eventually become sensitive to the small amounts of bovine protein remaining in these formulas and will do better on elemental diets.[50]

Some professionals, still eager to protect cows' reputations, insist that relief from intestinal diseases from an elemental diet does not prove there was an allergy at all; rather, this diet simply gives the intestines a rest. A rest from what? When elimination of most milk protein alone gives extremely high recovery rates, and additional elimination of other allergens provides even greater results, then clearly an elemental diet, which removes *all* traces of milk protein and other allergens, is an extension of the ability to successfully remove allergens.

A 1986 study helped to confirm the connection between bovine protein and colic from a different angle. A study performed on breast-feeding mothers and their infants demonstrated that the presence and extent of colic in infants (as well as diarrhea, vomiting, and eczema) strongly correlates to the levels of bovine protein in their mothers' milk.[51] The quantities of bovine milk proteins in these women's milk did not correlate well with their level of dairy intake, but varied from mother to mother. The amounts also did not correlate with the level of allergy in the mothers (leaving the question as to what does cause the appearance of cow's milk proteins in the mothers' milk). Cow's milk protein levels in mother's milk would certainly approach zero if dairy were eliminated from the mothers' diets.

When a breastfeeding mother eliminates dairy from her diet, her infant may still react to other foods she is eating. When mothers of breastfeeding infants who are sensitive to multiple foods take measures to find and eliminate all the offending foods, their children do just as well as those who are on elemental diets. Moreover, a breastfeeding infant's nutrition, development, and protection will be superior.

In comparison to the dietary changes above, a common drug shows about 54% effectiveness in reducing symptoms in these trials. No studies suggest whether intestinal damage is prevented by this drug, or whether long-term disease consequences are prevented. While anticholinergic drugs do inhibit gastric secretions, immune reactions can still be going on. In contrast to the safety of dietary alterations, Dicyclomine and similar infant colic medications occasionally lead to breathing difficulties, including cases of apnea (lack of breathing) and cyanosis (life threatening lack of oxygen).[52] A link to cancer has also been suggested.[53] More common side effects are constipation, irregular heart rhythms, and overheating in hot weather. Dental cavities may also result from these medications as salivation is decreased.

> *A study performed on breastfeeding mothers and their infants demonstrated that the presence and extent of colic in infants (as well as diarrhea, vomiting, and eczema) strongly correlates to the levels of bovine protein in their mothers' milk.*

Two investigations on the relationship between colic and gas formation in the infant colon were performed by measuring the amount of hydrogen released in the breath of infants. One study found that colicky infants produce 3 times the amount of gas as those without colic.[54] Another found a two-thirds reduction in gas formation when fussy infants who had been fed milk-based formula were placed on soy formulas, resulting in a 40% reduction in their usual fussing.[50] Excess gas formation results from the increase in undigested and unabsorbed proteins and carbohydrates passed into the colon as a result of immune system tagging of antigens. The gas is created by fermentation of this material by the colon flora. Excess gas distends the bowel and causes abdominal pain.

The colons of newborns are quite leaky to large proteins compared to mature, healthy systems. This is by design to take advantage of mother's milk antibodies. This situation allows for some of the sensitization to foods that occurs in young infants. In the food-sensitized individual, at any age, the inflammation and cellular damage that occurs as a result of immune responses causes the gut to be more leaky. A Swedish pediatrician and professor and her colleagues set out to demonstrate this and its relevance to colic.[56] They used a human milk protein as a marker protein. They found this protein in colicky breastfed infants at a level 6 times that in the non-colicky nursers, thereby demonstrating the amount of intact protein that was able to pass through the colon wall into the blood. This same marker protein was added to infant formulas and then found in formula-fed colicky infants at levels 12 times that of those without colic, again demonstrating the high level of leaking in colicky infant colons.

Constipation

There are many causes for constipation. Sometimes a child continually ignores the urge to pass stool. More and more water is then absorbed from the stool, making it harder and more uncomfortable to pass. This source of constipation may occur in an active child from the age of potty training on, but generally cannot be used as an explanation for infant constipation. Retraining of proper bowel habits can reverse this cycle. An Iowa doctor found relief in 52% of constipated infants one year after training treatment began.[57] Insufficient fluids, especially in hot weather, inactivity, and changes in diet or routine are other common causes. A formula-fed baby will generally have firmer stools than his breastfed counterpart.

Many cases diagnosed as chronic infectious diarrhea, colitis, or some other pathology are the end result of food hypersensitivity reactions.

Food sensitivity should be considered when constipation is very chronic, and simple measures such as fluids and exercise do not work. One study found that infants were relieved from chronic constipation in 21 out of 27 cases (78%) when cow's milk protein alone was removed from their diets.[58] Laboratory testing confirmed sensitivity in most of these, and constipation returned in all of the infants when milk was returned to their diets. A larger, double-blind study by the same researchers found the same improvement in 68% of those tested.[59] One fourth of these had other allergic symptoms such as rashes, runny noses, or asthma. Three fourths of them had laboratory confirmation of bovine protein sensitivity. Other studies have found strong correlation between cow's milk and constipation as well.[60]

Diarrhea

Diarrhea is the major manifestation of bovine protein sensitivity in infants and is a predominant symptom in children with other food intolerance. Food intolerance is the most likely cause of "nonspecific" or "non-infectious" diarrhea. However, as the inflammatory process continues, infection often sets in and many cases diagnosed as chronic infectious diarrhea, colitis, or some other pathology are the end result of food hypersensitivity reactions.

The following table summarizes the recovery rates reported with diets eliminating allergens and the improvement from common medication, for various diarrhea-related diagnoses. Some studies used only IgE antibody reactions when designing allergen-eliminating diets. IgE is associated mostly with immediate allergic reactions, which occur within minutes, not with delayed allergic reactions that may take hours or many days to manifest. These studies found lower success rates than more inclusive studies that tested for IgG antibodies and other indicators, especially those that included food challenges. Food challenges selectively offer suspect foods one at a time to see whether an allergic response is forthcoming.

In one study, which revealed 87% improvement in relieving diarrhea by eliminating milk and other allergic foods, 23% of the participants admitted they had not adhered well to the diet. This same finding had been reported in other dietary studies as well. The typical conclusion by researchers (well educated by the dairy industry) is that dietary management is too difficult to bother with. My

Recovery with Elimination Diet or Medication [61-68]

Study	Diagnosis	Sample	Non-allergenic Diet	Medication
Machida 1994	Colitis	31 infants	61%	
Jenkins 1984	Colitis	8 infants	100%	
Malchow 1990	Crohn's	40 adults	21/22 95%	80% for 6 weeks
Jones 1985	Crohn's	77 adults	80%	
Malchow 1984	Crohn's	192 adults		40% for 2 years
Meta-analysis 1994	Irritable Bowel	26 studies		27% standard medications
Grazioli 1993	Irritable Bowel	153 infants	87%	97% cromolyn
Jones 1982	Irritable bowel	21 adults	67%	

Figure 12-2 Percentage recovery seen for certain diseases in various studies using either elimination dieting or medication.

conclusion is that diet is apparently the cause of the disease in genetically susceptible children. People should at least be encouraged to try eliminating the cause first. This is rather simple in infants; simply use either elemental formula or control mother's diet. There are so many kinds of foods available today that it is unlikely that an adequately nutritious diet could not be found, except for in the most severe cases (which would not have been so severe had they been managed by diet sooner).

Infections are also responsible for several distinctive types of damage that will eventually earn diagnoses such as colitis, ulcer, or Crohn's disease, depending on the main organism involved.

In one investigation, 70 infants with food intolerance diarrhea were examined, and all had inflammation and infection of the stomach and duodenum (chronic gastroduodenitis). One third of these suffered from destruction of the nutrient absorbing villi of the intestinal lining.[69] An immune system attack on allergenic foods will cause diarrhea and will decrease the local defenses of the mucous lining of the intestines, allowing microorganisms to adhere to the digestive tract and multiply, resulting in infectious diarrhea.[70] This infection and damage leads to malabsorption of nutrients, and along with the diarrhea itself, is a very common source of failure to thrive in infants. These infections are also responsible for several distinctive types of damage that will eventually earn diagnoses such as colitis, ulcer, or Crohn's disease, depending on the main organism involved.[71] The microbe that causes the destructive infection in Crohn's disease (*Mycobacterium paratuberculosis*) happens to come from cow's milk as well.

The incidence of diarrhea in formula-fed infants from industrialized nations is at least double that in breastfed infants, with 5 to 7 times as many prolonged episodes in formula babies.[72-74] The immune properties of breastmilk and the more friendly flora of breastfed infants help to prevent infection of the intestinal walls.

Ear Infections

Middle ear fluid buildup (known as serous otitis, chronic otitis, or otitis media with effusion) and middle ear infections (acute otitis) have increased greatly over the last several decades, particularly in infants,[75] just as other symptoms of allergy and food sensitivity have. Two thirds of children in the U.S. experience at least one ear infection, and one third experience multiple episodes.[76] The small mucous membrane lining of children's ear tubes swells up with inflammatory allergic reactions, blocking off the middle ear and allowing fluid to accumulate and eventually bacteria to multiply. The evidence is unquestionable that food allergies are the most common cause for otitis when it is persistent in children, yet this is seldom told to parents, unless by another parent who has discovered it for themselves.

Shugrue Photography

One researcher using detailed laboratory techniques found allergies present in 97% of children who had persistent serous otitis.[77] Dr. Nsouli and his colleagues used food challenge testing and discovered food allergy in 78% of chronic otitis children.[78] Significant long-term improvement occurred in 86% of the food allergic children with food elimination diets. The source of this success was then confirmed when otitis returned in 94% of these children when they were challenged with foods that had been found suspect through laboratory testing and previous food challenges. Twenty-five percent of those with no dietary modification or medication improved.

Higher amounts of anti-bovine IgE and IgM antibodies have been found in children who suffer recurrent otitis than in those who do not.[79] Anti-bovine IgG antibodies have also been discovered within the fluid in otitis media cases, and it is proposed that these activate inflammatory chemical releases within the middle ear cavity.[80]

An investigation of the usefulness of "allergy shots" for recurring serous otitis media reported 65% recovery with this therapy and stated that all those who did not respond to therapy recovered on food elimination diets.[81] Another study used shots and diet, finding improvement in 80% of those found to be allergic. The adherence to diet was strongly associated with outcome.[82]

We have seen earlier that antibiotic treatments afford minimal, if any, help with ear infections. The inability of drug and surgical treatments to afford long-term recovery of otitis suggests the cause is not being addressed. In light of the positive and permanent results reported with dietary elimination, and the lack of side effects involved, it seems prudent to investigate this possibility in chronic cases of otitis media. It's difficult to find financial backers for food allergy studies, since the cure (eliminating allergenic foods) lines no pockets, while there is plenty of money to promote medications and to squash damaging rumors about certain foods. For this reason, many a family has had to reinvent the wheel in finding the sources of their child's chronic ear infections. Many more have had to just suffer through the ongoing illnesses and the side effects of medications and chronically impaired hearing.

Epilepsy

In a study on 63 children with epilepsy, 45 of them also had migraines, hyperactivity, and abdominal symptoms. Of the 45 with these food sensitivity symptoms, 25 were cured and 11 more improved on diets that eliminated most common allergens. Other symptoms improved in most of the 45 as well. None of the 18 who had epilepsy alone improved on the diet.[83]

> Psychiatrists have taken the symptoms commonly associated with fatigue syndromes and designed psychological diagnoses to fit them. When laboratory analyses or double-blind food challenge tests are performed, the relationship between a patient's fatigue and their reported food intolerance is generally found to be a valid physical immune reaction.

Eyes

Dark circles, bags, and skin folds under the eyes are visible signs of allergic children. Itchy eyes often result from allergies or sensitivities to airborne substances, although they have been reported in food sensitivities as well.

Fatigue

Studies often report links between fatigue in children (some with "chronic fatigue syndrome") and food or other allergies.[84] Studies on fatigue syndromes beyond infancy find a high correlation with other symptoms[85] such as irritable bowel and headache that have been found to be strongly associated with allergies and food intolerance in laboratory testing and double-blind challenges. One probe found irritable bowel syndrome in 63% of fatigue sufferers.[86]

Psychiatrists have taken the symptoms commonly associated with fatigue syndromes and designed psychological diagnoses to fit them. Now someone with these symptoms can easily be labeled as suffering a psychological problem. When laboratory analyses or double-blind food challenge tests are performed, the relationship between a patient's fatigue and their reported food intolerance is generally found to be a valid physical immune reaction. The younger the patient, the more likely it is that laboratory and diet testing will be performed, although many practitioners often do not have enough awareness to request the proper testing.

After performing detailed blood tests, one study found a very high correlation between allergy-related blood indicators and chronic fatigue syndrome complaints.[87] This study also found an absence of personality disorders in these subjects. It did, however, find some symptoms correlated with the psychiatric diagnoses (which, as we've said, are merely labels that were designed around typical fatigue reaction symptoms). The study concluded that the symptoms of fatigue syndrome resulted from "abnormal psychological response to the disordered expression" of allergic immune reactions, which degrades the fatigue sufferer, but I suppose it was an attempt to distinguish between allergy sufferers who complain of fatigue and those who do not. Interestingly, when fatigue (lethargy), gastrointestinal symptoms, and rashes are displayed in dogs, food sensitivity and not psychological disorder is assumed to be the cause. Elimination diet is the recommended course of care in dogs.[88,89]

Headaches

Headaches are not believed to be very common in young children, becoming more common and more severe after the age of 5 or so. Although headaches come from many different causes, the frequent relationship between headaches, especially migraine, and food or chemical sensitivities is well known and seldom disputed. A test of 88 children with migraine that provided non-allergenic diets found recovery in 93% of them.[90] Associated symptoms such as abdominal pain, behavior problems, tantrums, eczema, and asthma improved as well. A study of older children suffering from migraine found significant or complete remission from headaches in 92% of those who followed low antigen diets designed for each patient through elimination diets with double-blind challenges, as well as laboratory studies.[91] Hazelnuts, egg, and cocoa were among the foods implicated. Migraine is usually induced by different types of foods than most of what is being described in this chapter.[92] Cow's milk is not often connected with migraine headaches. A well-designed investigation found the immune system chemicals histamine and certain prostaglandins to be affecting the brain in people who suffer food-related headaches.[93] MSG (which goes under dozens of names) and aspartame cause headaches in some sensitive individuals, as confirmed by double-blind studies.[94,95] These are chemically induced effects that are different from the immune reactions we have covered.

Rashes

Eczema appears as dry, scaly, usually red, and often itchy patches of skin. Curiously, this type of rash is often called "atopic dermatitis," which means "allergic skin condition," even when the probability that allergy is causing the condition is not being acknowledged. The majority of eczema cases result from delayed intestinal food reactions, so it is often difficult to make the connection. Generally occurring on the face, especially the cheeks and around the mouth, as well as the upper chest, wrists, and hands, eczema may also occur inside the bends of the elbow and knees, and around the ankles and over the feet. Sometimes pimples concentrate around the mouth area. In others eczema may arise over the chest and low back. Sometimes it is accompanied by cradle cap.

Two other skin conditions that commonly go along with food sensitivities are angioedema, a swelling of the vasculature beneath the skin seen as redness and puffiness on the face and body, and hives, which are raised, red, itchy areas.[96] These conditions are loosely included when speaking about atopic dermatitis or eczema.

Eczema is commonly associated with other food sensitivity symptoms such as diarrhea or asthma. Sometimes other symptoms are not obvious, but the condition should still not be ignored. A *1992 study of 52 children with eczema and no intestinal complaints showed that all suffered immune compromising digestive tract inflammation, even if diarrhea was absent.*[97] Intestinal biopsy studies have demonstrated that intact proteins are being absorbed across the intestinal wall in children with eczema at a rate 10 times higher than in normal children.[98] This is the leaky gut described in the case of cow's milk and other food sensitivity reactions. Food hypersensitivity was found in 64% of children with eczema in one study that used double-blind, placebo-controlled challenges.[99] Other studies have reported higher correlations. Intestinal inflammation (gastro-duodenitis) and damage to villi contribute to the increased occur-rence of failure to thrive that is found with infants who have eczema. What does this mean? It means that lack of efforts to find and eliminate the sources of eczema (not just covering it up with steroid creams) can allow the child's health and development to be compromised.

Many food intolerant or otherwise allergic infants may display only a few little pimples around the mouth, or no rashes at all; eczema is the most commonly found of the many food-related symptoms. Eczema is also strongly associated with asthma and aller-gic rhinitis. I have described its prevalence in food sensitivities, and thus the association with bowel symptoms. Many researchers report its occurrence in association with other symptoms, often without recognizing the probable common origin. Dr. Kathi Kemper, author of *The Holistic Pediatrician*, notes that children with eczema often suffer sleep problems, behavior problems, and "difficult tempera-ments" as well. She associates these behaviors with the itching skin. She has found the correlations, but she may be missing the bigger picture.

Respiratory Symptoms: Runny Nose, Chronic Cough & Asthma

Chronic runny nose (rhinitis) and pulmonary (lung) symp-toms, common in the better-known airborne allergies, are some-times brought on by food sensitivity reactions. Lung symptoms include chronic coughing fits that can be either mild asthma or a pre-asthma condition. Coughing fits can also be caused by bron-chitis resulting from a bronchial infection, such as may occur after a cold. There is little shortness of breath involved, but by placing your ear on the chest, a rattling can be heard during deep breath-ing. The food sensitive individual with respiratory responses can be more disposed to chronic bronchitis because excess mucus in the airways provides a good breeding ground for microorganisms. Asthma presents itself as attacks of wheezing and the inability to catch your breath. Also referred to as bronchospasm, it results from contractions in the involuntary muscle tissues of the bronchi and the smaller bronchii (branching air tubes) of the lungs. Asthma attacks occur predominantly after exercise or other stress, or during the night.

Dr. D.S. Feigin describes the changes that occur in the lungs based on the type of sensitivity reaction experienced. Immediate (type 1) reactions obstruct the airways with mucus and produce the bronchial spasms of asthma with which we are most familiar. Delayed (type 2, 3, and 4) responses, which would be food reactions, come in a few varieties, causing hemorrhage, inflammation, or enlarged lymph nodes.[100] Airborne allergens have been cited as the most common irritants in asthma, including dust mites, animal dander, molds, and pollens. After these, foods, food additives, and certain drugs are indicted. Fumes such as fresh paint, perfumes, and pesticides can significantly provoke respiratory problems, evidently more often with age or chronic exposure. Smoking and air pollution are also major contributing factors,[101] and secondhand smoke has been shown to play a major role in childhood respiratory distress.

Hospital admissions for asthma have increased nearly twenty-fold over the last 35 years for young children to the age of 4.[102] Thousands of children and adults in the U.S. die each year of asthma (over 5,500 in 1996), even though asthma was almost never considered fatal before the 1950s. Certainly part of the problem is indoor and outdoor air pollution. While air pollution peaked in the 1960s, asthma death rates have grown, but cyclically, not steadily. Early introduction of formula and solids may account for much of the increase in this disease, but not the rise and falls in death rates. According to Dr. John Mansfield, author of *Asthma Epidemic*, death rates surge in accordance with increases

> *Thousands of children and adults in the U.S. die each year of asthma (over 5,500 in 1996), even though asthma was almost never considered fatal before the 1950s.*

in drug prescription rates with the advent of each new kind of asthma drug.[103]

Among children with food hypersensitivities and eczema, 59% also suffer respiratory reactions of some kind.[104] Children whose food allergies are persistent beyond two years of age have a 3.4 times higher incidence of rhinitis and a 5.5 times higher risk of becoming asthmatic than those who "grow out" of their food allergies early.[105]

While often little or no mention of allergy is made by a physician treating asthma, it has been determined that 80% of asthmatics and 90% of children with rhinitis suffer immediate type 1 allergies.[106] The remaining 20% and 10% respectively are most likely accounted for by delayed-reaction food sensitivities, with much overlap of conditions as well. The lungs are lined with a great number of H-1 histamine receptors and spasms of the little branches in the lungs (bronchioles) occur when these respond (or overrespond) to histamine releases. Unfortunately, to date, studies of asthma–food relationships tend to focus on immediate reactions; moreover, trials do not incorporate the common additional stressors. Typically, asthmatic reactions to foods require larger doses of allergen than do nasal reactions.[107] All asthma attacks are much more apt to occur when additional stressors such as exercise and emotional distress are added, as well as cigarette smoke and high pollen or smog counts. It is known that antihistamines, drugs that reduce histamine responses, are not always effective for asthmatics. This may be because susceptible lung tissues are being irritated by other chemicals and roaming antigen-antibody complexes created from intestinal reactions to foods. The actions of such chemicals and immune complexes are not well blocked by H-1 antihistamines alone.

> *Formula feeding before 3 months of age is a major risk factor for persistent asthma.*

The first link between asthma and food allergies is in the finding that formula feeding before 3 months of age is a major risk factor for persistent asthma.[108] About half of young asthmatic children are still suffering at age 4. Most who are still asthmatic at 4 will continue to suffer into adulthood. Some children first develop asthma after the age of 4. Often these children had earlier allergic signs, such as rashes or colic.

Reports that cow's milk is a mucus-producing food are strongly defended by some, but found not reproducible by others. Those who suffer chronic rhinitis or bronchial problems due to cow's milk sensitivity most likely account for the common reports of milk being a "mucus food."

Cow's milk sensitivity has been incriminated in some cases of pulmonary hemosiderosis — a condition where iron builds up in the lungs, causing iron deficiency anemia, poor lung performance, and eventually heart failure.[109]

Several studies report correlations between asthma and other sensitivity symptoms: One of these cites food allergy, eczema, frequent ear infections, and frequent sinus attacks.[110]

Short Stature

Several studies show that children with moderate to extensive eczema, and to a lesser extent those with asthma, grow to a shorter average height than do non-allergic children.[111] These children seem to obtain normal leg lengths, but shorter sitting statures.[112]

Children with untreated food sensitivities (those who don't successfully avoid foods to which they react) maintain high levels of inflammation and damaged villi much of the time and thus suffer from various degrees of malabsorption throughout their important growing years, and malabsorption means malnutrition. This could certainly explain the stunted growth seen in asthmatic and eczematous children. Medical studies express concern over the possibility that steroid medications used to treat asthma (inhaled) as well as eczema (applied topically) could be the cause of reduced growth, and this needs further investigation. However, the greatest reduction in expected height is seen in children with bedwetting problems, another symptom associated with food sensitivity reactions, for which corticosteroid medication is not standard treatment. Also, height reduction has been shown to occur chiefly in those asthmatic children who were considered the most allergic, as opposed to those who demonstrated little evidence of hypersensitivity reactions. The extent of stunting also correlated with the degree of allergic suffering.[113]

Dr. T. David suggests that if short stature is due to disease, and disease remits before puberty, then catch-up growth should occur. However if the stunted growth is caused by steroid therapy, or if allergic disease lasts into adult life, catch-up growth would not be expected.[114] He suggests that the sleeplessness of atopic children could contribute to stunting as well. Theoretically, according to Dr. David's suggestions, if allergens are avoided as much as possible, and if steroid use is avoided, the child should have a good chance of obtaining near-optimal growth.

Sleeplessness

Sleeplessness, frequent waking, and difficulty falling asleep are strongly associated with food intolerance and are mentioned by many food allergy researchers in their studies of other symptoms. One small study looked specifically at sleep difficulties. To investigate the sleeplessness of 17 children whose poor sleep could not be blamed on inappropriate sleep habits, cow's milk was experimentally removed from their diets. Sleep patterns normalized in 16 of the 17, and double-blind crossover challenges confirmed these results.[115]

Tonsillitis

We have seen that food and other allergies can lead to chronically inflamed mucous membranes and mucus production. The tonsils and adenoids are little bundles of immune-reacting tissues in the back of the throat situated right in the middle of these problems. These can become chronically congested by inflammatory immune cells in response to food or other allergy, even with little noticeable sinus congestion. When this occurs, they can then harbor viruses and bacteria, becoming very enlarged, and contributing to frequent throat infections and illnesses. This chronic enlargement also often leads to snoring. The huge trend of removing the tonsils in children, which became popular just after formula and cow's milk became very popular, has since settled down. Once they are removed, chronic congestion, leading to chronic illness, still occurs in the mucous membranes of the throat, nasal passages, and lungs. The procedure is often unsuccessful for reducing illness because the true source of the problem, allergy, is not being addressed.

> Among children with cystic fibrosis (a lung disease increasingly prevalent over the last century) who also suffered diarrhea, 90% improved when allergenic foods were discovered and eliminated from their diets.

Others

Furrows in the tongue, lacy tongue edges, geographic tongue (patterns of ulcers on tongue surface which incidentally are similar to damage seen in intestinal mucosa), and atrophic tongue (smooth surface portions where taste buds are barely apparent) are often seen in allergic and food intolerant children and adults.[116] Poor memory, learning disorders, autism,[117] muscle weakness, vertigo, palpitations, blurred vision, bad breath, and red ears, cheeks, and noses have at times been implicated as a result of allergy and food intolerance in certain children. The known allergy connections to autism are now building every day.

Several studies report a very high occurrence of allergy, and especially sensitivity to cow's milk protein, in several forms of glomerulonephritis, a degenerative disease of the kidney in children.[118,119]

Among children with cystic fibrosis (a lung disease increasingly prevalent over the last century) who also suffered diarrhea, 90% improved when allergenic foods were discovered and eliminated from their diets.[120] A study looked at infants who were admitted to a hospital due to diarrhea caused by cow or soy protein intolerance.

Conditions Responding to Elimination Diets

Symptom	Cow's Milk	Multiple Foods
ADHD		80%
Colic	67%	84%
Add Elemental Diet for Colic		98%
Constipation	71%	
Chronic otitis media		86%
Diarrheal diseases		82%
Migraines		93%
Sleeplessness	94%	

Figure 12-3 Weighted averages of cases shown to respond to eliminating cow's milk or multiple allergenic foods from the diet, taken from multiple studies, as presented in the text.

Six of these infants were also suffering a transient disorder of the oxygen-carrying capacity of their red blood cells (methemoglobinemia), and these six represented 65% of the total hospitalizations for methemoglobinemia.

Summary

Typically, food intolerance can be suspected when multiple symptoms are present, but it has also been shown that children whose parents report only eczema often harbor irritated or damaged intestinal linings. Symptoms such as diarrhea, constipation, mood swings, and rashes are very common indicators; however, everybody responds differently, presenting a wide range of symptoms. The number of infants and children whose comfort and health could be greatly improved through dietary corrections is staggering. The table above summarizes the percentage of patients found to recover from various problems through food elimination diets according to a review of medical literature.

Strange Genes

I present this section more for entertainment (mine) than for any kind of diagnostic value. The factors of cause and effect are unknown, although many plausible hypotheses could be made.

Many investigations over the last fifteen years have confirmed a significant prevalence of non-right-handedness (partial or dominant left-handedness) in allergic people.[121,122] At least one study ties in musical talent as well.[123] Several more studies also correlate near-sightedness, altered verbal skills, high IQ, and strong math abilities with allergics.[124-126] Other probes bring to light a high correlation between head circumference at birth and the possibility of developing allergies. Those with head circumferences of 14 inches or more (associated with higher IQ) develop allergies more than 4 times as often as those with head circumferences of 13 inches or less.[127,128] A 1998 report sites several chromosomes thought to be in play.[129] Type 1 immediate allergies are more common in males, while chemical sensitivities are more common in females.

If you find your child suffers from allergies, the evidence is that allergic individuals are more often intelligent (and some say limited in athletic abilities). Surely you have heard people say that a "difficult" baby's behavior could be a sign of intelligence. Fussiness, contrariness, and irritability are common symptoms of sensitivities. A restless fetus could be an early sign as well, as sensitization can begin in utero (thus, that kicker may not be the football hero).

The word for allergy, "atopy," means "strange disease."

13

Allergy Matters

THE NUMBER OF ADULTS SUFFERING FROM BOWEL SYNDROMES HAS
more than tripled over the last fifty years. Autoimmune diseases and
allergies have similarly increased. The percentage of children developing diabetes and hyperactivity has increased tremendously
throughout this century. What does all of this have to do with
hypersensitivity reactions in babies? Are these problems connected
to the decline in breastfeeding and to the new baby foods: cow's
milk formulas, soy formulas, and cow's milk?

Why the Concern?

A century ago, the incidence of childhood and adult allergies was reported to be 15%. Today, more than half of all infants suffer from some kind of sensitivity reactions. Changes in our environment and parenting styles are responsible. Colic, constipation, diarrhea, vomiting, failure to thrive, diaper rashes, eczema, fussiness, chronic middle ear fluid and infections, difficulty sleeping, waking with screams during naps, chronic stuffiness, asthma, loss of appetite or refusal of the breast — all these are signs of reactions to foods in the infant. The toddler may also exhibit uncharacteristic bouts of contrary and uncontrollable behavior. The school-age child may have daytime wetting and bedwetting problems, may suffer with headaches, or may be labeled with attention-deficit hyperactivity disorder (ADHD).

> When sensitivity reactions occur, the cellular damage that goes along with these inflammatory responses can predispose these children to developing many major diseases later in life.

Early introduction of solid foods, especially the heavy cow proteins present in infant formulas and in the breastmilk of mothers who drink cow's milk, has been the major cause of the growing sensitivity rates. While we certainly want to avoid the pain and suffering experienced by food sensitive infants in and of itself, we now also understand that when sensitivity reactions occur, the cellular damage that goes along with inflammatory responses can predispose children to developing many major diseases later in life. Additionally, in the case of intestinal reactions, malabsorption syndrome can occur, robbing a child of important immune-building, brain-building, and body-developing nutrients.

There are long-term ramifications to allowing babies to "tough it out," as some are advised to do. Treating only symptoms without attempting to find and eliminate the causes can lead to harm —

for instance, repeatedly applying steroid creams to baby rashes, or supplying sedatives and sleep aids to colicky infants. Taxing the immune system with allergens early on and ignoring the reactions has led to large increases in cases of arthritis and other autoimmune diseases, irritable bowel syndrome, colitis, Crohn's disease, diverticulitis, asthma, childhood diabetes, and certain forms of cancer.

Over 14.6 million Americans suffer from asthma. Over 35 million doctor visits per year are for disorders of the digestive system. The percentage of infants suffering from these diseases has rapidly increased over the last 75 years, and adult manifestations of disease have similarly risen over the last 50 years. A major portion of our society is suffering from annoying, weakening, or crippling, sensitivity-related conditions that we now have the knowledge and power to prevent, starting at infancy.

Bowel Diseases & Cancer

When food-related gastrointestinal complaints are dismissed, or more often, not even considered, children are diagnosed with colic, chronic gastroenteritis, colitis, irritable bowel syndrome, Crohn's disease, or ulcerative colitis. Research is now confirming that these diseases are caused by chronic delayed immune reactions to foods, which lead to serious complications that could have been prevented. In the absence of acute infection, symptoms such as abdominal pains, watery stools, bloody stools, chronic diarrhea, and even constipation are signs of inflammatory reactions going on in the intestines. Most often these are caused by food sensitivities.[1,2]

Childhood sensitivity symptoms may change with age, but, untreated, these problems often present themselves throughout much of the child's life. The more troubling symptoms may abate for many years, only to return after a stressful lifestyle reduces immune function in adulthood. The infant with chronic constipation or diarrhea and rashes very often becomes the adult with chronic headaches and troubling irritable bowel syndrome. The child with bouts of altered behavior, chronic fatigue syndrome, wild tantrums, or ADHD becomes the adult suffering from depression or schizophrenia.

Colitis is a term often used when inflammation and damage occur in the large intestine, the colon. The diagnosis of irritable bowel syndrome is often used for inflammatory conditions of either the large or small intestine. Crohn's disease is another such condition, with a slightly different and more severe diagnostic picture. With ulcerative colitis (or irritable bowel or whatever term is used) destruction of the intestinal walls is occurring with every reaction, and long-standing symptoms (eight years or more) predispose the individual not only to debilitating malabsorption syndrome, but also to the development of intestinal cancer.[3-5]

Those suffering from gluten sensitivity (celiac disease) are found to have a mortality rate nearly double that of the general population. A large study showed that increased deaths resulted from cancers of the digestive tract, including the throat.[6] Infection with *Helicobacter pylori*, especially common in dairy allergy, is associated with a tripled risk of stomach cancer.[7] *Even adolescents and young adults are at risk for intestinal cancer if they have suffered long-standing inflammatory intestinal conditions.* One probe found that nearly 25% of these young individuals presented precancerous cells, and 1 in the 35 studied was found to already have cancer.[8]

> If a parent could actually see this damage, they would probably be much more concerned. Additionally, it is this regular irritation of the digestive system linings that predisposes one to cancer.

Intestinal biopsies of food-sensitive infants have demonstrated that destructive inflammatory reactions occur deep in the mucosal linings of the intestines. Wasting of the tiny finger-like villi along the intestinal walls, important for exchange of nutrients, is seen, along with other destructive alterations.[9-11] Sometimes fissures and ulcers can be seen in the child's mouth and tongue, as can sores around the mouth. These provide a small picture of what may be going on in more important intestinal tissues.

Although often nothing is seen by parents using the naked eye, painful-looking destruction is occurring inside the infant who reacts to foods. If a parent could actually see this damage, they would probably be much more concerned. Additionally, it is this regular irritation of the digestive system linings that predisposes one to cancer.

More Diabetes Connections

In Chapter 11 we discussed the strong link between intolerance of cow's milk proteins and development of childhood diabetes. Other disorders that are highly associated with food intolerance are seen much more often in diabetics than in the non-allergic population. Ulcered tongue (atrophic and geographic tongue) is seen in 30% of diabetics.[12] There is a high rate of atrophic gastritis among diabetics as well, where the lining of the stomach is worn down by chronic inflammatory reactions. This condition has been shown to be strongly correlated with infection by *Helicobacter pylori* in childhood.[13] Other researchers point out that in diabetic children, childhood *H. pylori* infection is strongly associated with the presence of cow's milk antibodies in their blood.[14]

What Causes Hypersensitivity Reactions?

Various sources indicate that there is a 60 to 100% chance that when both parents have some kind of allergy, their children will have allergies. If only one parent has allergies, the likelihood for the children is quoted between 30 and 50%. While there are surely other causes, many children are genetically predisposed to overreact to certain allergens. The kinds of responses and the locations that will be affected seem to be predetermined to some degree, but the food and environment they are exposed to are the determining factors for the extent of their allergic disease. Approximately 20% of children with low genetic risk develop allergies as well.[15]

> Among all the potential causes for sensitivity problems, most studies point to cow's milk as the largest offender by far.

Gastrointestinal infections (more common in formula-feeding) can initiate food sensitivity problems as potential allergens are allowed to leak across irritated intestinal walls. Some other causes can be early introduction of solid foods, including formula, or high exposure to chemicals and allergens such as pets, perfumes, pollen, cigarette smoke, and dust mites. Stress can also make a child's body more reactive to allergens (and we know that babyhood and childhood have become more stressful). This can be clearly seen in asthmatics with certain allergies or sensitivities: They often become symptomatic only with exercise or stress.

Many look to our human roots to examine how our digestive system may have evolved to process a diet much different than the one we eat today. We did not evolve eating processed, refined, and drug-laden foods. Just as certainly we did not evolve on the milk of another very different kind of animal. The huge variety in the foods and spices we eat is also very new to our genome. Even grains are relatively new in human diets. Hunter–gatherers would most likely have had simple diets of meat, roots, and greens. Those who could not tolerate the diet of their people simply would not live to pass on their genes. Many children with multiple food sensitivities today are found to flourish on a simple meat, potato, and greens diet.

Among all the potential causes for sensitivity problems, most studies point to cow's milk as the largest offender by far.[16–22] We now know that, although it may be packed with certain nutrients, cow's milk is not meant for humans, especially for infants. We know that the intestinal irritation and bleeding commonly associated with consumption of bovine milk proteins in infants goes on to allow heavy proteins to pass through the intestinal protective barriers, causing deleterious immune reactions.

Mother's milk is designed to provide immunity and other components important to baby. It has special properties that prevent white blood cells, antibodies, hormones, and other chemicals in her milk from being broken down before they can be used by the infant. Cow's milk contains the same preventive media. Thus, the child drinking formula or milk from cows is exposed to whole bovine white blood cells, cow antibodies that cause negative reactions in the human system, cow hormones, many of which may have hormonal effects in human systems, antibiotics and other drugs in a highly absorbable media, and whole bacteria that exist in the highly infected cows, several strains of which easily escape the short low-temperature pasteurization process.[23]

Betalactoglobulin, one of the several bovine milk proteins, is much larger than the proteins found in human milk. In fact, it is probably larger than any proteins found in any other foods we eat. These poorly digested proteins react with intestinal tissues and are able to pass through the intestinal walls, causing havoc in the tiny immune system. Even infants who are breastfed may be subjected to cow's milk proteins from dairy products in their mothers' diets. Many breastfeeding mothers are encouraged to offer supplemental formula bottles to their babies as well.

What Can We Do?

Parental actions may help reduce the development of allergies; breastfeeding and delaying solid foods are two of the strongest. Beyond this, watching for signs of allergic reactions, such as rashes and stool abnormalities, is an important step in guarding the life-long health of your child. Prevention is the best health care for a baby and the adult he or she will become. Diminishing the amount of damage that occurs in infancy will provide a healthier and more comfortable childhood and can decrease the chance that diseases will develop in adulthood.

In many European countries, parents are advised to determine the likelihood of allergies before their child is born, based on family history. The mother can then avoid certain foods or other allergens during the second half of her pregnancy in an attempt to avoid sensitizing the baby's immune system. More apt to breastfeed, she may also automatically avoid key allergens in her diet while nursing, or she could provide a hypoallergenic formula to her child before sensitivities are ever detected. Good statistical results in reducing childhood and adult hypersensitivities are obtained using this procedure.[24,25] Food sensitivity rates in children are going back down in some countries, including Spain.[26]

The Ignored Diagnosis

Now that you're familiar with the major symptoms of allergies and the importance of recognizing them, you will need to know what to do if and when allergy is suspected. Because allergy is so widely prevalent in infants and at the same time so poorly recognized by a large portion of the medical community, I will give you a bare bones presentation of the science of these reactions, the diagnosis, and the treatment choices. If you don't need this information right now, you may wish to only glance through the rest of this book, saving it for future reference.

Some medical papers still report that only 15 to 25% of our population is suffering from allergies. These are not extensive studies however. These numbers come from confirmed standard IgE test results on complaining patients. They do not include most of those with delayed hypersensitivity reactions, those who do not consider themselves allergic, or those who do not demonstrate appropriate blood or skin test reactions.

I cannot recount the number of times I've observed congested patients or heard them complain about sinus pain during our infamous San Diego Santa Ana days, when the pollen count soars. In response to my remarks about their allergies, the common reply is: "No, I just have 'sinus.'" What exactly is "sinus"? It is inflamed membranes reacting to irritants — which are allergens. Some "sinus" is even less easily sleuthed, since it results from delayed sensitivity reaction to milk or other foods.

It is important to understand that frequent abdominal pain, gas, diarrhea, constipation, or vomiting are simply not normal to a healthy infant. Vomiting includes any excess spitting up. When these symptoms occur, it is apparent that some kind of less than desirable actions are occurring within the digestive system.

Before 1925, allergy was simply defined as any undesirable bodily response to something that is generally safe for most of the population. A patient would describe what symptoms he suffered, and the doctor would assist in tracing the causes.

Then IgE antibodies were discovered. These agents, found in the blood, are frequently overproduced when an allergic person is exposed to an allergen from the environment, such as pollen. Hives, difficulty breathing, itchy eyes, sneezing, and runny nose are some responses that are associated with this. Commonly associated with peanuts or sulfites, the severe allergic reaction of anaphylactic shock is generally an IgE-conducted response as well.

Once this discovery was made, the areas of the body generally associated with this type of reaction were defined. The most provable sources of this reaction were listed, and allergy was given a new, clean definition. There was certainly much excitement over this discovery, and it was thought the new definition of allergy would provide for more precise diagnoses. Unfortunately, in order for a patient's complaints or a child's colic to be diagnosed as an allergy, their symptoms had to fit into the new parameters, which covered only a small portion of the total allergic reactions to food, those with immediate manifestation. To be labeled allergic, patients had to exhibit IgE antibodies in their blood (RAST test) or have swelling in reaction to scratch tests. This new mindset about what defined an allergy arrived on the heels of a new explosion of delayed reactions such as rashes, asthma, and intestinal symptoms in infants who were progressively being fed more and more of the highly promoted milk formulas.

Since this time, when there are delayed allergic reactions, which most food reactions are, the diagnosis is usually missed altogether. When a child's symptoms do not fit the strict (limited) definition of allergy, it is considered an indication to perform more invasive diagnostic work-ups, which are either inconclusive or lead to one of many vague diagnoses, such as colitis or irritable bowel.

Most health practitioners insist that only the immediate, sneezy-wheezy kind of reactions (IgE antibody responses) are the result of immune system reactions. This is not true however. If one knows what to look for, like those who spend their lives researching such matters, there are many antibody responses that lead to delayed reactions. There are also other kinds of immune system responses, such as histamine and other chemical releases, inflammation, and altered behaviors of white blood cells. Informed researchers also use the term "allergy" for these delayed reactions, not just for immediate reactions. Today, with the voices of hundreds of thousands of food allergy sufferers trying to be heard, some who disallow the term "allergy" are allowing the use of "sensitivity" or "intolerance" for delayed allergic reactions. Here in this text, as is often done today, I use these terms interchangeably.

I just have to take you aside for a moment and tell you about my experience with a doctor whose anger was building to a face-reddening, vein-pulsating level over my attempts to explain that "these symptoms only happen when my husband has milk."

"Why does it make you so angry when I tell you this?" I asked him.

His frustrated response: "You wouldn't believe how many of my patients try to tell me that."

Well…what does that tell you???

Sometimes even double-blind studies do not confirm the patient's or parent's claims that food is causing symptoms. The reasons for this will be explained later. Around the 1940s, many adults and children whose complaints were not confirmed by IgE tests, and in whom no other diseases were found, were considered "frustrated" individuals (or babies with frustrated parents). Borrowing from the then rapidly growing field of psychology, it was often decided these complaints had psychological causes, and this mindset persists today.

It is true that certain psychological symptoms of stress and frustration are commonly found in people with diseases that can't be diagnosed. Actually, recent studies show these symptoms are found in asthma patients, heart patients, and others with chronic illnesses. Most people dealing with a frustrating disease, especially one that is not easily diagnosed by others, suffer some level of irritability, depression, or frustration — these being the result of the disease, not the cause.

The Immune Response

Airborne, food, or chemically-related sensitivity reactions are essentially caused by an overreaction of the immune system. The immune system is our body's defense against invasion; it uses antibodies and certain chemicals. Invasion is generally some kind of bacteria or virus, but in the case of allergy, the body treats some "non-harmful" agents as though they were invaders. In a food sensitive individual, the body may create an inordinate amount of antibody to certain foods, pollens, or other agents (antigens) that generally do not irritate other people. These antibodies then wait in their little forts, the mast cells residing in the respiratory, digestive, and urinary tissues, and deep in the skin. When antigens pass by, the antibodies signal for several chemical reactions to occur. Histamine and other chemicals are released in response to this adversarial encounter, which causes inflammation, tissue damage, and other symptoms.

Histamine can cause involuntary muscles to contract, such as those in the lungs (asthma) and intestines (colic). Breakdown products of serotonin cause irritation of the local tissues. Because it also acts as a neurotransmitter in the brain, serotonin is probably responsible for some of the behavioral changes or mood swings seen in sensitivity reactions. While serotonin is often thought to have a calming effect, elevated levels have also been linked with anxiety and aggressive behaviors.[27,28] Serotonin is often blamed for migraine headaches as well.[29] Prostaglandins and bradykinins cause pain. Prostaglandins, as well as histamine, may also be responsible for some mood effects.

Immediate Hypersensitivity Reactions

IgE antibodies are produced in allergic responses to airborne antigens such as pollen or animal dander. They are also produced in cases of sudden food allergic reactions. The ensuing histamine releases lead to symptoms such as coughing, wheezing, hives, sneezing, and runny nose. Hence, IgE antibodies are immensely involved in standard immediate or type 1 allergic reactions. These are the reactions that can be detected with RAST IgE blood testing and scratch tests.

A very intense immediate response is anaphylactic shock. In response to a strong allergen such as peanuts, shrimp, penicillin, insect venom, or a vaccine, the body of a highly sensitive individual can react very quickly and severely. Along with sudden anxiety, anaphylactic shock involves difficulty breathing, dropping blood pressure, and sometimes even death.

Chemical Sensitivity Reactions

Ill feelings resulting from airborne or internal exposure to various chemicals such as paint fumes, cigarette smoke, perfumes, cleaning agents, sulfites, and MSG are currently even more poorly understood than delayed food reactions. Characterized by symptoms such as fatigue, rash, rhinitis, headache, and drowsiness, IgE responses are occasionally detected,[30] but more often not. Little research exists on other types of detectable immune reactions, although this is changing as we speak. One third of the population report suffering ill feelings in response to some kind of chemical exposure.[31] Most rats also suffer ill effects when exposed to these chemicals in the lab.[32] Common drug reactions are chemical sensitivities too. Yet, many doctors claim chemical sensitivities are extremely rare, making the exception of sulfite reactions and recently recognized latex sensitivities. Over 70,000 different manmade chemicals are being used in our environment today, a very sharp contrast from only 100 years ago. Few of the 3,000 listed as high-volume usage have had even basic toxicity testing performed on them.[33] Since illness is known to occur in reaction to many chemical exposures, environmental medicine specialists assume that the enormous bombardment of chemicals may be causing illnesses in ways we are barely aware of.

Delayed Hypersensitivity Reactions

Delayed reactions are those that begin possibly 45 minutes to 36 hours after exposure to an allergen. They are typically in response to consumed foods or chemicals. As it takes time for food to empty from the stomach and reach the intestines, these reactions take time to mount. Reactions such as diarrhea and painful distention take time to build to noticeable levels once reactive chemical releases begin. Intestinal transit time varies greatly depending upon diet, stress, and other factors. Hence the delay and the wide variance in the time until symptoms are noticed.

Standard blood or scratch tests for allergies, which only measure IgE responses, will often be negative in cases of food reactions initiated in the intestines.

Only 10% of all food-related reactions are conducted very much by IgE, causing immediate reactions. Ninety percent of food sensitivity reactions occur as a result of immune responses other than IgE and will produce delayed reactions that start more than 20 minutes after exposure. The key antibody defenses launched by the intestinal tract generally include various antibodies, IgG, IgM, and IgA, and antibody-like T cells. These agents incite local release of histamine along with serotonin and other chemicals. These cause inflammation, intestinal muscle contractions, and tissue damage. Standard blood or scratch tests for allergies, which only measure IgE responses, will often be negative in cases of food reactions initiated in the intestines. New IgG blood tests provide fair results, but are only beginning to infiltrate medical education.

Following the Delayed Reaction

Although histamines are initially released in the intestines during delayed food sensitivity reactions, they often find their way into the bloodstream where they can alert histamine receptors in any organ that is genetically disposed to overreact. The bladder has many histamine receptors. Bedwetting problems (enuresis) can often be caused by swelling and contraction of the bladder lining in response to environmental or food sensitivity reactions.[34,35] Histamine receptors also reside in the walls of the uterus, and uterine contractions have been well demonstrated in response to histamine. I have not been able to find any studies investigating a relationship between allergic mothers and preterm contractions, although I personally know one very allergic mother who wishes she knew about this correlation during her months on horrible labor-inhibiting drugs.

In a sensitized system, many events occur after cow's milk proteins or other antigens enter the mouth and make their way into the small intestines. IgA antibodies tag the foods and try to rush them through the system without provoking irritation. When these tagged foods are rushed through, no digestion takes place, and the lack of symptoms may baffle an observer who suspected allergy.

Often, many of these proteins will find their way into the lining of the intestines and become recognized by waiting antibodies. As described before, inflammation occurs locally with tissue damage. As a result, the intestinal walls become more leaky, and some undigested proteins will pass through the intestinal walls.[36-38] This is very common in young infants, although it occurs throughout adulthood.[39,40] Once these proteins make their way into the bloodstream, more alarms go off and histamine is released throughout the system. Further and more varied delayed symptoms can now occur including eczema, nasal stuffiness, and asthma. Histamine receptors are located nearly everywhere in the body, including the brain. Symptoms of delayed food reactions can thus manifest in the muscles, joints, nasal passages, lungs, bladder, uterus, and altered behavior.

When antibodies attach to proteins to form immune complexes and deposit along the walls of blood vessels, arterial plaque gradually develops, and eventually, heart disease occurs. Deposits in the kidneys lead to kidney damage called "nephritis." Immune complexes can even deposit in the brain.[41] (One wonders whether this could be connected to Alzheimer's disease?)

While all this is going on in the blood, a cascade of chemical releases continues in the intestines, increasing inflammatory damage, and now causing the symptoms of diarrhea or constipation, along with decreased uptake of nutrients.

> Amazingly, milk provides a double assault in the case of Crohn's disease, acting as an allergen to cause reduced intestinal resistance, then supplying the infecting agent.

Infection & Disease: Beyond the Delayed Reaction

Now that the natural protective barrier of the intestinal walls has been compromised, the immune system has been taxed, and the nutrient status has diminished, the stage is set for opportunistic infection. With defenses down, bacteria or other microbes can establish themselves. Commonly, candida yeast will take hold in the intestinal walls. This reduces the protective barrier even more, allowing more proteins to pass through the walls, leading to more antibody reactions and chemical releases throughout the body.

Another common intestinal infection that follows the disrupted immune defenses of the intestinal wall is *Helicobacter pylori*, recently found to be present in most ulcers, and more recently suspected in some cases of SIDS. This bacterium is most likely responsible for much of the intestinal wall destruction (ulceration) in ulcerative colitis, common in infants.

A 1998 study found *Mycobacterium paratuberculosis* to be associated with the development of Crohn's disease.[42] This bacteria is passed to humans via cow's milk. Why doesn't everyone exposed to this bacteria develop Crohn's disease? Because the natural barrier defenses and immune defenses of the intestinal walls need to be regularly broken down by other frequent illness, such as hypersensitivity reactions to cow's milk, in order to allow the infection to take hold. *The bacteria are not the problem; they simply take advantage of a vulnerable situation, causing further disease.* Amazingly, milk provides a double assault in the case of Crohn's disease, acting as an allergen to cause reduced intestinal resistance, then supplying the infecting agent. Genetic susceptibility is the only other necessary ingredient.

Potentiation

Potentiation, aversion, and masking are processes that occur in delayed reactions that greatly complicate the diagnosis, misleading parent and health professional alike. Alone, infrequently, and in lesser quantities, a weaker allergen may cause no detectable reaction, but there is an additive effect of multiple irritants or of multiple exposures to the same irritant. This is called "potentiation."

One exposure to an antigen in an untaxed system may result in little symptomatic effect, but can still incite antibody production. If the same agent is introduced again in a day or so, the body is now armed with higher amounts of antibodies and ready to cause symptoms. Additionally, if the immune system is already in high gear from one kind of exposure or from stress, it may now react more strongly to other kinds of exposure. Since the leaking of undigested proteins through the intestinal linings may persist for several days, symptoms from one exposure can last for many days, and then a strong reaction can occur to what was previously only a mild irritant. As a result, the relationship between symptoms and foods ingested may not be at all obvious.[43]

Certainly, consuming several allergenic foods close together will create an enhanced reaction. At the same time, the presence of airborne allergies will increase food reactions. Seasonal colic is reported by some parents and could be related to the pollens of summer. Cigarette smoke, pet dander, and a high level of air pollutants can all add to the allergic response — so can stress, both mental and physical. It is well known that asthma attacks are much more common with exercise or on days of heavy smog. Many partially attribute the increasing occurrence of all kinds of sensitivities to our ever-growing environmental pollution. Diesel exhaust has been shown to be particularly offensive in promoting increased allergic reactions.[44]

Aversion

Animals and humans are born equipped with an innate ability to determine when a food has caused them to feel ill, so they can learn to avoid foods that are spoiled, poisonous, or otherwise undesirable. This instinctual ability, promoted by the nervous system, allows for the survival of a species.

In a child, and especially an infant, the body's natural system for learning to avoid poisonous and otherwise harmful foods is very much intact. For this reason, especially when the diet is simple, as it usually is for infants, these babies and young children will attempt to refuse a food that has previously caused an uncomfortable sensitivity reaction inside his body. These foods may be recognized by smell, taste, or sight. When a parent says, "My child won't eat much cheese or milk," there is probably a reason.

Even a breastfed baby will fuss or refuse the breast if he tastes or smells an odor that his body has associated with ill feeling. The avoidance may eventually become associated with the sight or smell of the breast itself. He may then accept breastmilk from a bottle for a while, but the refusal can return if the mother's diet does not change.

As one comes down from the morphine high or suffers a serotonin low, another dose of the allergenic food can relieve the down feeling. In this way, it is thought that individuals can start to crave the very food that is causing chronic destruction inside their bodies.

As we get older, our diets become more complicated, and we are taught to ignore our body's signals; as a result, the ability to subconsciously recognize offending foods is partially lost. Frequently, when forced to continually consume an offending food, a different phenomenon, the craving of such foods, will occur.

Masking

In one sense, the closer allergen exposures are in time, the greater the antibody and inflammatory reactions will be. With regular daily exposures however, the body learns to defend itself to some degree against the painful response. It is thought that in this case natural morphine-like chemicals are released by the body to make the individual more comfortable.[45] This can create a pleasant, almost "high" feeling for part of a day. At least it brings a reduction in the chronic symptoms from the chronic exposures. This masking effect, an addiction of sorts, can hide the exposure-to-symptom relationship, making diagnosis very difficult.[46] While the inflammatory destruction may be somewhat lessened, chronic damage definitely continues, often undetected, as does immune complex deposition — leading to the insidious development of chronic diseases.

As one comes down from the morphine high or suffers a serotonin low, another dose of the allergenic food can relieve the down feeling. In this way, it is thought that individuals can start to crave the very food that is causing chronic destruction inside their bodies. Eliminating the allergenic food for a day or two now brings about withdrawal symptoms. The morphine high is lost, serotonin is low, and one can now feel the pain from the low-level reactions going on — further complicating the ability to associate consumed foods with symptoms. Simply put, consuming an offending food actually makes you feel better for a while. This masks the damaging effect of eating a food. A person feels various symptoms of illness much of the time, but the foods causing it are not easily recognized.

It once was standard advice for ulcer sufferers to drink milk regularly. Since milk is commonly a cause of ulcers, a masking effect could bring about temporary relief for many — and initially increased pain when milk was withdrawn. Since it was learned that milk consumption actually causes ulcers to be prolonged (and that men on this milk sipping diet had high heart attack rates), this advice has been rescinded.

Protecting Baby

Allergic reactions, especially food allergies, rob baby of her greatest potential for lifelong health. Just waiting for her to "grow out" of her reactions allows ongoing damage to occur. While the number of children expressing certain kinds of food reactions drops with age, many retain their allergies. Fewer than we think "grow out" of their allergies; the way they express their discomfort merely changes with age. While they may have grown out of their colic, they have often grown into new problems such as tantrums, sleep difficulties, irritability, poor behavior, chronic diarrhea or constipation, vomiting, and so on. Eczema and other atopic rashes often give way to runny noses and respiratory symptoms.

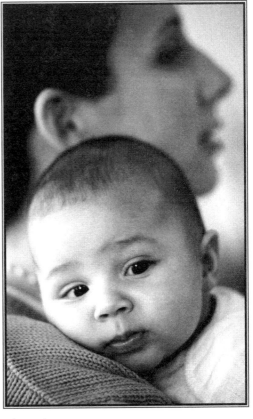

If no attempt is made to limit intestinal irritation, if it is indeed occurring, the child's chance of developing some form of irritable bowel syndrome or even cancer as an adult increases many times over. If immune complexes are allowed to roam through the child's body frequently, heart disease, stroke, arthritis, diabetes, or other debilitating disease may be waiting as well.

14

Discovering, Preventing & Treating Food Allergies

"A number of differences between medicine and pure science...can result in some medical innovations being ignored or rejected without an adequate assessment. Social-organizational factors in medicine appear to favor the acceptance of theoretically glamorous, pharmaceutical, and high technology innovations over simpler and less profitable ones."
— Dr. Robert Forman, University of Toledo[1]

"A wise man ought to realize that health is his most valuable possession and learn how to treat his illnesses by his own judgment."
— Hippocrates[2]

A VERY ANGRY PHONE CALL FROM A PATIENT OFTEN COMES TO MIND when I discuss diagnosis of food sensitivities.

Carol brought her 8-year-old daughter into my office one day to see if I had any ideas that could help with the child's daily abdominal pains. She had been to see many other doctors, and her 8-year-old was taking tranquilizers and sleep aids every day with no improvement. I took a thorough history, and based on some comments about the daughter's typical diet and the timing of the pains, I felt a rather strong possibility existed that she was sensitive to gluten. I provided materials to the mother and suggested she provide her daughter a gluten-free diet for a short trial.

Two days later came the phone call. Carol was upset and overwhelmed with the amount of work required to provide her daughter foods without wheat or any other source of gluten. She asked me where she was supposed to find the time. However, fourteen days later she called me again to say her daughter had been following the diet and was entirely free of symptoms. She couldn't have been more happy than to see the end to her daughter's constant suffering.

In attempting to diagnose and treat food hypersensitivity, remember that it is a means to an end — hopefully, a very happy, healthy end to pain or some other difficulty.

Food intolerance and other allergies are far more common in babies and children than most people think — and they are becoming more prevalent all the time. While medical acceptance of this scientific fact is slow in coming, many common difficulties with youngsters can be avoided by parents who work to prevent, diagnose, and treat hypersensitivity reactions. Moreover, the potential for adult allergies is decreased, and many diseases, including autoimmune diseases, bowel disease, and even cancer, may be thwarted by preventive measures such as avoiding foods or environmental allergens.

Not only are some of the better blood tests and hypoallergenic formulas not available in the U.S., but the ability of U.S. medical doctors to recognize food allergies is amazingly behind that in other nations. A University of Maryland report demonstrates this perfectly in a report on celiac disease occurrence in the U.S. and Europe.[3] While celiac disease remains the most accepted of any food-allergy diagnosis in this country, statistics reveal an amazing paucity of celiac cases in the U.S. compared to Europe. The author of this report has performed studies, however, that suggest the actual occurrence of celiac disease in Americans and Europeans is very similar — they are simply not being diagnosed in the U.S. Many Americans are suffering needlessly. Let us, as parents, make a change for our new generation.

Laboratory Diagnosis

Many parents have suspected food allergies in their children and have taken a child to a pediatrician or allergist. Generally, the doctor performs the standard tests for allergy, either a RAST IgE blood test or skin scratch tests. These two tests only look for IgE-conducted, immediate hypersensitivity (type 1) reactions — those that fit under the strict definition of allergy that was created *after* these tests were developed, to fit the limits of these tests. Most of the time these IgE tests come back negative. The parents are then told they are making too much of their child's symptoms, or when digestive tract symptoms are significant, that their child needs to see a gastroenterologist. In the latter case radiation tests and other procedures are performed to discover the underlying disease. Usually the "disease" turns out to be "nonspecific diarrhea of infancy," colic, colitis, or one of the other diagnoses that are known across Europe and in many a research laboratory as the result of non-IgE-dependent, immune-produced sensitivity reactions to foods. The proper referral at some point would be to a nutritionist or other practitioner interested in dietary disorders who could help discover a food intolerance, or could at least rule out this possibility.

A study done on how well immune reactions to foods are diagnosed in Crohn's disease sufferers illustrates the weakness of IgE testing for digestive disorders.[4] The patients were evaluated through extensive laboratory procedures and were compared to controls. All were found to have low to negative blood levels of IgE to all four major food allergens tested, while a few had elevated blood IgE levels to inhaled allergens. Scratch testing showed some positive reactions to foods. On the other hand, blood IgG levels were negative in all cases in response to inhaled allergens, but were quite elevated in response to various foods. Furthermore, a highly sensitive lymphocyte test, presently used only in research settings, was the most sensitive test for detecting an immune response to milk protein. Nearly all children and adults diagnosed with Crohn's disease remained in "remission" after allergenic foods were eliminated from their diets.

RAST IgE blood tests and skin scratch tests are valuable for diagnosing airborne allergens and immediate-reaction food allergies. These tests have very low sensitivity to the immune mechanisms in delayed-reaction food intolerance,[5] which are responsible for 90 to 95% of all hypersensitivity reactions to foods. Fortunately, for health care practitioners aware of the need, laboratory testing is now commercially available that can help diagnose delayed food reactions produced by IgG and other immune factors. An intestinal biopsy is very diagnostic as well, although it is generally too extreme unless someone is demanding empirical evidence. This procedure investigates the number and behavior of certain white blood cells in the intestinal walls and detects any damage to intestinal villi.[6,7] Biopsy provides visual evidence of the food reactions and the destruction they cause. In addition, colonoscopy (visually looking into the colon with a scope) will reveal signs such as erythema (redness), ulceration, bleeding, and loss of vascular pattern.[8]

Puzzled by the conflict between their observations and their education, doctors are currently ordering biopsies. These tests frequently find an increased number of eosinophils, the allergy-related blood cells of the immune system, so a diagnosis of "eosinophilia" is provided. Sometimes, mast cells are more numerous, and "mastocytosis" is the diagnosis. Since these diagnoses are merely descriptions of the ongoing allergic processes (except when parasitic infections or blood transfusions have occurred), they are empty findings, just like the vague terms "colitis" and "colic," with no recognition of the allergic causes. Common steroid treatment for these diagnoses is harmful to the body, and damage or illness will continue if irritating foods aren't avoided.

In the research laboratory, performing multiple tests for various immunological indicators provides high concordance with food challenge results ("challenging" the child by feeding of various foods to look for reactions). Of tests currently commercially available, even the best can only claim 75 to 85% sensitivity in detecting allergenic foods, with some false positive findings as well. One report found that only ELISA testing of IgM antibodies (not a commercially available test) is specific for diagnosing milk protein intolerance as it relates to chronic ear infections in 3-year-olds, while IgE testing was more accurate in 1-year-olds.[9] In a large base of patients who altered their diets based almost entirely on the results of an IgG test called ELISA, 67% found good improvement or recovered from symptoms.[10] Other investigations report a much higher recovery rate when actual food challenges are included in the diagnostic work-up.

Using IgE tests for immediate (type 1) allergic reactions is not foolproof: Scratch tests show only 60 to 70% sensitivity for detecting immediate reaction allergies (higher if fresh food extracts are used[11]). Some practitioners require positive test results to make their diagnosis, which makes these tests 100% reliable to them. I have shown that rhinitis and lung symptoms, usually assumed to be immediate allergic reactions, are often the result of IgG-conducted food sensitivities or other chemical sensitivity reactions. Children with these demonstrate obvious allergic symptoms, but may show up negative on all scratch and blood IgE tests. These children are often diagnosed with non-allergic (or non-atopic) rhinitis or asthma, but further investigation through other means can discover delayed reactions and chemical sensitivities in most, which can lead to relief from symptoms with proper diet. For reasons poorly understood, even children with anaphylactic (severe respiratory) reactions to certain elements, especially to a food, can come up with negative IgE results — but the majority of these will then show up positive on ELISA IgG testing.

The best way to diagnose which foods are causing symptoms is to use elimination diets. First you remove all possible allergens from the diet until the body recovers, then you offer each suspected food one at a time to see whether symptoms are reproduced. Many times, however, it makes sense to collect as much information as possible in advance to help make the best diagnosis or help design the elimination diet. Often the symptoms are so undesirable that any shortcuts to diagnosis are very beneficial. At other times, laboratory tests are of value simply to support one's own suspicions, or to help appease doubting family members or health care providers. While positive test results may help a parent decide about other kinds of medical procedures, it must be remembered that negative results from any laboratory tests do not necessarily mean that food reactions aren't taking place.

In blood testing, just as with food challenges, it is common for an allergenic food that has not been consumed for some time to produce a negative result, because over time, especially with mild offenders, the antibodies in the body diminish. But food challenges repeated two or three days in a row will discover these foods. To obtain the best blood test results, people must consume most of their dietary repertoire a few times during the weeks preceding their blood tests. This is not necessary, however, in the beginning of the discovery period for a young symptomatic child with a relatively simple diet. For this child or any person with very chronic symptoms, there is a good chance that the most strongly offending foods will show up in the proper blood test. Many times foods will provoke immune reactivity in the laboratory, but cause no apparent reactions in the patient. These are only some of the reasons why blood testing cannot be relied upon completely. Therefore, all blood test results, whether positive or negative, should be followed by food challenges to make sure that foods are not needlessly eliminated, that intolerant foods are not missed, and that foods are truly the problem.

ELISA is a standard test used in research laboratories — not only for IgG food antibodies, but for IgE and other antibodies and a very broad spectrum of blood components or contaminants of research interest. In clinical laboratory tests for food intolerance, the levels of IgG antibodies to various foods are measured in blood samples. ELISA is a highly dependable test, but high levels of IgG are not always indicative of, or always present in, food hypersensitivity reactions. In one study, ELISA IgG testing missed diagnoses for 20% of celiac disease patients, who had sensitivity to gluten from grains.[12]

RAST IgG blood testing is available in some areas as well, but is generally not as accurate as the ELISA.

Elimination Diets

We have arrived at the heart of diagnosing food intolerance — does an ingested food provoke a symptom in the body or not? Elimination dieting with sequential challenging of different foods works because all possible allergenic substances are removed from the diet for several days *before* the body is challenged with substances one at a time, then responses are observed. In this manner, chronic reactivity and masking efforts are removed, making positive reactions clear and definite.

For diagnosing food intolerance, there are two extremes of testing. For the greatest accuracy, one could fast for 3 days consuming only filtered water, then add foods at the rate of one new food every 2 or 3 days. On the other end of the spectrum, one can simply eliminate one food from the diet for a few days, look for improvement, and then reintroduce the food and watch for a response. Water fasting is not appropriate for an infant or child and is very seldom necessary for anyone. Eliminating only one food and then challenging with it may not tell the whole story, but it is simple and may be all that is needed. The real solution is generally somewhere between these two extremes. The first days of an elimination diet can be difficult, and the entire experiment can last for several weeks, making social eating and traveling difficult. Luckily, the diet is often simple for an infant and generally less arduous for a child than for an adult.

The gold standard medical version of elimination diet testing requires a patient to swallow capsules that contain either a suspected food or a placebo, then monitor medically for results. Because of placebo

Some doctors claim that since proving beyond a doubt that a food causes a symptom is so difficult, the diagnosis is not worth considering.

effects, many medical doctors will refuse to consider any diet conclusions not obtained in this fashion; however, they are not quick to
offer this testing either. To truly satisfy the criteria, a physician would
have to be present to observe a child's responses over a 48-hour
period for at least three separate challenges for every food of interest.
The quantity of food required to produce IgG-delayed reactions
would necessitate the use of many capsules
at a time. Additionally, accuracy cannot be
achieved unless all reactive antigens have
been eliminated from the diet for some days
prior to a food challenge to eliminate masking effects and reactions to foods consumed
prior the test. This kind of testing is far from
practical. In research studies, food samples
are provided in multiple double-blind challenges, and results are compared to one or
more blood studies, and in some cases, biopsies. Some doctors claim that since proving
beyond a doubt that a food causes a symptom is so difficult, the diagnosis is not worth
considering. This mindset is a product of a drug-oriented education
and a lack of appropriate education. Doctors have also been strongly
educated by industry partners to believe that there is a dangerous
health risk in any diet that excludes dairy, thus food elimination
should not be a consideration. I hope you understand by now that
this is far from true.

> When the desired improvement is seen, parents should not be pressured into believing that their conclusions are not valid.

Undoubtedly, the placebo effect is a confounding factor. The
attitude of the parent who provides the food and evaluates the
symptoms is just as suspect for lack of objectivity as is the child's
anticipation. The younger the child, however, the less placebo
effect there should be. In addition, one caretaker can be kept in the
dark about what is being tested so this individual will have more
objectivity while observing symptoms. In any event, the key is that
*over time, either the child's chronic symptoms will go away with food
elimination, or they won't.* If the symptoms are gone, there is no
other disease to be concerned with. If symptoms do not go away

with cautious elimination, something else is going on. When the desired improvement is seen, parents should not be pressured into believing that their conclusions are not valid.

Where to Begin

Several food allergy books recommend rotation diets for finding offending foods. Only members from a few food families are eaten at a time, eliminating other food families. Then a new set of food families is tried. While there is some treatment value to rotation dieting, this technique is weak diagnostically. A look at the lists of offending foods for many different people will actually reveal very little correlation between food families and sensitivity to the foods within these families. For instance, one may be very reactive to soy and peanuts, but thrive on peas, kidney beans, and carob, all members of the legume family. Then they may not tolerate strawberries or raspberries, in the rose family, but do fine with cherries, almonds and blackberries, all in this family as well. Rotary elimination diets are designed to allow ample food selection during the testing period, however, in practice, the entire experiment could be in vain.

The level of elimination attempted depends upon how chronic and severe baby's symptoms are, as well as the level of desire in the parent to relieve suffering, improve nutritional status, and prevent future disease. At the beginning of the test, the goal is to reduce all immune hyperactivity to a minimum level, so that the true effects of the food challenges can be seen.

To help determine the appropriate level of an elimination diet, refer to Figure 14-1. To use this table, find the appropriate level for each symptom listed, add up the numbers from each box, and use the point ranges below to select the appropriate food elimination process.

The Bottle-Fed Infant

Detecting food allergens in the bottle-fed infant is the easiest of all elimination diets — provided the child will accept a new formula. The easiest first attempt is a switch to soy-based formula. It is

Sensitivity Symptoms for Determining Level of Elimination Diet

Degree of Symptoms	Skin	Colic	Stools	Sinuses	Behavior
Mild	Light, occasional rash **1**	Occasional signs of intestinal discomfort **1**	Occasional loose stools or missed days **2**	Occasional stuffiness **1**	Occasional unexplained fussiness or misbehavior **1**
Moderate	Frequent light rash, occasional allergy rings or large rashes **2**	Frequent mild or occasional great discomfort **3**	Frequent loose or missed stools, occasional diarrhea or constipation **3**	Frequent stuffiness or occasional ear fluid **2**	Frequent fussiness, or occasional episodes of great contrariness **3**
Severe	Frequent large or open sore rashes, regular allergy rings **3**	Frequent great discomfort **4**	Frequent diarrhea or constipation **4**	Regular stuffiness or ear fluid, or occasional ear infection **3**	Frequent episodes of great fussiness or contrariness **4**

Figure 14-1 Based on the score from symptoms in chart, select the appropriate level of elimination diet.

LEVEL I (3 – 5 points) Try dairy elimination along with any suspected foods first.

LEVEL II (6 – 9 points) Try elimination of dairy, egg, wheat, corn, peanuts, fish, chicken, citrus, strawberry, and tomato, and any suspected foods first. Eliminate goat or soy also if has been regular in diet (not counting soy oil).

LEVEL III (10+ points) Best to start with comprehensive elimination diet.

LEVEL IV (Severe illness) Begin with elemental diet.

best to look for a soy formula that has no corn syrup, cornstarch, or corn solids. Sometime during the writing of this book, Wyeth dropped their Nursoy, which was the only soy formula I could find without corn products. They now distribute soy formula under various stores' brand names. Sadly, these all have corn syrup solids as their chief ingredient. Regardless, soy formula eliminates all dairy and may be tried for infants in any of the categories in Figure 14-1, with a better chance for success for lower scores. Try the new formula for 5 to 7 days. If desirable improvement is achieved, the soy formula can be used as the sole source of nutrition. Many infants who initially improve on soy formula eventually develop a sensitivity to the soy or corn, and a hydrolysate or elemental formula may then be needed.

If no improvement occurs with soy, try a protein hydrolysate. U.S. formulas labeled as hypoallergenic are made from cow's milk proteins that are mostly broken down (hydrolyzed by enzymes) into smaller pieces so the body will not recognize them as antigens. None of the hydrolysate formulas available presently in the U.S. are hydrolyzed enough to prevent eventual immune reactions in a moderate portion of sensitive infants. Hydrolyzed soy is available in some countries and has been found to be quite adequate for sensitive infants. Lamb-based formulas are also available in some other countries, as well as more completely hydrolyzed cow's milk formulas.

If adequate recovery is not seen with hydrolyzed formula, then the small remaining amounts of cow's milk protein could be the problem. The final effort is to try an elemental diet (such as Vivonex). Elemental formula is a complete nutrition formula with no intact proteins or complex sugars. It should be entirely hypoallergenic, that is, it should not cause allergic reactions. This formula contains all the essential amino acids (the building blocks of proteins), as well as other nutrients to create a diet as complete as other formulas. Some people with major digestive system errors can live for decades on this kind of diet. Elemental formula can be used by anyone who wants a simple way to start an elimination diet. This includes those who need to recover from major intestinal damage prior to beginning a diagnostic elimination diet.

Vivonex can be ordered without prescription through a pharmacy and is generally kept in stock in children's hospitals. It is very expensive and health insurance won't cover the cost. Each family needs to weigh the cost-to-benefit ratio based on the degree of symptoms and suffering in their child, as well as the prevalence of asthma, bowel disease, and diabetes in related family members — indicating the possible long-term need for preventive measures.

While Vivonex is expensive, remember it is only a test. Try it for at least 5 days. If the child recovers from his symptoms, then his health will improve if he stays on this formula. At 5 or 6 months of age, a nutritionist can help you figure out how to replace much of the formula with more affordable alternatives, such as fortified rice milk or oat milk, along with appropriate solid foods and nutrient supplements, to assure adequate nutrition while preventing further sensitization. Using rice, oat, almond, or soy milks instead of formula is not sufficient as a sole source of nutrition.

A child who initially improves on hydrolysate may eventually react to it as well and will need to be placed on an elemental diet.

Lactose-Free Is Not the Answer

Some formulas are made without lactose to help prevent gas and diarrhea in baby. Consider, however, that mother's milk contains far more lactose than cow's milk. Although testing sometimes suggests otherwise, lactose intolerance as a primary problem in infants is incredibly rare and would show up from the first days of an infant's life. True, when infants suffer from intestinal damage due to food intolerance reactions or infectious diarrhea, they may demonstrate lactase enzyme deficiency or sugar malabsorption, but they will also be deficient in many other enzymes and will suffer malabsorption in many other ways. Removing all cow's milk products from the diet is important for treating diarrhea from any cause, but as soon as any immune reactions are gone, an infant's body will straighten out the handling of lactose.

The Nursing Infant

The nursing mother of a symptomatic infant needs to follow an elimination diet herself, watching for symptoms in her child. She needs to eliminate a few more foods besides those listed in the diets.

Common Allergens in Commercial Formulas

Company	Brand (Type)	Cow's Milk Derivatives	Corn Derivatives	Soy Derivatives	Oils
Ross	Similac	Nonfat Milk** Whey**			Coconut, Soy, Safflower
Ross	Alimentum (Protein Hydrolysate)	Casein-Hydrolysate*			Coconut, Soy, Safflower
Wyeth Laboratory	Babysoy (Soy Protein Milk-Free)	Beef Fat (Oleo)	Corn Syrup Solids**	Soy Protein Isolate** Lecithin* Soy Oil*	Lard (Oleo) Coconut, Soy, Safflower
Mead Johnson	Enfamil LactoFree (Lactose Free)	Milk Protein Isolate**	Corn Syrup Solids**	Soy Oil*	Coconut, Palm, Soy, Sunflower
Mead Johnson	Enfamil Nutramigen (Hypoallergenic)	Casein-Hydrolysate*	Corn Syrup Solids** Corn Starch**	Soy Oil*	Coconut, Palm, Soy, Sunflower
Mead Johnson	Enfamil Next Step	Nonfat Milk**	Corn Syrup Solids**	Soy Oil*	Coconut, Palm, Soy, Sunflower

Figure 14-2 *Mild Allergen **Strong Allergen

Along with cow's milk, cruciferous vegetables in mother's diet are especially known for causing colic in breastfed infants.[13] These include cabbage, cauliflower, broccoli, and turnips. Onion and garlic, from a similar vegetable family, are often added to this list. It is not entirely understood whether colic from these is an allergic sort of reaction, or something else. Either way, if they cause symptoms, they must be discovered and eliminated. Chocolate and caffeine are also frequently implicated.

Once a mother finds which foods she needs to avoid to maintain the health and comfort of her infant, she can generally assume that these foods should not be fed to her child when he grows into solid foods. It is also likely the child will demonstrate reactions to other foods beyond these — but often only after the third or fourth exposure. If mother and child are happy with their nursing diet and relationship, there should be no rush to push solid foods. After a few bad experiences, the food intolerant infant often has less interest in solid foods beyond the curiosity and play opportunities. In the first two years, other foods are only replacing the higher nutrition of mother's milk and should be considered more as entertainment.

If the nursing child is eating solid foods and has had no problems before the introduction of supplemental formula or other foods, there is little need for the mother to follow the diet as well. It is good for mom to make some effort though, just in case her diet has an additive effect. If the nursing toddler has had long-term symptoms and is pretty attached to his solid foods, then mother and child need to follow the diet together. Still, only one food can be introduced at a time — in mother, child, or both at the same time. When a mother suspects or discovers for sure that her child is suffering reactions to foods in mother's milk, this is by no means an indication to stop nursing. This child will almost certainly have difficulties with formulas or solid foods. The best way to ensure optimum nutrition is to preserve the benefits of mother's wonderful milk, minus the offending foods in her diet. This will also provide baby with the healthiest possible digestive tract — thereby helping to prevent further sensitization and speed any "growing out" of sensitivities. Since allergy is a highly genetic condition, the mother may also end up reaping improved health from this process.

Elimination Diet on Solid Foods

If swelling of the tongue or difficulty breathing has ever been seen in a child, introduction of suspicious foods, especially nuts, shellfish, and sulfites, should only be made under medical supervision. Generally, anaphylactic attacks occur rapidly after ingestion of a food; determining which food is the problem is not difficult. Elimination dieting is most often used to discover regularly eaten foods that may be causing rashes, gastrointestinal problems, behavior changes, or other delayed reactions. In this case, eliminating and challenging is no more dangerous than feeding the child his normal diet.

For milder, less problematic symptoms, where there is less allergy-related "disease" running in the family, parents may choose to begin by eliminating only dairy products. Or, if any one food is highly suspect, it makes sense to eliminate this food first. If there is a good recovery, the answer is simple. If a good response is not seen, it is best to eliminate this food along with others in a new trial. Do not be discouraged if eliminating one food provides no answers. Immediate-response food allergy to one single food is common, but those who develop delayed food reactions more often develop sensitivity to a few or several foods.

The key to successfully eliminating offending foods is learning to read labels and being very thorough. So many times I've heard people say their dairy elimination provided no relief, only to find out later they were never quite able to give up that evening bowl of ice cream. Poor restriction will most likely invalidate your efforts, so the decision has to be made — either you want to find answers or you don't. You will best survive diet changes by learning to be proud and optimistic about your efforts, and by being creative. The elimination measures necessary to completely avoid certain foods for testing purposes may be more extreme than those eventually needed to maintain a symptom-free diet. Eventually, during the treatment phase, you learn which foods can be tolerated on an occasional basis in minute quantities as an added ingredient (like wheat starch), and which ones are highly reactive and need to be avoided at all cost.

Eating in restaurants is especially challenging and best avoided altogether in the first few weeks. Eating fast foods can be easier than other restaurant eating because fast-food restaurants are required to provide ingredient lists for their entire menu. Ask for these in your favorite spots and examine them ahead of time.

Where Do You find Milk Hidden in foods?

I've had many patients spout to me that dairy could not possibly be their problem because they eat dairy products all the time. To which I usually reply, "You tell me you are sick all the time." Eliminating dairy is much more complicated than you might think, but it is very possible once you learn to read labels and prepare simple foods at home.

Cheese and yogurt must be eliminated along with all other dairy products even though these two foods are reputed to be less problematic for a couple of reasons. For adolescents or adults who have decreasing lactose tolerance, much of the lactose has been consumed by the fungi or bacteria that produce the cheese or yogurt, making these more tolerable for lactase-deficient individuals. But this provides no protection from protein intolerance — the only concern in infants and young children. Also, cheese contains less whey, the more allergenic portion of the proteins in milk, which may make it slightly more tolerable for some protein sensitive individuals.

Of course, eliminating dairy means eliminating milk, cheese, butter, cottage cheese, cream, yogurt, and ice cream, but dairy products are hidden in at least half the packaged foods in the grocery store. Still, the grocery store or health food store is the safest source for meals for the elimination diet because the foods have ingredient labels.

The ingredients to look for on labels when eliminating dairy are milk, milk fat, milk solids, cheese, cream, butter, whey, casein, caseinate, and lactose. "Natural flavor" can be a problem because it can mean a lot of things, including hydrolyzed caseinate, which is a way to make MSG out of milk protein for flavor enhancement. Some foods that may sound very safe often are not:

- Margarine often contains whey, lactose, or casein.

- "Non-dairy" on a label usually indicates that the product contains the milk protein casein.
- Soy cheese almost always contains casein or whey.
- Chicken breasts in fast-food and most other restaurants, where they are purchased already infused with several flavorings, generally include whey, caseinate, or butter. Also breading and french fries often contain whey.
- In non-fast-food restaurants, hamburgers, meats, and fish are often grilled in butter, as are hamburger buns, and butter is commonly added to the vegetables. Fish is sometimes soaked in milk overnight.
- Some ingredients that sound like dairy derivatives that are not dairy are lactylate, calcium lactate, and cocoa butter.

One must read the label of any packaged food. Some form of dairy will be found in many foods:

- Most breads contain some whey. Ready-made pizza crusts usually contain cheese. Many fast-food buns are made with whey.
- Cereals, pastries, pancakes, waffles, muffins, cakes, cookies, crackers, granola bars, chocolates, soups, salad dressings, fat-free products, low-fat hot dogs, whole turkeys, and flavored chips often have dairy products in them.

When dairy products need to be avoided, remember that green vegetables and many other foods are superior sources of calcium (and other vitamins and minerals), and much less calcium is needed than the USRDA recommends when milk products and meat protein levels are not high in the diet. Remember also that *most products that claim to be non-dairy are full of the bovine protein caseinate, or some other dairy component.* Health food stores provide many good dairy alternatives.

Wheat

Due to marketing techniques, many people believe that white flour is not wheat. But any flour that does not specifically say otherwise is wheat flour. Some food labels list "starch" as an ingredient. This is more often corn, but could be wheat. Wheat is the main ingredient in nearly all breads, including white bread, corn bread, and rye bread, rolls, crackers, even graham crackers, cookies, even arrowroot cookies, cakes, waffles, pancakes, and most cereals. Wheat is a common thickener in ice creams, dressings, soups, and gravies, and it is the breading for foods such as fried chicken and onion rings.

Corn

Corn ranks up there with dairy for being difficult to avoid. Corn, popcorn, corn chips, and corn bread are obvious sources. Generally when a food item lists "starch," it is cornstarch, found in many foods. Asian sauces are thickened with cornstarch. Hydrolyzed vegetable protein (another source of MSG) is often made from corn, and 99.9% of all candies, condiments, and other sweetened treats or sauces are sweetened with corn syrup or another corn derivative. Dextrose, fructose, and glucose are all safe natural fruit sugars, but when they are added ingredients in foods, they are made from corn and will bother most moderately corn sensitive individuals. Corn syrup or dextrose is added to most hot dogs and hams. Sucrose is table sugar, (cane or beet sugar), and is safe for most people allergic to corn. A few are also allergic to cane, which is in the same food family as corn (the grass family), but they should tolerate beet sugar. Hypoglycemia is a different problem (of insulin regulation) and concerns all sugars.

The ingredients to look for on labels when avoiding corn are starch, cornstarch, corn syrup, dextrin, dextrose, malt, maltose, maltodextrin, maltitol, glucose, fructose, inulin syrup, invert sugar, caramel, sorbitol (also called starch hydrolysate), natural flavor, hydrolyzed vegetable protein, and corn oil.

Corn-derived sugars very occasionally make their way into orange juice, apple juice, honey, and maple syrup. This practice is illegal when the ingredient is not listed, but the FDA is well aware of its sporadic but continued occurrence. Companies are finding ways to make added ingredients rather "invisible" to laboratory tests. I used to avoid off-brands and trust the large brands. I once saw problems with these though and now stick to organic, without incident (so far). Corn is a prominent ingredient in many french fries, as is wheat. Someone who has anaphylactic reactions to corn should be aware that it is found in miniscule amounts in many more, often hard to believe places. These people should search ingredients on the World Wide Web; listing them all is beyond the scope of this book.

Other Foods Eliminated on a Level II Diet

Citrus includes orange, lemon, lime, citron, tangerine, kumquat, and grapefruit.

Peanuts can be hidden in some cereals and cookies, and some restaurants cook with peanut oil. Warnings about peanut contents are fairly common on labels nowadays. Tiny amounts of peanut are generally not much problem for those with food sensitivities, but anyone who displays breathing difficulties is at risk for anaphylactic shock from even very minute quantities of peanuts if they are allergic to them.

Eggs are common baking ingredients and are listed as eggs, egg whites, or albumin. Natural strawberry flavor contains strawberry antigens, but artificial strawberry flavor is "safe."

The best way to follow a level II elimination diet is to select most foods from the "low" and "seldom" columns in Figure 14-3.

Designing the Level III Diet

A highly restricted diet can be a problem for a young child, but with sincere effort, ample nutrition can be provided, especially since most of the restriction lasts for less than two weeks.

Allergy- or Sensitivity-Provoking Foods

High	Medium	Medium	Low	Seldom
Cow milk	Goat Milk	Goat Cheese		
	Yogurt			
Cheese	Rare Beef		Well Beef	Lamb
Egg	Chicken		Turkey	
Shellfish	Fish		Pork	
	Pecan	Walnut	Hazelnut	
Sunflower	Chocolate	Coconut	Avocado	Date
Peanut	Peas		Pod Beans	Tapioca
Soy	Kidney Bean		White Beans	
Wheat	Kamut	Buckwheat	Oat	
Corn	Rye		Rice	
	Millet		Barley	
	Citrus		Apple	Pear
	Grape		Raisin	Cream of Tartar
	Plum		Prune	
Strawberry	Raspberry		Blackberry	
	Pineapple		Cranberry	
	Banana	Ginger	Peach	Arrowroot
			Apricot	
			Cherry	
	Mango	Cashew	Almond	
	Squash	Melon	Papaya	Persimmon
	Cucumber	Mushroom		
	Yam		Beet	Poi
Tomato	White Potato	Bell Pepper	Sweet Potato	
	Sesame	Pepper		
	Cabbage	Broccoli	Cauliflower	
	Onion		Garlic	
	Mustard		Asparagus	
	Celery		Carrot	Lettuce
	Honey		Cane	Maple

Figure 14-3 Foods known for high, medium, or low capacity to provoke allergy or sensitivity reaction, and those seldom implicated. From multiple sources.

For the first days of the diet, select one or two meats, fruits, veg-etables, and grains from the last two columns of Figure 14-3. Choose foods that were seldom consumed, that are not suspect, and for infants, that were not often consumed by mom during the second half of her pregnancy (if possible). Lamb, whole oats, sweet potato, and pear provide more than adequate nutrition for a week or two, and with the addition of a green vegetable, will provide a complete diet. Remember, the more foods included, the greater the chance you will include a food your child is sensitized to, and the less the chance there is for diagnostic success. I generally push for only one food from each of the meat or nut, vegetable, fruit, and grain groups.

You should be eliminating and challenging with spices as well, except for salt, which is never a problem. Testing food colorings and other additives may be advisable, since the prevalence of additive intolerance is thought to be between .15 and 2%,[14,15] and is probably much higher. The most commonly implicated additives are sulfites (metabisulfite, disulfite), benzoates (in Sprite but not 7UP for exam-ple), and tartrazine (FD&C Yellow No. 5). The drug aspirin, which is salicylate, is also known to provoke reactions. These are all better known for their type 1 allergic associations, but other types of intol-erance have been reported.[16] MSG sensitivity is more common, but less likely to cause several of the food sensitivity symptoms discussed. In most cases MSG causes headaches, nausea, or sudden, over-whelming fatigue. Accent is a pure source of MSG that can be used in testing if desired. Truly, MSG is a dangerous neurotoxin and should not be in the diet of an infant or child regardless of reaction.

MSG (monosodium glutamate) is a concentrated form of an amino acid that occurs naturally in small quantities in many foods, and in moderate levels in yeast, soy, tomatoes, mushrooms, and sea-weed. High amounts of MSG or free glutamates are often an intended component of "natural flavor" as well as "spice," and "seasoning." Often it is referred to as "broth," or "vegetable broth," which does not include all broth. Bouillon is almost entirely MSG (hydrolyzed veg-etable protein). Be especially wary if the label says "No MSG;" you can be sure it's in there as part of some other ingredient. MSG is dis-guised under many names, or is the major component of them.

The ingredients to look for on labels when avoiding MSG are monosodium glutamate, natural flavor, spice, spice extract, seasoning, broth, hydrolyzed vegetable protein, hydrolyzed caseinate, any hydrolyzed vegetables or proteins, yeast extract, autolyzed yeast, torula yeast, (occasionally labels just say "yeast," although generally yeast in bread or someplace it belongs is not an added source of glutamate), disodium guanylate and disodium inosinate, kombu, and seaweed extract.

Preventing Allergies

Attempting to prevent sensitization to foods and other factors is often a valuable first step for protecting at-risk babies. Hypersensitive individuals exhibit more than one kind of sensitivity reaction just as often as not, and at least half of the infants who are intolerant of one or more foods will also have allergies to airborne allergens to some degree, generally beginning around the age of three. A mother with a strong allergy to pollens may have a child with a strong sensitivity to corn. Therefore, one may wish to cover airborne as well as food exposures in their preventive efforts.

When allergies run in a family or have been experienced by either parent, or if irritable bowel syndrome, colitis, Crohn's, arthritis, or asthma are found in the family, many researchers suggest that attempts should be made to prevent sensitization. The intensity of the preventive measures implemented should depend on the frequency and severity of the symptoms in the family. After efforts to prevent sensitization are in effect, a reduced level of allergic reaction seems to maintain throughout the growing years.

Expecting parents can attempt to avoid sensitization in their unborn child by reducing potential allergens in the pregnant mother's environment and diet, especially during the last 3 months of pregnancy. Enough research has been performed that we can be relatively certain that elimination will help to some degree, but there has not been enough study for us to know which kinds of allergens are more or less apt to cause fetal sensitization, or for us to predict the actual degree of protection and lifetime benefit.

The effect of cow's milk in the mother's diet has been studied the most. While some trials show reduced childhood allergies when mothers avoid milk during the latter part of pregnancy, one investigation found no long-term statistical reduction of allergies in children whose mothers avoided cow's milk and egg during the last 12 weeks of gestation.[17] Maternal smoking during pregnancy certainly affects development of asthma in the child,[18] as does secondhand smoke exposure.

Avoiding milk during the last third of pregnancy as well as during lactation has been shown to provide a definite benefit, at least against early allergy.

The next, more certain step is to prevent sensitizing the infant after birth by reducing potential environmental irritants and allergens. Although factors such as pollen and air pollution may be difficult to avoid, the best technique is to reduce overall exposure by removing all irritants you can control, such as pet dander, cigarette smoke, and fragrances. Such measures are more convincingly beneficial after a child has been born.

The child's diet is the other concern. Many times it has been shown that breastfeeding provides good protection against the development of allergies. When the lactating mother avoids dairy and other common allergens, this is even better. Avoiding milk during the last third of pregnancy as well as during lactation has been shown to provide a definite benefit, at least against early allergy.[19] (This will also reduce mom's chances of developing toxemia.) The artificially fed infant can be started on hydrolysate immediately, avoiding any exposure to regular milk formula, and the nursing infant who is weaned early or who starts on supplements can receive the same. Although dairy hydrolysate is often poorly tolerated by infants already sensitized to bovine proteins, either from regular milk formulas or in utero, infants without this exposure are less likely to develop bovine protein intolerance from the lower concentrations in hydrolysates. These measures have been shown to reduce the chances of allergic disease in at-risk children (those with allergic parents) by 50% in a 5-year follow-up study.[20] This same Canadian study revealed no long-term preventive benefit with soy formulas.

The longer you wait before exposing your child to bovine proteins and other likely allergens, the less your child's chances of developing sensitivity. A Belgian investigation that evaluated hydrolysate formula against regular formula found a sixfold reduction in bovine protein sensitivity in the hydrolysate group at the age of 6 months, and just as above, a 50% advantage after 5 years, measured in terms of milk protein sensitivity.[21] Colic in infants was reduced fourfold. Researchers who previously discovered these effects suggested that no infant should ever be exposed to cow's milk proteins during their first four weeks of life.[22] All the evidence strongly agrees with this conclusion. In fact, *the American Academy of Pediatrics released an advisory stating that milk products should not be provided during the first year of life*. Milk formulas should certainly be included in this advisory since the chief motivation for this announcement was development of childhood diabetes. Studies report that cow's milk exposure from formula feeding during the first few months of life is the biggest risk from dairy for developing diabetes. Since formula companies provide large amounts of monetary funding to pediatric schools, associations, researchers, and practitioners, it is difficult for the AAP to promote their recommendation to any extent.[23]

Developing food intolerances or other allergies may be unavoidable in those with stronger genetic programming because allergic responses are highly hereditary maladies. Attempting to prevent reactions may at least reduce or delay symptoms. The big disappointment (and benefit) in preventive medicine is that you generally don't know what has been prevented in any individual case. Therefore, without having a certain sense of purpose, it is often difficult to implement preventive measures unless a problem in a previous child provides strong incentive. Remember, preventive decisions are based chiefly on family history, but certainly also must be predicated on their feasibility in any given situation.

Treatment Choices

There are some old and new immune therapies that aim to reduce sensitivity reactions, and there are also medicines that may reduce or prevent symptoms, all with varying levels of success and drawbacks. There are times when one may wisely decide to try immune therapies, and possibly more times when one may wish to use medication to relieve the symptoms of accidental or unavoidable exposures. One medication (cromolyn) is sometimes quite valuable in preventing reactions to exposures when mystery foods must be consumed, but it is costly and not approved for this kind of use in the U.S.

The best treatment today is to avoid aggravating factors. Even though Drs. F. Savino and R. Oggero suggest drugs as the second treatment of choice for colic (after comforting), they go on to state that dietary modifications (their third choice) provide superior results, and without the side effects of medications.[24] In many cases, long-term avoidance can reduce or erase one's sensitivity to a given allergen.[25] However, almost all medically documented studies that report this kind of success fail to look at the long-term consequences of reintroducing past allergens into a diet. Clinical experience of practitioners reveals that although one or two trial challenges may cause no reaction, regular reintroduction of past allergens will eventually result in resensitization. Studies on celiac disease (gluten intolerance), the best researched of all food intolerances, show this to be true in almost all cases.[26]

Clinical Treatment Methods

For nearly a century allergy shots have been given for type 1 allergies (immunotherapy). Progress has been made, but results are still only moderate, and the therapy must be received several times per month for 3 to 5 years. Benefit is mostly found for pollen, dust mite, and bee venom allergies. To date, this therapy is not recommended for food sensitivities and is not useful for food-related symptoms such as eczema. Therapy for severe anaphylactic food reactions such as peanut allergies is sometimes tried in an attempt to prevent disastrous results from accidental exposure. Doctors from the National Jewish Center for Immunology and Respiratory Medicine are having excellent results with this.[27] On the other hand, doctors at John Hopkins University found no reduction in the need for medications in an immunotherapy-treated group of allergic children with seasonal asthma.[28] Sometimes immunotherapy only makes symptoms worse, as often occurs with animal dander treatments.[29]

Provocation-neutralization is an evolving technique popular in many ear, nose, and throat and environmental medicine practices. The largest study of the provocation-neutralization method, performed by supporters of the technique but following a study design approved by the American Academy of Otolaryngic Allergy, seems to be the best source for judging the efficacy of the technique. This multicenter triple-blind placebo-controlled study reports 75% beneficial outcomes.[30] In reviewing their reports, I find apparent weaknesses in their study design and conclusions. Still, one can see benefits in more than half the subjects. Although good benefits resulted for rhinitis, headache, and lung symptoms — symptoms that also generally respond to traditional allergen injection therapy — gastrointestinal symptoms do not appear to have improved.

Medications

Medications are commonly used to reduce symptoms of disorders such as asthma and gastrointestinal problems. Dicyclomine has been in recent use for colic, with about 54% effectiveness and some serious side effects (remember, dietary measures safely provide very high percentages of relief). Due to some adverse effects of this medication in infants, similar ones are now being used, but with similar risks. Steroids are used for many symptoms that relate to hypersensitivity reactions — everything from eczema to bowel syndromes to asthma — offering temporary relief but also potentially serious side effects. Epinephrine is a lifesaving emergency drug for anaphylactic reactions. Many drugs available for asthma can assist with acute reactions, but have serious side effects and (as previously discussed) are possibly responsible for the cyclical increases in asthma deaths.

The good news is that some of the best medications for food sensitivity reactions are over-the-counter drugs with minimal side effects. While your doctor may be less aware of their food allergy values, he may be ready to guide you in what would be safe to try. Histamine-1 blockers (antihistamines), such as Chlortrimeton, are very valuable for allergic rhinitis and other allergic symptoms. What is not commonly known is that medications such as Zantac (ranitidine) and Tagamet (cimetadine), commonly called histamine-2 blockers, are valuable drugs for reducing the effects of food intolerance reactions,[31,32] since most histamine receptors in the intestines are histamine 2 type. These drugs, popularly known for their use with ulcers, can block H-2 receptors from responding to histamine releases related to food sensitivity and thus can reduce symptoms from food reactions — hopefully reducing damage as well. This effect often unknowingly accounts for some of the success of these drugs in ulcer treatment. H-1 blockers may be somewhat beneficial in reducing some intestinal reactions as well, and a medically supervised combination of these two drugs may work well for many. Since many chemicals are released by mast cells, and these drugs chiefly block the histamine action, the entire reaction is not necessarily prevented. Simple anti-inflammatory medications such as ibuprofen (Advil) and aspirin may be helpful too, affecting different parts of the reaction. Unfortunately, these can also damage some already irritated stomachs and need to be used with care, but they are worth trying.

Other symptoms associated with a child's intestinal food sensitivities should respond to all of these drugs as well. Improvement is often seen in behavior, eczema, and other symptoms. Serotonin action is only partly blocked by H-2 blockers,[33] so all behavioral effects may not be mitigated by H-2 blockers, or by any one drug. H-2 blockers work better for symptom treatment than for prevention. By reducing stomach secretions, they reduce the ability to digest proteins. Most allergens are proteins, and less-digested proteins will only cause more reactions.

Ketotifen is a prescription drug with H-1 antihistamine activity and mast cell stabilizing action as well. Used only outside of the U.S., it has been proven in many trials to be especially beneficial for treating food sensitive patients.[34,35]

Cytoprotective drugs, prescription drugs that help to protect the intestinal mucosal lining in other ways, can be very helpful for reducing food reaction symptoms and damage,[36,37] but these have more potential side effects (and should never be used during pregnancy). Pepto-Bismol is a mild and reportedly safe over-the-counter cytoprotective drug used by some.

Cromolyn sodium seems to be a valuable prescription for preventing hypersensitivity reactions in many.[38,39] Cromolyn is sometimes used in preemies experiencing various allergic reactions who cannot tolerate riskier drugs. This drug works preventively when taken one half hour before consuming an offending food (or a mystery meal). It is not useful once a reaction is already occurring. Cromolyn works very well for some people and not for others.[40] This is a result of the wide variation of immune response mechanisms between individuals and the amount of damage already present. Cromolyn, like any other drug, should not be used in place of sincere attempts at food allergen elimination. Some of these are for the occasional meal out that cannot be trusted, others are for reducing symptoms after an accidental exposure has occurred.

In the U.S., however, this drug is not legally classified to be prescribed for food hypersensitivity reactions (since we all know they don't really exist). Technically, cromolyn *is* prescribed here for the condition called "mastocytosis." This disease is described as extremely rare. It is defined as having too many mast cells and is diagnosed with biopsy. Remember, mast cells are responsible for recognizing food allergens and initiating the allergic inflammatory response. While this condition is described as severe (or needs to be severe in order to be diagnosed as mastocytosis), and it reportedly more commonly affects the skin, the symptoms of intestinal mastocytosis are indistinguishable from those of intestinal food sensitivity.

Natural Treatments

Antioxidants have been shown to reduce intestinal allergic reactions. Vitamin C has been shown in several small studies to reduce histamine levels. Selenium and zinc were found to be low in children with allergic colitis, probably used up by the inflammatory process.[41] Thus, supplementing these elements might be beneficial. Fatty acids are known to be associated with allergic reactions. While one author suggests reducing hydrogenated fats, another suggests reducing unsaturated fats. Fat soluble antioxidants, vitamins A and E, have been shown to reduce the negative effects of fats.[42] Since the jury is out on the fats, and antioxidants help to block their deleterious effects, taking antioxidant vitamins (A, C, and E) and minerals (selenium and zinc) that are highly beneficial for many other reasons seems to be a better choice than attempting to alter fat intake in children.

It has been proven that *Lactobacillus acidophilus* supplements reduce the gastrointestinal side effects and intestinal yeast infections that result from antibiotic use.[43] In trials on food allergic infants, Finnish researchers have shown that this bacteria is also beneficial for further reducing symptoms when used with dietary measures, as compared with using dietary measures alone.[44] Because this bacteria is able to survive stomach conditions, especially the very neutral stomachs of infants and children, it can adhere to the intestinal lining,[45] providing competition for yeast. These researchers have shown that Lactobacillus may actually promote the protective IgA immune response and reduce permeability defects in the intestinal lining. Dairy yogurt would not be my choice as a source of this beneficial bacteria; fortunately, soy yogurt is available. For daily use, non-dairy Lactobacillus supplements can be given (keep refrigerated). Powder form works well for infants. Many brands offer a broader spectrum of flora including *L. bifidus* and bifidobacteria, probably providing superior results.

Many practitioners also recommend building up the body's overall health for better immune system function by using good nutrition, regular exercise, stress reduction, and ample rest. There is certainly nothing wrong with this advice, and it will probably help. The immune system certainly functions best when nutrition, exercise, and rest are plentiful. Asthma attacks, even when surely allergy-related, are very well known to increase with stress, including the stress of otherwise poor health. Cortisol (the stress hormone) release alerts the immune system, and any allergic reactions can increase in response.

Information can be found on many herbal remedies — there are certainly some real gems here. Many other natural modalities can also be explored such as massage, chiropractic, naturopathy, and acupuncture. Many of these minimize allergic responses by reducing the body's stress level or stress reactions and improving the body's overall functioning. Nutritional guidance can often be obtained from such practitioners as well.

Once they are able to remember and recognize the source of their uncomfortable symptoms, children will want to avoid the bad feelings that allergenic foods cause. For many, by the time they are more aware of the outside world of food, their own dietary restrictions are as much a way of life as getting dressed. Sometimes those of us around a child with a restricted diet feel much more sorry for them

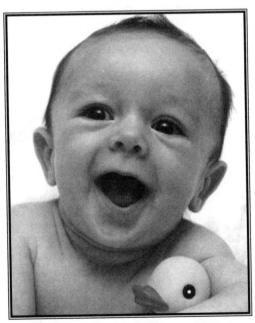

than they do for themselves. Having an awareness of diet at a young age, and of one's own special chemistry, can only be helpful with future nutritional choices, even if many foods become tolerated.

Knowing and avoiding the potentially harmful effects sensitivity reactions can have on your child is just as important and loving as nursing, close bonding, and informed health care decisions. What we feed our children matters; how we parent them matters. These measures will lead to the best health, comfort, and happiness available to a child. Parents have the power to create and enjoy healthier, happier children with brighter futures.

Epilogue

The New Old Way

The baby care practices that attachment parents have found to provide optimal physical and emotional health and intellectual development include:

- Responding to baby's cries
- Holding and carrying baby closely much of the day
- Nighttime parenting promoted by flexible sleep arrangements, especially sharing sleep with baby
- Exclusive breastfeeding on cue
- Continued breastfeeding beyond solid foods; avoiding forced premature weaning
- Speaking to and interacting with baby frequently, responding to cues
- Interpreting exploration as mind development rather than as "naughty behavior"
- Validating baby's feelings
- Enriching dialog and guidance as opposed to violent discipline or meaningless dogma
- Non-violent toys and play

Respecting the feelings and needs of every member in the household is just as important, albeit giving baby some priority.

Notes

Chapter 2: The Attachment Advantage

1. John B. Watson, *Psychological Care of Infant and Child* (New York: W. W. Norton, 1928).
2. D.R. Pederson et al., "Maternal sensitivity and the security of infant–mother attachment: a Q-sort study," *Child Dev* (Canada) 61, no. 6 (Dec 1990): 1974–83.
3. T. Jacobsen et al., "Children's ability to delay gratification: longitudinal relations to mother–child attachment," *J Genet Psychol* 158, no. 4 (Dec 1997): 411–26.
4. M.H. van Ijzendoorn and S. van Vliet-Visser, "The relationship between quality of attachment in infancy and IQ in kindergarten," *J Genet Psychol* (Netherlands) 149, no. 1 (Mar 1988): 23–8.
5. A.G. Bus and M.H. van Ijzendoorn, "Attachment and early reading: a longitudinal study," *J Genet Psychol* (Netherlands) 149, no. 2 (Jun 1988): 199–210.
6. E.S. Harris et al., "Quality of mother–infant attachment and pediatric health care use," *Pediatrics* 84, no. 2 (Aug 1989): 248–54.
7. D.C. van den Boom, "The influence of temperament and mothering on attachment and exploration: an experimental manipulation of sensitive responsiveness among lower-class mothers with irritable infants," *Child Dev* (Netherlands) 65, no. 5 (Oct 1994): 1457–77.
8. D.C. van den Boom, "Do first-year intervention effects endure? Follow-up during toddlerhood of a sample of Dutch irritable infants," *Child Dev* (Netherlands) 66, no. 6 (Dec 1995): 1798–816.
9. G. Kochanska, "Multiple pathways to conscience for children with different temperaments: from toddlerhood to age 5," *Dev Psychol* 33, no. 2 (Mar 1997): 228–40.
10. E. B. Lehman et al., "Soft object and pacifier attachments in young children: the role of security of attachment to the mother," *J Child Psychol Psychiatry* 33, no. 7 (Oct 1992): 1205–15.
11. A.W. Wolf and B. Lozoff, "Object attachment, thumb-sucking, and the passage to sleep," *J Am Acad Child Adolesc Psychiatry* 28, no. 2 (Mar 1989): 287–92.
12. K.D. Mickelson et al., "Adult attachment in a nationally representative sample," *J Pers Soc Psychol* 73, No. 5 (Nov 1997): 1092–106.
13. E.A. Carlson, "A prospective longitudinal study of attachment disorganization/disorientation," *Child Dev* 69, no. 4 (Aug 1998): 1107–28.
14. M. Mikulincer and I. Erev, "Attachment style and the structure of romantic love," *Br J Soc Psychol* (Israel) 30, part 4 (Dec 1991): 273–91.
15. T.L. Morrison et al., "Attachment and the representation of intimate relationships in adulthood," *J Psychol* 131, no. 1 (Jan 1997): 57–71.
16. E. Moss et al., "Correlates of attachment at school age: maternal reported stress, mother–child interaction, and behavior problems," *Child Dev* 69, no. 5 (Oct 1998): 1390–405.
17. S.L. Warren et al., "Child and adolescent anxiety disorders and early attachment," *J Am Acad Child Adolesc Psychiatry* 36, no. 5 (May 1997): 637–44.
18. J.P. Allen et al., "Attachment and adolescent psychosocial functioning," *Child Dev* 69, no. 5 (Oct 1998): 1406–19.
19. K.A. Brennan and P.R. Shaver, "Attachment styles and personality disorders: their connections to each other and to parental divorce, parental death, and perceptions of parental care-giving," *J Pers* 66, no. 5 (Oct 1998): 835–78.

20. B.A. van der Kolk and R.E. Fisler, "Childhood abuse and neglect and loss of self-regulation," *Bull Menninger Clin* 58, no. 2 (Spring 1994): 145–68.

21. D.S. Rosenstein and H.A. Horowitz, "Adolescent attachment and psychopathology," *J Consult Clin Psychol* 64, no. 2 (Apr 1996): 244–53.

22. J.P. Allen et al., "Attachment theory as a framework for understanding sequelae of severe adolescent psychopathology: an 11-year follow-up study," *J Consult Clin Psychol* 64, no. 2 (Apr 1996): 254–64.

23. K.D. Mickelson et al., "Adult attachment in a nationally representative sample," *J Pers Soc Psychol* 73, no. 5 (Nov 1997): 1092–106.

24. T. Sato et al., "Dysfunctional parenting as a risk factor to lifetime depression in a sample of employed Japanese adults: evidence for the 'affectionless control' hypothesis," *Psychol Med* (Japan) 28, no. 3 (May 1998): 737–42.

25. C. Duggan et al., "Quality of parenting and vulnerability to depression: results from a family study," 28, no. 1 (Jan 1998): 185–91.

26. J.I. Escobar, "Immigration and mental health: why are immigrants better off?" *Arch Gen Psychiatry* 55, no. 9 (Sep 1998): 781–2.

27. W.A. Vega et al., "Lifetime prevalence of DSM-III-R psychiatric disorders among urban and rural Mexican Americans in California," *Arch Gen Psychiatry* 55, no. 9 (Sep 1998): 771–8.

28. National Research Council and the Institute of Medicine, "From generation to generation: The health and well-being of children in immigrant families," *National Research Council and the Institute of Medicine Report* (Washington, D.C.: National Academy Press, 1998).

29. B. Bower, "Immigrants go from health to worse," *Science News* 154, no. 12 (Sep 19, 1998): 180.

30. D.A. Cohn, "Child–mother attachment of six-year-olds and social competence at school," *Child Dev* 61, no. 1 (Feb 1990): 152–62.

31. B. Renken et al., "Early childhood antecedents of aggression and passive withdrawal in early elementary school," *J Pers* 57, no. 2 (Jun 1989): 257–81.

32. F.I. De Zulueta, "Human violence: a treatable epidemic," *Med Confl Surviv* (London) 14, no. 1 (Jan–Mar 1998): 46–55.

33. J.N. Constantino, "Early relationships and the development of aggression in children," *Harv Rev Psychiatry* 2, no. 5 (Jan–Feb 1995): 259–73.

34. J.D. Coie et al., "Predicting early adolescent disorder from childhood aggression and peer rejection," *J Consult Clin Psychol* 60, no. 5 (Oct 1992): 783–92.

35. J.A. Graber et al., "The antecedents of menarcheal age: heredity, family environment, and stressful life events," *Child Dev* 66, no. 2 (Apr 1995): 346–59.

36. M. Wierson et al., "Toward a new understanding of early menarche: the role of environmental stress in pubertal timing," *Adolescence* 28, no. 112 (Winter 1993): 913–24.

37. T.E. Moffitt et al., "Childhood experience and the onset of menarche: a test of a sociobiological model," *Child Dev* 63, no. 1 (Feb 1992): 47–58.

38. B.A. Stroll, "Western diet, early puberty, and breast cancer risk," *Breast Cancer Res Treat* (England) 49, no. 3 (Jun 1998): 187–93.

39. J.S. Suh et al., "Menstrual and reproductive factors related to the risk of breast cancer in Korea. Ovarian hormone effect on breast cancer," *J Korean Med Sci* (Korea) 11, no. 6 (Dec 1996): 501–8.

40. J. Belsky et al., "Childhood experience, interpersonal development, and reproductive strategy: an evolutionary theory of socialization," *Child Dev* 62, no. 4 (Aug 1991): 647–70.

41. Dr. Ken Magid and Carole A. McKelvey, *High Risk: Children without a Conscience* (New York: Bantam Books, 1987), 61–3.

42. Lawrence Wright, *Twins and What They Tell Us About Who We Are* (New York: John Wiley & Sons, Inc., 1997).

43. V. Jockin et al., "Personality and divorce: a genetic analysis," *J Pers Soc Psychol* 71, no. 2 (Aug 1996): 288–99.

44. Dr. Ken Magid and Carole A. McKelvey, *High Risk: Children without a Conscience* (New York: Bantam Books, 1987).

45. J.L. Phelps, J. Belsky, and K. Crnic, "Earned security, daily stress, and parenting: a comparison of five alternative models," *Dev Psychopathol* 10, no. 1 (Winter 1998): 21–38.

46. M. Main, "Introduction to the special section on attachment and psychopathology: 2. Overview of the field of attachment," *J Consult Clin Psychol* 64, no. 2 (Apr 1996): 237–43.

47. K.D. Mickelson et al., "Adult attachment in a nationally representative sample," *J Pers Soc Psychol* 73, no. 5 (Nov 1997): 1092–106.

Chapter 3: Bonding: The Inside Story

1. C.S. Carter, "Neuroendocrine perspectives on social attachment and love," *Psychoneuroendocrinology* 23, no. 8 (Nov 1998): 779–818.

2. S.S. Knox and K. Uvnas-Moberg, "Social isolation and cardiovascular disease: an atherosclerotic pathway?" *Psychoneuroendocrinology* 23, no. 8 (Nov 1998): 877–90.

3. N. Frasure-Smith et al., "Gender, depression, and one-year prognosis after myocardial infarction," *Psychosom Med* (Canada) 61, no. 1 (Jan–Feb 1999): 26-37.

4. T.R. Insel, "Oxytocin — a neuropeptide for affiliation: evidence from behavioral, receptor autoradiographic, and comparative studies," *Psychoneuroendocrinology* 17, no. 1 (1992): 3–35.

5. E. Nissen et al., "Elevation of oxytocin levels early post partum in women," *Acta Obstet Gynecol Scand* (Sweden) 74, no. 7 (Aug 1995): 530–3.

6. K.M. Kendrick et al., "Changes in the sensory processing of olfactory signals induced by birth in sheep," *Science* (England) 256, no. 5058 (May 1992): 833–6.

7. K. de Geest et al., "Plasma oxytocin in human pregnancy and parturition," *J Perinat Med* 13, no. 1 (1985): 3–13.

8. E. Nissen et al., "Different patterns of oxytocin, prolactin but not cortisol release during breastfeeding in women delivered by caesarean section or by the vaginal route," *Early Hum Dev* (Sweden) 45, nos. 1–2 (Jul 1996): 103–18.

9. E. Nissen et al., "Oxytocin, prolactin, milk production and their relationship with personality traits in women after vaginal delivery or Cesarean section," *J Psychosom Obstet Gynaecol* (Sweden) 19, no. 1 (Mar 1998): 49–58.

10. T.R. Insel and T.J. Hulihan, "A gender-specific mechanism for pair bonding: oxytocin and partner preference formation in monogamous voles," *Behav Neurosci* 109, no. 4 (Aug 1995): 782–9.

11. P. Popik and J. Vetulani, "Opposite action of oxytocin and its peptide antagonists on social memory in rats," *Neuropeptides* (Poland) 18, no. 1 (Jan 1991): 23–7.

12. D.A. Battin et al., "Effect of suckling on serum prolactin, luteinizing hormone, follicle-stimulating hormone, and estradiol during prolonged lactation," *Obstet Gynecol* 65, no. 6 (Jun 1985): 785–8.

13. K. Uvnas-Moberg et al., "Oxytocin and prolactin levels in breast-feeding women. Correlation with milk yield and duration of breast-feeding," *Acta Obstet Gynecol Scand* (Sweden) 69, no. 4 (1990): 301–6.

14. H. Varendi et al., "Attractiveness of amniotic fluid odor: evidence of prenatal olfactory learning?" *Acta Paediatr* (Estonia) 85, no. 10 (Oct 1996): 1233–7.

15. J.C. Molina and M.G. Chotro, "Association between chemosensory stimuli and cesarean delivery in rat fetuses: neonatal presentation of similar stimuli increases motor activity," *Behav Neural Biol* (Argentina) 55, no. 1 (Jan 1991): 42–60.

16. H. Varendi et al., "Soothing effect of amniotic fluid smell in newborn infants," *Early Hum Dev* (Estonia) 51, no. 1 (Apr 1998): 47–55.

17. R.H. Porter et al., "An assessment of the salient olfactory environment of formula-fed infants," *Physiol Behav* 50, no. 5 (Nov 1991): 907–11.

18. S. Takeda et al., "Concentrations and origin of oxytocin in breast milk," *Endocrinol Jpn* (Japan) 33, no. 6 (Dec 1986): 821–6.

19. A. Powell, "Children need touching and attention, Harvard researchers say," *Harvard University Gazette*, (Apr 9, 1998).

20. D.J. Gubernick et al., "Oxytocin changes in males over the reproductive cycle in the monogamous, biparental California mouse, *Peromyscus californicus,*" *Horm Behav* 29, no. 1 (Mar 1995): 59–73.

21. B. Schaal and L. Marlier, "Maternal and paternal perception of individual odor signatures in human amniotic fluid — potential role in early bonding?" *Biol Neonate* (France) 74, no. 4 (Oct 1998): 266–73.

22. D.M. Witt et al., "Enhanced social interactions in rats following chronic, centrally infused oxytocin," *Pharmacol Biochem Behav* 43, no. 3 (Nov 1992): 855–61.

23. Theresa L. Crenshaw, M.D., *The Alchemy of Love and Lust* (New York, New York: Pocket Books, 1997), 117.

24. M. Bamshad et al., "Cohabitation alters vasopressin innervation and paternal behavior in prairie voles (*Microtus ochrogaster*)," *Physiol Behav* 56, no. 4 (Oct 1994): 751–8.

25. Z. Wang et al., "Role of septal vasopressin innervation in paternal behavior in prairie voles (*Microtus ochrogaster*)," *Proc Natl Acad Sci USA* 91, no. 1 (Jan 1994): 400–4.

26. T.R. Insel and T.J. Hulihan, "A gender-specific mechanism for pair bonding: oxytocin and partner preference formation in monogamous voles," *Behav Neurosci* 109, no. 4 (Aug 1995): 782–9.

27. Theresa L. Crenshaw, M.D., *The Alchemy of Love and Lust* (New York, New York: Pocket Books, 1997), 106.

28. C.S. Carter, Neuroendocrine perspectives on social attachment and love," *Psychoneuroendocrinology* 23, no. 8 (Nov 1998): 779–818.

29. M. Engelmann et al., "Behavioral consequences of intracerebral vasopressin and oxytocin: focus on learning and memory," *Neurosci Biobehav Rev* (Germany) 20, no. 3 (Autumn 1996): 341–58.

30. E.E. Nelson and J. Panksepp, "Brain substrates of infant–mother attachment: contributions of opioids, oxytocin, and norepinephrine," *Neurosci Biobehav Rev* 22, no. 3 (1998): 437–452.

31. R.S. Bridges, "The role of lactogenic hormones in maternal behavior in female rats," *Acta Paediatr Suppl* 397 (Jun 1994): 33–9.

32. R.E. Brown et al., "Hormonal responses of male gerbils to stimuli from their mate and pups," Horm Behav (Canada) 29, no. 4 (Dec 1995): 474–91.

33. W.L. Castro and K.S. Matt, "The importance of social condition in the hormonal and behavioral responses to an acute social stressor in the male Siberian dwarf hamster (Phodopus sungorus)," Horm Behav 32, no. 3 (Dec 1997): 209–16.

34. R.J. Windle et al., "Endocrine and behavioral responses to noise stress: comparison of virgin and lactating female rats during non-disrupted maternal activity," J Neuroendocrinol 9, no. 6 (Jun 1997): 407–14.

35. T.E. Ziegler et al., "Hormonal responses to parental and nonparental conditions in male cotton-top tamarins, Saguinus oedipus, a New World primate," Horm Behav 30, no. 3 (Sep 1996): 287–97.

36. L.G. Sobrinho, "Emotional aspects of hyperprolactinemia," Psychother Psychosom (Portugal) 67, no. 3 (1998): 133–9.

37. B. Lozoff et al., "Serum prolactin levels and behavior in infants," Biol Psychiatry 37, no. 1 (Jan 1995): 4–12.

38. W.G. Roper, "The etiology of male homosexuality," Med Hypotheses 46, no. 2 (Feb 1996): 85–8.

39. E.M. Alder et al., "Hormones, mood and sexuality in lactating women," Br J Psychiatry 148 (Jan 1986): 74–9.

40. L.G. Sobrinho, "The psychogenic effects of prolactin," Acta Endocrinol (Copenh) (Portugal) 129, suppl. 1 (Jul 1993): 38–40.

41. Concept Fertility Centre, "Prolactin" conceptfert.com.au/infosht/pro.htm (Dec 1996).

42. E.E. Nelson and J. Panksepp, "Brain substrates of infant–mother attachment: contributions of opioids, oxytocin, and norepinephrine," Neurosci Biobehav Rev 22, no. 3 (1998): 437–452.

43. S.R. Robinson et al., "Experience with milk and an artificial nipple promotes conditioned opioid activity in the rat fetus," Dev Psychobiol 26, no. 7 (Nov 1993): 375–87.

44. E.E. Nelson and J. Panksepp, "Brain substrates of infant–mother attachment: contributions of opioids, oxytocin, and norepinephrine," Neurosci Biobehav Rev 22, no. 3 (1998): 441.

45. W.P. Smotherman and S.R. Robinson, "Prenatal experience with milk: fetal behavior and endogenous opioid systems," Neurosci Biobehav Rev 16, no. 3 (Fall 1992): 351–64.

46. L.G. Sobrinho, "The psychogenic effects of prolactin," Acta Endocrinol (Copenh) (Portugal) 129, suppl. 1 (Jul 1993): 38–40.

47. G.L. Kovacs et al., "Oxytocin and addiction: a review," Psychoneuroendocrinology (Hungary) 23, no. 8 (Nov 1998): 945–62.

48. Theresa L. Crenshaw, M.D., The Alchemy of Love and Lust (New York, New York: Pocket Books, 1997), 134–5.

49. G.W. Kraemer et al., "A longitudinal study of the effect of different social rearing conditions on cerebrospinal fluid norepinephrine and biogenic amine metabolites in rhesus monkeys," Neuropsychopharmacology 2, no. 3 (Sep 1989): 175–89.

50. J. Winberg and R.H. Porter, "Olfaction and human neonatal behavior: clinical implications," Acta Paediatr (Sweden) 87, no. 1 (Jan 1998): 6–10.

51. K. Stern and M.K. McClintock, "Regulation of ovulation by human pheromones," Nature 392, no. 6672 (Mar 1998): 177–9.

52. J. Winberg and R.H. Porter, "Olfaction and human neonatal behavior: clinical implications," Acta Paediatr (Sweden) 87, no. 1 (Jan 1998): 6–10.

53. D. Trotier et al., "[The vomeronasal organ—a rediscovered sensory organ]," Tidsskr Nor Laegeforen (Norway) 116, no. 1 (Jan 1996): 47–51.

54. M.K. McClintock, "On the nature of mammalian and human pheromones," Ann N Y Acad Sci 855 (Nov 30, 1998): 390–2.

55. L.M. Katz et al., "Inhibition of GH in maternal separation may be mediated through altered serotonergic activity at 5-HT2A and 5-HT2C receptors," Psychoneuroendocrinology 21, no. 2 (Feb 1996): 219–35.

56. M.S. Oitzl et al., "Continuous blockade of brain glucocorticoid receptors facilitates spatial learning and memory in rats," Eur J Neurosci (Netherlands) 10, no. 12 (Dec 1998): 3759–66.

57. E.E. Gilles et al., "Abnormal corticosterone regulation in an immature rat model of continuous chronic stress," Pediatr Neurol 15, no. 2 (Sep 1996): 114–9.

58. D. Liu et al., "Maternal care, hippocampal glucocorticoid receptors, and hypothalamic–pituitary–adrenal responses to stress," Science (Canada) 277, no. 5332 (Sep 1997): 1659–62.

59. K. Lyons-Ruth, "Attachment relationships among children with aggressive behavior problems: the role of disorganized early attachment patterns," J Consult Clin Psychol 64, no. 1 (Feb 1996): 64–73.

60. L. Hertsgaard et al., "Adrenocortical responses to the strange situation in infants with disorganized/disoriented attachment relationships," Child Dev 66, no. 4 (Aug 1995): 1100–6.

61. M. Altemus et al., "Suppression of hypothalamic–pituitary–adrenal axis responses to stress in lactating women," J Clin Endocrinol Metab 80, no. 10 (Oct 1995): 2965–9.

62. M.L. Laudenslager et al., "Total cortisol, free cortisol, and growth hormone associated with brief social separation experiences in young macaques," Dev Psychobiol 28, no. 4 (May 1995): 199–211.

63. P. Rosenfeld et al., "Maternal regulation of the adrenocortical response in preweanling rats," Physiol Behav 50, no. 4 (Oct 1991): 661–71.

64. H.J. van Oers et al., "Maternal deprivation effect on the infant's neural stress markers is reversed by tactile stimulation and feeding but not by suppressing corticosterone," *J Neurosci* 18, no. 23 (Dec 1, 1998): 10171–9.

65. M.A. Smith of Dupont Merck Research Labs as reported by John Travis of *Science News* 152 (Nov 8, 1997): 298.

66. E.R. de Kloet et al., "Brain–corticosteroid hormone dialogue: slow and persistent," *Cell Mol Neurobiol* (Netherlands) 16, no. 3 (Jun 1996): 345–56.

67. H. Anisman et al., "Do early-life events permanently alter behavioral and hormonal responses to stressors?" *Int J Dev Neurosci* 16, no. 3–4 (Jun–Jul 1998): 149–64.

68. M. Nachmias et al., "Behavioral inhibition and stress reactivity: the moderating role of attachment security," *Child Dev* 67, no. 2 (Apr 1996): 508–22.

69. M.R. Gunnar et al., "Stress reactivity and attachment security," *Dev Psychobiol* 29, no. 3 (Apr 1996): 191–204.

70. G. Spangler and K.E. Grossmann, "Biobehavioral organization in securely and insecurely attached infants," *Child Dev* 64, no. 5 (Oct 1993): 1439–50.

71. M.R. Gunnar, "Quality and buffering of neuroendocrine stress reactions: potential effects on the developing human brain," *Prev Med* 27, no. 2 (Mar–Apr 1998): 208–11.

72. C. Caldji et al., "Maternal care during infancy regulates the development of neural systems mediating the expression of fearfulness in the rat," *Proc Natl Acad Sci* (Canada) 95, no. 9 (Apr 1998): 5335–40.

73. L.J. Luecken, "Childhood attachment and loss experiences affect adult cardiovascular and cortisol function," *Psychosom Med* 60, no. 6 (Nov–Dec 1998): 765–72.

74. D.M. Vazquez et al., "Regulation of glucocorticoid and mineralcorticoid receptor mRNAs in the hippocampus of the maternal deprived infant rat," *Brain Res* 731, no. 1–2 (Aug 1996): 79–90.

75. J. Raber, "Detrimental effects of chronic hypothalamic–pituitary–adrenal axis activation. From obesity to memory deficits," *Mol Neurobiol* 18, no. 1 (Aug 1998): 1–22.

76. H.J. Krugers et al., "Exposure to chronic psychosocial stress and corticosterone in the rat: effects on spatial discrimination learning and hippocampal protein kinase Cgamma immunoreactivity," *Hippocampus* (Netherlands) 7, no. 4 (1997): 427–36.

77. M. Carlson and F. Earls, "Psychological and neuroendocrinological sequelae of early social deprivation in institutionalized children in Romania," *Ann N Y Acad Sci* 807 (Jan 15, 1997): 419–28.

78. L.D. Dorn et al., "Biopsychological and cognitive differences in children with premature vs. on-time adrenarche," *Arch Pediatr Adolesc Med* 153, no. 2 (Feb 1999): 137–46.

79. E. Redei et al., "Corticotropin release-inhibiting factor is preprothyrotropin-releasing hormone-(178-199)," *Endocrinology* 136, no. 8 (Aug 1995): 3557–63.

80. J. Raber, "Detrimental effects of chronic hypothalamic–pituitary–adrenal axis activation. From obesity to memory deficits," *Mol Neurobiol* 18, no. 1 (Aug 1998): 1–22.

81. M. Deuschle et al., "Effects of major depression, aging and gender upon calculated diurnal free plasma cortisol concentrations: a reevaluation study," (Germany) *Stress* 2, no. 4 (Jan 1999): 281–87.

82. C.L. Coe and C.M. Erickson, "Stress decreases lymphocyte cytolytic activity in the young monkey even after blockade of steroid and opiate hormone receptors," *Dev Psychobiol* 30, no. 1 (Jan 1997): 1–10.

83. G.R. Lubach et al., "Effects of early rearing environment on immune responses of infant rhesus monkeys," *Brain Behav Immun* 9, no. 1 (Mar 1995): 31–46.

Chapter 4: Crying & Caring

1. B.S. McEwen, "Steroid hormones and the brain: linking 'nature' and 'nurture,'" *Neurochem Res* 13, no. 7 (Jul 1998): 663–9.

2. L. Eisenberg, "The social construction of the human brain," *Am J Psychiatry* 152, no. 11 (Nov 1995): 1563–75.

3. C. Acebo and E.B. Thoman, "Role of infant crying in the early mother–infant dialogue," *Physiol Behav* 57, no. 3 (Mar 1995): 541–7.

4. G.C. Anderson, "Risk in mother–infant separation postbirth," *Image J Nurs Sch* 21, no. 4 (Winter 1989): 196–9.

5. W.H. Frey II and M. Langseth, *Crying: The Mystery of Tears* (San Francisco: Harper, 1985).

6. J.E. Brazy, "Effects of crying on cerebral blood volume and cytochrome aa3," *J Pediatr* 112, no. 3 (Mar 1998): 457–61.

7. S.M. Labott et al., "The physiological and psychological effects of the expression and inhibition of emotion," *Behav Med* 16, no. 4 (Winter 1990): 182–9.

8. J.J. Gross et al., "The psychophysiology of crying," *Psychophysiology* 31, no. 5 (Sep 1994): 460–8.

9. C.C. Lambesis et al., "Effects of surrogate mothering on physiologic stabilization in transitional newborns," *Birth Defects Orig Artic Ser* 15, no. 7 (1979): 201–3.

10. P.M. Taylor et al., "Extra early physical contact and aspects of the early mother–infant relationship," *Acta Paediatr Scand Suppl* 316 (1985): 3–14.

11. R.G. Barr et al., "Crying in !Kung San infants: a test of the cultural specificity hypothesis," *Dev Med Child Neurol* (Canada) 33, no. 7 (Jul 1991): 601–10.

12. K. Lee, "The crying pattern of Korean infants and related factors," *Dev Med Child Neurol* (Korea) 36, no. 7 (Jul 1994): 601–7.

13. Sharon Heller, Ph.D. *The Vital Touch* (New York: Henry Holt and Co., 1997).

14. S.K. Dihigo, "New strategies for the treatment of colic: modifying the parent/infant interaction," *J Pediatr Health Care* 12, no. 5 (Sep–Oct 1998): 256–62.

15. R.G. Barr and M.F. Elias, "Nursing interval and maternal responsivity: effect on early infant crying," *Pediatrics* (Canada) 81, no. 4 (Apr 1988): 529–36.

16. E.M. Baildam et al., "Duration and pattern of crying in the first year of life," *Dev Med Child Neurol* 37, no. 4 (Apr 1995): 345–53.

17. B. Lozoff and G. Brittenham, "Infant care: cache or carry," *J Pediatr* 95, no. 3 (Sep 1979): 478–83.

18. J.R. Bemporad, "Cultural and historical aspects of eating disorders," *Theor Med* 18, no. 4 (Dec 1997): 401–20.

19. J.E. Pate et al., "Cross-cultural patterns in eating disorders: a review," *J Am Acad Child Adolesc Psychiatry* 31, no. 5 (Sep 1992): 802–9.

20. S.W. Hurt et al., "A comparison of psychopathology in eating disorder patients from France and the United States," *Int J Eat Disord* 22, no. 2 (Sep 1997): 153–8.

21. D. Neumark-Sztainer et al., "Lessons learned about adolescent nutrition from the Minnesota Adolescent Health Survey," *J Am Diet Assoc* 98, no. 12 (Dec 1998): 1449–56.

22. P.S. Zeskind and R.G. Barr, "Acoustic characteristics of naturally occurring cries of infants with "colic," *Child Dev* 68, no. 3 (Jun 1997): 394–403.

23. B.F. Fuller et al., "Acoustic analysis of cries from "normal" and "irritable" infants," *West J Nurs Res* 16, no. 3 (Jun 1994): 243–53.

24. V.A. Howard and F.W. Thurber, "The interpretation of infant pain: physiological and behavioral indicators used by NICU nurses," *J Pediatr Nurs* 13, no. 3 (Jun 1998): 164–74.

25. Aletha J. Solter, Ph.D., *Tears and Tantrums* (Goleta, California: Shining Star Press, 1998.)

26. J.J. Gross and R.W. Levenson, "Hiding feelings: the acute effects of inhibiting negative and positive emotion," *J Abnorm Psychol* 106, no. 1 (Feb 1997): 95–103.

27. Benjamin Spock, M.D. and Michael B. Rothenberg, M.D., *Dr. Spock's Baby and Child Care*, (New York: Pocket Books, 1998), 237, 257–8.

28. F.E. Gardner, "The quality of joint activity between mothers and their children with behaviour problems," *J Child Psychol Psychiatry* 35, no. 5 (Jul 1994): 935–48.

29. S.M. Labott et al., "The physiological and psychological effects of the expression and inhibition of emotion," *Behav Med* 16, no. 4 (Winter 1990): 182–9.

30. J.S. Rosenblatt, "Psychobiology of maternal behavior: contribution to the clinical understanding of maternal behavior among humans," *Acta Paediatr Suppl* 397 (Jun 1994): 3–8.

31. Ashley Montagu, *Touching, The Human Significance of the Skin*, third edition (New York: Perennial Library, 1986).

32. C.M. Kuhn and S.M. Schanberg, "Responses to maternal separation: mechanisms and mediators," *Int J Dev Neurosci* 16, no. 3–4 (Jun–Jul 1998): 261–70.

33. T.M. Field et al., "Tactile/kinesthetic stimulation effects on preterm neonates," *Pediatrics* 77, no. 5 (May 1986): 654–8.

34. D. Acolet et al., "Changes in plasma cortisol and catecholamine concentrations in response to massage in preterm infants," *Arch Dis Child* 68, no. 1 (Jan 1993): 29–31.

35. G. Ironson et al., "Massage therapy is associated with enhancement of the immune system's cytotoxic capacity," *Int J Neurosci* 84, no. 1–4 (Feb 1996): 205–17.

36. H.J. Polan and M.J. Ward, "Role of mother's touch in failure to thrive: a preliminary investigation," *J Am Acad Child Adolesc Psychiatry* 33, no. 8 (Oct 1994): 1098–105.

37. S. Lowinger et al., "Maternal social and physical contact: links to early infant attachment behaviors," *J Genet Psychol* 156, no. 4 (Dec 1995): 461–76.

38. H. Lugt-Tappeser and B. Wiese, "[Prospective study of maternal behavior in the neonatal period: a pilot study]," *Prax Kinderpsychol Kinderpsychiatr* (Germany) 43, no. 9 (Nov 1994): 322–30.

39. D. Liu et al., "Maternal care, hippocampal glucocorticoid receptors, and hypothalamic–pituitary–adrenal responses to stress," *Science* 277, no. 5332 (Sep 1997): 1659–62.

40. G.E. Carvell and D.J. Simons, "Abnormal tactile experience early in life disrupts active touch," *J Neurosci* 16, no. 8 (Apr 15, 1996): 2750–7.

41. Sharon Heller, Ph.D., *The Vital Touch* (New York: Henry Holt and Co., 1997), 83.

42. E. Anisfeld et al., "Does infant carrying promote attachment? An experimental study of the effects of increased physical contact on the development of attachment," *Child Dev* 61, no. 5 (Oct 1990): 1617–27.

43. U.A. Hunziker and R.G. Barr, "Increased carrying reduces infant crying: a randomized controlled trial," *Pediatrics* 77, no. 5 (May 1986): 641–8.

44. R.G. Barr et al., "Carrying as colic "therapy": a randomized controlled trial," *Pediatrics* 87, no. 5 (May 1991): 623–30.

45. B. Lozoff, "Birth and 'bonding' in non-industrial societies," *Dev Med Child Neurol* 25, no. 5 (Oct 1983): 595–600.
46. K. Christensson, "Fathers can effectively achieve heat conservation in healthy newborn infants," *Acta Paediatr* (Sweden) 85, no. 11 (Nov 1996): 1354–60.
47. J Bauer et al., "Metabolic rate and energy balance in very low birth weight infants during kangaroo holding by their mothers and fathers," *J Pediatr* (Germany) 129 no. 4 (Oct 1996): 608–11.
48. K. Christensson et al., "Separation distress call in the human neonate in the absence of maternal body contact," *Acta Paediatr* (Sweden) 84, no 5 (May 1995): 468–73.
49. C.C. Lambesis et al., "Effects of surrogate mothering on physiologic stabilization in transitional newborns," *Birth Defects Orig Artic Ser* 15, no. 7 (1979): 201–23.
50. L. Vaivre-Douret et al., "[Kangaroo method and care]," *Arch Pediatr* (France) 3, no. 12 (Dec 1996): 1262–9.
51. R.A. Kambarami et al., "Kangaroo care versus incubator care in the management of well preterm infants — a pilot study," *Ann Trop Paediatr* 18, no. 2 (Jun 1998): 81–6.
52. P.R. Messmer et al., "Effect of kangaroo care on sleep time for neonates," *Pediatr Nurs* 23, no. 4 (Jul–Aug 1997): 408–14.
53. S.M. Ludington-Hoe et al., "Birth-related fatigue in 34–36-week preterm neonates: rapid recovery with very early kangaroo (skin-to-skin) care," *J Obstet Gynecol Neonatal Nurs* 28, no. 1 (Jan–Feb 1999): 94–103.
54. C.J. Tornhage et al., "Plasma somatostatin and cholecystokinin levels in preterm infants during kangaroo care with and without nasogastric tube-feeding," *J Pediatr Endocrinol Metab* 11, no. 5 (Sep–Oct 1998): 645–51.
55. K. Gloppestad, *Vard Nord Utveckl Forsk* (Norway) 16, no. 1 (spring 1996): 22–7.
56. N.M. Hurst et al., "Skin-to-skin holding in the neonatal intensive care unit influences maternal milk volume," *J Perinatol* 17, no. 3 (May–Jun 1997): 213–7.
57. P. De Chateau and B. Wiberg, "Long-term effect on mother–infant behavior of extra contact during the first hour post partum. I. First observations at 36 hours," *Acta Paediatr Scand* 66, no. 2 (Mar 1977): 137–43.
58. G. Gale et al., "Skin-to-skin (kangaroo) holding of the intubated premature infant," *Neonatal Netw* 12, no. 6 (Sep 1993): 49–57.
59. A. Tan et al., "The characterization and outcome of stereotypical movements in nonautistic children," *Mov Disord* 12, no. 1 (Jan 1997): 47–52.
60. W.E. MacLean Jr. and A.A. Baumeister, "Effects of vestibular stimulation on motor development and stereotyped behavior of developmentally delayed children," *J Abnorm Child Psychol* 10, no. 2 (Jun 1982): 229–45.
61. T. Farrimond, "Sudden infant death syndrome and possible relation to vestibular function," *Percept Mot Skills* (New Zealand) 71, no. 2 (Oct 1990): 419–23.
62. J. Groswasser et al., "Reduction in obstructive breathing events during body rocking: a controlled polygraphic study in preterm and full-term infants," *Pediatrics* (Belgium) 96, no. 1 pt. 1 (Jul 1995): 64–8.
63. M.P. Sammon and R.A. Darnall, "Entrainment of respiration to rocking in premature infants: coherence analysis," *J Appl Physiol* 77, no. 3 (Sep 1994): 1548–54.
64. G. Malcuit et al., "Cardiac and behavioral responses to rocking stimulations in one- and three-month-old infants," *Percept Mot Skill* (Canada) 66, no. 1 (Feb 1988): 207–17.
65. T. Farrimond, "Sudden infant death syndrome and possible relation to vestibular function," *Percept Mot Skills* (New Zealand) 71, no. 2 (Oct 1990): 419–23.
66. D.L Clark et al., "Effects of rocking on neuromuscular development in the premature," *Biol Neonate* 56, no. 6 (1989): 306–14.
67. L. Cordero et al., "Effects of vestibular stimulation on sleep states in premature infants," *Am J Perinatol* 3, no. 4 (Oct 1986): 319–24.
68. K.E. Barnard and H.L. Bee, "The impact of temporally patterned stimulation on the development of preterm infants," *Child Dev* 54, no. 5 (Oct 1983): 1156–67.
69. A.F. Korner et al., "Effects of vestibular-proprioceptive stimulation on the neurobehavioral development of preterm infants: a pilot study," *Neuropediatrics* 14, no. 3 (Aug 1983): 170–5.
70. K.A. Waters et al., "Neuronal apoptosis in sudden infant death syndrome," *Pediatr* (Canada) 45, no. 2 (Feb 1999): 166–72.
71. J. Lehtonen et al., "The effect of nursing on the brain activity of the newborn," *J Pediatr* (Finland) 132, no. 4 (Apr 1998): 646–51.
72. R.G. Campos, "Rocking and pacifiers: two comforting interventions for heelstick pain," *Res Nurs Health* 17, no. 5 (Oct 1994): 321–31.
73. N.F. Butte et al., "Heart rates of breast-fed and formula-fed infants," *J Pediatr Gastroenterol Nutr* 13, no. 4 (Nov 1991): 391–6.
74. N.F. Butte et al., "Sleep organization and energy expenditure of breast-fed and formula-fed infants," *Pediatr Res* 32, no. 5 (Nov 1992): 514–9.
75. J.A. Bier et al., "Comparison of skin-to-skin contact with standard contact in low-birth-weight infants who are breast-fed," *Arch Pediatr Adolesc Med* 150, No. 12 (Dec 1996): 1265–9.
76. D.M. Treloar, "The effect of nonnutritive sucking on oxygenation in healthy, crying full-term infants," *Appl Nurs Res* 7, no. 2 (May 1994): 52–8.

77. G.C. McCain, "Facilitating inactive awake states in preterm infants: a study of three interventions," *Nurs Res* 41, no. 3 (May–Jun 1992): 157–60.

78. E.A. Mitchell et al., "Dummies and the sudden infant death syndrome," *Arch Dis Child* (New Zealand) 68, no. 4 (Apr 1993): 501–4.

79. M. Arnestad et al., "Is the use of dummy or carry-cot of importance for sudden infant death?" *Eur J Pediatr* 156, no. 12 (Dec 1997): 968–70.

80. Laura Flynn McCarthy, "Snooze Alarm," *Parenttime* Web site, www.pathfinder.com, 1998.

81. B. Ogaard et al., "The effect of sucking habits, cohort, sex, intercanine arch widths, and breast or bottle feeding on posterior crossbite in Norwegian and Swedish 3-year-old children," *Am J Orthod Dentofacial Orthop* (Norway) 106, no. 2 (Aug 1994): 161–6.

82. H. Turgeon-O'Brien et al., "Nutritive and nonnutritive sucking habits: a review," *ASDC J Dent Child* 63, no. 5 (Sep–Oct 1996): 321–7.

83. P. Ollila et al., "Prolonged pacifier-sucking and use of a nursing bottle at night: possible risk factors for dental caries in children," *Acta Odontol Scand* (Finland) 56, no. 4 (Aug 1998): 233–7.

84. L. Righard and M.O. Alade, "Breastfeeding and the use of pacifiers," *Birth* (Sweden) 24, no. 2 (Jun 1997): 116–20.

85. L. Righard, "Are breastfeeding problems related to incorrect breastfeeding technique and the use of pacifiers and bottles?" *Birth* (Sweden) 25, no. 1 (Mar 1998): 40–4.

86. E. Larsson, "Orthodontic aspects on feeding of young children. 1. A comparison between Swedish and Norwegian-Sami children," *Swed Dent J* (Sweden) 22, no. 3 (1998): 117–21.

87. K. A. Freudigman and E.B. Thoman, "Infants' earliest sleep/wake organization differs as a function of delivery mode," *Dev Psychobiol* 32, no. 4 (May 1998): 293–303.

88. K.A. Waters et al., "Neuronal apoptosis in sudden infant death syndrome," *Pediatr* (Canada) 45, no. 2 (Feb 1999): 166–72.

89. M.P. L'Hoir et al., "Sudden unexpected death in infancy: epidemiologically determined risk factors related to pathological classification," *Acta Paediatr* (Holland) 87, no. 12 (Dec 1998): 1279–87.

90. S. Farooqi et al., "Ethnic differences in infant-rearing practices and their possible relationship to the incidence of sudden infant death syndrome (SIDS)," *Paediatr Perinat Epidemiol* (England) 7, no. 3 (Jul 1993): 245–52.

91. R.K. Scragg et al., "Infant room-sharing and prone sleep position in sudden infant death syndrome. New Zealand Cot Death Study Group," *Lancet* (New Zealand) 347, no. 8993 (Jan 1996): 7–12.

92. R. Scragg et al., "Public health policy on bed sharing and smoking in the sudden infant death syndrome," *N Z Med J* (New Zealand) 108, no. 1001 (Jun 14, 1995): 218–22.

93. H. Brooke et al., "Case-control study of sudden infant death syndrome in Scotland, 1992–5," *BMJ* (Scotland) 14, no. 7093 (May 24, 1997): 1516–20.

94. R.E. Gilbert et al., "Bottle feeding and the sudden infant death syndrome," *BMJ* (England) 310, no. 6972 (Jan 14, 1995): 88–90.

95. H.S. Klonoff-Cohen et al., "The effect of passive smoking and tobacco exposure through breast milk on sudden infant death syndrome," *JAMA* 273, no. 10 (Mar 1995): 795–8.

96. J. Schellscheidt et al., "Epidemiological features of sudden infant death after a German intervention campaign in 1992," *Eur J Pediatr* (Germany) 156, no. 8 (Aug 1997): 655–60.

97. J.J. McKenna et al., "Bedsharing promotes breastfeeding," *Pediatrics* 100, no. 2, part 1 (Aug 1997): 214–9.

98. D. Weinert et al., "The development of circadian rhythmicity in neonates," *Early Hum Dev* (Germany) 36, no. 2 (Feb 1994): 117–26.

99. P.J. Schwartz, et al., "Prolongation of the QT interval and the sudden infant death syndrome," *N Engl J Med* 338, no. 24 (June 11, 1998): 1709–14.

100. R.M. Harper et al., "Periodicity of sleep states is altered in infants at risk for the sudden infant death syndrome," *Science* 213, no. 4511 (Aug 28, 1981): 1030–2.

101. V.L. Schechtman et al., "Sleep state organization in normal infants and victims of the sudden infant death syndrome," *Pediatrics* 89, no. 5, pt. 1 (May 1992): 865–79.

102. J.B. Gould et al., "The relationship between sleep and sudden infant death," *Ann N Y Acad Sci* 533 (1988): 62–77.

103. J.J. McKenna et al., "Sleep and arousal patterns of co-sleeping human mother/infant pairs: a preliminary physiological study with implications for the study of sudden infant death syndrome (SIDS)," *Am J Phys Anthropol* 83, no. 3 (Nov 1990): 331–47.

104. S. Mosko et al., "Infant arousals during mother–infant bed sharing: implications for infant sleep and sudden infant death syndrome research," *Pediatrics* 100, no. 5 (Nov 1997): 841–9.

105. S. Mosko et al., "Maternal sleep and arousals during bedsharing with infants," *Sleep* 20, no. 2 (Feb 1997): 142–50.

106. M. Gantley et al., "Sudden infant death syndrome: links with infant care practices," *BMJ* 306, no. 6869 (Jan 1993): 16–20.

107. J. Winberg and R.H. Porter, "Olfaction and human neonatal behavior: clinical implications," *Acta Paediatr* 87, no. 1 (Jan 1998): 6–10.

108. S. Farooqi et al., "Ethnic differences in infant-rearing practices and their possible relationship to the incidence of sudden infant death syndrome (SIDS)," *Paediatr Perinat Epidemiol* (England) 7, no. 3 (Jul 1993): 245–52.

109. N. Watanabe et al., "Epidemiology of sudden infant death syndrome in Japan," *Acta Paediatr Jpn* (Japan) 36, no. 3 (Jun 1994): 329–32.

110. E.J. Adams et al., "Changes in the epidemiologic profile of sudden infant death syndrome as rates decline among California infants: 1990–1995," *Pediatrics* 102, no. 6 (Dec 1998): 1445–51.

111. B.H. Wolf and M.O. Ikeogu, *Ann Trop Paediatr* (Zimbabwe) 16, no. 2 (Jun 1996): 149–53.

112. C.L. Lee and T.L. Chung, "The trend of sudden infant death syndrome in Taiwan from 1984 to 1993," *Chung Hua Min Kui Hsiao Erh Ko I Hsueh Hui Tsa Chih* (Taiwan) 36, no. 6 (Nov–Dec 1995): 431–3.

113. J. McKenna, International Lactation Consultants Association Conference in Atlanta Georgia, July 1994.

114. Nakamura et al., "Review of hazards associated with children placed in adult beds." *Arch Pediatr Adolesc Med* Oct. 1999 153 (10):1019-23

115. D.P. Southall et al., "Severe hypoxaemia in pertussis," *Arch Dis Child* (England) 63, no. 6 (Jun 1988): 598–605.

116. Centers for Disease Control statistics.

117. Tine Thevenin, *The Family Bed* (Wayne, New Jersey: Avery, 1987), 35.

118. Tine Thevenin, *The Family Bed* (Wayne, New Jersey: Avery, 1987), 42.

119. W.P. Fifer and C.M. Moon, "The role of mother's voice in the organization of brain function in the newborn," *Acta Paediatr Suppl* 397 (Jun 1994): 86–93.

120. A.W. Wolf and B. Lozoff, Object attachment, thumbsucking, and the passage to sleep," *J Am Acad Child Adolesc Psychiatry* 28, no. 2 (Mar 1989): 287–92.

121. V. Gedaly-Duff and J. Huff Slankard, "Sleep as an indicator for pain relief in an infant: a case study," *J Pediatr Nurs* 13, no. 1 (Feb 1998): 32–40.

122. A. Kahn et al., "Insomnia and cow's milk allergy in infants," *Pediatrics* 76, no. 6 (Dec 1985): 880–4.

123. A. Kahn et al., "Milk intolerance in children with persistent sleeplessness: a prospective double-blind crossover evaluation," *Pediatrics* (Belgium) 84, no. 4 (Oct 1989): 595–603.

Chapter 5: Brighter Babies, Not Super Babies

1. J. Lehtonen et al., "The effect of nursing on the brain activity of the newborn," *J Pediatr* (Finland) 132, no. 4 (Apr 1998): 646–51.

2. M.C. Temboury et al., "Influence of breast-feeding on the infant's intellectual development," *J Pediatr Gastroenterol Nutr* (Spain) 18, no. 1 (Jan 1994): 32–6.

3. C.D. Florey et al., "Infant feeding and mental and motor development at 18 months of age in first born singletons," *Int J Epidemiol* (England) 24, suppl. 1 (1995): S21–6.

4. D. L. Johnson et al., "Breast feeding and children's intelligence," *Psychol Rep* 79, no. 3, part 2 (Dec 1996): 1179–85.

5. A. Lucas et al., "Breast milk and subsequent intelligence quotient in children born preterm," *Lancet* 339, no. 8788 (Feb 1992): 261–4.

6. J.L. Pollock, "Long-term associations with infant feeding in a clinically advantaged population of babies," *Dev Med Child Neurol* 36, no. 5 (May 1994): 429–40.

7. C.I. Lanting et al., "Neurological differences between 9-year-old children fed breast-milk or formula-milk as babies," *Lancet* (Holland) 344, no. 8933 (Nov 1994): 1319–22.

8. L.J. Horwood and D.M. Fergusson, "Breastfeeding and later cognitive and academic outcomes," *Pediatrics* (New Zealand) 101, no. 1 (Jan 1998): E9.

9. J. Golding et al., "Association between breast feeding, child development and behavior," *Early Hum Dev* (England) 49, suppl. (Oct 1997): S175–84.

10. C.R. Gale and C.N. Martyn, "Breastfeeding, dummy use, and adult intelligence," *Lancet* 347 no. 9008 (Apr 1996): 1072–5.

11. F.C. Barros et al., "Breastfeeding, pacifier use and infant development at 12 months of age: a birth cohort study in Brazil," *Paediatr Perinat Epidemiol* (Brazil) 11, no. 4 (Oct 1997): 441–50.

12. J. Worobey, "Feeding method and motor activity in 3-month-old human infants," *Percept Mot Skills* 86, no. 3, part 1 (Jun 1998): 883–95.

13. C.I. Lanting et al., "Breastfeeding and neurological outcome at 42 months," *Acta Paediatr* (Holland) 87, no. 12 (Dec 1998): 1224–9.

14. B. Lozoff et al., "Iron-deficiency anemia and infant development: effects of extended oral iron therapy," *J Pediatr* 129, no. 3 (Sep 1996): 382–9.

15. E. Riva et al., "Early breastfeeding is linked to higher intelligence quotient scores in dietary treated phenylke-tonuric children," *Acta Paediatr* (Italy) 85, no. 1 (Jan 1996): 639.
16. I.F. Wallace et al., "Interactions of African American infants and their mothers: relations with development at 1 year of age," *J Speech Lang Hear Res* 41, no. 4 (Aug 1998): 900–12.
17. D.L. Coates and M. Lewis, "Early mother-infant interaction and infant cognitive status as predictors of school performance and cognitive behavior in six-year-olds," *Child Dev* 55, no. 4 (Aug 1984): 1219–30.
18. J.R. Smith et al., "Correlates and consequences of harsh discipline for young children," *Arch Pediatr Adolesc Med* 151, no. 8 (Aug 1997): 777–86.
19. J. Raber, "Detrimental effects of chronic hypothalamic–pituitary–adrenal axis activation. From obesity to memory deficits," *Mol Neurobiol* 18, no. 1 (Aug 1998): 1–22.
20. H.J. Krugers et al., "Exposure to chronic psychosocial stress and corticosterone in the rat: effects on spatial dis-crimination learning and hippocampal protein kinase C gamma immunoreactivity," *Hippocampus* 7, no. 4 (1997): 427–36.
21. M. Carlson and F. Earls, "Psychological and neuroendocrinological sequelae of early social deprivation in insti-tutionalized children in Romania," *Ann N Y Acad Sci* 807 (Jan 15, 1997): 419–28.
22. M.M. McGrath et al., "Maternal interaction patterns and preschool competence in high-risk children," *Nurs Res* 47, no. 6 (Nov–Dec 1998): 309–17.
23. B.M. Lester et al., "Developmental outcome as a function of the goodness of fit between the infant's cry char-acteristics and the mother's perception of her infant's cry," *Pediatrics* 95, no. 4 (Apr 1995): 516–21.
24. J. Belsky et al., "Maternal stimulation and infant exploratory competence: cross-sectional, correlational, and experimental analyses," *Child Dev* 51, no. 4 (Dec 1980): 1168–78.
25. M.W. Yogman et al., "Father involvement and cognitive/behavioral outcomes of preterm infants," *J Am Acad Child Adolesc Psychiatry* 34, no. 1 (Jan 1995): 58–66.
26. S.E. Cohen and L. Beckwith, "Preterm infant interaction with the caregiver in the first year of life and com-petence at age two," *Child Dev* 50, no. 3 (Sep 1979): 767–76.
27. J.D. Morrow, "The eyes have it: visual attention as an index of infant cognition," *J Pediatr Health Care* 74, no. 4 (Aug–Jul 1993): 150–5.
28. M. Zuckerman, "Attention must be paid," *U.S. News and World Report* (Aug 18 and Aug 25, 1997): 92.
29. K.E. Smith et al., "The relation of medical risk and maternal stimulation with preterm infants' development of cognitive, language and daily living skills," *J Child Psychol Psychiatry* 37, no. 7 (Oct 1996): 855–64.
30. N. Weisglas-Kuperus et al., "Effects of biological and social factors on the cognitive development of very low birth weight children," *Pediatrics* (Netherlands) 92, no. 5 (Nov 1993): 658–65.
31. L. Beckwith and A.H. Parmelee, Jr., "EEG patterns of preterm infants, home environment, and later IQ," *Child Dev* 57, no. 3 (Jun 1986): 777–89.
32. R.L. Goldenberg et al., "Pregnancy outcome and intelligence at age five years," *Am J Obstet Gynecol* 175, no. 6 (Dec 1996): 1511–5.
33. K.E. Barnard and H.L. Bee, "The impact of temporally patterned stimulation on the development of preterm infants," *Child Dev* 54, no. 5 (Oct 1983): 1156–67.
34. D.L. Clark et al., "Effects of rocking on neuromuscular development in the premature," *Biol Neonate* 56, no. 6 (1989): 306–14.
35. T. Field et al., "Massage therapy reduces anxiety and enhances EEG pattern of alertness and math computa-tions," *Int J Neurosci* 86, nos. 3–4 (Sep 1996): 197–205.
36. H. Montgomery-Downs and E.B. Thoman, "Biological and behavioral correlates of quiet sleep respiration rates in infants," *Physiol Behav* 64, no. 5 (Jul 1998): 637–43.
37. Robert Karen, Ph.D., *Becoming Attached* (New York: Oxford University Press, 1998), 21–2.
38. P.A. Ferchmin et al., "Genetic learning deficiency does not hinder environment-dependent brain growth," *Physiol Behav* 24, no. 1 (Jan 1980): 45–50.
39. F. Gonzalez-Lima et al., "Metabolic activation of the brain of young rats after exposure to environmental com-plexity," *Dev Psychobiol* 27, no. 6 (Sep 1994): 343–51.
40. P.D. Wadhwa et al., "Prenatal psychosocial factors and the neuroendocrine axis in human pregnancy," *Psychosom Med* 58, no. 5 (Sep–Oct 1996): 432–46.
41. K. Sjostrom et al., "Maternal anxiety in late pregnancy and fetal hemodynamics," *Eur J Obstet Gynecol Reprod Biol* 74, no. 2 (Aug 1997): 149–55.
42. L.K. Takahashi et al., "*Psychoneuroendocrinology* 23, no. 6 (Aug 1998): 571–81.
43. C. Brezinka et al., "[The fetus and noise]," *Gynakol Geburtshilfliche Rundsch* (Germany) 37, no. 3 (1997): 119–29.
44. D.S. Richards et al., "Sound levels in the human uterus," *Obstet Gynecol* 80, no. 2 (Aug 1992): 186–90.
45. F.H. Rauscher et al., "Improved maze learning through early music exposure in rats," *Neurol Res* 20, no. 5 (Jul 1998): 427–32.
46. B. Bower, "Language's great innate debate continues to make noise," *Science News* 151 (May 3, 1997): 276–77.
47. W.H. Dietz and V.C. Strasburger, "Children, adolescents, and television," *Curr Probl Pediatr* 21, no. 1 (Jan 1991): 8–32.

48. Ulric Neisser (Editor), *The Rising Curve: Long-Term Gains in IQ and Related Measures*, Apa Science Volumes, (American Psychological Association, 1998).
49. R.B. Tower et al., "Differential effects of television programming on preschoolers' cognition, imagination, and social play," *Am J Orthopsychiatry* 49, no. 2 (Apr 1979): 265–81.
50. Judith Van Evra, "Television and Child Development" (Canada: University of Minnesota Children Youth and Family Consortium, 1990) www.cyfc.umn.edu.
51. B.S. Centerwall, "Television and violence. The scale of the problem and where to go from here," *JAMA* 267, no. 22 (Jun 1992): 3059–63.
52. R.A. Gibson et al., "Effect of dietary docosahexaenoic acid on brain composition and neural function in term infants," *Lipids* 31, suppl. (Mar 1996): S177–81.
53. R.A. Gibson and M. Makrides, "The role of long chain polyunsaturated fatty acids (LCPUFA) in neonatal nutrition," *Acta Paediatr* (Australia) 87, no. 10 (Oct 1998): 1017–22.
54. H.A. Woltil et al., "Long-chain polyunsaturated fatty acid status and early growth of low birth weight infants," *Eur J Pediatr* (Holland) 157, no. 2 (Feb 1998): 146–52.
55. C.L. Jensen et al., "Effect of dietary linoleic/alpha-linolenic acid ration on growth and visual function of term infants," *J Pediatr* 131, no. 2 (Aug 1997): 200–9.
56. J. Woods et al., "Is docosahexaenoic acid necessary in infant formula? Evaluation of high linolenate diets in the neonatal rat," *Pediatr Res* 40, no. 5 (Nov 1996): 687–94.
57. C. Young et al., "Fatty acid compositions of colostrum, cord blood, maternal blood and major infant formulas in Japan," *Acta Paediatr Jpn* (Japan) 39, no. 3 (Jun 1997): 299–304.

Chapter 6: Immune Protection Matters

1. S.P. Srivastava et al., "Mortality patterns in breast versus artificially fed term babies in early infancy: a longitudinal study," *Indian Pediatr* 31, no. 11 (Nov 1994): 1393–6.
2. B. Kuate Defo, "Effects of infant feeding practices and birth spacing on infant and child survival: a reassessment from retrospective and prospective data," *J Biosoc Sci* (Canada) 29, no. 3 (Jul 1997): 303–26.
3. A. Palloni and M. Tienda, "The effects of breastfeeding and pace of childbearing on mortality at early ages," *Demography* 23, no. 1 (Feb 1986): 31–52.
4. S. Awasthi et al., "Mortality patterns in breast versus artificially fed term babies in early infancy: a longitudinal study," *Indian Pediatr* 28, no. 3 (Mar 1991): 243–8.
5. D.C. Nath et al., "Birth spacing, breastfeeding, and early child mortality in a traditional Indian society: a hazards model analysis," *Soc Biol* 41, nos. 3–4 (Fall–Winter 1994): 168–80.
6. A. Palloni et al., "The effects of breast-feeding and the pace of childbearing on early childhood mortality in Mexico," *Bull Pan Am Health Organ* 28, no. 2 (Jun 1994): 93–111.
7. J.P. Habicht et al., "Does breastfeeding really save lives, or are apparent benefits due to biases?" *Am J Epidemiol* 123, no. 2 (Feb 1986): 279–90.
8. C.G. Victora et al., "Infant feeding and deaths due to diarrhea. A case-control study," *Am J Epidemiol* 129, no. 5 (May 1989): 1032–41.
9. A. Lucas and T.J. Cole, "Breast milk and neonatal necrotising enterocolitis," *Lancet* (England) 336, no. 8730 (Dec 1990): 1519–23.
10. M.K. Davis, "Review of the evidence for an association between infant feeding and childhood cancer," *Int J Cancer Suppl* 11 (1998): 29–33.
11. G.P. Mathur et al., "Breastfeeding and childhood cancer," *Indian Pediatr* (India) 30, no. 5 (May 1993): 651–7.
12. M. Xanthou, "Immune protection of human milk," *Biol Neonate* (Greece) 74, no. 2 (1998): 121–33.
13. A.L. Wright et al., "Increasing breastfeeding rates to reduce infant illness at the community level," *Pediatrics* 101, no. 5 (May 1998): 837–44.
14. Y.S. Wang and S.Y. Wu, "The effect of exclusive breastfeeding on development and incidence of infection in infants," *J Hum Lact* 12, no. 1 (Mar 1996): 27–30.
15. O.S. Levine et al., "Risk factors for invasive pneumococcal disease in children: a population-based case-control study in North America," *Pediatrics* 103, no. 3 (Mar 1999): E28.
16. S.M. Bass and M.W. Groër, "Relationship of breastfeeding and formula-feeding practices with infant health outcomes in an urban poor population," *J Perinat Neonatal Nurs* 11, no. 2 (Sep 1997): 1–9.
17. M. Lopez-Alarcon et al., "Breast-feeding lowers the frequency and duration of acute respiratory infection and diarrhea in infants under six months of age," *J Nutr* (Mexico) 127, no. 3 (Mar 1997): 436–43.
18. H. Palti, "Episodes of illness in breast-fed and bottle-fed infants in Jerusalem," *Isr J Med Sci* 20, no. 5 (May 1984): 395–9.
19. J. Raisler et al., "Breast-feeding and infant illness: a dose-response relationship?" *Am J Public Health* 89, no. 1 (Jan 1999): 25–30.
20. C. van den Bogaard et al., "The relationship between breast-feeding and early childhood morbidity in a general population," *Fam Med* (Holland) 23, no. 7 (Oct–Sep 1991): 510–5.

21. M.K. Davis, "Review of the evidence for an association between infant feeding and childhood cancer," *Int J Cancer Suppl* 11 (1998): 29–33.

22. S.A. Silfverdal et al., "Protective effect of breastfeeding: an ecologic study of Haemophilus influenzae meningitis and breastfeeding in a Swedish population," *Int J Epidemiol* (Sweden) 28, no. 1 (Feb 1999): 152–6.

23. A.C. Wilson et al., "Relation of infant diet to childhood health: seven year follow up of cohort of children in Dundee infant feeding study," *BMJ* (England) 316, no. 7124 (Jan 1998): 21–5.

24. L.A. Hanson, "Breastfeeding provides passive and likely long-lasting active immunity," *Ann Allergy Asthma Immunol* (Sweden) 81, no. 6 (Dec 1998): 523–33.

25. P.G. Quie, "Antimicrobial defenses in the neonate," *Semin Perinatol* 14, no. 4, suppl. 1 (Aug 1990): 2–9.

26. M. Haeney, "Infection determinants at extremes of age," *J Antimicrob Chemother* 34, suppl. A (Aug 1994): 1–9.

27. S. Agrawal et al., "Comparative study of immunoglobulin G and immunoglobulin M among neonates in caesarean section and vaginal delivery," *J Indian Med Assoc* 94, no. 2 (Feb 1996): 43–4.

28. G. Goncalves et al., "[Anti-measles IgG concentration in maternal blood: according to the mother's vaccination status]," *Acta Med Port* (Portugal) 11, no. 10 (Oct 1998): 847–53.

29. L.A. Hanson, "Breastfeeding provides passive and likely long-lasting active immunity," *Ann Allergy Asthma Immunol* 81, no. 6 (Dec 1998): 523–33.

30. L.A. Hanson et al., "The immune response of the mammary gland and its significance for the neonate," *Ann Allergy* 53, no. 6, part 2 (Dec 1984): 576–82.

31. J.A. Peterson et al., "Milk fat globule glycoproteins in human milk and in gastric aspirates of mother's milk-fed preterm infants," *Pediatr Res* 44, no. 4 (Oct 1998): 499–506.

32. D. Newburg, "Human milk glycoconjugates that inhibit pathogens," *Curr Med Chem* 6, no. 2 (Feb 1999): 117–27.

33. D.S. Newburg, "Role of human-milk lactadherin in protection against symptomatic rotavirus infection," *Lancet* 351, no. 9110 (Apr 18, 1998): 1160–4.

34. Mark Gladwin, M.D. and Bill Trattler, M.D., *Clinical Microbiology* (Miami, Florida: MedMaster, Inc., 1997), 56, 219.

35. B. Fornarini et al., "Human milk 90K (Mac-2 BP): possible protective effects against acute respiratory infections," *Clin Exp Immunol* 115, no. 1 (Jan 1999): 91–4.

36. P. McVeagh and J.B. Miller, "Human milk oligosaccharides: only the breast," *J Paediatr Child Health* 33, no. 4 (Aug 1997): 281–6.

37. D.S. Newburg, "Human milk glycoconjugates that inhibit pathogens," *Curr Med Chem* 6, no. 2 (Feb 1999): 117–27.

38. J. Portelli et al., "Effect of compounds with antibacterial activities in human milk on respiratory syncytial virus and cytomegalovirus in vitro," *J Med Microbiol* 47, no. 11 (Nov 1998): 1015–8.

39. D.V. Semenov et al., "Human milk lactoferrin binds ATP and dissociates into monomers," *Biochem Mol Biol Int* 47, no. 2 (Feb 1999): 177–84.

40. S.A. Dolan, "Inhibition of enteropathogenic bacteria by human milk whey in vitro," *Pediatr Infect Dis J* 8, no.7 (Jul 1989): 430–6.

41. J. Portelli et al., "Effect of compounds with antibacterial activities in human milk on respiratory syncytial virus and cytomegalovirus in vitro," *J Med Microbiol* 47, no. 11 (Nov 1998): 1015–8.

42. M. Hamosh, "Protective function of proteins and lipids in human milk," *Biol Neonate* 74, no. 2 (1998): 163–76.

43. A. Lucas and T.J. Cole, "Breast milk and neonatal necrotising enterocolitis," *Lancet* 336, no. 8730 (Dec 1990): 1519–23.

44. Ramzi S. et al., *Pathologic Basis of Disease* (Philadelphia: Harcourt Brace Jovanovich, Inc., 1989), 890.

45. D. Dia and W.A. Walker, "Role of bacterial colonization in neonatal necrotizing enterocolitis and its prevention," *Chung Hua Min Kuo Hsiao Erh Ko I Hsueh Hui Tsa Chih* (China) 39, no. 6 (Nov–Dec 1998): 357–65.

46. F.R. Moya et al., "Platelet-activating factor acetylhydrolase in term and preterm human milk: a preliminary report," *J Pediatr Gastroenterol Nutr* 19, no. 2 (Aug 1994): 236–9.

47. A.S. Goldman and R.M. Goldblum, "Transfer of maternal leukocytes to the infant by human milk," *Curr Top Microbiol Immunol* 222, no. 205 (1997): 205–13.

48. R.P. Garofalo and A.S. Goldman, "Cytokines, chemokines, and colony-stimulation factors in human milk: the 1997 update," *Biol Neonate* 74, no. 2 (1998): 134–42.

49. M. Hamosh, "Protective function of proteins and lipids in human milk," *Biol Neonate* 74, no. 2 (1998): 163–76.

50. O.H. Braun, "[The protective effect of human milk against infections and its potential causes,]" *Klin Padiatr* (Germany) 188, no. 4 (Jul 1976): 297–310.

51. J. Levy, "Immunonutrition: the pediatric experience," *Nutrition* 14, nos. 7–8 (Jul–Aug 1998): 641–7.

52. L. Thorell et al., "Nucleotides in human milk: sources and metabolism by the newborn infant," *Pediatr Res* (Sweden) 40, no. 6 (Dec 1996): 845–52.

53. G. Capano et al., "Polyamines in human and rat milk influence intestinal cell growth in vitro," *J Pediatr Gastroenterol Nutr* 27, no. 3 (Sep 1998): 281–6.

54. A.S. Goldman et al., "Anti-inflammatory systems in human milk," *Adv Exp Med Biol* 262 (1990): 69–76.

55. E.S. Buescher and I. Malinowska, "Soluble receptors and cytokine antagonists in human milk," *Pediatr Res* 40, no. 6 (Dec 1996): 839–44.

56. N. D'Ostilio et al., "90K (Mac-s BP) in human milk," *Clin Exp Immunol* 104, no. 3 (Jun 1996): 543–6.

57. R. J. Schanler, "The role of human milk fortification for premature infants," *Clin Perinatol* 25, no. 3 (Sep 1998): 645–57.

58. G. Schoch, "[Immunologic and ethologic aspects of breast feeding]," *Monatsschr Kinderheilkd* (Germany) 134, no. 6 (Jun 1986): 396–402.

59. A.S. Goldman et al., "Immunologic factors in human milk during the first year of lactation," *J Pediatr* 100, no. 4 (Apr 1982): 563–7.

60. L.A. Hanson, "Breastfeeding provides passive and likely long-lasting active immunity," *Ann Allergy Asthma Immunol* 81, no. 6 (Dec 1998): 523–33.

61. K.I. Kennedy et al., "Do the benefits of breastfeeding outweigh the risk of postnatal transmission of HIV via breast milk?" *Trop Doct* 20, no. 1 (Jan 1990): 25–9.

62. R.W. Ryder et al., "Evidence from Zaire that breast-feeding by HIV-1-seropositive mothers is not a major route for perinatal HIV-1 transmission but does decrease morbidity," *AIDS* (Zaire) 5, no. 6 (Jun 1991): 709–14.

63. H. Hasselbalch et al., "Decreased thymus size in formula-fed infants compared with breastfed infants," *Acta Paediatr* 85, no. 9 (Sep 1996): 1029–32.

64. M. Aronson, "Involution of the thymus revisited: immunological trade-offs as an adaptation to aging," *Mech Ageing Dev* 72, no. 1 (Nov 1993): 49–55.

65. N.C. Klein and B.A. Cunha, "Treatment of fever," *Infect Dis Clin North Am* 10, no. 1 (Mar 1996): 211–6.

66. M.J. Kluger et al., "The adaptive value of fever," *Infect Dis Clin North Am* 10, no. 1 (Mar 1996): 1–20.

67. H.A. Bernheim et al., "Fever: effect of drug-induced antipyresis on survival," *Science* 193, no. 4249 (Jul 1976): 237–9.

68. M.J. Kluger et al., "Role of fever in disease," *Ann N Y Acad Sci* 856 (Sep 29, 1998): 224–33.

69. D.M. Zerr et al., "A case-control study of necrotizing fasciitis during primary varicella," *Pediatrics* 103, no. 4, part 1 (Apr 1999): 783–90.

70. TF Doran et al., Acetaminophen: more harm than good for chickenpox? *J Pediatr* 114 no.6 (1989 Jun): 1045–8

71. N. Nathanson at al., "The evolution of virus diseases: their emergence, epidemicity, and control," *Virus Res* 29, no. 1 (Jul 1993): 3–20.

72. D.P. Hoa et al., "Young child feeding in a rural area in the Red River delta, Vietnam," *Acta Paediatr* (Vietnam) 84, no. 9 (Sep 1995): 1045–9.

73. J. Storsaeter et al., "Mortality and morbidity from invasive bacterial infections during a clinical trial of acellular pertussis vaccines in Sweden," *Pediatr Infect Dis J* (Sweden) 7, no. 9 (Sep 1988): 637–45.

74. M.R. Griffin et al., "No increased risk for invasive bacterial infection found following diphtheria–tetanus–pertussis immunization," *Pediatrics* 89, no. 4, part 1 (Apr 1992): 640–2.

75. Centers for Disease Control, 11/17/98, www.cdc.gov

76. H. Yoshida et al., "Circulation of type 1 wild poliovirus in northern Vietnam during 1991–1994," *Am J Trop Med Hyg* (Japan) 55, no. 5 (Nov 1996): 531–5.

77. S. Khalfan et al., "Epidemics of aseptic meningitis due to enteroviruses following national immunization days in Baharain," *Ann Trop Paediatr* (Arabia) 18, no. 2 (Jun 1998): 101–9.

78. S. Takimoto et al., "Enterovirus 71 infection and acute neurological disease among children in Brazil (1988–1990)," *Trans R Soc Trop Med Hyg* (Brazil) 92, no. 1 (Jan–Feb 1998): 25–8.

79. T.A. Popova et al., "[The results of monitoring enterovirus circulation among the population and in the environment of Tula Province over 10 years (1985–1994)]," *Zh Mikrobiol Epidemiol Immunobiol* (Japan) 1 (Jan–Feb 1997): 35–9.

80. E. Druyts-Voets, "Epidemiological features of entero non-poliovirus isolations in Belgium 1980–94," *Epidemiol Infect* (Belgium) 119, no. 1 (Aug 1997): 71–7.

81. K. Ishii et al., "[Epidemiology of virus-related nervous infections in Japan]," *Nippon Rinsho* (Japan) 55, no. 4 (Apr 1997): 839–48.

82. Naomi Baumslag, M.D. and Dia L. Michels, *Milk, Money, and Madness* (Westport, Connecticut: Bergin and Garvey, 1995).

83. B.F. Elswood and R.B. Stricker, "Polio vaccines and the origin of AIDS," *Med Hypotheses* 42, no. 6 (Jun 1994): 347–54.

84. V. Reinhardt and A. Roberts, "The African polio vaccine-acquired immune deficiency syndrome connection," *Med Hypotheses* 48, no. 5 (May 1997): 367–74.

85. F. Brown, "Review of accidents caused by incomplete inactivation of viruses," *Dev Biol Stand* 81, no. 103 (1993).

86. W.J. Martin, "Simian cytomegalovirus-related stealth virus isolated from the cerebrospinal fluid of a patient with bipolar psychosis and acute encephalopathy," *Pathobiology* 64, no. 2 (1996): 64–6.

87. W.J. Martin and D. Anderson, "Stealth virus epidemic in the Mohave Valley. I. Initial report of virus isolation," *Pathobiology* 65, no. 1 (1997): 51–6.

88. F. Friedrich, "Rare adverse events associated with oral poliovirus vaccine in Brazil," *Braz J Med Biol Res* (Brazil) 30, no. 6 (Jun 1997): 695–703.

89. C.P. Howson and H.V. Fineberg, "Adverse events following pertussis and rubella vaccines. Summary of a report of the Institute of Medicine," *JAMA* 267, no. 3 (Jan 1992): 392–6.

90. M.M. Braun et al., "Report of a US public health service workshop on hypotonic-hyporesponsive episode (HHE) after pertussis immunization," *Pediatrics* 102, no. 5 (Nov 1998): E52.

91. K.R. Wentz and E.K. Marcuse, "Diphtheria–tetanus–pertussis vaccine and serious neurologic illness: an updated review of the epidemiologic evidence," *Pediatrics* 87, no. 3 (Mar 1991): 287–97.

92. D.P. Southall et al., "Severe hypoxaemia in pertussis," *Arch Dis Child* 63, no. 6 (Jun 1988): 598–605.

93. C. Lindgren et al., "Sudden infant death and prevalence of whooping cough in the Swedish and Norwegian communities," *Eur J Pediatr* 156, no. 5 (May 1997): 405–9.

94. S. Schmitt-Groge et al., "Pertussis in German adults," *Clin Infect Dis* (Germany) 21, no. 4 (Oct 1995): 860–6.

95. C.M. Ausiello et al., "Cell-mediated immune response of healthy adults to Bordetella pertussis vaccine antigens," *J Infect Dis* (Italy) 178, no. 2 (Aug 1998): 466–70.

96. J. Isacson et al., "How common is whooping cough in a nonvaccinating country?" *Pediatr Infect Dis J* (Sweden) 12, no. 4 (Apr 1993): 284–8.

97. L. Gustafsson et al., "A controlled trial of a two-component acellular, a five-component acellular, and a whole-cell pertussis vaccine," *N Engl J Med* 334, no. 6 (Feb 1996): 349–55.

98. M.A. Uberall et al., "Severe adverse events in a comparative efficacy trial in Germany in infants receiving either the Lederle/Takeda acellular pertussis component DTP (DtaP) vaccine, the Lederle whole-cell component DTP (DTP) or DT vaccine. The Pertussis Vaccine Study Group," *Dev Biol Stand* 89 (1997): 83–9.

99. J.H. Menkes and M. Kinsbourne, "Workshop on neurologic complications of pertussis and pertussis vaccination," *Neuropediatrics* 21, no. 4 (Nov 1990): 171–6.

100. J.D. Cherry et al., "The effect of investigator compliance (observer bias) on calculated efficacy in a pertussis vaccine trial," *Pediatrics* 102, no. 4, part 1 (Oct 1998): 909–12.

101. L. Gustafsson et al., "A controlled trial of a two-component acellular, a five-component acellular, and a whole-cell pertussis vaccine," *N Engl J Med* 334, no. 6 (Feb 1996): 349–55.

102. T.A. Kenyon et al., "Persistent low immunization coverage among inner-city preschool children despite access to free vaccine," *Pediatrics* 101, no. 4, part 1 (Apr 1998): 612–6.

103. L. Squeri and A. Ioli, "[A few viral infections in the recent epidemiological evolution]," *Ann Sclavo* (Italy) 19, no. 3 (May–Jun 1977): 313–46.

104. E. Kinnunen et al., "Nationwide oral poliovirus vaccination campaign and the incidence of Guillain-Barre Syndrome," *Am J Epidemiol* (Finland) 147, no. 1 (Jan 1998): 69–73.

105. T. Lasky et al., "The Guillain-Barre syndrome and the 1992–93 and 1993–94 influenza vaccines," *N Engl J Med* 339, no. 25 (Dec 1998): 1797–802.

106. F. Friedrich, "Neurologic complications associated with oral poliovirus vaccine and genomic variability of the vaccine strains after multiplication in humans," *Acta Virol* (Brazil) 42, no. 3 (Jun 1998): 187–94.

107. N.P. Thompson et al., "Is measles vaccination a risk factor for inflammatory bowel disease?" *Lancet* (England) 345, no. 8957 (Apr 1995): 1071–4.

108. P. Duclos and B.J. Ward, "Measles vaccines: a review of adverse events," *Drug Saf* (Canada) 19, no. 6 (Dec 1998): 435–54.

109. S. Bachmann and J. Kesselring, "Multiple sclerosis and infectious childhood diseases," *Neuroepidemiology* 17, no. 3 (1998): 154–60.

110. "Rotavirus vaccine for the prevention of rotavirus gastroenteritis among children." *MMWR Morb Mortal Wkly Rep* 48, (RR-2) (Mar 19, 1999): 1–20.

111. "Rotavirus vaccine for the prevention of rotavirus gastroenteritis among children." *MMWR Morb Mortal Wkly Rep* 48, (RR-2) (Mar 19, 1999): 1–20.

112. "Withdrawal of rotavirus vaccine recommendation," *MMWR Morb Mortal Wkly Rep* 48, no. 43 (Nov 5, 99): 1007.

113. S. Deguen et al., "Epidemiology of chicken pox in France (1991–1995)," 52, suppl. 1 (Apr 1998): 46S–49S.

114. K.R. Stratton et al., "Adverse events associated with childhood vaccines other than pertussis and rubella. Summary of a report from the Institute of Medicine," *JAMA* 271, no. 20 (May 25, 1994): 1602–5.

115. M. Rey et al., "Impact of measles in France," *Rev Infect Dis* 5, no. 3 (May–Jun 1983): 433–8.

116. www.infactcanada.ca

117. J.B. McCormick, "Epidemiology of emerging/re-emerging antimicrobial-resistant bacterial pathogens," *Curr Opin Microbiol* (France) 1, no. 1 (Feb 1998): 125–129.

118. M. Inoue et al., "Why do antimicrobial agents become ineffectual?" *Yonsei Med J* 39, no. 6 (Dec 1998): 502–13.

119. Stuart B. Levy, M.D., *The Antibiotic Paradox* (New York: Plenum Press, 1992).

120. O.S. Levine et al., "Risk factors for invasive pneumococcal disease in children: a population-based case-control study in North America," *Pediatrics* 103, no. 3 (Mar 1999): E28.

121. N. Cimolai et al., "Invasive Streptococcus pyogenes infections in children," *Can J Public Health* 83, no. 3 (May–Jun 1992): 230–3.

122. L.V. McFarland, "[Risk factor for antibiotic-associated diarrhea. A review of the literature]," *Ann Med Interne Paris* (France) 149, no. 5 (Sep 1998): 261–6.

123. B.A. Jobe et al., "Clostridium difficile colitis: an increasing hospital-acquired illness," *Am J Surg* 169, no. 5 (May 1995): 480–3.

124. F.L. van Buchem et al., "Primary-care-based randomised placebo-controlled trial of antibiotic treatment in acute maxillary sinusitis," *Lancet* 349, no. 9053 (Mar 8, 1997): 683–7.

125. N.T. el-Daher et al., "Immediate vs. delayed treatment of group A beta-hemolytic streptococcal pharyngitis with penicillin V," *Pediatr Infect Dis J* 10, no. 2 (Feb 1991): 126–30.

126. The National Center for Health Statistics.

127. K.G. Dewey et al., "Differences in morbidity between breast-fed and formula-fed infants," *J Pediatr* 126, no. 5, part 1 (May 1995): 696–702.

128. M.L. Sassen et al., "Breast-feeding and acute otitis media," *Am J Otolaryngol* 15, no. 5 (Sep–Oct 1994): 351–7.

129. A. Khafif et al., "Acute mastoiditis: a 10-year review," *Am J Otolaryngol* 19, no. 3 (May–Jun 1998): 170–3.

130. P.T. Yen et al., "Brain abscess: with special reference to otolaryngologic sources of infection," *Otolaryngol Head Neck Surg* (Taiwan) 113, no. 1 (Jul 1995): 15–22.

131. Dr. Patrick Antonelli, "Doctor's Guide to Medical and Other News: Ear infection complications on the rise, researchers report," www.pslgroup.com, P\S\L Consulting Group Inc. Healthcare Research Partners, (Sep 17, 1998): 1–3.

132. F. Tovi et al., "[Latent, non-suppurative mastoiditis. Apropos of 62 cases]," *Ann Otolaryngol Chir Cervicofac* (France) 112, no. 6 (1995): 275–8.

133. Dr. Robert Steele, "Ask the doctor — Contagiousness of sore throat and ear infection," www.parentsplace.com, Village Inc., (1998): 1–2.

134. S.R. Cohen and J.W. Thompson, "Otitic candidiasis in children: an evaluation of the problem and effectiveness of ketoconazole in 10 patients," *An Otol Rhinol Laryngol* 99, no. 6, part 1 (Jun 1990): 427–31.

135. R.M. Rosenfeld et al., "Clinical efficacy of antimicrobial drugs for acute otitis media: meta-analysis of 5400 children from thirty-three randomized trials," *J Pediatr* 124, no. 3 (Mar 1994): 355–67.

136. R.L. Williams et al., "Use of antibiotics in preventing recurrent acute otitis media and in treating otitis media with effusion. A meta-analytic attempt to resolve the brouhaha," *JAMA* 270, no. 11 (Sep 1993): 1344–51.

137. E.I. Cantekin et al., "Antimicrobial therapy for otitis media with effusion," *JAMA* 266, no. 23 (Dec 1991): 3309–17.

138. C.T. Le at al "Evaluation of ventilating tubes and myringotomy in the treatment of recurrent or persistent otitus media," *Pediatr Infect Dis J* 10, no. 1 (Jan 1991):2–11.

139. F.L. van Buchem et al., "Acute otitis media: a new treatment strategy," *Br Med J (Clin Res Ed)* 290, no. 6474 (Apr 6, 1985): 1033–7.

140. M.L. Garland and K.O. Hagmeyer, "The role of zinc lozenges in treatment of the common cold," *Ann Pharmacother* 32, no. 1 (Jan 1998): 63–9.

141. R. Bauer, "[Echinacea drugs—effects and active ingredients]," *Z Arztl Fortbild (Jena)* (Germany) 90, no. 2 (Apr 1996): 111–5.

142. J.T. Giles et al., "Evaluation of echinacea for treatment of common cold," *Pharmacotherapy* 20, no. 6 (June 2000): 690–7.

143. S.S. Percival, "Use of echinacea in medicine," *Biochem Pharmacol* 60, no. 2 (Jul 15, 2000): 155–8.

144. H. Hemila, "Does vitamin C alleviate the symptoms of the common cold?—a review of current evidence," *Scand J Infect Dis* (Finland) 26, no. 1 (1994): 1–6.

Chapter 7: Digestion Matters

1. L.T. Weaver et al., "Small intestinal length: a factor essential for gut adaptation," *Gut* 32, no. 11 (Nov 1991): 1321–3.

2. V.M. Houle et al., "Small intestinal disaccharidase activity and ileal villus height are increased in piglets consuming formula containing recombinant human insulin-like growth factor-I," *Pediatr Res* 42, no. 1 (Jul 1997): 78–86.

3. M.A. Ortega et al., "Maturation status of small intestine epithelium in rats deprived of dietary nucleotides," *Life Sci* 56, no. 19 (1995): 1623–30.

4. L. Thorell et al., "Nucleotides in human milk: sources and metabolism by the newborn infant," *Pediatr Res* (Sweden) 40, no. 6 (Dec 1996): 845–52.

5. *Gastroenterol Nutr* 27, no. 3 (Sep 1998): 281–6.

6. E.C. Dickinson et al., "Immunoglobulin A supplementation abrogates bacterial translocation and preserves the architecture of the intestinal epithelium," *Surgery* 124, no.2 (Aug 1998): 284–90.

7. L.L. Go et al., "Quantitative and morphologic analysis of bacterial translocation in neonates," *Arch Surg* 129, no. 11 (Nov 1994): 1184–90.

8. James M. Orten and Otto W. Neuhaus, *Human Biochemistry*, ninth edition (St. Louis: The C.V. Mosby Co., 1975): 695.

9. Y. Wang et al., "The genetically programmed down-regulation of lactase in children," *Gastroenterology* (London) 114, no. 5 (June 1998): 1230–6.

10. J.J. Ellestad-Sayed and J.C. Heworth, "Disaccharide consumption and malabsorption in Canadian Indians," *Am J Clin Nutr* 30, no. 5 (May 1977): 698–703.

11. N.W. Solomons, "[Lactose and its implications in gastroenterology. Nutrition and food sciences.]" *Rev Invest Clin* (Guatemala) 48, suppl. (Nov 1996): 1–13.

12. E. Savilahti et al., "Congenital lactase deficiency. A clinical study on 16 patients." *Arch Dis Child* 58, no. 4 (Apr 1983): 246–52.

13. C.L. James et al., "Neonatal screening for hereditary fructose intolerance: frequency of the most common mutant aldolase B allele in the British population," *J Med Genet* 33, no. 10 (Oct 1996): 837–41.

14. E. Gudmand-Hoyer and H. Skovbjerg, "Disaccharide digestion and maldigestion," *Scand J Gastroenterol Suppl* (Denmark) 216 (1996): 111–21.

15. G. Eschenburg et al., "[Fecal sIgS and lysozyme excretion in breast feeding and formula feeding]," *Kinderarztl Prax* (Germany) 58, no. 5 (May 1990): 225–60.

16. D.G. Schmidt et al., "Raising the pH of the pepsin-catalysed hydrolysis of bovine whey proteins increases the antigenicity of the hydrolysates," *Clin Exp Allergy* (Netherlands) 25, no. 10 (Oct 1995): 1007–17

17. S.E. Balmer et al., "Diet and faecal flora in the newborn: lactoferrin," *Arch Dis Child* 64, no. 12 (Dec 1989): 1685–90.

18. G. Eschenburg et al., "[Fecal sIgS and lysozyme excretion in breast feeding and formula feeding]," *Kinderarztl Prax* (Germany) 58, no. 5 (May 1990): 225–60.

19. M. Armand et al., "Effect of human milk or formula on gastric function and fat digestion in the premature infant," *Pediatr Res* 40, no. 3 (Sep 1996): 429–37.

20. E. Freudenberg, "A lipase in the milk of the gorilla," *Experientia* 22 (1966): 317.

21. Jonathan Brostoff and Stephen J. Challacombe, eds., *Food Allergy and Intolerance*, chapter 12 by Charlotte Cunningham-Rundles (London: Baillière Tindall, 1987): 224.

22. C. Catassi et al., "Intestinal permeability changes during the first month: effect of natural versus artificial feeding," *J Pediatr Gastroenterol Nutr* 21, no. 4 (Nov 1995): 383–6.

23. La Leche League Intl., *The Womanly Art of Breastfeeding*, sixth edition (New York: pub. by Plume, a part of Penguin Putnam Inc. by arrangement with La Leche League Intl., 1997), 341–2.

24. A.G. Marsh et al., "Cortical bone density of adult lacto–ovo–vegetarian and omnivorous women," *J Am Diet Assoc* 76, no. 2 (Feb 1980): 149–51.

25. R. Itoh et al., "Dietary protein intake and urinary excretion of calcium: a cross-sectional study in a healthy Japanese population," *Am J Clin Nutr* (Tokyo) 67, no. 3 (Mar 1998): 438–44.

26. M. Hegsted and H.M. Linkswiler, "Long-term effects of level of protein intake on calcium metabolism in young adult women," *J Nutr* 111, no. 2 (Feb 1981): 244–51.

27. R. Chierici, "Supplementation of an adapted formula with bovine lactoferrin. 2. Effects on serum iron, ferritin and zinc levels," *Acta Paediatr* 81, nos. 6–7 (Jun–Jul 1992): 475–9.

28. C.P. Anyon, "Normal haemoglobin values in urban Polynesian infants: the possible deleterious influence of artificial feeding," *N Z Med J* 84, no. 578 (Dec 1976): 474–6

29. M.F. Deshchekina et al., "[Study of the formation of intestinal microflora in newborn infants staying with or separated from their mothers]," *Pediatria* (Russia) 1 (1990): 13–18.

30. O.H. Braun and W.E. Heine, "[The physiologic significance of Bifidobacteria and fecal lysozyme in the breast fed infant. A contribution on the microecology of the intestine]," *Klin Padiatr* (Germany) 207, no. 1 (Jan–Feb 1995): 4–7.

31. S.S. Arnon, "Breast feeding and toxigenic intestinal infections: missing links in crib deaths?" *Rev Infect Dis* 6, suppl. 1 (Mar–Apr 1984): S193–201.

32. F. Balli et al., "[High-dose oral bacteria-therapy for chronic non-specific diarrhea of infancy,]" *Pediatr Med Chir* (Italy) 14, no. 1 (Jan–Feb 1992): 13–15.

33. M.J. Hill, "Intestinal flora and endogenous vitamin synthesis," *Eur J Cancer Prev* 6 suppl. 1 (Mar 1997): S43–5.

34. K. Fujita et al., "Vitamin K_1 and K_2 status and faecal flora in breast fed and formula fed 1-month-old infants," *Eur J Pediatr* 152, no. 10 (Oct 1993): 852–5.

35. A. Mohan et al., "The relationship between bottle usage/content, age, and number of teeth with mutans streptococci colonization in 6–24-month-old children," *Community Dent Oral Epidemiol* 26, no.1 (Feb 1998): 12–20.

36. R.O. Mattos-Graner et al., "Association between caries prevalence and clinical, microbial and dietary variables in 1.0 to .5-year-old Brazilian children," *Caries Res* (Brazil) 32, no. 5 (1998): 319–23.

37. M.C. Moreau et al., "[Effect of orally administered bovine lactoferrin and bovine IgG on the establishment of *Escherichia coli* in the digestive tract of gnotobiotic mice and human newborn infants]," *Ann Microbiol* (France) 134B, no. 3 (Nov–Dec 1983): 429–41.

38. J.M. Dolby et al., "Bacteriostasis of *Escherichia coli* by milk. II. Effect of bicarbonate and transferrin on the activity of infant feeds," *J Hyg* (London) 78 no. 2 (Apr 1977): 235–42.

39. P.T. Quinlan et al., "The relationship between stool hardness and stool composition in breast- and formula-fed infants," *J Pediatr Gastroenterol Nutr* 20, no. 1 (Jan 1995): 81–90.

40. G. Iacono et al., "Chronic constipation as a symptom of cow milk allergy," *J Pediatr* 126, no. 1 (Jan 1995): 34–9.

41. G. Iacono, "Intolerance of cow's milk and chronic constipation in children," *N Engl J Med* 339, no. 16 (Oct 15, 1998): 1100–4.

Chapter 8: In the Womb & the First Few Days

1. C.A. Sandman et al., "Maternal stress, HPA activity, and fetal/infant outcome," *Ann N Y Acad Sci* 814 (Apr 1997): 266–75.

2. M. Weinstock, "Does prenatal stress impair coping and regulation of hypothalamic–pituitary–adrenal axis?," *Neurosci Biobehav Rev* 21, no. 1 (Jan 1997): 1–10

3. S.K. Sobrian et al., "Gestational exposure to loud noise alters the development and postnatal responsiveness of humoral and cellular components of the immune system in offspring," *Environ Res* 73, nos. 1–2 (1997): 227–41.

4. F. Benini et al., "Evaluation of noise in the neonatal intensive care unit," *Am J Perinatol* 13, no. 1 (Jan 1996): 37–41.

5. P.J. Landrigan et al., "Children's health and the environment: a new agenda for prevention research," *Environ Health Perspect* 106, suppl. 3 (Jun 1998): 787–94.

6. Richard Wiles et al., "How 'bout them apples? Pesticides in children's food ten years after alar," Environmental Working Group, www.ewg.org (Feb 1999).

7. T.L. Copeland et al., "Use of probabilistic methods to understand the conservatism in California's approach to assessing health risks posed by air contaminants," *Air Waste* 44, no. 12 (Dec 1994): 1399–413.

8. L.F. Paulozzi et al., "Hypospadias trends in two US surveillance systems," *Pediatrics* 100, no. 5 (Nov 1997): 831–4.

9. J.G. Koppe, "Nutrition and breast-feeding," *Eur J Obstet Gynecol Reprod Biol* (Holland) 61, no. 1 (1995): 73–8.

10. G. Ohi, "[Endocrine disrupting chemicals and carcinogenicity]," *Gan To Kagaku Ryoho* (Japan) 26, no. 3 (Feb 1999): 263–8.

11. L.E. Gray Jr. et al., "Environmental antiandrogens: low doses of the fungicide vinclozin alter sexual differentiation of the male rat," *Toxicol Ind Health* 15, nos. 1–2 (Jan–Mar 1999): 48–64.

12. I.S. Weidner et al., "Cryptorchidism and hypospadias in sons of gardeners and farmers," *Environ Health Perspect* 106, no. 12 (Dec 1998): 793–6.

13. A.M. Garcia et al., "Parental agricultural work and selected congenital malformations," *Am J Epidemiol* 149, no. 1 (Jan 1999): 64–74.

14. C. Gupta, "Reproductive malformation of the male offspring following maternal exposure to estrogenic chemicals," *Proc Soc Exp Biol Med* 224, no. 2 (Jun 2000): 61–8.

15. K.L. Howdeshell et al., "Exposure to bisphenol A advances puberty," *Nature* 401, no. 6755 (Oct 21, 1999): 763–4

16. D. Mukerjee, "Health impact of polychlorinated dibenzo-p-dioxins: a critical review," *J Air Waste Manag Assoc* 48, no. 2 (Feb 1998): 157–65.

17. S. Patandin et al., "Dietary exposure to polychlorinated biphenyls and dioxins from infancy until adulthood: A comparison between breast-feeding, toddler, and long-term exposure," *Environ Health Perspect* (Holland) 107, no. 1 (Jan 1999): 45–51.

18. S. Patandin et al., "Effects of environmental exposure to polychlorinated biphenyls and dioxins on cognitive abilities in Dutch children at 42 months of age," *J Pediatr* 134, no. 1 (Jan 1999): 33–41.

19. B.E. Richardson and D.D. Baird, "A study of milk and calcium supplement intake and subsequent preeclampsia in a cohort of pregnant women," *Am J Epidemiol* 141, no. 7 (Apr 1995): 667–73.

20. H.C. Bucher et al., "Effect of calcium supplementation on pregnancy-induced hypertension and preeclampsia: a meta-analysis of randomized controlled trials," *JAMA* (Canada) 276, no. 17 (Nov 6, 1996): 1388.

21. C.A. Aligne and J.J. Stoddard, "Tobacco and children. An economic evaluation of the medical effects of parental smoking," *Arch Pediatr Adolesc Med* 151, no. 7 (Jul 1997): 648–53.

22. Monthly Vital Statistics Report, Centers for Disease Control and Prevention 45, no. 11, suppl. (Jun 10, 1997): 2.

23. B.A. Finette et al., "Gene mutations with characteristic deletions in cord blood T lymphocytes associated with passive maternal exposure to tobacco smoke," *Nat Med* 4, no. 10 (Oct 1998): 1144–51.

24. H. Witschi et al., "The toxicology of environmental tobacco smoke," *Annu Rev Pharmacol Toxicol* 37 (1997): 29–52

25. B.T. Ji, "Paternal cigarette smoking and the risk of childhood cancer among offspring of nonsmoking mothers," *J Natl Cancer Inst* 5, no. 89 (Feb 1997): 238–44.

26. N.G. Beratis et al., "Prolactin, growth hormone and insulin-like growth factor-1 in newborn children of smoking mothers," *Clin Endocrinol (Oxf)* 40, no. 2 (Feb 1994): 179–85.

27. H. Nakajima, "Response of the newborn when gently accosted by the mother immediately after birth and subsequent growth and development," *Keio J Med* (Japan) 43, no. 3 (Sep 1994): 167–70.

28. L.G. Israels et al., "The riddle of vitamin K$_1$ deficit in the newborn," *Semin Perinatol* 21, no. 1 (Feb 1997): 90–6.

29. P. Reverdiau-Moalic et al., "Evolution of blood coagulation activators and inhibitors in the healthy human fetus," *Blood* (France) 88, no. 3 (Aug 1996): 900–6.

30. A.H. Sutor et al., "Late form of vitamin K deficiency bleeding in Germany," *Klin Padiatr* (Germany) 207, no. 3 (May–Jun 1995): 89–97.

31. L. Parker et al., "Neonatal vitamin K administration and childhood cancer in the north of England: retrospective case-control study," *BMJ* (England) 316, no. 7126 (Jan 1998): 189–93.

32. S.J. Passmore et al., "Case-control studies of relation between childhood cancer and neonatal vitamin K administration," *BMJ* 316, no. 7126 (Jan 1998): 178–84.

33. M. Andrew, "The relevance of developmental hemostasis to hemorrhagic disorders of newborns," *Semin Perinatol* 21, no. 1 (Feb 1997): 70–85.

34. E. Bourrat et al., "[Scleroderma-like patch on the thigh in infants after vitamin K injection at birth: six observations]," *Ann Dermatol Venereol* (France) 123, no. 10 (1996): 634–8.

35. A.H. Sutor, "Vitamin K deficiency bleeding in infants and children," *Semin Thromb Hemost* (Germany) 21, no. 3 (1995): 317–29.

36. S. Bolisetty, "Vitamin K in preterm breast milk with maternal supplementation," *Acta Paediatr* (Australia) 87, no. 9 (Sep 1998): 960–2.

37. K. Hogenbirk et al., "The effect of formula versus breast feeding and exogenous vitamin K1 supplementation on circulating levels of vitamin K1 and vitamin K-dependent clotting factors in newborns," *Eur J Pediatr* 152, no. 1 (Jan 1993): 72–4.

38. A. Stewart, "Etiology of childhood leukemia: a possible alternative to the Greaves hypothesis," *Leuk Res* (England) 14, nos. 11–12 (1990): 937–9.

39. D.L. Gollaher, "From ritual to science: The medical transformation of circumcision in America," *Journal of Social History* 28, no. 1 (Fall 1994): 5–36.

40. T. To et al., "Cohort study on circumcision of newborn boys and subsequent risk of urinary-tract infection," *Lancet* (Canada) 352 no. 9143 (Dec 1998): 1813–6.

41. D.M. Fergusson et al., "Neonatal circumcision and penile problems: an 8-year longitudinal study," *Pediatrics* 81, no. 4 (Apr 1988): 537–41.

42. K.A. Gracely-Kilgore, "Penile adhesion: the hidden complication of circumcision," *Nurse Pract* 9, no. 5 (May 1984): 22–4.

43. C. Tomasini et al., "Multiple pyogenic granuloma of the penis," *Sex Transm Infect* 74, no. 3 (Jun 1998): 221–2.

44. J.R. Taylor et al., "The prepuce: specialized mucosa of the penis and its loss to circumcision," *Br J Urol* 77, no. 2 (Feb 1996): 291–5.

45. W.L. Robson and A.K. Leung, "The circumcision question," *Postgrad Med* 91, no. 6 (May 1992): 237–42.

46. Y. Erk and O. Kocabalkan, "A case report of penis reconstruction for partial penis necrosis following circumcision," *Turk J Pediatr* (Turkey) 37, no. 1 (Jan–Mar 1995): 79–82.

47. J. Orozco-Sanchez and R. Neri-Vela, "[Total denudation of the penis in circumcision. Description of a plastic technique for repair of the penis]," *Bol Med Hosp Infant Mex* (Mexico) 48, no. 8 (Aug 1991): 565–9.

48. N.K. Bissada et al., "Post-circumcision carcinoma of the penis: I. Clinical aspects," *J Urol* (135, no. 2 (Feb 1986): 283–5.

49. N. Williams and L. Kapila, "Complications of circumcision," *Br J Surg* (England) 80, no. 10 (Oct 1993): 1231–6.

50. H.J. Stang and L.W. Snellman, "Circumcision practice patterns in the United States," *Pediatrics* 101, no. 6 (Jun 1998): E5.

51. Taddio et al., "Effect of neonatal circumcision on pain response during subsequent routine vaccination," *Lancet* 349, no. 9052 (Mar 1997): 599–603.

52. C. Maden et al., "History of circumcision, medical conditions, and sexual activity and risk of penile cancer," *J Natl Cancer Inst* 85, no. 1 (Jan 1993): 19–24.

53. A.G. Maiche, "Epidemiological aspects of cancer of the penis in Finland," *Eur J Cancer Prev* (Finland) 1, no. 2 (Feb 1992): 153–8.

54. F. Levi et al., "Descriptive epidemiology of vulvar and vaginal cancers in Vaud, Switzerland, 1974–1994," *Ann Oncol* 9, no. 11 (Nov 1998): 1229–32.

55. U. Kohler et al., "[Results of an individualized surgical therapy of vulvar carcinoma from 1973–1993,]" *Zentralbl Gynakol* (Germany) 119, suppl. 1 (1997): 8–16.

56. V. Mayatula and T.R. Mavundla, "A review on male circumcision procedures among South African Blacks," *Curationis* 20, no. 3 (Sep 1997): 16–20.

57. A.J. Sasco and I. Gendre, "[Current epidemiology of vulvar cancer]," *Contracept Fertil Sex* (France) 26, no. 12, (Dec 1998): 858–64.

58. R. Barrasso, "[Cancer of the uterine cervix: epidemiology and virology]," *Rev Prat* (France) 40, no. 1 (Jan 1990): 9–11.
59. S.K. Kjaer et al., "Case-control study of risk factors for cervical neoplasia in Denmark. I: Role of the "male factor" in women with one lifetime sexual partner," *Int J Cancer* 48, no. 1 (Apr 1991): 39–44.
60. E.O. Laumann et al., "Circumcision in the United States. Prevalence, prophylactic effects, and sexual practice," *JAMA* 277, no. 13 (Apr 1997): 1052–7.
61. S. Troisier, "[Sexual mutilation in women]," *Bull Acad Natl Med* (France) 179, no. 1 (Jan 1995): 135–42.
62. R. Kelly et al., "Age of male circumcision and risk of prevalent HIV infection in rural Uganda," *AIDS* 13, no. 3 (Feb 1999): 399–405.
63. E.O. Laumann et al., "Circumcision in the United States. Prevalence, prophylactic effects, and sexual practice," *JAMA* 277, no. 13 (Apr 1997): 1052–7.
64. J. Seed et al., "Male circumcision, sexually transmitted disease, and risk of HIV," *J Acquir Immune Defic Syndr Hum Retrovirol* 8, no. 1 (Jan 1995): 83–90.
65. E.O. Laumann et al., "Circumcision in the United States. Prevalence, prophylactic effects, and sexual practice," *JAMA* 277, no. 13 (Apr 1997): 1052–7.
66. American Academy of Pediatrics, Task Force on Circumcision, Circumcision policy statement, *Pediatrics* 103, no. 3 (Mar 1999): 686–93.
67. National Organization of Circumcision Information Resource Centers (NOCIRC), "Medical association position papers," www.nocirc.org, (Apr 1999).
68. M. Brophy Marcus, "Questioning an old assumption," *U.S. News & World Report* (Apr 14, 1997): 15.
69. R.N. Musoke et al., "Breastfeeding promotion: feeding the low birth weight infant," *Int J Gynaecol Obstet* (Kenya) 31, suppl. 1 (1990): 57–9.
70. G.P. Mathur et al., "Breastfeeding in babies delivered by cesarean section," *Indian Pediatr* 30, no. 11 (Nov 1993): 1285–90.
71. J. Contreras-Lemus J et al., "[Morbidity reduction in preterm newborns fed with milk of their own mothers]," *Bol Med Hosp Infant Mex* 49, no. 10 (Oct 1992): 671–7.
72. M.A. Hylander et al., "Human milk feedings and infection among very low birth weight infants," *Pediatrics* 102, no. 3 (Sep 1998): E38.
73. S.P. Srivastava et al., "Mortality patterns in breast versus artificially fed term babies in early infancy: a longitudinal study," *Indian Pediatr* 31, no. 11 (Nov 1994): 1393–6.
74. S. Awasthi et al., "Mortality patterns in breast versus artificially fed term babies in early infancy: a longitudinal study," *Indian Pediatr* 28, no. 3 (Mar 1991): 243–8.
75. M. Armand et al., "Effect of human milk or formula on gastric function and fat digestion in the premature infant," *Pediatr Res* 40, no. 3 (Sep 1996): 429–37.
76. R.J. Schanler et al., "Bone mineralization outcomes in human milk-fed preterm infants," *Pediatr Res* 31, no. 6 (Jun 1992): 583–6.
77. J. Ramasethu et al., "Weight gain in exclusively breastfed preterm infants," *J Trop Pediatr* (India) 39, no. 3 (Jun 1993): 152–9.
78. N.J. Bishop et al., "Early diet of preterm infants and bone mineralization at age five years," *Acta Paediatr* (England) 85, no. 2 (Feb 1996): 230–6.
79. G. Putet et al., "Nutrient balance, energy utilization, and composition of weight gain in very-low-birth-weight infants fed pooled human milk or a preterm formula," *J Pediatr* 105, no. 1 (Jul 1984): 79–85.
80. A. Lucas et al., "A randomised multicentre study of human milk versus formula and later development in preterm infants," *Arch Dis Child Fetal Neonatal Ed* (England) 70, no. 2 (Mar 1994): F141–6.
81. M.E. Wegman, "Infant mortality: some international comparisons," *Pediatrics* 98, no. 6, part 1 (Dec 1996): 1020–7.
82. M.J. Martin Puerto et al., "[Early discharge of low-birth-weight neonates. 5-year experience]," *An Esp Pediatr* (Spain) 38, no. 1 (Jan 1993): 20–4
83. L.S. Adair et al., "The duration of breast-feeding: How is it affected by biological, sociodemographic, health sector, and food industry factor?" *Demography* 30, no. 1 (Feb 1993): 63–80.
84. K. Aisaka et al., "[Effects of mother-infant interaction on maternal milk secretion and dynamics of maternal serum prolactin levels in puerperium]," *Nippon Sanka Fujinka Gakkai Zasshi* (Japan) 37, no. 5 (May 1985): 713–20.
85. V. Nedkova and S. Tanchev, "[Serum levels of prolactin, progesterone and estradiol in nursing mothers,]" *Akush Ginedol (Solfiia)* (Bulgaria) 34, no. 3 (1995): 22–3.
86. S.J. Gross, "Growth and biochemical response of preterm infants fed human milk or modified infant formula," *N Engl J Med* 308, no. 5 (Feb 3 1983): 237–41.
87. G. Boehm et al., "[Consequences of the composition of breast milk for the nutrition of underweight newborn infants. II. Lipids and lactose]," *Kinderärztl Prax* (Germany) 57, no. 9 (Sep 1989): 443–50.
88. Narayanan, "Human milk for low birthweight infants: immunology, nutrition and newer practical technologies," *Acta Paediatr Jpn* (Japan) 31, no. 4 (Aug 1989): 455–61.

89. K. Pridham et al., "The effects of prescribed versus ad libitum feedings and formula caloric density on premature infant dietary intake and weight gain," *Nurs Res* 48, no. 2 (Mar–Apr 1999): 86–93.

90. R.J. Schanler and S.A. Abrams, "Postnatal attainment of intrauterine macromineral accretion rates in low birth weight infants fed fortified human milk," *J Pediatr* 126, no. 3 (Mar 1995): 441–7.

91. S. Awasthi et al., "Is high protein milk beneficial for SGA-terms?" *Indian Pediatr* 26, no. 1 (Jan 1989): 45–51.

92. G. Boehm et al., "[Protein utilization by premature infants with a birth weight less than 1,500 g during nutrition with MANSAN or breast milk protein]," *Kinderarztl Prax* (German) 59, no. 1–2 (Jan–Feb 1991): 26–30.

93. R. Quan et al., "The effect of nutritional additives on anti-infective factors in human milk," *Clin Pediatr (Phila)* 33, no. 6 (Jun 1994): 325–8.

94. A. Lucas et al., "Randomized outcome trial of human milk fortification and developmental outcome in preterm infants," *Am J Clin Nutr* (England) 64, no. 2 (Aug 1996): 142–51.

95. J. Kreuder et al., "[Efficacy and side effects of differential calcium and phosphate administration in prevention of osteopenia in premature infants]," *Monatsschr Kinderheilkd* (Germany) 138, no. 11 (Nov 1990): 775–9.

96. S.J. Gross, "Bone mineralization in preterm infants fed human milk with and without mineral supplementation," *J Pediatr* 111, no. 3 (Sep 1987): 450–8.

97. J. Neuzil et al., "Oxidation of parenteral lipid emulsion by ambient and phototherapy lights: potential toxicity of routine parenteral feeding," *J Pediatr* 126, no. 5, part 1 (May 1995): 785–90.

98. D.A. Kelly, "Liver complications of pediatric parenteral nutrition — epidemiology," *Nutrition* 14, no. 1 (Jan 1998): 153–7.

99. R.L. Fisher, "Hepatobiliary abnormalities associated with total parenteral nutrition," *Gastroenterol Clin North Am* 18, no. 3 (Sep 1989): 645–66.

100. K. Simmer et al., "The use of breast milk in a neonatal unit and its relationship to protein and energy intake and growth," *J Paediatr Child Health* 33, no. 1 (Feb 1997): 55–60.

101. A. Lucas and T.J. Cole, "Breast milk and neonatal necrotising enterocolitis," *Lancet* (England) 336, no. 8730 (Dec 1990): 1519–23.

102. V. Araujo et al., "Impact of oxygen therapy on antioxidant status in newborns," *Biofactors* 8, nos. 1–2 (1998): 143–7.

103. L. Daniels et al., "Selenium status of preterm infants: the effect of postnatal age and method of feeding," *Acta Paediatr* 86, no. 3 (Mar 1997) 281–8.

104. G.P. Mathur et al., "Breastfeeding in babies delivered by cesarean section," *Indian Pediatr* 30, no. 11 (Nov 1993): 1285–90.

105. J. Martin-Calama et al., "The effect of feeding glucose water to breastfeeding newborns on weight, body temperature, blood glucose, and breastfeeding duration," *J Hum Lact* 13, no. 3 (Sep 1997): 209–13.

Chapter 9: Baby's Nutritional Beginnings

1. S.E. Nelson, "Absorption of fat and calcium by infants fed a milk-based formula containing palm olein," *J Am Coll Nutr* 17, no. 4 (Aug 1998): 327–32.

2. L.A. Baur et al., "The fatty acid composition of skeletal muscle membrane phospholipid: its relationship with the type of feeding and plasma glucose levels in young children," *Metabolism* (Australia) 47, no. 1 (Jan 1998): 106–12.

3. P.T. Quinlan et al., "The relationship between stool hardness and stool composition in breast- and formula-fed infants," *J Pediatr Gastroenterol Nutr* 20, no. 1 (Jan 1995): 81–90.

4. C.P. Anyon, "Normal haemoglobin values in urban Polynesian infants: the possible deleterious influence of artificial feeding," *NZ Med J* 84 (1976): 474–476.

5. J. Williams et al., "Iron supplemented formula milk related to reduction in psychomotor decline in infants from inner city areas: randomised study," *BMJ* 318, no. 7185 (Mar 1999): 693–7.

6. E.K. Hurtado et al., "Early childhood anemia and mild or moderate mental retardation," *Am J Clin Nutr* 69, no. 1 (Jan 1999): 115–9.

7. P. MacDougall, "Breast milk versus cow's milk," *BC Ped Res*, www.childhosp.bc.ca, (1997).

8. J. Williams et al., "Iron supplemented formula milk related to reduction in psychomotor decline in infants from inner city areas: randomised study," *BMJ* 318, no. 7185 (Mar 1999): 693–7.

9. E.A. Mevissen-Verhage et al., "Effect of iron on serotypes and haemagglutination patterns of Escherichia coli in bottle-fed infants," *Eur J Clin Microbiol* 4, no. 6 (Dec 1985): 570–4.

10. B. Lönnerdal and O. Hernell, "Iron, zinc, copper and selenium status of breast-fed infants and infants fed trace element fortified milk-based infant formula," *Acta Paediatr* 83, no. 4 (Apr 1994): 367–73.

11. F. Haschke et al., "Iron nutrition and growth of breast- and formula-fed infants during the first 9 months of life," *J Pediatr Gastroenterol Nutr* (Austria) 16, no. 2 (Feb 1993): 151–6.

12. T. Walter et al., "Prevention of iron-deficiency anemia: comparison of high- and low-iron formulas in term healthy infants after six months of life," *J Pediatr* 132, no. 4 (Apr 1998): 635–40.

13. B. Lönnerdal and O. Hernell, "Iron, zinc, copper and selenium status of breast-fed infants and infants fed trace element fortified milk-based infant formula," *Acta Paediatr* 83, no. 4 (Apr 1994): 367–73.

14. M.A. Siimes et al., "Exclusive breast-feeding for 9 months: risk of iron deficiency," J Pediatr 104, no. 2 (Feb 1984): 196–9.

15. B. Duncan et al., "Iron and the exclusively breast-fed infant from birth to six months," J Pediatr Gastroenterol Nutr 4, no. 3 (Jun 1985): 421–5.

16. M.A. Siimes et al., "Exclusive breast-feeding for 9 months: risk of iron deficiency," J Pediatr 104, no. 2 (Feb 1984): 196–9.

17. P.D. Scariati et al., "Risk of diarrhea related to iron content of infant formula: lack of evidence to support the use of low-iron formula as a supplement for breastfed infants," Pediatrics 99, no. 3 (Mar 1997): E2.

18. M.A. Siimes et al., "Exclusive breast-feeding for 9 months: risk of iron deficiency," J Pediatr 104, no. 2 (Feb 1984): 196–9.

19. F.A. Oski and S.A. Landaw, "Inhibition of iron absorption from human milk by baby food," Am J Dis Child 134, no. 5 (May 1980): 459–60.

20. E.B. Calvo et al., "Iron status in exclusively breast-fed infants," Pediatrics (Argentina) 90, no. 3 (Sep 1992): 375–9.

21. M. Makrides et al., "A randomized controlled clinical trial of increased dietary iron in breast-fed infants," J Pediatr 133, no. 4 (Oct 1998): 559–62.

22. A. Pisacane et al., "Iron status in breast-fed infants," J Pediatr (Italy) 127, no. 3 (Sep 1995): 429–31.

23. Figure 9-1 was extracted from the USDA Nutrient Database for Standard Reference (1998).

24. P. Hemalatha et al., "Zinc status of breastfed and formula-fed infants of different gestational ages," J Trop Pediatr 43, no. 1 (Feb 1997): 52–4.

25. R.M. Ortega et al., "[Supplementation with iron and folates during gestation: influence on the zinc status in the mother and on the zinc content in the maternal milk]," Med Clin (Barc) (Spain) 111, no. 8 (Sep 1998): 281–5.

26. D. Chlubek, "[Interaction of fluoride with milk constituents]," Ann Acad Med Stetin (Poland) 39 (1993): 23–38.

27. K.E. Heller et al., "Dental caries and dental fluorosis at varying water fluoride concentrations," J Public Health Dent 57, no. 3 (Summer 1997): 136–43.

28. D.J. Brothwell and H. Limeback, "Fluorosis risk in grade 2 students residing in a rural area with widely varying natural fluoride," Community Dent Oral Epidemiol (Canada) 27, no. 2 (Apr 1999): 130–6.

29. M. Diesendorf et al., "Aust N Z J Public Health (Australia) 21, no. 2 (Apr 1997): 187–90.

30. E.H. Abdennebi et al., "Human fluorosis in Morocco: analytical and clinical investigations," Vet Hum Toxicol (Morocco) 37 no. 5 (Oct 1995): 465–8.

31. S Dasarathy et al., "Gastroduodenal manifestations in patients with skeletal fluorosis," J Gastroenterol (India) 31, no. 3 (Jun 1996): 333–7.

32. P.K. DenBesten, "Biological mechanisms of dental fluorosis relevant to the use of fluoride supplements," Community Dent Oral Epidemiol 27, no. 1 (Feb 1999): 41–7.

33. N.J. Wang and P.J. Riordan, "Fluoride supplements and caries in a non-fluoridated child population," Community Dent Oral Epidemiol (Norway) 27, no. 2 (Apr 1999): 117–23.

34. A.I. Ismail and R.R. Bandekar, "Fluoride supplements and fluorosis: a meta-analysis," Community Dent Oral Epidemiol 27, no. 1 (Feb 1999): 48–56.

35. P.J. Riordan, "Dental fluorosis, dental caries and fluoride exposure among 7-year-olds," Caries Res 27, no. 1 (1993): 71–7.

36. D.J. Brothwell and H. Limeback, "Fluorosis risk in grade 2 students residing in a rural area with widely varying natural fluoride," Community Dent Oral Epidemiol (Canada) 27, no. 2 (Apr 1999): 130–6.

37. C.J. Spak et al., "Fluoride in human milk," Acta Paediatr Scand 72, no. 5 (Sep 1983): 699–701.

38. P.J. Riordan, "The place of fluoride supplements in caries prevention today," Aust Dent J (Australia) 41, no. 5 (Oct 1996): 335–42.

39. M.T. Pugliese et al., "Nutritional rickets in suburbia," J Am Coll Nutr 17, no. 6 (Dec 1998): 637–41.

40. M.J. Park, "Bone mineral content is not reduced despite low vitamin D status in breast milk-fed infants versus cow's milk based formula-fed infants," J Pediatr 132, no. 4 (Apr 1998): 641–5.

41. M. Cosgrove, "Perinatal and infant nutrition. Nucleotides," Nutrition (England) 14, no. 10 (Oct 1998): 748–51.

42. V.Y. Yu, "The role of dietary nucleotides in neonatal and infant nutrition," Singapore Med J (Australia) 39, no. 4 (Apr 1998): 145–50.

43. G. Sarwar et al., "Free amino acids in milks of human subjects, other primates and non-primates," Br J Nutr 79, no. 2 (Feb 1998): 129–31.

44. S Desantiago et al., "[Free amino acids in plasma and milk of Mexican rural lactating women]," Rev Invest Clin (Mexico) 50, no. 5 (Sep–Oct 1998): 405–12.

45. Z. Kurugöl et al., "Comparison of growth, serum prealbumin, transferrin, IgG and amino acids of term infants fed breast milk or formula," Turk J Pediatr 39, no. 2 (Apr 1997): 195–202.

46. W.E. Heine et al., "The importance of alpha-lactalbumin in infant nutrition," J Nutr 121, no. 3 (Mar 1991): 277–83.

47. B. Lönnerdal, "Effects of milk and milk components on calcium, magnesium, and trace element absorption during infancy," *Physiol Rev* 77, no. 3 (Jul 1997): 643–669.
48. B. Lönnerdal et al., "Effect of reducing the phytate content and of partially hydrolyzing the protein content in soy formula on zinc and copper absorption and status in infant rhesus monkeys and rat pups," *Am J Clin Nutr* 69, no. 3 (Mar 1999): 490–6.
49. S.R. Lynch et al., "Inhibitory effect of a soybean-protein-related moiety on iron absorption in humans," *Am J Clin Nutr* 60, no. 4 (Oct 1994): 567–72.
50. B. Lönnerdal, "Nutritional aspects of soy formula," *Acta Paediatr Suppl* 402 (Sep 1994): 105–8.
51. K.D. Setchell et al., "Isoflavone content of infant formulas and the metabolic fate of these phytoestrogens in early life," *Am J Clin Nutr* 68, no. 6, suppl. (Dec 1998): 1453S–61S.
52. A.A. Franke et al., "Isoflavones in human breast milk and other biological fluids," *Am J Clin Nutr* 68, no. 6, suppl. (Dec 1998): 1466S–73S.
53. D.M. Sheehan, "Herbal medicines, phytoestrogens and toxicity: risk:benefit considerations," *Proc Soc Exp Biol Med* 217, no. 3 (Mar 1998): 379–85.
54. James M. Orten and Otto W. Neuhaus, *Human Biochemistry*, ninth edition (St. Louis: The C.V. Mosby Co., 1975): 248–9, 694–5.
55. K. Yoneyama et al., "[Change in the concentrations of nutrient components of human milk during lactation]," *Nippon Koshu Eisei Zasshi* (Japan) 42, no. 7 (Jul 1995): 472–81.
56. G.V. Coppa et al., "Changes in carbohydrate composition in human milk over 4 months of lactation," *Pediatrics* (Italy) 91, no. 3 (Mar 1993): 637–41.
57. M.V. Karra et al., "Zinc, calcium, and magnesium concentrations in milk from American and Egyptian women throughout the first 6 months of lactation," 47, no. 4 (Apr 1988): 642–8.
58. M.A. Laskey et al., "Breast-milk calcium concentrations during prolonged lactation in British and rural Gambian mothers," *Acta Paediatr Scand* (England) 79, no. 5 (May 1990): 507–12.
59. B. Fournier et al., "Variations of phylloquinone concentration in human milk at various stages of lactation and in cow's milk at various seasons," *Am J Clin Nutr* 45, no. 3 (Mar 1987): 551–8.
60. K.G. Dewey, "Growth of breast-fed and formula-fed infants from 0 to 18 months: the DARLING Study," *Pediatrics* 89, no. 6, part 1 (Jun 1992): 1035–41.
61. K.G. Dewey et al., "Breast-fed infants are leaner than formula-fed infants at 1 year of age: the DARLING Study," *Am J Clin Nutr* 57, no. 2 (Feb 1993): 140–5.
62. M. Prokopec and F. Bellisle, "Adiposity in Czech children followed from 1 month of age to adulthood: analysis of individual BMI patterns," *Ann Hum Biol* (Czech Republic) 20, no. 6 (Nov–Dec 1993): 517–25.
63. B.S. Simic, "Childhood obesity as a risk factor in adulthood and its prevention," *Prev Med* 12, no. 1 (Jan 1983): 47–51.
64. B. Lönnerdal, "Effects of milk and milk components on calcium, magnesium, and trace element absorption during infancy," *Physiol Rev* 77 (1997): 643–669.
65. D.R. Woodward et al., "Human milk fat content: within-feed variation," *Early Hum Dev* (Australia) 19, no. 1 (Apr 1989): 39–46.
66. X. Casabiell at al., "Presence of leptin in colostrum and/or breast milk from lactating mothers: a potential role in the regulation of neonatal food intake," *J Clin Endocrinol Metab* (Spain) 82, no. 12 (Dec 1997): 4270–3.
67. S.J. Fomon et al., "Infant formula with protein-energy ratio of 1.7 g/100 kcal is adequate but may not be safe," *J Pediatr Gastroenterol Nutr* 28, no. 5 (May 1999): 495–501.
68. K.G. Dewey et al., "Do exclusively breast-fed infants require extra protein?" *Pediatr Res* 39, no. 2 (Feb 1996): 303–7.
69. K.G. Dewey et al., "Breast-fed infants are leaner than formula-fed infants at 1 year of age: the DARLING Study," *Am J Clin Nutr* 57, no. 2 (Feb 1993): 140–5.
70. E.A. Simoes and S.M. Pereira, "The growth of exclusively breastfed infants," *Ann Trop Paediatr* 6, no. 1 (Mar 1986): 17–21.
71. Naomi Baumslag, M.D. and Dia L. Michels, *Milk, Money, and Madness: The culture and politics of breastfeeding* (Westport, Connecticut: Bergin & Garvey, 1995).
72. R. von Kries et al., "Breast feeding and obesity: cross sectional study," *Br Med J* 319, no. 7203 (Jul 17, 1999): 147–50.
73. K.G. Dewey et al., "Adequacy of energy intake among breast-fed infants in the DARLING study: relationships to growth velocity, morbidity, and activity levels. Davis Area Research on Lactation, Infant Nutrition and Growth," *J Pediatr* 119, no. 4 (Oct 1991): 538–47.
74. D. Skuse et al., "Postnatal growth and mental development: evidence for a "sensitive period," *J Child Psychol Psychiatry* 35, no. 3 (Mar 1994): 521–45.
75. K.C. Mehta et al., "Trial on timing of introduction to solids and food type on infant growth," *Pediatrics* 102, no. 3, part 1 (Sep 1998): 569–73.
76. H.C. Borresen, "[A questionable guideline on introduction of solid food to breast-fed infants]," *Tidsskr Nor Laegeforen* (Norway) 114, no. 26 (Oct 30, 1994): 3087–9.
77. K.B. Simondon and F. Simondon, "Age at introduction of complementary food and physical growth from 2 to 9 months in rural Senegal," *Eur J Clin Nutr* 51, no. 10 (Oct 1997): 703–7.

78. S. Cosminsky et al., "Child feeding practices in a rural area of Zimbabwe," *Soc Sci Med* 36, no. 7 (Apr 1993): 937–47.

79. S.A. Quandt, "The effect of beikost on the diet of breast-fed infants," *J Am Diet Assoc* 84, no. 1 (Jan 1984): 47–51.

80. B. Kuate Defo, "Effects of infant feeding practices and birth spacing on infant and child survival: a reassessment from retrospective and prospective data," *J Biosoc Sci* (Canada) 29, no. 3 (Jul 1997): 303–26.

81. L.L. Birch, "Development of food acceptance patterns in the first years of life," *Proc Nutr Soc* 57, no. 4 (Nov 1998): 617–24.

Chapter 10: Baby Feeding: Facts & Fallacies

1. F.A. Oski, "Infant nutrition, physical growth, breastfeeding, and general nutrition," *Curr Opin Pediatr* 5, no. 3 (Jun 1993): 385–8.

2. H.C. Borresen, "[A questionable guideline on introduction of solid food to breast-fed infants,]" *Tidsskr Nor Laegeforen* (Norway) 114, no. 26 (Oct 30, 1994): 3087–9.

3. D.J. Chapman and R. Perez-Escamilla, "Identification of risk factors for delayed onset of lactation," *J Am Diet Assoc* 99, no. 4 (Apr 1999): 450–4.

4. K. Nemba, "Induced lactation: a study of 37 non-puerperal mothers," *J Trop Pediatr* 40, no. 4 (Aug 1994): 240–2.

5. M.L. Macknin et al., "Infant sleep and bedtime cereal," *Am J Dis Child* 143, no. 9 (Sep 1989): 1066–8.

6. R.R. Bainbridge et al., "Effect of rice cereal feedings on bone mineralization and calcium homeostasis in cow milk formula fed infants," *J Am Coll Nutr* 15, no. 4 (Aug 1996): 383–8.

7. R.J. Shulman et al., "Impact of dietary cereal on nutrient absorption and fecal nitrogen loss in formula-fed infants," *J Pediatr* 118, no. 1 (Jan 1991): 39–43.

8. S.R, Orenstein et al., "Thickening of infant feedings for therapy of gastroesophageal reflux," *J Pediatr* 110, no. 2 (Feb 1987): 181–6.

9. A.A. al-Dashti et al., "Breast feeding, bottle feeding and dental caries in Kuwait, a country with low-fluoride levels in the water supply," *Community Dent Health* (England) 12, no. 1 (Mar 1995): 42–7.

10. R.O. Mattos-Graner et al., "Association between caries prevalence and clinical, microbiological and dietary variables in 1.0 to 2.5-year-old Brazilian children," *Caries Res* 32, no. 5 (1998): 319–23.

11. N. Kanou et al., "[Investigation into the actual condition of outpatients. II. Correlation between the daily habits of eating and toothbrushing and the prevalence of dental caries incidence]," *Shoni Shikagaku Zasshi* (Japan) 27, no. 2 (1989): 467–74.

12. A. Mohan et al., "The relationship between bottle usage/content, age, and number of teeth with mutans streptococci colonization in 6–24-month-old children," *Comm Dent Oral Epidemiol* 26, no. 1 (Feb 1998): 12–20.

13. K.L. Weerheijm et al., "Prolonged demand breast-feeding and nursing caries," *Caries Res* (Holland) 21, no. 1 (1998): 46–50.

14. L. Lopez Del Valle et al., "Early childhood caries and risk factors in rural Puerto Rican children," *ASDC J Dent Child* 65, no. 2 (Mar–Apr 1998): 132–5.

15. A.L. Hallonsten et al., "Dental caries and prolonged breast-feeding in 18-month-old Swedish children," *Int J Paediatr Dent* (Sweden) 5, no. 3 (Sep 1995): 149–55.

16. M.I. Matee et al., "Mutans streptococci and lactobacilli in breast-fed children with rampant caries," *Caries Res* (Tanzania) 26, no. 3 (1992): 183–7.

17. P.R. Erickson and E. Mazhari, "Investigation of the role of human breast milk in caries development," *Pediatr Dent* 21, no. 2 (Mar–Apr 1999): 86–90.

18. C. Sheikh and P.R. Erickson, "Evaluation of plaque pH changes following oral rinse with eight infant formulas," *Pediatr Dent* 18, no. 3 (May–Jun 1996): 200–4.

19. D. Birkhed et al., "pH changes in human dental plaque from lactose and milk before and after adaptation," *Caries Res* 27, no. 1 (1993): 43–50.

20. P. Ollila et al., "Prolonged pacifier-sucking and use of a nursing bottle at night: possible risk factors for dental caries in children," *Acta Odontol Scand* 56, no. 4 (Aug 1998): 233–7.

21. H.J. Kalkwarf et al., "The effect of calcium supplementation on bone density during lactation and after weaning," *N Engl J Med* 337, no. 8 (Aug 1997): 523–8.

22. K.D. Little and J.F. Clapp III, "Self-selected recreational exercise has no impact on early postpartum lactation-induced bone loss," *Med Sci Sports Exerc* 30, no. 6 (Jun 1998): 831–6.

23. M. Sowers et al., "Changes in bone density with lactation," *JAMA* 269, no. 24 (Jun 23–30, 1993): 3130–5.

24. R.G. Cumming and R.J. Klineberg, "Breastfeeding and other reproductive factors and the risk of hip fractures in elderly women," *Int J Epidemiol* (Australia) 22, no. 4 (Aug 1993): 684–91.

25. J.H. Himes et al., "Maternal supplementation and bone growth in infancy," *Paediatr Perinat Epidemiol* 4, no. 4 (Oct 1990): 436–47.

26. L.H. Amir et al., "*Candida albicans*: is it associated with nipple pain in lactating women?" *Gynecol Obstet Invest* (Australia) 41, no. 1 (1996): 30–4.

27. L. Amir, "Candida and the lactating breast: predisposing factors," *J Hum Lact* 7, no. 4 (Dec 1991): 177–81.

28. P. Thomassen et al., "Breast-feeding, pain and infection," *Gynecol Obstet Invest* 46, no. 2 (Aug 1998): 73–4.

29. S. Matsuda, "Transfer of antibiotics into maternal milk," *Biol Res Pregnancy Perinatol* 5, no. 2 (1984): 57–60.

30. K.E. Tanguay et al., "Nipple candidiasis among breastfeeding mothers. Case-control study of predisposing factors," *Can Fam Physician* (Canada) 40 (Aug 1994): 1407–13.

31. K. Katsouyanni et al., "A case-control study of lactation and cancer of the breast," *Br J Cancer* (Greece) 73, no. 6 (Mar 1996): 814–8.

32. F.D. Gilliland et al., "Reproductive risk factors for breast cancer in Hispanic and non-Hispanic white women: the New Mexico Women's Health Study," *Am J Epidemiol* 148, no. 7 (Oct 1998): 683–92.

33. L.G. Ries et al., "SEER Cancer Statistics Review, 1973–94: Tables and Graphs," National Cancer Institute, Bethesda, MD, NIH Publication No. 97-2789, (1997)

34. V. Siskind et al., "Breastfeeding, menopause, and epithelial ovarian cancer," *Epidemiology* (Australia) 8, no. 2 (Mar 1997): 188–91.

35. M. Altemus et al., "Suppression of hypothalamic–pituitary–adrenal axis responses to stress in lactating women," *J Clin Endocrinol Metab* 80, no. 10 (Oct 1995): 2954–9.

36. K. Uvnas-Moberg et al. "Oxytocin and prolactin levels in breast-feeding women. Correlation with milk yield and duration of breast-feeding," *Acta Obstet Gynecol Scand* (Sweden) 69, no. 4 (1990): 301–6.

37. M. Petersson et al., "Oxytocin causes a long-term decrease of blood pressure in female and male rats," *Physiol Behav* 60, no. 5 (Nov 1996): 1311–5.

38. Naomi Baumslag, M.D. and Dia L. Michels, "Milk, Money, and Madness, The Culture and Politics of Breastfeeding," (Westport, Connecticut: Bergin & Garvey, 1995).

39. A. Pallone and M. Tienda, "The effects of breastfeeding and pace of childbearing on mortality at early ages," *Demography* 23, no. 1 (Feb 1986): 31–52.

40. B. Kuate Defo, "Effects of infant feeding practices and birth spacing on infant and child survival: a reassessment from retrospective and prospective data," *J Biosoc Sci* (Canada) 29, no. 3 (Jul 1997): 303–26.

41. R.K. Valaitis and E. Shea, "An evaluation of breastfeeding promotion literature: does it really promote breastfeeding?" *Can J Public Health* (Canada) 84, no. 1 (Jan–Feb 1993): 24–7.

42. J. Wise, "Companies still breaking milk marketing code," *BMJ* 316, no. 7138 (April 11, 1998): 1115.

43. L.S. Adair et al., "The duration of breast-feeding: How is it affected by biological, sociodemographic, health sector, and food industry factors?" *Demography* 30, no. 1 (Feb 1993): 63–80.

44. "Yes! The Nestlé boycott is on!!" www.infactcanada, (Spring 95).

45. E. Romero-Gwynn, "Breast-feeding pattern among Indochinese immigrants in northern California, *Am J Dis Child* 143, no. 7 (Jul 1989): 804–8.

46. R.J. Schanler et al., "Pediatricians' practices and attitudes regarding breastfeeding promotion," *Pediatrics* 103, no. 3 (Mar 1999): E35.

47. G.L. Freed et al., "Pediatrician involvement in breast-feeding promotion: a national study of residents and practitioners," *Pediatrics* 96, no. 3, part 1 (Sep 1995): 490–4.

48. P.P. Meier et al., "Breastfeeding support services in the neonatal intensive-care unit," *J Obstet Gynecol Neonatal Nurs* 22, no. 4 (Jul–Aug 1993): 338–47.

49. J.M. Riordan, "The cost of not breastfeeding: a commentary," *J Hum Lact* 13, no. 2 (Jun 1997): 93–7.

50. J.D. Skinner et al., "Transitions in infant feeding during the first year of life," *J Am Coll Nutr* 16, no. 3 (Jun 1997): 209–15.

51. A.H. Goodman et al., "The chronological distribution of enamel hypoplasias from prehistoric Dickson Mounds populations," *Am J Phys Anthropol* 65, no. 3 (Nov 1984): 259–66.

52. L.E. Wright and H.P. Schwarcz, "Stable carbon and oxygen isotopes in human tooth enamel: identifying breastfeeding and weaning in prehistory," *Am J Phys Anthropol* 106, no. 1 (May 1998): 1–18.

53. K.M. Lanphear, "Frequency and distribution of enamel hypoplasias in a historic skeletal sample," *Am J Phys Anthropol* 81, no. 1 (Jan 1990): 35–43.

54. J. Moggi-Cecchi et al., "Enamel hypoplasias in a 19th century population from northern Italy," *Anthropol Anz* 51, no. 2 (Jun 1993): 123–9.

55. J. Wallis, "A survey of reproductive parameters in the free-ranging chimpanzees of Gombe National Park," *J Reprod Fertil* 109, no. 2 (Mar 1997): 297–307.

56. L.D. Hammer et al., "Development of feeding practices during the first 5 years of life," *Arch Pediatr Adolesc Med* 153, no. 2 (Feb 1999): 189–94.

Chapter 11: The Dangers of Cow's Milk

1. J.M. Norris et al., "Lack of association between early exposure to cow's milk protein and beta-cell autoimmunity. Diabetes autoimmunity study in the young," *JAMA* 276, no. 8 (Aug 1996): 609–14.

2. R.B. Elliott et al., "Type I (insulin-dependent) diabetes mellitus and cow milk: casein variant consumption," *Diabetologia* (New Zealand) 42, no. 3 (Mar 1999): 292–6.

3. S.G. Gimeno and J.M. deSouza, "IDDM and milk consumption: A case-control study in Sao Paulo, Brazil," *Diabetes Care* (Brazil) 20, no. 8 (Aug 1997): 1256–60.

4. J. Karjalainen et al., "A bovine albumin peptide as a possible trigger of insulin-dependent diabetes mellitus," *N Engl J Med* (Canada) 327, no. 5 (Jul 30, 1992): 302–7.

5. T. Saukkonen et al., "Significance of cow's milk protein antibodies as risk factor for childhood IDDM: interactions with dietary cow's milk intake and HLA-DQB1 genotype. Childhood Diabetes in Finland Study Group," *Diabetologia* (Finland) 41, no. 1 (Jan 1998): 72–8.

6. S.M. Virtanen et al., "Diet, cow's milk protein antibodies and the risk of IDDM in Finnish children. Childhood Diabetes in Finland Study Group," *Diabetologia* (Finland) 37, no. 4 (Apr 1994): 381–7.

7. P. Vähäsalo et al., "Relation between antibodies to islet cell antigens, other autoantigens, and cow's milk proteins in diabetic children and unaffected siblings as the clinical manifestation of IDDM," *Autoimmunity* (Finland) 23, no. 3 (1996): 165–74.

8. B. Rami et al., "Risk factors for type I diabetes mellitus in children in Austria," *Eur J Pediatr* (Austria) 158,no. 5 (May 1999): 362–6.

9. Y. Fukushima et al., "Consumption of cow milk and egg by lactating women and the presence of beta-lactoglobulin and ovalbumin in breast milk," *Am J Clin Nutr* (Japan) 65, no. 1 (Jan 1997): 30–5.

10. R. Sorva et al., "Beta-lactoglobulin secretion in human milk varies widely after cow's milk ingestion in mothers of infants with cow's milk allergy," *J Allergy Clin Immunol* (Finland) 93, no. 4 (Apr 1994): 787–92.

11. F. Perez Bravo et al., "Genetic predisposition and environmental factors leading to the development of insulin-dependent diabetes mellitus in Chilean children," *J Mol Med* (Chile) 74, no. 2 (Feb 1996): 105–9.

12. D.J. Pettitt et al., "Breastfeeding and incidence of non-insulin-dependent diabetes mellitus in Pima Indians," *Lancet* 350, no. 9072 (Jul 1997): 166–8.

13. K. Dahl-Jorgensen et al., "Relationship between cows' milk consumption and incidence of IDDM in childhood," *Diabetes Care* (Norway) 14, no. 11 (Nov 1991): 1081–3.

14. A.L. Drash et al., "The interface between epidemiology and molecular biology in the search for the causes of insulin-dependent diabetes mellitus," *Ann Med* 23, no. 4 (Oct 1991): 463–71.

15. G. Dahlquist et al., "An increased level of antibodies to beta-lactoglobulin is a risk determinant for early-onset type I (insulin-dependent) diabetes mellitus independent of islet cell antibodies and early introduction of cow's milk," *Diabetologia* (Sweden) 35, no. 10 (Oct 1992): 980–4.

16. D. Cislak et al., "[Frequency of appearance of antibodies to bovine serum albumin in children with diabetes type I]," *Pol Arch Med Wewn* (Poland) 100, no. 2 (Aug 1998): 106–10.

17. M.G. Cavallo et al., "Cell-mediated immune response to beta casein in recent-onset insulin-dependent diabetes: implications for disease pathogenesis," *Lancet* (Italy) 348, no. 9032 (Oct 1996): 926–8.

18. O. Vaarala et al., "Cow milk feeding induces antibodies to insulin in children — a link between cow milk and insulin-dependent diabetes mellitus?" *Scand J Immunol* (Finland) 47, no. 2 (Feb 1998): 131–5.

19. G. Dahlquist, "The aetiology of type 1 diabetes: an epidemiological perspective," *Acta Paediatr Suppl* (Sweden) 425 (Oct 1998): 5–10.

20. G.G. Dahlquist, "Viruses and other perinatal exposures as initiating events for beta-cell destruction," *Ann Med* (Sweden) 29, no. 5 (Oct 1997): 413–7.

21. S.M. Virtanen et al., "Cow's milk consumption, disease-associated autoantibodies and type-1 diabetes mellitus: a follow-up study in siblings of diabetic children. Childhood Diabetes in Finland Study Group," *Diabet Med* (Finland) 15, no. 9 (Sep 1998): 730–8.

22. D. Kitts, Y. Yaun et al., "Adverse reactions to food constituents: allergy, intolerance, and autoimmunity," *Can J Physiol Pharmacol* (Canada) 75, no. 4 (April 1997): 241–54.

23. D. Malosse et al., "Correlation between milk and dairy product consumption and multiple sclerosis prevalence: a worldwide study," *Neuroepidemiology* (France) 11, no. 4–6 (1992): 304–12.

24. J. Butcher, "The distribution of multiple sclerosis in relation to the dairy industry and milk consumption," *N Z Med J* 83, no. 566 (Jun 1976): 427–30.

25. A.C. Wilson et al. "Relation of infant diet to childhood health: seven year follow up of cohort of children in Dundee infant feeding study," *BMJ* (England) 316, no. 7124 (Jan 1998): 21–5.

26. R.M. Bostick et al., "Relation of calcium, vitamin D, and dairy food intake to ischemic heart disease mortality among postmenopausal women," *Am J Epidemiol* 149, no. 2 (Jan 1999): 151–61.

27. R.B. Singh et al., "Association of trans fatty acids (vegetable ghee) and clarified butter (Indian ghee) intake with higher risk of coronary artery disease in rural and urban populations with low fat consumption," *Int J Cardiol* (India) 56, no. 3 (Oct 1996): 289–98.

28. L.H. Kushe et al., "Health implications of Mediterranean diets in light of contemporary knowledge. 1. Plant foods and dairy products," *Am J Clin Nutr* 61, no. 6, suppl. (Jun 1995): 1407S–15S.

29. S. Seely, "Diet and coronary arterial disease: a statistical study," *Int J Cardiol* (England) 20, no. 2 (Aug 1988): 183–92.

30. W.B. Grant, "Milk and other dietary influences on coronary heart disease," *Altern Med Rev* 3, no. 4 (Aug 1998): 281–94.

31. M. Cecim et al., "Increased plasma corticosterone levels in bovine growth hormone (bGH) transgenic mice: effects of ACTH, GH, and IGF-I on in vitro adrenal corticosterone production," *Transgenic Res* 5, no. 3 (May 1996): 187–92.

32. S. Seely, "Diet and coronary disease: a survey of mortality rates and food consumption statistics of 24 countries," *Med Hypotheses* 7, no. 7 (Jul 1981): 907-18.

33. N.S. Scrimshaw and E.B. Murray, "The acceptability of milk and milk products in populations with a high prevalence of lactose intolerance," *Am J Clin Nutr* 48, no. 4, suppl. (Oct 1988): 1079–159.

34. L.D. McBean and G.D. Miller, "Allaying fears and fallacies about lactose intolerance," *J Am Diet Assoc* 98, no. 6 (Jun 1998): 671–6.

35. James M. Orten and Otto W. Neuhaus, *Human Biochemistry*, ninth edition (St. Louis: The C.V. Mosby Co., 1975): 249.

36. "Don't Drink Your Milk," *Natural Health* (July–Aug 1994).

37. I. Birlouez-Aragon et al., "Disturbed galactose metabolism in elderly and diabetic humans is associated with cataract formation," *J Nutr* (France) 123, no. 8 (Aug 1993): 1370–6.

38. J.F. Ferrer et al., "Milk of dairy cows frequently contains a leukemogenic virus," *Science* 213, no. 4511 (Aug 1981): 1014–6.

39. P. Kristensen et al., "Incidence and risk factors of cancer among men and women in Norwegian agriculture," *Scand J Work Environ Health* 22, no. 1 (Feb 1996): 14–26.

40. A.S. Cunningham, "Lymphomas and animal-protein consumption," *Lancet* 2, no. 7996 (Nov 27, 1976): 1184–6.

41. K.J. Donham et al., "Epidemiologic relationships of the bovine population and human leukemia in Iowa," *Am J Epidemiol* 112, no. 1 (Jul 1980): 80–92.

42. A. Tavani et al., "Diet and risk of lymphoid neoplasms and soft tissue sarcomas," *Nutr Cancer* 27, no. 3 (1997): 256–60.

43. A. Kwiatkowski, "Dietary and other environmental risk factors in acute leukaemias: a case-control study of 119 patients," *Eur J Cancer Prev* 2, no. 2 (Mar 1993): 139–46.

44. K. Klintevall et al., "Evaluation of an indirect ELISA for the detection of antibodies to bovine leukemia virus in milk and serum," *J Virol Methods* 33, no. 3 (Aug 1991): 319–33.

45. M.C. Wu et al., "Milk and fat production in dairy cattle influenced by advanced subclinical bovine leukemia virus infection," *Proc Natl Acad Sci U S A* 8a6, no. 3 (Feb 1989): 993–6.

46. F.L. Pollari et al., "Effects of bovine leukemia virus infection on production and reproduction in dairy cattle," *Can J Vet Res* 56, no. 4 (Oct 1992): 289–95.

47. Y. Da et al., "Milk and fat yields decline in bovine leukemia virus-infected Holstein cattle with persistent lymphocytosis," *Proc Natl Acad Sci U S A* 90, no. 14 (Jul 1993): 6538–41.

48. M.C. Alavanja et al., "Estimating the effect of dietary fat on the risk of lung cancer in nonsmoking women," *Lung Cancer* 14, suppl. 1 (Mar 1996): S63–74.

49. E. De Stefani et al., "Fatty foods and the risk of lung cancer: a case-control study from Uruguay," *Int J Cancer* (Uruguay) 71, no. 5 (May 29, 1997): 760–6.

50. M.B. Veierod et al., "Dietary fat intake and risk of lung cancer: a prospective study of 51,452 Norwegian men and women," *Eur J Cancer Prev* (Norway) 6, no. 6 (Dec 1997): 540–9.

51. R. Rylander et al., "Lung cancer, smoking and diet among Swedish men," *Lung Cancer* (Sweden) 14, suppl. 1 (Mar 1996): S75–83.

52. F. Nyberg et al., "Dietary factors and risk of lung cancer in never-smokers," *Int J Cancer* (Sweden) 78, no. 4 (Nov 1998): 430–6.

53. M.B. Veierod et al., "Dietary fat intake and risk of prostate cancer: a prospective study of 25,708 Norwegian men," *Int J Cancer* (Norway) 73, no. 5 (Nov 1997): 634–8.

54. C. La Vecchia et al., "Dairy products and the risk of prostatic cancer," *Oncology* 48, no. 5 (1991): 406–10.

55. W.B. Grant, "An ecologic study of dietary links to prostate cancer," *Altern Med Rev* 4, no. 3 (Jun 1999): 162–9.

56. F.F. Angwafo, "Migration and prostate cancer: an international perspective," *J Natl Med Assoc* (Cameroon) 90, no. 11, suppl. (Nov 1998): S720–3.

57. Y. Kakehi, "[Epidemiology and clinical features of prostate cancer in Japan]," *Nippon Rinsho* (Japan) 56, no. 8 (Aug 1998): 1969–73.

58. J.O. Ogunbiyi and O.B. Shittu, "Increased incidence of prostate cancer in Nigerians," *J Natl Med Assoc* (Nigeria) 91, no. 3 (Mar 1999): 159–64.

59. A.R. Walker, "Prostate cancer—some aspects of epidemiology, risk factors, treatment and survival," *S Afr Med J* 69, no. 1 (Jan 1986): 44–7.

60. C.J. Mettlin and P.S. Piver, "A case-control study of milk-drinking and ovarian cancer risk," *Am J Epidemiol* 132, no. 5 (Nov 1990): 871–6.

61. D.W. Cramer, "Lactase persistence and milk consumption as determinants of ovarian cancer risk," *Am J Epidemiol* 130, no. 5 (Nov 1989): 904–10.

62. G. Tortolero-Luna and M.F. Mitchell, "The epidemiology of ovarian cancer," *J Cell Biochem Suppl* 23 (1995): 200–7.

63. D.W. Cramer et al., "Adult hypolactasia, milk consumption, and age-specific fertility," *Am J Epidemiol* 139, no. 3 (Feb 1994): 282–9.

64. I. Kato et al., "Factors related to late menopause and early menarche as risk factors for breast cancer," *Jpn J Cancer Res* (Japan) 79, no. 2 (Feb 1988): 165–72.

65. B.A. Stoll, "Western diet, early puberty, and breast cancer risk," *Breast Cancer Res Treat* 49, no. 3 (Jun 1998): 187–93.

66. L. Ibanez et al., "Hyperinsulinemia and decreased insulin-like growth factor-binding protein-1 are common features in prepubertal and pubertal girls with a history of premature pubarche," *J Clin Endocrinol Metab* (Spain) 82, no. 7 (Jul 1997): 2283–8.

67. M.E. Herman-Giddens et al., "Secondary sexual characteristics and menses in young girls seen in office practice: a study from the Pediatric Research in Office Settings network," *Pediatrics* 99, no. 4 (Apr 1997): 505–12.

68. P. Pasquet et al., "Age at menarche and urbanization in Cameroon: current status and secular trends," *Ann Hum Biol* (France) 26, no. 1 (Jan–Feb, 1999): 89–97.

69. L Spinney, "Hispanic Girls Reach Puberty Later," *BioMednews*, report on AACR conference, www.biomednet.com, (April 12, 1999).

70. R.M. Malina et al., "Age of menarche in Oaxaca, Mexico, schoolgirls, with comparative data for other areas of Mexico," *Ann Hum Biol* (Mexico) 4, no. 6 (Nov 1977): 551–8.

71. S. Tsuzaki et al., "Lack of linkage between height and weight and age at menarche during the secular shift in growth of Japanese children," *Ann Hum Biol* 16, no. 5 (Sep–Oct 1989): 429–36.

72. K. Liestol and M. Rosenberg, "Height, weight and menarcheal age of schoolgirls in Oslo — an update," *Ann Hum Biol* (Norway) 22, no. 3 (May–Jun 1995): 199–205.

73. B.A. Stoll, "Western diet, early puberty, and breast cancer risk," *Breast Cancer Res Treat* 49, no. 3 (Jun 1998): 187–93.

74. J.S. Suh et al., "Menstrual and reproductive factors related to the risk of breast cancer in Korea. Ovarian hormone effect on breast cancer," *J Korean Med Sci* (Korea) 11, no. 6 (Dec 1996): 501–8.

75. C.C. Hsieh et al., "Age at menarche, age at menopause, height and obesity as risk factors for breast cancer: associations and interactions in an international case-control study," *Int J Cancer* 46, no. 5 (Nov 15, 1990): 796–800.

76. C.S. Berkey, "Adolescence and breast carcinoma risk," *Cancer* 85, no. 11 (Jun 1999): 2400–9.

77. B.A. Stoll, "Western nutrition and the insulin resistance syndrome: a link to breast cancer," *Eur J Clin Nutr* 53, no. 2 (Feb 1999): 83–7.

78. *MMWR Morb Mortal Wkly Rep* 43, no. 15 (Apr 22, 1994): 279–81.

79. S.P. Gaskill et al., "Breast cancer mortality and diet in the United States," *Cancer Res* 39, no. 9 (Sep 1979): 3628, no. 37.

80. H. Ishimoto et al., "Epidemiological study on relationship between breast cancer mortality and dietary factors," *Tokushima J Exp Med* (Japan) 41, nos. 3–4 (Dec 1994): 103–14.

81. S. Mannisto et al., "Diet and the risk of breast cancer in a case-control study: does the threat of disease have an influence on recall bias? *J Clin Epidemiol* (Finland) 52, no. 5 (May 1999): 429–39.

82. J.L. Freudenheim et al., "Exposure to breastmilk in infancy and the risk of breast cancer," *Epidemiology* 5, no. 3 (May 1994): 324–31.

83. H.A. Weiss et al., "Prenatal and perinatal risk factors for breast cancer in young women," *Epidemiology* 8, no. 2 (Mar 1997): 181–7.

84. A. Mbakop et al., "[Current epidemiology of cancers in Cameroon]," *Bull Cancer* (France) 79, no. 11 (1992): 1101–4.

85. *MMWR Morb Mortal Wkly Rep* 43, no. 15 (Apr 22, 1994): 279–81.

86. K.B. Simondon et al., "Preschool stunting, age at menarche and adolescent height: a longitudinal study in rural Senegal," *Eur J Clin Nutr* (France) 52, no. 6 (Jun 1998): 412–8.

87. F. La Rosa et al., "[Descriptive epidemiology of malignant tumors of the colon and rectum]," *Ann Ig* (Italy) 1, no. 5 (Sep–Oct 1989): 899–922.

88. W. Harris, "Breast Cancer Statistics," vegsource.com, (Oct 15, 1998): 2–3.

89. A. Honegger and R.E. Humbel, "Insulin-like growth factors I and II in fetal and adult bovine serum. Purification, primary structures, and immunological cross-reactivities," *J Biol Chem* 261, no. 2 (Jan 1986): 569–75.

90. T. Nickerson and H. Huynh, "Vitamin D analogue EB1089-induced prostate regression is associated with increased gene expression of insulin-like growth factor binding proteins," *J Endocrinol* 160, no. 2 (Feb 1999): 223–9.

91. E. Petridou et al., "Insulin-like growth factor-I and binding protein-3 in relation to childhood leukaemia," *Int J Cancer* (Greece) 80, no. 4 (Feb 9, 1999): 494–6.

92. J.L. Outwater et al., "Dairy products and breast cancer: the IGF-I, estrogen, and bGH hypothesis," *Med Hypotheses* 48, no. 6 (Jun 1997): 453–61.

93. K. Robbins et al., "Immunological effects of insulin-like growth factor-I—enhancement of immunoglobulin syntheses," *Clin Exp Immunol* 95, no. 2 (Feb 1994): 337–42.

94. P. Cohen et al., "Biological effects of prostate specific antigen as an insulin-like growth factor binding protein-3 protease," *J Endocrinol* 142, no. 3 (Sep 1994): 407–15.

95. D.M. Peehl et al., "The insulin-like factor system in the prostate," World J Urol 13, no. 5 (1995): 306–11.

96. J.C. Chen et al., "Insulin-like growth factor-binding protein enhancement of insulin-like growth factor-I (IGF-I)-mediated DNA synthesis and IGF-I binding in a human breast carcinoma cell line," J Cell Physiol 159, no. 1 (Jan 1994): 69–78.

97. N. Rosen et al., "Insulin-like growth factors in human breast cancer," Breast Cancer Res Treat 18, suppl. 1 (May 1991): S55–62.

98. A.V. Lee et al., "Enhancement of insulin-like growth factor signaling in human breast-cancer: estrogen regulation of insulin receptor substrate-1 expression in vitro and in vivo," Mol Endocrinol 13, no. 5 (May 1999): 787–96.

99. E.P. Beck et al., "Identification of insulin and insulin-like growth factor I (IGF I) receptors in ovarian cancer tissue," Gynecol Oncol (Germany) 53, no. 2 (May 1994): 196–201.

100. M. Resnicoff et al., "Insulin-like growth factor-1 and its receptor mediate the autocrine proliferation of human ovarian carcinoma cell lines," Lab Invest 69, no. 6 (Dec 1993): 756–60.

101. M.S. Piver, "Prophylactic oophorectomy: Reducing the U.S. death rate from epithelial ovarian cancer. A continuing debate," Oncologist 1, no. 5 (1996): 326–330.

102. R.P. Glick et al., "Insulin-like growth factors in central nervous system tumors," J Neurooncol 35, no. 3 (Dec 1997): 315–25.

103. E.E. Wheeler and D.N. Challacombe, "The trophic action of growth hormone, insulin-like growth factor-I, and insulin on human duodenal mucosa cultured in vitro," Gut 40, no. 1 (Jan 1997): 57–60.

104. C.C. Kappel et al., "Human osteosarcoma cell lines are dependent on insulin-like growth factor I for in vitro growth," Cancer Res 54, no. 10 (May 15, 1994): 2803–7.

105. S.T. Wolford and C.J. Argoudelis, "Measurement of estrogens in cow's milk, human milk, and dairy products," J Dairy Sci 62, no. 9 (Sep 1979): 1458–63.

106. E.P. Diamandis and H. Yu, "Nonprostatic sources of prostate-specific antigen," Urol Clin North Am 24, no. 2 (May 1997): 275–82.

107. S.S. Epstein, "Unlabeled milk from cows treated with biosynthetic growth hormones: a case of regulatory abdication," Int J Health Serv 26, no. 1 (1996): 173–85.

108. Robert Cohen, Milk, The Deadly Poison (Englewood Cliffs, N.J.: Argus, 1998): 310.

109. www.foxBGHsuit.com.

110. W.T. Lee et al., "Relationship between long-term calcium intake and bone mineral content of children aged from birth to 5 years," Br J Nutr (Hong Kong) 70, no. 1 (Jul 1993): 235–48.

111. W.T. Lee et al., "A randomized double-blind controlled calcium supplementation trial, and bone and height acquisition in children," Br J Nutr (Hong Kong) 74, no. 1 (Jul 1995): 125–39.

112. J.C. Cheng et al., "Determinants of axial and peripheral bone mass in Chinese adolescents," Arch Dis Child (Hong Kong) 78, no. 6 (Jun 1998): 524–30.

113. J.C. Cheng et al., "Axial and peripheral bone mineral acquisition: a 3-year longitudinal study in Chinese adolescents," Eur J Pediatr (Hong Kong) 158, no. 6 (Jun 1999): 506–12.

114. A.M. Fehily et al., "Factors affecting bone density in young adults," Am J Clin Nutr (England) 56, no. 3 (Sep 1992): 579–86.

115. J. Cadogan et al., "Milk intake and bone mineral acquisition in adolescent girls: randomised, controlled intervention trial" BMJ (England) 315, no. 7118 (Nov 15, 1997): 1255–60.

116. I.D. Griffiths and R.M. Francis, "Results in two groups are not so different," BMJ (England) 316, no. 7146 (Jun 6, 1998): 1747–8.

117. C.C. Johnston et al., "Calcium supplementation and increases in bone mineral density in children," N Engl J Med 327, no. 2 (Jul 1992): 82–7.

118. N.A. Breslau et al., "Relationship of animal protein-rich diet to kidney stone formation and calcium metabolism," J Clin Endocrinol Metab 66, no. 1 (Jan 1988): 140–6.

119. U.S. Barzel and L.K. Massey, "Excess dietary protein can adversely affect bone," J Nutr 128, no. 6 (Jun 1998): 1051–3.

120. L.H. Allen et al., "Protein-induced hypercalcuria: a long term study" Am J Clin Nutr 32, no. 4 (Apr 1979): 741–9.

121. M.B. Zemel, "Calcium utilization: effect of varying level and source of dietary protein," Am J Clin Nutr 48, no. 3, suppl. (Sep 1988): 880–3.

122. D.M. Hegsted, "Calcium and Osteoporosis?" Adv Nutr Res 9 (1994): 119–28.

123. B.L. Riggs et al., "Dietary calcium intake and rates of bone loss in women," J Clin Invest 80, no. 4 (Oct 1987): 979–82.

124. A. Tavani et al., "Calcium, dairy products, and the risk of hip fracture in women in northern Italy" Epidemiology (Italy) 6, no. 5 (Sep 1995): 554–7.

125. D. Feskanich et al., "Milk, dietary calcium, and bone fractures in women: a 12-year prospective study," Am J Public Health 87, no. 6 (Jun 1997): 992–7.

126. W. Owusu et al., "Calcium intake and the incidence of forearm and hip fractures among men," J Nutr 127, no. 9 (Sep 1997): 1782–7.

127. D. M. Hegsted, "Calcium and Osteoporosis," *J Nutr* 116, no 11 (Nov 1986): 2316–9.

128. R.L. Bauer, "Ethnic differences in hip fracture: a reduced incidence in Mexican Americans," *Am J Epidemiol* 127, no. 1 (Jan 1988): 145–9.

129. B.J. Abelow et al., "Cross-cultural association between dietary animal protein and hip fracture: a hypothesis," *Calcif Tissue Int* 50, no. 1 (Jan 1992): 14–8.

130. C. Cooper et al., "Hip fractures in the elderly: a world-wide projection," *Osteoporosis Int* 2, no. 6 (Nov 1992): 285–9.

131. T. Fujita, "Osteoporosis in Japan: factors contributing to the low incidence of hip fracture," *Adv Nutr Res* (Japan) 9 (1994): 89–99.

132. W.J. MacLennan, "History of arthritis and bone rarefaction evidence from paleopathology onwards," *Scott Med J* (England) 44, no. 1 (Feb 1999): 18–20.

133. R. Cohen, "Who is behind the National Osteoporosis Foundation and what is their agenda?" Dairy Education Board Archives, www.notmilk.com, (May 23, 1999): 1–5.

134. "Optimal calcium intake" *NIH Consens Statement* 12, no. 4 (Jun 6–8, 1994): 1–31.

135. K.K. Kim et al., "Nutritional status of Chinese-, Korean-, and Japanese-American elderly," *J Am Diet Assoc* 93, no. 12 (Dec 1993): 1416–22.

136. E.C. van Beresteijn et al., "Relationship between the calcium-to-protein ratio in milk and the urinary calcium excretion in healthy adults — a controlled crossover study," *Am J Clin Nutr* (Netherlands) 52, no. 1 (Jul 1990): 142–6.

137. M.F. Rolland-Cachera et al., "Influence of macronutrients on adiposity development: a follow up study of nutrition and growth from 10 months to 8 years of age," *Int J Obes Relat Metab Disord* (France) 19, no. 8 (Aug 1995): 573–8.

138. L.H. Kushi et al., "Health implications of Mediterranean diets in light of contemporary knowledge. 1. Plant foods and dairy products," *Am J Clin Nutr* 61, suppl 6 (Jun 1995): 1407S–1415S.

139. M. Nestle, "Food lobbies, the food pyramid, and U.S. nutrition policy," *Int J Health Serv* 23, no. 3 (1993): 483–96.

140. W.C. Willett, Department of Nutrition, Harvard School of Public Health, in the *Boston Globe*, June 8, 1999.

Chapter 12: Colic to Ear infections, Behavior to Bedwetting

1. E. Odak, "The incidence and clinical manifestation of food allergy in unselected Polish infants: follow-up from birth to one year of age," *Rocz Akad Med Bialymst* (Poland) 42, no. 1 (1997): 196–204.

2. Heather M. Little, "Food may be causing kids' problems," *WOMANEWS*, 29 October 1995, sec. 13.

3. F. Savino and R. Oggero, "[Management of infantile colics]," *Minerva Pediatr* (Italy) 48 (July 1996): 7–8, 313–19.

4. R. Oggero et al., "Dietary modifications versus Dicyclomine hydrochloride in the treatment of severe infantile colics," *Acta Paediatr* (Italy) 83, no. 2 (Feb 1994): 222–5.

5. G. Iacono et al., "Severe infantile colic and food intolerance: a long-term prospective study," *J Pediatr Gastroenterol Nutr* 12, no. 3 (April 1991): 332–5.

6. J.P. Campbell, "[Dietary therapy of infant colic: a double-blind study]," *Cesk Pediatr* (Czechoslovakia) 48, no. 4 (April 1993): 199–202.

7. J.J. Verwimp et al., "Symptomatology and growth in infants with cow's milk protein intolerance using two different whey-protein hydrolysate based formulas in a primary health care setting," *Eur J Clin Nutr* (Netherlands) 49, suppl. 1 (Sept 1995): S39–48.

8. T.M. Nsouli et al., "Role of food allergy in serous otitis media," *Ann Allergy* 73, no. 3 (Sep 1994): 215–9.

9. A. Ojuawo et al., "Non-infective colitis in infancy: evidence in favour of minor immunodeficiency in its pathogenesis," *Arch Dis Child* (London) 76, no. 4 (April 1997): 345–8.

10. A. Armisén Pedrejon et al., "[Colitis induced by a food allergen. A report of 20 cases]," *An Esp Pediatr* (Spain) 44, no. 1 (Jan 1996): 21–4.

11. H.R. Jenkins et al., "Food Allergy: the major cause of infantile colitis," *Arch Dis Child* 59 (1984): 326–9.

12. Jonathan Brostoff and Stephen J. Challacombe, eds., *Food Allergy and Intolerance*, chapter 6 by Stephan Strobel and John G. Shields (London: Baillière Tindall, 1987), 112–5.

13. V. Alun Jones et al., "Crohn's disease: maintenance of remission by diet," *Lancet* 2 (1985): 177–80.

14. H. Malchow et al., "European cooperative Crohn's disease study: results of drug treatment," *Gastroenterol* 86 (1984): 249–66.

15. J.O. Hunter, "Nutritional factors in inflammatory bowel disease," *Eur J Gastroenterol Hepatol* 10, no. 3 (1998): 235–7.

16. P. Knoflach et al., "Serum antibodies to cow's milk proteins in ulcerative colitis and Crohn's disease," *Gastroenterology* 92, no. 2 (Feb 1987): 479–85.

17. I. Grazioli, et al., "[Food intolerance and irritable bowel syndrome of childhood: clinical efficacy of oral sodium cromoglycate and elimination diet]," *Minerva Pediatr* (Italy) 45, no. 6 (Jun 1993): 253–8.

18. J. Egger et al., "Is migraine food allergy?" *Lancet* 2 (1983): 865–9.

19. M. Boris and F.S. Mandel, "Foods and additives are common causes of the attention-deficit hyperactive disorder in children," *Ann Allergy* 72, no. 5 (May 1994): 462–8.

20. W.G. Crook et al., "Systemic manifestations due to allergy," *Pediatric* 27 (1961): 790–9.

21. T. Uhlig et al., "Topographic mapping of brain electrical activity in children with food-induced attention-deficit hyperkinetic disorder," *Eur J Pediatr* 156, no. 7 (July 1997): 557–61.

22. J. Egger et al., "Effect of diet treatment on enuresis in children with migraine or hyperkinetic behavior," *Clin Pediatr* (Philadelphia) 31, no. 5 (May 1992): 302–7.

23. W.L. Robson et al., "Enuresis in children with attention-deficit hyperactivity disorder," *South Med J* 90, no. 5 (May 1997): 503–5.

24. Jonathan Brostoff and Stephen J. Challacombe, eds., *Food Allergy and Intolerance*, chapter 11 by W. Allen Walker (London: Baillière Tindall, 1987), 219.

25. G. Iacono et al., "Persistent cow's milk protein intolerance in infants: the changing faces of the same disease," *Clin Exp Allergy* (Italy) 28, no. 7 (Jul 1998): 817–23.

26. J.L. Eseverri et al., "[Epidemiology and chronology of allergic diseases and their risk factors]," *Allergol Immunopathol* (Spain) 26, no. 3 (May–Jun 1998): 90–7.

27. F. Cavataio et al., "Gastroesophageal reflux associated with cow's milk allergy in infants: which diagnostic examinations are useful?" *Am J Gastroenterol* 91, no. 6 (Jun 1996): 1215–20.

28. Jonathan Brostoff and Stephen J. Challacombe, eds., *Food Allergy and Intolerance*, chapter 18 by John W. Gerrard (London: Baillière Tindall, 1987), 349–50.

29. C. Power and O. Manor, "Asthma, enuresis, and chronic illness: long term impact on height," *Arch Dis Child* 73, no. 4 (Oct 1995): 298–304.

30. J. Egger et al., "Effect of diet treatment on enuresis in children with migraine or hyperkinetic behavior," *Clin Pediatr* 31, no. 5 (May 1992): 302–7.

31. W.L. Robson et al., "Enuresis in children with attention-deficit hyperactivity disorder," *South Med J* 90, no. 5 (May 1997): 503–5.

32. M. Boris and F.S. Mandel, "Foods and additives are common causes of the attention-deficit hyperactive disorder in children," *Ann Allergy* 722, no. 5 (May 1994): 462–8.

33. J. Egger et al., "Controlled trial of oligoantigenic treatment in the hyperkinetic syndrome," *Lancet* 1, no. 8428 (Mar 1985): 540–5.

34. J. Breakey, "The role of diet and behaviour in childhood," *J Paediatr Child Health* 33, no. 3 (Jun 1997): 190–4.

35. T. Uhlig, "Topographic mapping of brain electrical activity in children with food-induced attention-deficit hyperkinetic disorder," *Eur J Pediatr* (Australia) 156, no. 7 (Jul 1997): 557–61.

36. B.J. Kaplan et al., "Dietary replacement in preschool-aged hyperactive boys," *Pediatrics* (Canada) 83, no. 1 (Jan 1989): 7–17.

37. N. Roth et al., "Coincidence of attention-deficit disorder and atopic disorders in children: empirical findings and hypothetical background," *J Abnorm Child Psychol* (Germany) 19, no. 1 (Feb 1991): 1–13.

38. C.E. Price et al., "Associations of excessive irritability with common illnesses and food intolerance," *Paediatr Perinat Epidemiol* (London) 4, no. 2 (Apr 1990): 156–60.

39. U.A. Hunziker and R.G. Barr, "Increased carrying reduces infant crying: a randomized controlled trial," *Pediatrics* 77, no. 5 (May 1986): 641–8.

40. R.G. Barr et al., "Carrying as colic 'therapy': a randomized controlled trial," *Pediatrics* 87, no. 5 (May 1991): 623–30.

41. R. Oggero, et al., "Dietary modifications versus dicyclomine hydrochloride in the treatment of severe infantile colics," *Acta Paediatr* (Italy) 83, no. 2 (Feb 1994): 222–5.

42. G. Iacono, et al., "Severe infantile colic and food intolerance: a long-term prospective study," *J Pediatr Gastroenterol Nutr* (Italy) 12, no. 3 (Apr 1991): 332–335.

43. R.J. Merritt, et al., "Whey protein hydrolysate formula for infants with gastrointestinal intolerance to cow milk and soy protein in infant formulas," *J Pediatr Gastroenterol Nutr* 11, no. 1 (Jul 1990): 78–82.

44. J.P. Campbell, "Dietary treatment of infant colic: a double-blind study," *J R Coll Gen Pract* 39, no. 318 (Jan 1989): 11–14.

45. L. Lothe and T. Lindberg, "Cow's milk whey protein elicits symptoms of infantile colic in colicky formula-fed infants: a double-blind crossover study," *Pediatrics* (Sweden) 83, no. 2 (Feb 1989): 262–6.

46. M. Weissbluth, et al., "Treatment of infantile colic with dicyclomine hydrochloride," *J Pediatr* 104, no. 6 (Jun 1984): 951–5.

47. L. Lothe, et al., "Cow's milk formula as a cause of infantile colic: a double-blind study," *Pediatrics* (Sweden) 70, no. 1 (Jul 1982): 7–10.

48. I. Jakobsson and T. Lindberg, "Cow's milk proteins cause infantile colic in breast-fed infants: a double-blind crossover study," *Pediatrics* (Sweden) 71, no. 22 (Feb 1983): 268–71.

49. J.A. Vanderhoof et al., "Intolerance to protein hydrolysate infant formulas: an underrecognized cause of gastrointestinal symptoms in infants," *J Pediatr* 131, no. 5 (Nov 1997): 741–4.

50. D.J. Hill et al., "Challenge confirmation of late-onset reactions to extensively hydrolyzed formulas in infants with multiple food protein intolerance," *J Allergy Clin Immunol* 96, no. 3 (Sep 1995): 386–94.

51. I. Axelsson et al., "Bovine beta-lactoglobulin in the human milk. A longitudinal study during the whole lactation period," *Acta Paediatr Scand* (Sweden) 75, no. 5 (Sep 1986): 702–7.

52. R.A. Hardoin et al., "Colic medication and apparent life-threatening events," *Clin Pediatr (Phila)* 30, no. 5 (May 1991): 281–5.

53. D. Satge et al., "Antenatal therapeutic drug exposure and fetal/neonatal tumours: review of 89 cases," *Paediatr Perinat Epidemiol* (France) 12, no. 1 (Jan 1998): 84–117.

54. J.J. Miller et al., "Breath hydrogen excretion in infants with colic," *Arch Dis Child* (Australia) 64, no. 5 (May 1989): 725–9.

55. R.G. Barr et al., "Effects of formula change on intestinal hydrogen production and crying and fussing behavior," *J Dev Behav Pediatr* (Canada) 12, no. 4 (Aug 1991): 248–53.

56. L. Lothe et al., "Macromolecular absorption in infants with infantile colic," *Acta Paediatr Scand* (Sweden) 79, no. 4 (Apr 1990): 417–21.

57. V. Loening-Baucke, "Urinary incontinence and urinary tract infection and their resolution with treatment of chronic constipation of childhood," *Pediatrics* 100, no. 2, part 1 (Aug 1997): 228–32.

58. G. Iacono et al., "Chronic constipation as a symptom of cow milk allergy," *J Pediatr* 126, no. 1 (Jan 1995): 34–9.

59. G. Iacono et al., "Intolerance of cow's milk and chronic constipation in children," *N Engl J Med* 339, no. 16 (Oct 15, 1998): 1100–4.

60. J. McGrath, "Allergy to cow's milk presenting as chronic constipation," *Br Med J (Clin Res Ed)* 288, no. 6412 (Jan 21, 1984): 36.

61. H.M. Machida, et al., "Allergic colitis in infancy: clinical and pathologic aspects," *J Pediatr Gastroenterol Nutr* (Canada) 19, no. 1 (Jul 1994): 22–6.

62. H.R. Jenkins, et al., "Food allergy: the major cause of infantile colitis," *Arch Dis Child* 59, no. 4 (Apr 1984): 326–9.

63. H. Malchow, et al., "Feasibility and effectiveness of a defined-formula diet regimen in treating active Crohn's disease. European Cooperative Crohn's Disease Study III," *Scand J Gastroenterol* (Denmark) 25, no. 3 (Mar 1990): 235–44.

64. V.A. Jones, et al., "Crohn's disease: maintenance of remission by diet," *Lancet* 2, no. 8448 (Jul 1985): 177–80.

65. H. Malchow, et al., "European Cooperative Crohn's Disease Study (ECCDS): results of drug treatment," *Gastroenterology* 86, no. 2 (Feb 1984): 249–66.

66. T. Poynard, et al., "Meta-analyses of smooth muscle relaxants in the treatment of irritable bowel syndrome," *Aliment Pharmacol Ther* 8, no. 5 (Oct 1994): 499–510.

67. I. Grazioli, et al., "[Food intolerance and irritable bowel syndrome of childhood: clinical efficacy of oral sodium cromoglycate and elimination diet]," *Minerva Pediatr* (Italy) 45, no. 6 (Jun 1993): 253–8.

68. V.A. Jones, et al., "Food intolerance: a major factor in the pathogenesis of irritable bowel syndrome," *Lancet* 2, no. 8308 (Nov 1982): 1115–7.

69. N.E. Sazanova et al., "[Immunological aspects of food intolerance in children during first years of life]," *Pediatriia* (Russia) 3 (1992): 14–18.

70. U. Fagundes-Neto, "Nutritional impact and ultrastructural intestinal alterations in severe infections due to enteropathogenic *Escherichia coli* strains in infants," *J Am Coll Nutr* (Brazil) 15, no. 2 (Apr 1996): 180–5.

71. P. McClean et al., "Surface features of small-intestine mucosa in childhood diarrheal disorders," *J Pediatr Gastroenterol Nutr* (Ireland) 23, no. 5 (Dec 1996): 538–46.

72. K.G. Dewey et al., "Differences in morbidity between breast-fed and formula-fed infants," *J Pediatr* 126, no. 5, part 1 (May 1995): 696–702.

73. Y. Lerman et al., "Epidemiology of acute diarrheal diseases in children in a high standard of living rural settlement in Israel," *Pediatr Infect Dis J* (Israel) 13, no. 2 (Feb 1994): 116–22.

74. S.C. Fuchs et al., "Case-control study of risk of dehydrating diarrhoea in infants in vulnerable period after full weaning," *BMJ* (Brazil) 313, no. 7054 (Aug 1996): 391–4.

75. B.P. Lanphear et al., "Increasing prevalence of recurrent otitis media among children in the United States," *Pediatrics* 99, no. 3 (Mar 1997): E1.

76. Kathi Kemper, M.D., M.P.H., *The Holistic Pediatrician*, (New York: HarperCollins, 1996), 180.

77. D.S. Hurst, "Association of otitis media with effusion and allergy as demonstrated by intradermal skin testing and eosinophil cationic protein levels in both middle ear effusions and mucosal biopsies," *Laryngoscope* 106, no. 9, part 1 (Sep 1996): 1128–37.

78. T.M. Nsouli et al., "Role of food allergy in serous otitis media," *Ann Allergy* 73, no. 3 (Sep 1994): 215–9.

79. U.M. Saarinen et al., "Increased IgM-type betalactoglobulin antibodies in children with recurrent otitis media," *Allergy* 38, no. 8 (Nov 1983): 571–6.

80. M. Tachibana et al., "Experimental immune complex otitis media: localization of IgG by protein A-gold technique," *Auris Nasus Larynx* 12, suppl. 1 (1985): S86–8.

81. D.S. Hurst, "Allergy management of refractory serous otitis media," *Otolaryngol Head Neck Surg* 102, no. 6 (Jun 1990): 664–9.

82. M.J. Derebery and K.I. Berliner, *Am J Otol* 18, no. 2 (Mar 1997): 160–5.

83. J. Egger et al., "Oligoantigenic diet treatment of children with epilepsy and migraine," *J Pediatr* (England) 114, no. 1 (Jan 1989): 51–8.

84. K.M. Bell et al., "Risk factors associated with chronic fatigue syndrome in a cluster of pediatric cases," *Rev Infect Dis* 13, suppl. 1 (Jan–Feb 1991): S32–8.

85. D.J. Clauw, "The pathogenesis of chronic pain and fatigue syndromes, with special reference to fibromyalgia," *Med Hypotheses* 44, no. 5 (May 1995): 369–78.

86. J.E. Gomborone et al., "Prevalence of irritable bowel syndrome in chronic fatigue," *J R Coll Physicians Lond* (England) 30, no. 6 (Nov 1996): 512–3.

87. L. Borish et al., "Chronic fatigue syndrome: identification of distinct subgroups on the basis of allergy and psychologic variables," *J Allergy Clin Immunol* 102, no. 2 (Aug 1998): 222–30.

88. S. Paterson, "Food hypersensitivity in 20 dogs with skin and gastrointestinal signs," *J Small Anim Pract* 36, no. 12 (Dec 1995): 529–34.

89. B. Ballauf, "[Feed allergy in dogs and cats — not only a gastrointestinal problem]," *Tierarztl Prax* (Germany) 21, no. 1 (Feb 1993): 53–6.

90. J. Egger et al., "Is migraine food allergy? A double-blind controlled trial of oligoantigenic diet treatment," *Lancet* 2, no. 8355 (Oct 1983): 865–9.

91. G. Guariso et al., "[Migraine and food intolerance: a controlled study in pediatric patients]," *Pediatr Med Chir* (Italy) 15, no. 1 (Jan–Feb 1993): 57–61.

92. M.L. Pacor et al., "[Migraine and food]," *Recenti Prog Med* (Italy) 80, no. 2 (Feb 1989): 53–5.

93. J.A. Anderson, "Mechanisms in adverse reactions to food: The brain," *Allergy* 50, no. 20 suppl. (1995): 78–81.

94. W.H. Yang et al., "The monosodium glutamate symptom complex: assessment in a double-blind, placebo-controlled, randomized study," *J Allergy Clin Immunol* 99, no. 6, part 1 (Jun 1997): 757–62.

95. S.K. Van den Eeden et al., "Aspartame ingestion and headaches: a randomized crossover trial," *Neurology* 44, no. 10 (Oct 1994): 1787–93.

96. A. Oehling et al., "Skin manifestations and immunological parameters in childhood food allergy," *J Investig allergol clin immunol* (Spain) 7, no. 3 (May–Jun 1997): 155–9.

97. N.E. Sazanova et al., "[Immunological aspects of food intolerance in children during first years of life]," *Pediatriia* (Russia) 3 (1992): 14–8.

98. H. Majamaa and E. Isolauri, "Evaluation of the gut mucosal barrier: evidence for increased antigen transfer in children with atopic eczema," *J Allergy Clin Immunol* (Finland) 97, no. 4 (Apr 1996): 985–90.

99. J.M. James et al., "Respiratory reactions provoked by double-blind food challenges in children," *Am J Respir Crit Care Med* 149, no. 1 (Jan 1994): 59–64.

100. D.S. Feigin, "Allergic diseases in the lungs," *Crit Rev Diagn Imaging*, 25, no. 2 (1986): 159–76.

101. N.S. Zhong, "New insights into risk factors of asthma," *Respirology*, (China) 1, no. 3 (Sep 1996): 159–66.

102. John Mansfield, *Asthma Epidemic*, (London: HarperCollins, 1997), 1.

103. John Mansfield, *Asthma Epidemic*, (London: HarperCollins, 1997), 14–27.

104. J.M. James et al., "Respiratory reactions provoked by double-blind food challenges in children," *Am J Respir Crit Care Med* 149, no. 1 (Jan 1994): 59–64.

105. M. Kulig et al., "Long-lasting sensitization to food during the first two years precedes allergic airway disease. The MAS Study Group, Germany," *Pediatr Allergy Immunol* (Germany) 9, no. 2 (May 1998): 61–7.

106. E.R. Weeke, "Epidemiology of allergic diseases in children," *Rhinol Suppl* 13 (Sep 1992): 5–12.

107. D.C. Heiner, "Respiratory diseases and food allergy," *Ann Allergy* 53, no. 6, part 2 (Dec 1984): 657–64.

108. S.M. Tariq et al., "The prevalence of and risk factors for atopy in early childhood: a whole population birth cohort study," *J Allergy Clin Immunol* 101, no. 5 (May 1998): 587–93.

109. T.F. Boat et al., "Hyperreactivity to cow milk in young children with pulmonary hemosiderosis and cor pulmonale secondary to nasopharyngeal obstruction," *J Pediatr* 87, no. 1 (Jul 1975): 23–9.

110. U. Ones et al., "Prevalence of childhood asthma in Istanbul, Turkey," *Allergy* (Turkey) 52, no. 5 (May 1997): 570–5.

111. L.D. Voss et al., "Short stature at school entry — an index of social deprivation? (The Wessex Growth Study)," *Child Care Health Dev* (England) 24, no. 2 (Mar 1998): 145–56.

112. F. Kristmundsdottir and T.J. David, "Growth impairment in children with atopic eczema," *J R Soc Med* 80, no. 1 (Jan 1987): 9–12.

113. W.F. Baum et al., "Effect of bronchial asthma on growth and physical development," *Arztl Jugendkd* 81, no. 5 (1990): 379–83.

114. T.J. David, "Short stature in children with atopic eczema," *Acta Derm Venereol Suppl (Stockh)* (England) 144 (1989): 41–4.

115. A. Kahn et al., "Milk intolerance in children with persistent sleeplessness: a prospective double-blind crossover evaluation," *Pediatrics* 84, no. 4 (Oct 1989): 595–603.

116. J. Jarvinen et al., "Some local and systemic factors related to tongue inflammation," *Proc Finn Dent* 85, no. 3 (1989): 199–209.

117. S. Lucarelli et al., "Food allergy and infantile autism," *Panminerva Med* (Italy) 37, no. 3 (Sep 1995): 137–41.

118. G. Rostoker et al., "Mucosal immunity in primary glomerulonephritis: II. Study of the serum IgA subclass repertoire to food and airborne antigens," *Nephron* 59, no. 4 (1991): 561–6.

119. S. Jackson et al., "IgA-containing immune complexes after challenge with food antigens in patients with IgA nephropathy," *Clin Exp Immunol* 89, no. 2 (Aug 1992): 315–20.

120. S. Lucarelli et al., "Food allergy in cystic fibrosis," *Minerva Pediatr* (Italy) 46, no. 12 (Dec 1994): 543–8.

121. S. Coren, "Handedness and allergic response," *Int J Neurosci* (Canada) 76, nos. 3–4 (Jun 1994): 231–6.

122. R.E. Weinstein and D.R. Pieper, "Altered cerebral dominance in an atopic population," *Brain Behav Immun* 2, no. 3 (Sep 1988): 235–41.

123. M. Hassler and D. Gupta, "Functional brain organization, handedness, and immune vulnerability in musicians and non-musicians," *Neuropsychologia* (Germany) 31, no. 7 (Jul 1993): 655–60.

124. C.P. Benbow, "Physiological correlates of extreme intellectual precocity," *Neuropsychologia* 24, no. 5 (1986): 719–25.

125. G. Martino and E. Winner, "Talents and disorders: relationships among handedness, sex, and college major," *Brain Cogn* 29, no. 1 (Oct 1995): 66–84.

126. V. Dolezalova and D. Mottlova, "[Relation between myopia and intelligence]," *Cesk Oftalmol* (Czechoslovakia) 51, no. 4 (Sep 1995): 235–9.

127. D.M. Fergusson et al., "Perinatal factors and atopic disease in childhood," *Clin Exp Allergy* (New Zealand) 27, no. 12 (Dec 1997): 1394–401.

128. K.M. Godfrey et al., "Disproportionate fetal growth and raised IgE concentration in adult life," *Clin Exp Allergy* (England) 24, no. 7 (Jul 1994): 641–8.

129. F. Lorente et al., "[Preventive measures for allergic disease]," *Allergol Immunopathol (Madr)* (Spain) 26, no. 3 (May–Jun 1998): 101–13.

Chapter 13: Allergy Matters

1. A. Ojuawo et al., "Non-infective colitis in infancy: evidence in favour of minor immunodeficiency in its pathogenesis," *Arch Dis Child* (London) 76, no. 4 (April 1997): 345–8.

2. A. Armisén Pedrejon et al., "[Colitis induced by a food allergen. A report of 20 cases]," *An Esp Pediatr* (Spain) 44, no. 1 (Jan 1996): 21–4.

3. M.J. Solomon and M. Schnitzler, "Cancer and inflammatory bowel disease: bias, epidemiology, surveillance, and treatment," *World J Surg* (Australia) 22, no. 4 (April 1998): 352–8.

4. M.B. Ribeiro et al., "Colorectal adenocarcinoma in Crohn's disease," *Ann Surg* 2, no. 223 (Feb 1996): 186–93.

5. P. Karlen et al., "Increased risk of cancer in ulcerative colitis: a population-based cohort study," *Am J Gastroenterol* (Sweden) 94, no. 4 (Apr 1999): 1047–52.

6. A. Ferguson and K. Kingstone, "Coeliac disease and malignancies," *Acta Paediatr* suppl (UK) 412 (May 1996): 78–81.

7. R. Barreto-Zuniga et al., "Significance of *Helicobacter pylori* infection as a risk factor in gastric cancer: serological and histological studies," *J Gastroenterol* (Mexico) 32, no. 3 (Jun 1997): 289–94.

8. J. Markowitz et al., "Endoscopic screening for dysplasia and mucosal aneuploidy in adolescents and young adults with childhood-onset colitis," *Am J Gastroenterol* 92, no. 11 (Nov 1997): 2001–6.

9. K. Wasowska Królikowska et al., "[Morphological, microstereological, and immunohistoenzymological studies of the jejuni of infants with recurrent constructive bronchitis and chronic diarrhea due to cow's milk protein allergy]," *Pediatr Pol* (Poland) 71, no. 5 (May 1996): 397–403.

10. Jonathan Brostoff and Stephen J. Challacombe, *Food Allergy and Intolerance* (London: Baillière Tindall, 1987), 22, 112, 129, 243–5, 575.

11. Jonathan Brostoff et al., *Immunology*, fifth edition (London: Mosby, 1998), 58.

12. T. Voros-Balog et al., "[Epidemiologic survey of tongue lesions and analysis of the etiologic factors involved,]" *Fogorv Sz* (Hungary) 92, no. 5 (May 1999): 157–63.

13. S. Salardi et al., "*Helicobacter pylori* and type 1 diabetes mellitus in children," *J Pediatr Gastroenterol Nutr* (Italy) 28, no. 3 (Mar 1999): 307–9.

14. M Pocecco et al., "High risk of *Helicobacter pylori* infection associated with cow's milk antibodies in young diabetics." *Acta Paediatr* 86, no. 7 (Jul 1997): 700–3.

15. E. Odak, "The incidence and clinical manifestation of food allergy in unselected Polish infants: follow-up from birth to one year of age," *Rocz Akad Med Bialymst* (Poland) 42, no. 1 (1997): 196–204.

16. A. Armisén Pedrejon et al., "[Colitis induced by a food allergen. A report of 20 cases]," *An Esp Pediatr* (Spain) 44, no. 1 (Jan 1996): 21–4.

17. I. Polanco, "Current status of digestive intolerance to food protein," *J Pediatr* 121 (Nov 1992): S108–10.

18. H.R. Jenkins et al., "Food Allergy: the major cause of infantile colitis," *Arch Dis Child* 59 (1984): 326–9.

19. J.W. Gerrard, "Familial recurrent rhinorrhea and bronchitis due to cow's milk," *JAMA* 198 (1966): 605–7.

20. J. Egger et al., "Is migraine food allergy?" *Lancet* 2 (1983): 865–9.

21. A.S. Goldman et al., "Milk allergy: I. Oral challenge with milk and isolated proteins in allergic children," *Pediatrics* 32 (1963): 425–43.

22. Jonathan Brostoff and Stephen J. Challacombe, eds., *Food Allergy and Intolerance*, chapter 18 by John W. Gerrard (London: Baillière Tindall, 1987), 344–55.

23. John Hermon-Taylor et al., "Grand Round: Mycobacterium paratuberculosis cervical lymphadenitis, followed five years later by terminal ileitis similar to Crohn's disease," *BMJ* 316 (1998): 449–453.

24. R.K. Chandra, "Five-year follow-up of high-risk infants with family history of allergy who were exclusively breast-fed or fed partial whey hydrolysate, soy, and conventional cow's milk formulas," *J Pediatr Gastroenterol Nutr* (Canada) 24, no. 4 (April 1997): 380–8.

25. S. Halken, A. Host et al., "[Prevention of allergy in infants. A prospective study of 159 high-risk children]," *Ugeskr Laeger* (Denmark) 156, no. 3 (Jan 17 1994): 308–12.

26. I. Polanco, "Current status of digestive intolerance to food protein," *J Pediatr* 121 (Nov 1992): S108–10.

27. F.G. Graeff et al., "Dual role of 5-HT in defense and anxiety," *Neurosoc Biobehav Rev* (Brazil) 21, no. 6 (Nov 1997): 791–9.

28. J.C. Shih et al., "Role of MAO A and B in neurotransmitter metabolism and behavior," *Pol J Pharmacol* 51, no. 1 (Jan–Feb 1999): 25–9.

29. M. Nicolodi et al., "The way to serotonergic use and abuse in migraine," *Int J Clin Pharmacol* (Italy) 17, nos. 2–3 (1997): 79–84.

30. X. Baur and A. Czuppon, "Diagnostic validation of specific IgE antibody concentrations, skin prick testing, and challenge tests in chemical workers with symptoms of sensitivity to different anhydrides," *J Allergy Clin Immunol* (Germany) 96, no. 4 (Oct 1995): 489–94.

31. W.J. Meggs et al., "Prevalence and nature of allergy and chemical sensitivity in a general population," *Arch Environ Health* 51, no. 4 (Jul–Aug 1996): 275–82.

32. B.A. Sorg et al., "Proposed animal neurosensitization model for multiple chemical sensitivity in studies with formalin," *Toxicology* 111, nos. 1–3 (Jul 17, 1996): 135–45.

33. L.R. Goldman, "Chemicals and children's environment: what we don't know about risks" *Environ Health Perspect* 106, suppl. 3 (Jun 1998): 875–80.

34. Jonathan Brostoff and Stephen J. Challacombe, eds., *Food Allergy and Intolerance*, chapter 18 by John W. Gerrard (London: Baillière Tindall, 1987), 349–50.

35. J. Egger et al., "Effect of diet treatment on enuresis in children with migraine or hyperkinetic behavior," *Clin Pediatr* (Philadelphia) 31, no. 5 (May 1992): 302–7.

36. P.F. Kilshaw and H. Hester-Slade, "Passage of ingested protein into the blood during gastrointestinal hypersensitivity reactions experiments in the preruminant calf," *Clin Exp Immunol* 6 (1980): 45.

37. P.L. Lim and D. Rowley, "The effect of antibody on the intestinal absorption of macromolecules and on intestinal permeability in adult mice," *Int Arch Allergy Appl Immunol* 68 (1982): 41–6.

38. S. Husby, "Dietary antigens: uptake and humoral immunity in man," *Institute of Medical Microbiology APMIS Suppl* (Denmark) 1 (1988): 1–40.

39. Jonathan Brostoff and Stephen J. Challacombe, eds., *Food Allergy and Intolerance*, chapter 2 by C. N. Mallinson (London: Baillière Tindall, 1987), 45.

40. J.A. Lovegrove et al., "Transfer of cow's milk beta-lactoglobulin to human serum after a milk load: a pilot study," *Gut* 34, no. s (Feb 1993): 203–7.

41. Jonathan Brostoff et al., *Immunology*, fifth edition (London: Mosby, 1998), 336.

42. John Hermon-Taylor et al., "Grand Round: Mycobacterium paratuberculosis cervical lymphadenitis, followed five years later by terminal ileitis similar to Crohn's disease," *BMJ* 316 (1998): 449–53.

43. G.C.L. Du Mont et al., "Gastrointestinal permeability in food allergic eczematous children," *Clin Allergy* 14 (1984): 55–9.

44. Jonathan Brostoff et al., *Immunology*, fifth edition (London: Mosby, 1998), 315.

45. James Braly, M.D., *Dr. Braly's Food Allergy and Nutrition Revolution* (New Canaan, Connecticut: Keats Publishing, Inc., 1992), 59.

46. C.S. Miller, "Chemical sensitivity: symptom, syndrome or mechanism for disease?" *Toxicology* 111, nos. 1–3 (Jul 17, 1996): 69–86.

Chapter 14: Discovering, Preventing & Treating Food Allergies

1. R. Forman, "Medical resistance to innovation," *Med Hypotheses* 7, no. 8 (Aug 1981): 1009.

2. *Hippocrates Writings*, edited with an introduction by G.E.R. Lloyd (Harmondsworth: Penguin, 1978), 266.

3. A. Fasano, "Where have all the American celiacs gone?," *Acta Paediatr Suppl* 412 (May 1996): 20–4.

4. M. Frieri et al., "Preliminary investigation on humoral and cellular immune responses to selected food proteins in patients with Crohn's disease," *Ann Allergy* 64, no. 4 (Apr 1990): 345–51.

5. P. Juvonen et al., "Macromolecular absorption and cow's milk allergy," *Arch Dis Child* (Sweden) 66, no. 3 (Mar 1991): 300–3.

6. G.F. Hankard et al., "Increased TIA1-expressing intraepithelial lymphocytes in cow's milk protein intolerance," *J Pediatr Gastroenterol Nutr* (France) 25, no. 1 (Jul 1997): 79–83.

7. K. Wasowska Królikowska et al., "[Morphological, microstereological, and immunohistoenzymological studies of the jejuni of infants with recurrent constructive bronchitis and chronic diarrhea due to cow's milk protein allergy]," *Pediatr Pol*, (Poland) 71, no. 5 (May 1996): 397–403.

8. A. Armisén Pedrejón et al., "[Colitis induced by a food allergen. A report of 20 cases]," *An Esp Pediatr* (Spain) 44, no. 2 (Jan 1996): 21–4.

9. U.M. Saarinen et al., *Allergy* 38, no. 8 (Nov 1983): 571–6.

10. J. Graham, "Food intolerance and its impact on the nation's health. Patient survey," (York, England: York Nutritional Laboratory, 1998).

11. F. Rance et al., "Correlations between skin prick tests using commercial extracts and fresh foods, specific IgE, and food challenges," *Allergy* (France) 52, no. 10 (Oct 1997): 1031–5.

12. H. Scott et al., "Measurements of serum IgA and IgG activities to dietary antigens: A prospective study of the diagnostic usefulness in adult coeliac disease," *Scand J Gastroenterol* 25, no. 3 (Mar 1990): 287–92.

13. K.D. Lust et al., "Maternal intake of cruciferous vegetables and other foods and colic symptoms in exclusively breast-fed infants," *J Am Diet Assoc* 96, no. 1 (Jan 1996): 46–8.

14. B. Wutrich, "Adverse reactions to food additives," *Ann Allergy* 71, no. 4 (Oct 1993): 379–84.

15. G. Fuglsang et al., "Adverse reactions to food additives in children with atopic symptoms," *Allergy* 49, no. 1 (Jan 1994): 31–7.

16. E. Novembre et al., "[Unusual reactions to food additives]," *Pediatr Med Chir* (Italy) 14, no. 1 (Jan–Feb 1992): 39–42.

17. K. Falth-Magnusson and N.I. Kjellman, "Allergy prevention by maternal elimination diet during late pregnancy — a 5-year follow-up of a randomized study," *J Allergy Clin Immunol* (Sweden) 89, no. 3 (Mar 1992): 709–13.

18. J.P. Hanrahan and M. Halonen, "Antenatal interventions in childhood asthma," *Eur Respir J Suppl* 27 (Jul 1998): 46S–51S.

19. J.A. Lovegrove et al., "Dietary factors influencing levels of food antibodies and antigens in breast milk," *Acta Paediatr* (England) 85 no. 7 (Jul 1996): 778–84.

20. R.K. Chandra, "Five-year follow-up of high-risk infants with family history of allergy who were exclusively breast-fed or fed partial whey hydrolysate, soy, and conventional cow's milk formulas," *J Pediatr Gastroenterol Nutr* (Canada) 24, no. 4 (Apr 1997): 380–8.

21. Y. Vandenplas et al., "The long-term effect of a partial whey hydrolysate formula on the prophylaxis of atopic disease," *Eur J Pediatr* (Belgium) 154 no. 6 (Jun 1995): 488–94.

22. G. Stintzing and R. Zetterstrom, "Cow's milk allergy, incidence, and pathogenetic role of early exposure to cow's milk formula," *Acta Paediatr Scand* 68, no. 3 (May 1979): 383–7.

23. Naomi Baumslag, M.D., M.P.H. and Dia L. Michels, *Milk, Money, and Madness: The Culture and Politics of Breastfeeding* (Westport, Connecticut: Bergin & Garvey, 1995), 171–2.

24. F. Savino and R. Oggero, "[Management of infantile colics]," *Minerva Pediatr* (Italy) 48, nos. 7–8 (Jul 1996): 313–9.

25. G. Patriarca et al., "Food allergy in children: results of a standardized protocol for oral desensitization," *Hepatogastroenterology* (Italy) 45, no. 19 (Jan–Feb 1998): 52–8.

26. L.J. Chartrand and E.G. Seidman, "Celiac disease is a lifelong disorder," *Clin Invest Med* 19, no. 5 (Oct 1996): 357–61.

27. J.J. Oppenheimer et al., "Treatment of peanut allergy with rush immunotherapy," *J Allergy Clin Immunol* 90, no. 2 (Aug 1992): 256–62.

28. N.F. Adkinson Jr. et al., "A controlled trial of immunotherapy for asthma in allergic children," *N Engl J Med* 336, no. 5 (Jan 30, 1997): 324–31.

29. Alan Pressman, D.C., Ph.D. and Herbert D. Goodman, M.D., Ph.D., *Treating Asthma, Allergies, and Food Sensitivities* (New York: Berkley Books, 1997), 29–30.

30. W.P. King et al., "Provocation-neutralization: A two-part study. Part II. Subcutaneous neutralization therapy: A multi-center study," *Otolaryngol Head Neck Surg* 99, no. 3 (Sep 1988): 272–7.

31. G.W. Canonica et al., "Cytoprotective drugs: a new perspective in the treatment of adverse reactions to foods," *Ann Allergy* (Italy) 60, no. 6 (Jun 1988): 541–5.

32. M. Kaliner and R. Lemanske, "Inflammatory responses to mast cell granules," *Fed Proc* 43, no. 13 (Oct 1984): 2846–51.

33. B. Skyzydlo-Radomanska et al., "The effect of stimulation and blocking of histamine H-2 receptors on the turnover of the serotonin in different parts of the alimentary tract and the brain of the rat," *Agents Actions* 16, nos. 3–4 (Apr 1985): 183–6.

34. N. Kondo et al., "Suppression of proliferative responses of lymphocytes to food antigens by an anti-allergic drug, ketotifen fumerate, in patients with food sensitive atopic dermatitis," *Int Arch Allergy Immunol* (Japan) 103, no. 3 (1994): 234–8.

35. G. Ciprandi et al., "Ketotifen treatment of adverse reactions to foods: clinical and immunological effects," *Curr Med Res Opin* (Italy) 10, no. 5 (1986): 346–50.

36. G.W. Canonica et al., "Cytoprotective drugs: a new perspective in the treatment of adverse reactions to foods," *Ann Allergy* (Italy) 60, no. 6 (Jun 1988): 541–5.

37. G. Ciprandi et al., "Pirenzepine treatment in urticaria-angioedema syndrome caused by adverse reactions to foods," (Italy) 17, no. 4 (Jul–Aug 1989): 189–92.

38. L. Businco et al., "Evaluation of the efficacy of oral cromolyn sodium or an oligoantigenic diet in children with atopic dermatitis: a multi-center study of 1085 patients," *J Investig Allergol Clin Immunol* (Italy) 6, no. 2 (Mar–Apr 1996): 103–9.

39. A.M. Edwards, "Oral sodium cromoglycate: its use in the management of food allergy," *Clin Exp Allergy* 25, suppl. 1 (Jul 1995):31–3.

40. R.M. Van Elburg et al., "Effect of disodiomcromoglycate on intestinal permeability changes and clinical response during cow's milk challenge," *Pediatr Allergy Immunol* (Netherlands) 4, no. 2 (May 1993): 79–85.

41. A. Ojuawo et al., "Serum zinc, selenium, and copper concentration in children with allergic colitis," *East Afr Med J* (Nigeria) 73, no. 4 (Apr 1996): 236–8.

42. K. Yamada et al., "Effect of unsaturated fatty acids and antioxidants on immunoglobulin production by mesenteric lymph node lymphocytes of Sprague-Dawley rats," *J Biochem* (Japan) 120 no. 1 (Jul 1996): 138–44.

43. D.L. Witsell et al., "Effect of *Lactobacillus acidophilus* on antibiotic-associated gastrointestinal morbidity: a prospective randomized trial," *J Otolaryngol* 24, no. 4 (Aug 1995): 230–3.

44. H. Majamaa and E. Isolauri, "Probiotics: a novel approach in the management of food allergy," *J Allergy Clin Immunol* (Finland) 99, no. 2 (Feb 1997): 179–85.

45. S. Salminen et al., "Clinical uses of probiotics for stabilizing the gut mucosal barrier: successful strains and future challenges," *Antonie Van Leeuwenhoek* (Finland) 70, nos. 2–4 (Oct 1996): 347–58.

Recommended Reading

Bonding & Attachment

Karen, Robert, Ph.D. *Becoming Attached.* New York: Oxford University Press, 1998. Covers the development and findings of attachment research, and the discovered ramifications.

Montagu, Ashley, Ph.D. *Touching.* New York: Harper & Row, 1986. A must-read about the importance of touching and bonding to healthy development.

Heller, Sharon, Ph.D. *The Vital Touch.* New York: Henry Holt and Co., 1997. An important complement to Montagu's *Touching*, incorporating current research and addressing modern questions, with strong documentation.

Food Allergy

Braly, James, M.D. *Dr. Braly's Food Allergy and Nutrition Revolution.* New Canaan, CT: Keats Publishing, Inc., 1992. An excellent resource for understanding, diagnosing, and treating food allergies.

Buist, Robert, Ph.D. *Food Chemical Sensitivity.* New York: Avery Publishing, 1986. A comprehensive guide to the chemicals in our food and environment and their known and possible effects.

Rapp, Doris J., M.D. *Is This Your Child?* New York: William Morrow, 1991. Contains good explanations of hyperactivity and other food allergy symptoms and reactions. The diagnosis and treatment method is weak for delayed food reactions.

Rona, Zoltan P., M.D. *Childhood Illness and the Allergy Connection.* Rocklin, CA: Prima Publishing, 1996. Lots of nutrition-based ideas for treating food allergies and their related symptoms.

milk Dangers & Politics

Oski, Frank A., M.D. *Don't Drink Your Milk!* New York: TEACH Services, 1992. First printed in 1977, Pediatrician Oski, author of renowned standard pediatric textbooks, was well ahead of his time recognizing the medical dangers of cow's milk.

Cohen, Robert. *Milk, the Deadly Poison.* Englewood Cliffs, NJ: Argus Publishing, 1998. Touching on other concerns over milk as well, Mr. Cohen provides 300 pages of eye-opening detailed information about how money and politics supercede health concerns in federal handling of milk safety issues.

Baumslag, Naomi, M.D. *Milk, Money, and Madness, the Culture and Politics of Breastfeeding.* Westport, CT: Bergin & Garvey, 1995. A detailed and extremely eye-opening book about the history of breastfeeding and the politics of formula promotion.

Gordon, David B., Ph.D. *Milk and Mortality.* Livermore, CA: Gordon Books, 1999. A well-documented, in-depth presentation of the connections between milk drinking and coronary heart disease.

Twogood, Daniel A., D.C. *No Milk.* Victorville, CA: Wilhelmina Books, 1991. A discussion about the negative aspects of milk and its relation to back pain and headaches.

Plant, Jane, Ph.D. *Your Life in Your Hands, Understanding, Preventing and Overcoming Breast Cancer.* St Martin's Press: New York, 2000. 250 pages and hundreds of references on how dairy consumption leads to breast cancer.

Parenting & Health

Granju, Katie Allison. *Attachment Parenting.* New York: Pocket Books, 1999. A resource manual for attachment parenting.

Frissell-Deppe, Tammy. *Every Parent's Guide to Attachment Parenting.* Dracut, MA: JED Publishing, 1998. A question-and-answer resource for attachment parenting.

Magid, Ken, Ph.D. *High Risk, Children without a Conscience.* New York: Bantam, 1989. About the consequences to society of children raised without good attachment. Once you read it, you will wish to prevent it.

Mendelsohn, Robert S., M.D. *How to Raise a Healthy Child...in Spite of Your Doctor.* New York, NY: Ballantine Books, 1987. Solid revelation about the pediatric care industry and their motives, and how and why 95% of medical treatments offered to children can be avoided.

Sears, William, M.D. *The Baby Book, Everything You Need to Know about Your Baby — from Birth to Age Two.* New York: Little, Brown and Co.,

1993. A complete infant care guide using attachment parenting. Dr. Sears has other valuable parenting books as well.

Smith, Lendon H., M.D. *How to Raise a Healthy Child, Medical and Nutritional Advice.* New York, NY: M. Evans and Company, Inc., 1996. From pregnancy to feeding baby to bug bites to neurological disorder, a caring manual for understanding common childhood illnesses and disorders, wisely offering healthy options and solutions.

Small, Meredith. *Our Babies, Ourselves.* New York: Dell Publishing Co., 1999. A look at how worldwide cultures promote infant care practices that either accommodate or neglect (such as U.S.) various biological needs of infants, and the apparent outcomes of these assorted practices.

Thevenin, Tine. *The Family Bed.* Wayne, NJ: Avery Publishing, 1987. An irrefutable discussion of the values of cosleeping.

Vaccination

Scheibner, Viera, Ph.D. *Vaccination.* Victoria, Australia: Australian Print Group, 1993. The most scholarly coverage of the dangerous side of vaccination.

Miller, Neil Z. *Vaccines: Are They Really Safe and Effective?* Santa Fe, NM: New Atlantean Press, 1994. A brief guide documenting recent historical statistics.

Murphy, Jamie. *What Every Parent Should Know about Childhood Immunization.* Boston: Earth Healing Products, 1994. A sensational but very informative discussion of vaccinations.

Magazines & Organizations

Attachment Parenting International (615) 298-4334 Parenting information and direction to local attachment parenting support groups. www.AttachmentParenting.org

INFACT Canada On-line newsletter and valuable links. Excellent health-oriented and political action-oriented breastfeeding information. www.INFACTCanada.ca

La Leche League International (847) 519-7730 Information and support for breastfeeding. Telephone support and local meetings. www.LaLecheLeague.org

LLL Intl. Publishes *New Beginnings,* a magazine that contains much information and support for the breastfeeding mother.

Mothering magazine (800) 984-8116 Excellent natural parenting wisdom and information. www.Mothering.com